Northern Michigan Almanac

ACKNOWLEDGEMENTS

I owe thanks to many people who at some point during this 14-month project have either provided help, or at least tolerated me as I lived in a near constant state of distraction.

Thank you Brian Lewis of Petoskey Publishing for the opportunity, for believing in me, and for the friendship; Mary Erwin of the University of Michigan Press for the vote of confidence; Rick Coates for writing and research help in the Music and Movies section; Sarah Wichtner for her research prowess; Kimber Bilby for research assistance and ongoing support; Mike "The Professor" Sheehan for advice – always solicited - and the encouragement; to the talented JimDeWildt for his calm and cool deadline demeanor; Terry Phipps and John Russell for the great photos; to Dave Barrons, chief meteorologist for TV 9 & 10 News for his time and expertise; Charles Ferguson Barker for his perspectives on prehistoric Michigan to historian Steve Harold for the inspiration; to local historical groups like the Grand Traverse Pioneer & Historical Society, Leelanau Historical Society, Little Traverse Bay Historical Society and Beaver Island Historical Society for preserving our heritage; to the many kind and helpful employees of the State of Michigan for their efficiency and willingness to help; to county-level employees around northern Michigan for their ability to find and share information; ditto to the staffs of the Traverse Area District Library and Osterlin Library of Northwestern Michigan College; to the following Realtors for their insights and time: Jack Lane, Ken Schmidt, Judy Levin, Mark Carlson, Lynn Delling, Matt Case, Don Toffolo, Joe Blachy, Kerry Hollingshead and Michael Banninga; to Ross Biederman, President of Midwestern Broadcasting for the opportunity and support; to my mother, from whom I developed an early love of books and reading; to my wife Laura, who watched me disappear into our basement office (the dungeon) night after night, and weekend after weekend: thank you my love, for your unselfishness, patience, support and love. I am the lucky one. Finally, to the Detroit Red Wings Hockey Club and NHL Players Association: thanks for taking the 2004-05 season off so I could get some work done!

Northern Michigan
Almanac

by
Ron Jolly

The University of Michigan Press
Ann Arbor
&
The Petoskey Publishing Company
Traverse City

Published in the United States of America by
The University of Michigan Press
&
The Petoskey Publishing Company

Manufactured in the United States of America

2008   2007   2006   2005   4   3   2   1

ISBN 0-472-03088-4

Library of Congress Cataloging-in-Publication Data on File

Cover photography
courtesy of Terry Phipps

Dedicated to my wife,
the Lovely Laura

CONTENTS

POPULATION & HOUSING   119

COUNTIES & TOWNS   143

BUSINESS   217

SPORTS & RECREATION 555

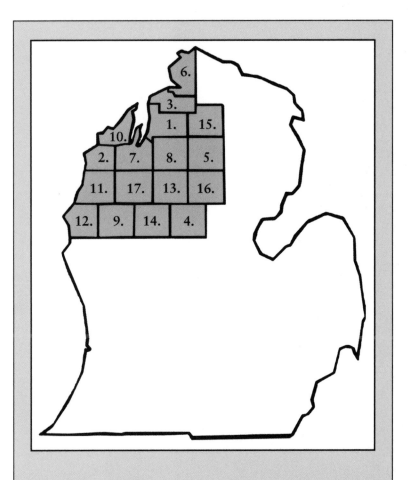

1. Antrim
2. Benzie
3. Charlevoix
4. Clare
5. Crawford
6. Emmet
7. Grand Traverse
8. Kalkaska
9. Lake

10. Leelanau
11. Manistee
12. Mason
13. Missaukee
14. Osceola
15. Otsego
16. Roscommon
17. Wexford

OFFICIAL STATE SYMBOLS

Several symbols chosen to represent Michigan are unique to northern Michigan, or common in the North Country. For instance...

Official State Stone of Michigan

State Stone: The Petoskey stone is actually a fossilized coral *(Hexagonaria pericarnata)* from a coral reef that existed in the northern Lower Peninsula during the Devonian era, 350 million years ago. Adopted as the State stone by Public Act 89 of 1965.

State Soil: Kalkaska sand was first identified as a soil type in 1927. It has distinctive layers ranging in color from black to yellowish brown, and covers nearly a million acres in 29 Upper and Lower Peninsula counties. Designated as the State soil by Public Act 302 of 1990.

State Flower: The apple blossom became the State flower after introduction of a bill by State Representative, William Harris of Norwood. Harris lived in the first house built in Norwood with his wife, Marion and son and daughter. *(Marion Township is named after Marion Harris.)* He was the town's first postmaster, held several posts in local government, and was elected to the State House to represent Charlevoix, Antrim, and the now defunct Manitou County. He earned the name "Apple-Blossom William" the Sage of Norwood. Designated the State flower by Joint Resolution 10 of 1897.

For more reading

Norwood: A Legacy of North Woods Living, copyright 2001 by Nancy Ritsema, Norwood Historical Society, Norwood, Michigan

State Tree: The white pine symbolizes the lumber industry which created tremendous wealth and provided lumber for thousands of homes and buildings around the Midwest. Most northern Michigan towns were formed during the lumber era. Public Act 7 of 1955 designated the white pine as the State tree.

White pine

State Fish: The Brook Trout, which is found in some of the top fishing streams and rivers around the north. Native to Michigan, the brook trout was adopted as the State fish by Public Act 5 of 1988.

State Game Mammal: White-tailed deer is found throughout Michigan and is certainly

White-tailed deer (photo courtesy of Travel Michigan)

associated with the great outdoors of northern Michigan. Designated by Public Act 15 of 1997, after Zeeland fourth-graders lobbied the State Legislature.

State Gem: Chlorastrolite Primarily found in the Upper Peninsula, chlorastrolite was adopted as the State gem by Public Act 56 of 1972

State Reptile: The painted turtle *(Chysemys picta)* was another classroom project. Fifth graders from Niles lobbied lawmakers after discovering that Michigan had no official State reptile. Public Act 281 of 1995.

State Wildflower: Dwarf Lake Iris grows mostly along the northern shores of Lake Michigan and Lake Huron. First discovered in 1810, it is now considered endangered. Public Act 454 of 1998 designated the dwarf lake iris (iris lacustris) as Michigan's official State wildflower.

Retreiving Michigan's Buried Past, edited by John R. Halsey, Associate editor, Michael D. Stafford 1999, Cranbrook Institute of Science

TIMELINE_*

Hundreds of millions of years ago. Michigan rested in the middle of a bowl-like basin created over 400 million years ago as continents drifted and collided to change the geologic formation of the planet. Over a long period of time this shifting of the earth caused the area around Michigan to sink. The outer ridge of this basin can be seen today in the islands around Green Bay, Wisconsin, and the islands of Georgian Bay in Lake Huron.

When ancient salt-water seas advanced over the continent they spilled over the rim of the Michigan basin. Coral reefs developed, blocking the flow of the tropical sea into the Michigan basin, which led to evaporation – a process that repeated several times over hundreds of millions of years. Each time the water flowed in and evaporated, it left behind layers of limestone, sandstone, shale, salt, gypsum, and other minerals.

Two million years ago. *(Pleistocene Period)* The tropical seas were gone, and Michigan was buried under a mass of ice. As the Pleistocene glacier advanced, it shattered and scraped the bedrock, scattering stones across the Great Lakes region. Today many of them wash up on our Lake Michigan beaches, and one of them is our official State stone.

The Petoskey Stone

The Petoskey stone is a type of coral that lived in the ancient warm sea that covered Michigan about 350 million years ago. The coral is found in what's known as Alpena limestone, which was deposited by the ancient sea that spilled into Michigan long ago. It was left behind when the sea evaporated, and eventually buried beneath layers of other rock.

Petoskey stones are made primarily of calcite, but can also include quartz, pyrite and other minerals. They are found along the shores of northern Lake Michigan, some inland lakes, and as far away as Iowa, Illinois, New York, and even in parts of Europe.

The Petoskey became Michigan's official State stone on June 28, 1965. Joining then-Governor George Romney was Miss Ella Jane Petoskey, a grand child of Chief Petosegay, the man whom the town of Petoskey is named after.

Glaciers advanced and retreated over Michigan four times during the Pleistocene. As these ice masses, some as high as two miles, melted and moved, they compressed the earth and in some places dug out canyons. When the last glacier retreated about 12,000 years ago its runoff water filled the canyons to create our Great Lakes.

25-50,000 years ago.
Many scientists believe the first people arrived in North America by crossing an ice bridge from Siberia.

8-12,000 years ago.
Paleo-Indians arrive in northern Michigan after the last glacier retreats. It was a food chain in motion as the Indians pursued wild game, which migrated north where trees and other vegetation had begun growing.

Archeological evidence indicates there was a temporary village of prehistoric Indians in Antrim County as many as 10,000 years ago. Artifacts associated with this time period have been found on the Samels farm between Lake Skegemog and Elk Lake.

The Samels Farm:
One of Michigan's Most Important Archeological Sites

Frank Samels, born in 1868 on a farm in Williamsburg, grew up working in the lumber camps where he saved enough money to buy his own farm on Skegemog Point. He ignored warnings from friends about poor quality soil, and bought 64 acres full of tree stumps. Working the fields, either pulling stumps or planting crops, Samels found many Indian artifacts. There were Indian mounds and pits, and dozens of points and blades.

In the late 1920's an archeologist from the University of Michigan found out about this farm up north with the Indian mounds and artifacts, and paid a visit. He was allowed to view the property and take notes. Later the head of his department also visited, and took more notes. As Frank and his team of oxen worked the fields he continued to find ancient Indian artifacts.

In 1965, after Frank had passed away, his sons gave permission to researchers from Michigan State University to excavate some of the land. In addition to the hundreds of relics already collected by the Samels family, the MSU team unearthed blades, projectile points and scrapers associated with Early Archaic Indians *(8,000-10,000 years ago).*

Most of the unearthed artifacts were probably used by late woodland Indians between the years of 600-1650 A.D. Some of the found objects were associated with Late Archaic *(1,000 – 2,000 years ago)*, and Middle Woodland Indians *(1 – 600 A.D.)* Archeologists believe large groups of Native Americans, from different eras, used the site as a base camp, and that it was connected by a trail to the Saginaw area. Researchers call the Samels Farm a "spectacular site that yielded a wealth of information."

The collection of artifacts, numbering over one thousand, is now housed at Michigan State University. The farm, which was a great success agriculturally and archeologically, has been designated a Michigan Centennial Farm, and in 1972 was placed on the National Register of Historic Places. Frank's sons, working with the Archeology Conservancy, have preserved the entire farm, and in 2002 a Samels Family Heritage Society was founded to further preserve the farm buildings, antique equipment, and land.

3,000 to 4,000 years ago. Evidence of Late Archaic Indians in northern Michigan has been found near Burt Lake *(the Screaming Loon site)*, Reed Lake in Lake County and on North Manitou Island.

Indians of this period built temporary hunting and fishing camps. Evidence discovered near Burt Lake indicate there was a fire pit where fish and small mammals may have been roasted, and a place for butchering and hide processing.

1,400 to 2,000 years ago.
Indians during this period *(Middle Woodland)* were becoming domesticated even though they spent only the warm months in northern Michigan. They were cultivating wild rice, using ceramics, and families lived together in the seasonal camps where they developed burial sites and rituals for their dead. Artifacts associated with this period have been found in the following areas: Platte River Campground *(Benzie)*, Fisher Lake and Dunn Farm *(Leelanau)*, Lake Skegemog and two other Antrim County sites, Pine River Channel *(Charlevoix)*, and several locations in Emmet County including Wycamp Creek and Fort Michilimackinac.

600 to 1650
The modern Indians lived on lakeshores and riverbanks to take advantage of the plentiful supply of fish. After the fall spawning cycle, many Indian families moved downstate, while some remained in northern Michigan, moving inland where they turned to hunting. They raised crops, and started trading with Europeans, who began arriving in the mid-1600's.

There are two noteworthy burial sites from this period in Missaukee County.

Around 1000 the Anishinabeg *(or Anishnabek)* migrated from northeastern United States. Spiritual leaders said they would find food near the water, which they did in the form of wild rice around the Great Lakes.

The Anishinabeg consisted of the Odawa *(Ottawa)*, the Ojibwa *(Chippewa)* and Bodowadomi (Pottawatomi), or Three Fires Confederacy. The Chippewa lived in the eastern Upper Peninsula, the Ottawa around northern lower Michigan, and the Pottawatomi in western Michigan. All three tribes spoke the Algonquin language, which gave the State its name. Michi gami means "large lake" in Algonquin.

Around 1640 Iroquoian tribes from the east coast along with British troops moved west looking to expand fur-trapping enterprise. Ottawa tribes around southern Ontario moved to northern Michigan and Wisconsin to avoid the invading Iroquois.

1619
Etienne Brule becomes first European to see Lake Superior or Lake Huron. Indian guides from New France *(Quebec)* take him to "the big lake."

The French Period
1634-1763

Fur traders and voyageurs from New France *(Montreal)* begin relations with the natives – the Chippewa and Ottawa – during the 1600's. The Ottawa of the northern Lower Peninsula trapped beaver and traded furs to Chippewa tribes from the U.P. and Canada, in exchange for handcrafted goods. The Chippewa traded the furs to the French in exchange for money, clothing, tools and weapons. The two tribes and the French maintained friendly relations during this period.

1634

Jean Nicolet becomes the first known European to see Mackinac Island, the Straits, and Lake Michigan. Nicolet's mission was to find the water route from New France *(Montreal)* to the Orient. He paddled his canoe west through the Straits, and across Lake Michigan to what he thought was China. When Nicolet ran out of water, he assumed he had landed on the shore of China. He dressed in an Oriental robe given to him by the French government, and as he approached the curious natives on shore, he fired two pistols, before discovering it was not China, but Green Bay, Wisconsin.

1641

First interaction between native Indians and Europeans on Michigan soil. Fathers Jogues and Raymbault, Jesuit priests, paddle down the St. Mary's River and land near Sault Ste. Marie where they are greeted by thousands of Indians. It was a peaceful meeting, as the priests shared the Christian gospel with the natives.

1668

Father Jacques Marquette establishes the first permanent European settlement in Michigan at Sault Ste. Marie.

1670

Fathers Dablon and Allouez establish a mission and trading post at Mackinac.

1671

Marquette established a mission at St. Ignace.

1674

Father Marquette dies near Frankfort or Ludington upon return from Missisiippi River adventure.

1679

LaSalle, sails through the Straits on the *Griffin*, the first commercial sailing ship on the Great Lakes.

1690

French build Fort de Buade at St. Ignace.

1695

Antonie de Cadillac observes Ottawa fishing near Mackinac

Father Jacques Marquette (photo courtesy of Terry Phipps)

Island and writes: "…no family does not catch an abundance of fish…better fish can not be eaten…they are bathed and nourished in the purest water…."

1690's through early 1700's
Michilimackinac described by historian as "most important place in the west."

1715
The French build Fort Mackinac at Mackinaw City to protect from British moving into region.

1742
Ottawa establish L'Arbre Croche, at present day Cross Village.

1760
French-Indian War ends as French surrender Montreal to the British.

1761
Fort Mackinac taken over by British.

The British Period
1761 - 1814

1763
Fort captured by Chippewa who massacred most of the garrison.

Revolutionary War:
1763-1775

1766
Fort re-occupied by British until 1796, when it and most of Michigan was handed over to the United States.

For the next thirty years the international fur trade was centered on Mackinac Island where John Jacob Astor built his American Fur Co. headquarters.

1805
Michigan becomes a territory; only the eastern half of the U.P. was included.

1812
War of 1812. British, with help from Ottawa and Chippewa, re-capture Fort Mackinac.

The American Period
1815 - present

1815
Official survey of Michigan begins. Lasts into the 1850's.

1818
Michigan Territory expanded to include the rest of the U.P., Wisconsin and part of Minnesota.

Federal surveyors describe Michigan as a land of sand and swamp, unfit for farming.

1819
First steamship, *Walk-in-the-Water*, passes through Straits.

1820
Governor of the territory, Lewis Cass, organizes an expedition of scientists and

engineers to explore the State. First stop: Mackinac Island. Among those on the expedition, Henry Rowe Schoolcraft, who described the Straits region as a place "celebrated for the salubrity of its atmosphere." He saw about 100 houses and many whitefish!

1825
Erie Canal completed, opening Lake Michigan to boating traffic from the East Coast.

1829
Father Pete DeJean and other missionaries along with local Odawa members build the Holy Childhood of Jesus Boarding School in Harbor Springs.

1830's –1900
The lumber boom in northern Michigan: Estimated output of pine lumber between 1834 and 1897 from Clare and Muskegon County north to the Straits of Mackinac: 36.5 billion board feet.

1836
Chippewa and Ottawa leaders sign Treaty of Washington ceding most land in the northern Lower Peninsula to the United States Government.

1837
January 26, Michigan achieves statehood.

Charles Mears builds the first sawmill in Mason County. He eventually builds six mills shipping lumber to Milwaukee and Chicago.

1839
Reverend Peter Dougherty, the area's first Caucasian settler, arrives on the Old Mission Peninsula and establishes a Presbyterian Mission for the Indians. He was so small and accomplished so much work that the Indians called him Little Beaver.

1840
Most counties in northern lower Michigan are formed and renamed.

1841
The Stronach family opens the first sawmill in Manistee County. They go on to operate seven mills, and by 1854 they employed over 60 men and produced nearly 14 million board feet of lumber per year–the highest production in the State.

1842
Dougherty builds the first frame house on Old Mission.

1846
First settlers arrive in Traverse City.

1847
Horace Boardman builds sawmill along Kid's Creek – the first one in Grand Traverse County.
James Jesse Strang, Mormon

leader, arrives on Beaver Island.

1848
Chief Peter Waukazoo and Reverend George alarmed by a smallpox epidemic, relocate their Ottawa mission from Black River to present day Northport.

1850
James Jesse Strang is crowned "King of Beaver Island."

1850's and 60's
Lumber industry booming in Clare as logs are floated west down the Muskegon River, and east down the Tobacco River to Saginaw.

1851
Three businessmen from Chicago, Perry Hannah, Albert Tracy Lay, and James Morgan buy a mill on the Boardman River along with 200 acres of land and plat out the city of Traverse City.

Over the next 35 years Hannah and Lay enterprises will produce and sell over 400 million board feet of lumber.

1852
Reverend Dougherty plants the first cherry orchard in Old Mission.

Dougherty moves across the bay to Omena where he and his flock could buy and own the land they lived on.

1853
The Antoine Manseau family arrives in Leland from N. Manitou Island. Manseau and John Miller build a dam, sawmill and dock, which leads to new jobs, new homes, and a population of 200 by the year 1867.

1854
Harry C. Sutton builds a fuel station for wood-burning steamboats on the shore of present day Suttons Bay.

Northport founded.

1856
"King" James Strang is assassinated on Beaver Island. Mormon followers are chased from the island, and former residents return.

1860
A Hannah & Lay steamer begins weekly service between Chicago and Traverse City.

1861-1865
Civil War.

1862
Traverse City population 300.

1871
Fire! Manistee hit hardest in northern Michigan. Fire broke out in Holland and spread quickly. Most of Holland was destroyed, and half the town of Manistee was lost. The fire caused

James Strang

damage in Lake, Osceola and other counties as it burned all the way to Saginaw.

In Chicago, fire burned for two days klling 200 people. In Wisconsin the entire town of Peshtigo was wiped out. Fires caused by a combination of farmers burning slash, sparks from trains running through dry cutover lands, and the weather-very hot with high winds.

1872
First railroad, Grand Rapids & Indiana, arrives in Traverse City.

1873
Henry Campbell builds Campbell House *(later called Park Place Hotel)*.

1876
Michigan Campground Association, the forerunner to the Bay View Association, holds its first meeting near Petoskey.

1877
Angry residents burn down the courthouse in Farwell, and the Clare County seat is moved to Harrison.

1879
Susan B. Anthony lectures at Traverse City Ladies Library on Woman's Suffrage.

1881
First regular ferry service established for railroad cars from Mackinaw City to St. Ignace.

Traverse City incorporated as a village.

Traverse City chosen as site for the new Northern Michigan Asylum, which becomes key employer, providing almost 1,000 jobs.

1884
First telephone service in Traverse City.

First European Brown Trout planted in Pere Marquette River near Baldwin.

1887
Grand Hotel opens on Mackinac Island.

1896
First golf courses in northern Michigan open at Harbor Point and Wequetonsing in Harbor Springs, and the Charlevoix Country Club in Charlevoix.

1899
R.B. Cobb drives first automobile in Traverse City on July 7.

1921
Charles Fowler, a civil engineer, proposes a bridge that would leapfrog from island to island to cross the Straits of Mackinac.

1923
State starts up ferry service across the Straits.

1924
The first cherry harvest celebration "Blessing of the Blossoms" *(precursor to, National Cherry Festival)* attracted 3,000 people.

1926
New Munson Hospital dedicated.

1928
Interlochen Music Camp opens.

1935
First National Trout Festival held in Kalkaska.

1951
Northwestern Michigan College founded.

1953
Grandview Parkway built along West Bay in Traverse City.

1957
Mackinac Bridge opens in November.

1969
Oil and natural gas boom begins with discovery of the Niagaren Reef Trend. Traverse City becomes the hub.

1970's
First wineries become established on Old Mission and Leelanau peninsulas.

1978
Northern Michigan's first mall, the Cherryland Mall opens in Traverse City.

1983
The Grand Traverse Band of Ottawa and Chippewa Indians opens the Leelanau Sands Casino, the first legal gaming facility in northern Michigan.

1992
Grand Traverse Mall opens on South Airport Drive.

1997
Grand Traverse Band of Ottawa and Chippewa Indians opens Turtle Creek Casino in Acme.
For further information on Traverse City history, see *Anishnaabek: Artists of Little Traverse* by M. MacDowell, 1996, and *Queen of the North* by Lawrence Wakefield, 1998.

NATIONAL HISTORIC LANDMARKS

There are 33 National Historic Landmarks in the State of Michigan. Of those, seven are located in northern lower Michigan and Mackinac Island. Emmet County, with three, has the most National Historic Landmarks.

Windemere. The Hemingway family cottage on the shore of Walloon Lake (photo courtesy of John F. Kennedy Library)

Site: Windemere *(the Ernest Hemingway Cottage)*
County: Emmet
Date listed: November 24, 1968

Ernest Hemingway spent every summer of his youth at the family cottage on Walloon Lake. His father, Dr. Clarence Hemingway, had the cottage built in 1899 after spending the previous summer vacationing in the area. Hemingway developed his passions of fishing, hunting, and writing while on vacation at Windemere.

Site: Bay View Association
County: Emmet
Date listed: December 23, 1987

The Victorian community overlooking Little Traverse Bay was founded in 1876 as a Methodist camp meeting and resort. The summer community includes 437 privately owned cottages, 2 hotels and 29 other structures belonging to the Bay View Association. The 338-acre neighborhood owned by the association is perched on a terrace 200 feet over the water. Most of the Victorian-style homes are over 100 years old and shaded by large hardwood trees on curved streets.

Historians praise the "ongoing collective values" of the religious community as one

North Manitou Life Saving Station –1900 (photo courtesy of G. T. Pioneer & Historical Society)

of the reasons it has been so well preserved.

Site: Fort Michilimackinac
County: Emmet
Date listed: October 9, 1960

The French built the fort in 1715 to serve as a fur trading post. It was one of the first European settlements on the mainland of northern Michigan. In 1761 the British, having taken control of Canada from the French, took over Fort Michilimackinac, and continued using it as a fur trading post. Two years later angry Ottawa and Chippewa killed most of the soldiers and residents of the fort, and by 1781 it was abandoned by the Brits, who built a new fort on Mackinac Island. Fort Michilimackinac, with its re-enactments and pageantry, is one of the most popular tourist attractions in northern Michigan.

Site: North Manitou Island Lifesaving Station
County: Leelanau
Date listed: August 5, 1998

Started in 1854 as a volunteer lifesaving station for the many shipwrecks in the narrow Manitou Passage. The station was taken over in 1874 by the U.S. Life-Saving Service, and in 1915 became part of the U.S. Coast Guard. The buildings were sold in 1938 to the private Manitou Island Association, and became part of the Sleeping Bear Dunes National

Lakeshore in 1984. The North Manitou Island Station is the only remaining station that represents the entire life-saving service history from the volunteer era through the Coast Guard era.

Site: City of Milwaukee Car Ferry
County: Manistee
Date listed:
December 14, 1990
The last remaining Great Lakes railroad car ferry from the classic period before 1940, the City of Milwaukee is in near original condition. The steel-hulled, twin pro-peller, steam-powered ship was built in 1931 by the Manitowoc Ship-building Company in Wisconsin. With a capacity of 22 rail cars the City of Milwaukee ferried rail cars between Michigan ports – Frankfort and Ludington – and other ports of the Great Lakes. It was part of the largest open lake train ferry system in the world. Today the ferry in its temporary home on Manistee Lake is visible from US 31 just north of Manistee.

Site: Grand Hotel
County: Mackinac
Date listed: June 29, 1989
Railroad and steamship inter-ests chipped in to build a summer destination at the northern end of their lines. Today the Grand remains as one of the top summer

resorts in the world, famous for its 660-foot long front porch – the longest in the world. The Mackinac Island Hotel Company consisted of the Michigan Central and the Grand Rapids & Indiana Railroads along with the Detroit and Cleveland Navigation Company (steam-boats). Michigan architect, George D. Mason, designed the hotel, and Charles Caskey of Allegan was the builder. Major additions were built in 1918, and the last addition, the Millennium Wing, opened in 2000.

Site: Mackinac Island
County: Mackinac
Date listed: October 9, 1960
Mackinac Island was the country's second national park, established in 1875, just three years after Yellowstone Park. By 1875 the island was already developing a reputa-tion as a summer resort. In 1895 most of the island, was turned over to the State, be-coming Michigan's first State Park. Island life of the 18th and 19th century is preserved in its Victorian homes, small commercial buildings and churches. Some of the oldest existing buildings in Michigan are located on Mackinac Island.

Grand Hotel

WEATHER, WATER & WOODS

WEATHER

Climate

Some people say northern Michigan has a four season climate: early winter, winter, late winter, and construction season. It is due to this deep cynicism that I avoided asking any of *them* to help describe the climate. Instead, I turned to meteorologist, Dave Barrons, who has been closely observing and reporting on every aspect of northern Michigan's weather for the past 20 years.

Barrons, the Chief Meteorologist for TV 9 & 10 News keeps viewers informed on all things outdoors from bird watching tips to the latest hunting conditions to space station sightings! The native of Midland, Michigan holds a masters of political science from Purdue and a masters in education from North Carolina. He started his television career as a reporter and back up meteorologist, before becoming a full time Chief Meteorologist for WWTV and WWUP-TV (www.9and10news.com). The northern Michigan climate according to Dave...

"The effects of the Great Lakes in general and Lake Michigan dominate the weather of northwest Lower Michigan specifically. 'Lake-effect' is one of the most commonly used weather-terms in the region and though it usually is linked to the word snow, it is the essence of our weather, year round.

"Let's start with winter. During the cold season the waters of the big lakes remain warmer than the air temperature, even by just a few degrees. The warmth of the water provides the heat-units needed to evaporate the water into the air above. The rising, warmer air cools and sheds its load of moisture as snow. The Northwest is one of the principle snow belts in the state, though only parts of Antrim and Kalkaska counties would rank near the very top for state snowfall. Lake effect snows do give the entire region a better shot at winter's white covering, consistently. The lakes also affect temperatures, which are much less extreme (cold) on this side of the lake than they are in Wisconsin. We can turn cold enough but it would really be worse without the moderating effects of the big lakes.

"By spring, the 'lake-effect' continues to be one of warmth, especially overnight warmth. Because of the overall heating effect of the lakes, a strip of land up to 10 miles wide all along the Lake Michigan shoreline suffers less, late-season frost than areas inland. It's significantly less frost, and this fact alone accounts for the precise location of the 'fruit-belt' along the lakeshore; that region where cherries, apples and now grapes are so successfully cultivated. The spring lake effect makes northwest Michigan the Cherry Capital of the World, and is rapidly turning it into a fine wine-producing region as well.

"Springtime and summer time weather both show a very beneficial lake effect. That is, the lake takes the 'umph' out of thunderstorms, and protects northern Michigan from the development of really big tornados. Tornados can and do occur, but most are short-lived and of the small, rattail kind. The moderating effect of Lake Michigan's cool waters prevents storm size and development that is likely to produce big grinding tornados. So Lake Michigan acts like a big fence in the atmosphere protecting our region from the worst kind of severe weather.

"Lake effect in the heat of the summer is also beneficial. Even on the stickiest of dog days, one can usually find a cooling breeze on our many beautiful beaches. It may be only a faint breeze, though usually a steady lake breeze sets up every summer day. A cooling breeze and one that gives our region top marks from sailors looking for the big-water, cruising experience available on the lakes.

"In the fall the effects of the Great Lakes on our weather may be less apparent but still goes on. By keeping the fruit growing region a little warmer into autumn, wine grapes get a few extra heat-units to help the ripening process and to stretch it out. That leads to what is becoming the region's signature wine, late-harvest Riesling.

"It's back to winter and our weather cycle begins again. Year round north west lower Michigan benefits from Great Lakes in so many ways, and when it comes to the weather it is no different. Lake effect weather gives our region one of its most attractive physical attributes; four seasons of change, each with its own beauty and distinctive qualities."

HOTTEST DAYS IN NORTHERN MICHIGAN

Highest recorded temp.	Town	Date
108	Vanderbilt	July 11, 1936
107	Houghton Lake	July 13, 1936
107	Fife Lake	July 13, 1936
106	Grayling	June 28, 1887
106	Lake City	July 12, 1936
106	Higgins Lake	July 13, 1936
105	Traverse City	July 7, 1936
104	Mackinaw City	July 29, 1916
104	Grayling	July 1, 1936
104	Cadillac	July 13, 1936
104	Baldwin	June 27, 1949
104	Cheboygan	August 6, 1947
103	E. Jordan	July 13, 1936
103	Pellston	August 6, 1947
102	Baldwin	August, 1955
102	Boyne Falls	August 18, 1955
102	Houghton Lake	June 18, 1994
102	Maple City	July 14, 1995
101	Gaylord	July 1, 1901
101	Petoskey	July 31, 1917
100	Manistee	August 5, 1947
100	Higgins Lake	August, 1955
100	Grayling	July, 1977
100	Houghton Lake	July, 1977
100	Evart	August 2, 1988

COLDEST DAYS IN NORTHERN MICHIGAN

Coldest recorded temp.	Town	Date
-51	Vanderbilt	February 9, 1934
-48	Houghton Lake	February 1, 1918
-49	Baldwin	February 11, 1899
-45	Grayling	February 3, 1898
-45	Fife Lake	March 3, 1943
-43	Cadillac	January 30, 1951
-42	Grayling	February 17, 1979
-41	Lake City	February 11, 1899
-41	E. Jordan	February 17, 1979

Coldest recorded temp.	Town	Date
-39	Gaylord	January 6, 1912
-39	Higgins Lake	February 1, 1918
-38	Cheboygan	February 6, 1895
-38	Ludington	February 11, 1899
-38	Houghton Lake	February 17, 1979
-38	Manistee	February 11, 1899
-37	Traverse City	February 17, 1979
-37	Pellston	January 23, 1948
-37	Pellston	February 17, 1979
-37	Baldwin	January, 1951
-35	Petoskey	February 9, 1934
-35	Boyne Falls	February 17, 1979
-34	Kalkaska	February 4, 1996
-33	Mackinaw City	February 6, 1885
-32	Higgins Lake	January, 1951
-30	Evart	January 21, 1984
-29	Cross Village	February 2, 1976
-29	St. Ignace Mackinac Bridge	February 16, 1987
-28	St. James Beaver Island	December 28, 1917

1934 snowplow on County Road 633 (old M-22) (photo courtesy of Leelanau Historical Society)– snowiest winter on record

Owner, Kieth Miles, takes a snowblower to the roof of Fay's Motel in Grayling, a favorite of snow-mobilers using the Lovells trail system (photo courtesy of Sandy Miles)

HIGHEST DAILY SNOWFALL

Amount (inches)	Town	Date
33.5	Baldwin	November 30, 1960
27.1	Ludington	December 9, 1962
24	Manistee	January 23, 1898
24	Kalkaska	February 15, 1985
24	Petoskey	December 26, 2001
20.5	Charlevoix	November 11,1950
20	Gaylord	November 23, 1893
20	Vanderbilt	March 24, 1951
19.3	Cheboygan	December 4, 1970
18	Harrison	March 13, 1901
18	Mackinaw City	February 1, 1908

Amount (inches)	Town	Date
18	Lake City	February 1, 1908
18	Petoskey	December 15, 1955
18	Maple City	January 7, 1962
18	Kalkaska	January 27, 1978
18	E. Jordan	December 9, 1995
18	Cross Village	January 12, 1999
17.1	Cross Village	March 6, 1959
17	Boyne Falls	January 26, 1978
16	Grayling	March 21, 1913
16	Traverse City	November 29, 1924
16	East Jordan	January 10, 1969
16	Scottville	November 14, 1969
16	Pellston	January 26, 1978
16	Wellston	January 27, 1978
16	Frankfort	December 22, 1989

Snowy Hartwick Pines picnic tables

SNOWIEST WINTERS OF RECORD

Amount (inches)	Town	Winter
219.6	Maple City	1996-97
212	Maple City	1976-77
211.9	Kalkaska	1996-97
207.5	Gaylord	1996-97
205.5	Gaylord	1970-71
200.2	Pellston	1971-72
199.1	Vanderbilt	1970-71
194.9	Traverse City	1996-97
187	Kalkaska	1984-85
184.9	Petoskey	1970-71
181.8	Boyne Falls	1970-71
181	Cadillac	1984-85
172.1	Grayling	1989-90
166.8	E. Jordan	2000-01
164.5	Charlevoix	1978-79
162.6	Thompsonville	1976-77
159.7	Ludington	1985-86
154.6	East Jordan	1984-85
151.8	Fife Lake	1959-60
147.8	Grayling	1984-85

AVERAGE MONTHLY WEATHER

ANTRIM COUNTY - BELLAIRE

	J	F	M	A	M	J	J	A	S	O	N	D
High temp	27.3	30.1	39.7	53.0	67.1	75.8	79.9	77.7	69.7	58.0	43.5	32.3
Low temp	11.3	10.4	18.5	29.8	40.2	49.4	54.4	53.2	46.1	36.8	28.1	18.5
Cloudy days	22	17	18	17	14	12	10	12	14	18	23	23
Snowfall	19.9	13.3	11.7	4.4	0.2	0.7					10.0	17.1

BENZIE COUNTY - BENZONIA

	J	F	M	A	M	J	J	A	S	O	N	D
High temp	28.5	31.2	40.1	52.1	65.1	73.9	78.4	76.5	69.0	57.7	44.1	32.9
Low temp	16.7	17.4	24.1	34.1	44.3	53.1	58.8	58.9	51.9	42.1	32.3	22.3
Cloudy days	22	17	18	17	14	12	10	12	13	17	22	23
Snowfall	19.6	12.5	10.9	3.6	0.2	0.6					8.7	16.3

CHARLEVOIX COUNTY - CHARLEVOIX

	J	F	M	A	M	J	J	A	S	O	N	D
High temp	27.8	30.6	40.2	53.0	66.6	75.1	79.7	77.6	69.9	58.6	44.1	32.7
Low temp	12.7	11.6	20.0	31.0	41.1	50.3	55.8	54.6	47.5	38.2	29.2	19.7
Cloudy days	22	17	17	16	14	12	10	12	15	18	23	23
Snowfall	22.2	14.9	12.5	4.8	0.3	1.0					10.8	20.5

CLARE COUNTY - CLARE

	J	F	M	A	M	J	J	A	S	O	N	D
High temp	27.8	30.8	41.3	54.9	68.7	77.8	82.3	79.6	71.3	59.0	44.6	32.9
Low temp	12.1	13.4	21.8	32.9	43.9	53.5	57.9	56.1	47.9	37.4	28.5	18.9
Cloudy days	22	17	18	17	14	12	10	12	14	18	23	23
Snowfall	18.8	12.4	11.1	4.0	0.2	0.7					9.6	15.9

CRAWFORD COUNTY - GRAYLING

	J	F	M	A	M	J	J	A	S	O	N	D
High temp	25.4	28.2	38.3	52.1	66.7	75.8	79.9	77.3	68.3	56.0	41.8	30.1
Low temp	6.6	6.3	15.2	28.1	38.9	48.4	53.1	51.2	43.6	33.8	25.1	14.5
Cloudy days	22	17	18	17	14	12	10	12	14	18	23	23
Snowfall	19.2	12.6	11.4	4.2	0.2	0.7					10.1	16.1

EMMET COUNTY - PETOSKEY

	J	F	M	A	M	J	J	A	S	O	N	D
High temp	26.2	27.5	36.6	47.8	59.6	69.4	74.9	73.6	66.6	55.6	42.3	31.6
Low temp	14.0	12.1	21.0	32.5	43.2	53.1	59.3	58.0	50.6	40.4	30.5	21.2
Cloudy days	22	17	17	16	14	12	10	12	15	18	23	23
Snowfall	22.5	15.2	12.6	4.9	0.3	1.0					10.6	20.8

GRAND TRAVERSE COUNTY - TRAVERSE CITY

J	F	M	A	M	J	J	A	S	O	N	D
High temp											
27.4	30.0	39.6	53.1	67.0	76.3	81.0	78.5	69.9	57.9	43.8	32.3
Low temp											
14.3	13.7	21.5	31.9	41.8	51.9	57.7	56.8	49.5	39.5	30.5	20.5
Cloudy days											
22	17	18	17	14	12	10	12	14	18	23	23
Snowfall											
19.9	13.0	11.5	4.2	0.2	0.7					9.9	16.6

KALKASKA COUNTY - KALKASKA

J	F	M	A	M	J	J	A	S	O	N	D
High temp											
24.4	27.5	37.6	51.1	65.3	74.5	77.9	76.0	67.2	55.3	40.8	29.8
Low temp											
7.9	6.8	15.7	28.8	40.6	50.3	45.0	52.5	45.2	35.9	26.9	16.4
Cloudy days											
22	17	18	17	14	12	10	12	14	18	23	23
Snowfall											
19.4	12.8	11.4	4.2	0.2	0.7					10.0	16.2

LAKE COUNTY - BALDWIN

J	F	M	A	M	J	J	A	S	O	N	D
High temp											
28.6	32.4	42.7	56.0	69.8	78.0	82.1	79.8	71.4	59.1	44.8	33.2
Low temp											
10.8	10.7	19.1	30.4	40.8	48.8	53.2	52.1	44.8	35.3	27.0	17.3
Cloudy days											
24	20	18	16	14	12	10	11	13	16	23	25
Snowfall											
26.0	15.1	11.1	3.1	0.1	0.6					9.1	21.2

LEELANAU COUNTY - SUTTONS BAY

J	F	M	A	M	J	J	A	S	O	N	D
High temp											
27.7	30.1	39.2	52.2	65.8	75.2	79.8	77.6	69.5	50.6	43.8	32.6
Low temp											
13.9	13.4	20.6	30.8	40.8	50.6	56.4	55.6	48.5	38.6	29.6	20.0
Cloudy days											
22	17	18	17	14	12	10	12	14	18	23	23
Snowfall											
20.3	13.6	11.8	4.4	0.2	0.8					10.2	17.7

MANISTEE COUNTY - MANISTEE

J	F	M	A	M	J	J	A	S	O	N	D
High temp											
29.9	33.3	42.3	55.0	67.4	76.4	80.7	78.5	71.3	59.8	45.9	34.2
Low temp											
17.1	18.0	24.6	34.3	43.9	52.7	58.3	57.7	51.2	41.9	32.5	22.6
Cloudy days											
22	18	17	16	14	12	10	11	13	16	22	23
Snowfall											
22.3	13.5	10.8	3.2	0.1	0.5					8.2	18.2

MASON COUNTY - LUDINGTON

J	F	M	A	M	J	J	A	S	O	N	D
High temp											
29.0	33.3	42.8	56.2	68.6	76.7	81.2	79.1	70.7	58.8	44.8	33.3
Low temp											
15.6	17.3	23.5	33.1	42.7	52.2	57.5	56.7	49.4	39.9	30.7	20.9
Cloudy days											
24	20	18	16	14	12	10	11	13	16	22	23
Snowfall											
27.2	15.4	10.8	2.7	0.5						8.2	22.0

MISSAUKEE COUNTY - LAKE CITY

J	F	M	A	M	J	J	A	S	O	N	D
High temp											
25.9	29.3	39.0	52.6	66.7	75.5	79.9	77.2	68.6	56.3	42.1	30.6
Low temp											
7.9	8.1	17.2	29.9	40.3	49.3	53.6	52.1	44.1	34.3	25.5	14.7
Cloudy days											
22	17	18	17	14	12	10	12	14	18	23	23
Snowfall											
19.3	12.6	11.4	4.2	0.2	0.7					10.1	16.1

OSCEOLA COUNTY - REED CITY

J	F	M	A	M	J	J	A	S	O	N	D
High temp											
28.4	32.1	41.9	55.3	69.0	77.4	81.7	79.0	70.6	58.3	44.0	32.8
Low temp											
11.0	11.8	20.1	31.5	42.4	51.1	55.9	54.3	46.2	36.0	27.4	17.4
Cloudy days											
23	18	18	17	14	12	10	11	13	17	23	24
Snowfall											
22.8	13.8	11.1	3.5	0.1	0.7					9.4	19.0

OTSEGO COUNTY - GAYLORD

J	F	M	A	M	J	J	A	S	O	N	D
High temp											
25.2	29.0	39.4	53.4	67.8	76.1	80.0	77.3	68.3	56.4	41.3	29.8
Low temp											
9.6	10.1	18.3	29.5	41.0	50.1	55.0	53.9	46.7	36.8	26.8	16.2
Cloudy days											
22	17	18	17	14	12	10	12	14	18	23	23
Snowfall											
20.3	13.9	11.9	4.5	0.2	0.7					9.7	17.7

ROSCOMMON COUNTY - HOUGHTON LAKE

J	F	M	A	M	J	J	A	S	O	N	D
High temp											
26.0	29.3	39.5	53.0	67.2	75.7	80.2	77.4	68.6	56.2	42.1	30.6
Low temp											
8.9	9.4	18.0	29.7	39.9	48.4	52.8	51.1	44.0	34.9	26.7	16.1
Cloudy days											
22	17	18	17	14	12	10	12	14	18	23	23
Snowfall											
19.2	12.6	11.4	4.2	0.2	0.7					10.1	16.0

WEXFORD COUNTY - CADILLAC

J	F	M	A	M	J	J	A	S	O	N	D
High temp											
25.9	28.9	38.7	52.0	66.3	74.8	79.2	76.7	68.3	55.9	42.0	30.6
Low temp											
9.1	8.7	17.2	29.8	40.4	49.9	54.5	52.6	44.7	35.2	26.3	16.0
Cloudy days											
22	17	18	17	14	12	10	12	14	18	23	23
Snowfall											
19.5	12.7	11.4	4.1	0.2	0.7					10.0	16.3

ANNUAL PRECIPITATION AND GROWING SEASONS

County	Annual Precipitation	Annual Snowfall	Growing Season (days)
Antrim	30-33"	80-120"	100-130
Benzie	28-32"	80-100"	130-160
Charlevoix	30-32"	80-120"	80-140
Clare	29-31"	40 - 60"	90-130
Crawford	29-33"	70-100"	100-120
Emmet	30-33"	90-110"	90-140
Grand Traverse	30-32"	80-100"	90-130
Kalkaska	31-33"	80-100"	100-120
Lake	31-33"	60 - 80"	130-150
Leelanau	29-31"	80-100"	130-150
Manistee	30-32"	80-100"	130-160
Mason	30-34"	60 - 90"	160-180
Missaukee	29-33"	60 - 80"	90-110
Osceola	29-33"	50- 70"	100-130
Otsego	28-33"	90-160"	70-110
Roscommon	29-32"	50- 90"	90-110
Wexford	29-32"	70-90"	100-140

THE FROZEN BAY

Since 1851 the Traverse City Chamber of Commerce has tracked how often, and for how long the west arm of Grand Traverse Bay freezes. It's considered frozen when the ice stretches from the downtown Traverse City shore out to Power Island, some six-and-a-half miles to the north. Confirmation comes from the U.S. Coast Guard based in Traverse City.

The longest duration was in 1874 when the Bay was a sheet of ice for 116 days, January 13 through May 8th. The shortest duration on record is a five day freeze between February 28th and March 4th, 1973.

The longest consecutive streak of West Bay freezing over is 20 years between 1883 and 1902. In the last twenty years, between 1984 and 2003 the Bay has frozen over only eight times.

When the Bay does freeze over it usually occurs in February. The earliest point in the season it froze over was January 10th in 1856, and again in 1857. The latest it remained frozen was until May 4th in 1873.

Year	Freeze-up	Break-up	Duration (days)
1852	March 11	March 22	12
1853	March 01	April 06	37
1854	January 25	April 11	77
1856	January 10	April 26	107
1857	January 10	April 30	111
1858	March 04	March 20	17
1859	February 23	March 12	18
1860	February 17	March 03	15
1861	January 22	March 20	58
1862	February 15	April 04	49
1864	February 18	April 25	69
1865	January 17	April 05	79
1866	January 25	April 06	72
1867	January 26	April 14	79
1868	February 09	March 17	37
1869	February 20	April 13	53
1870	February 02	April 24	82

1871	February 10	March 10	29
1872	January 27	April 25	89
1873	January 13	May 04	112
1874	January 13	May 08	116
1875	January 16	April 29	104
1876	February 23	April 20	57
1877	January 13	April 23	101
1879	February 14	April 23	69
1881	January 17	May 01	105
1883	February 03	April 15	72
1884	January 15	April 26	102
1885	January 27	April 29	93
1886	February 01	April 22	81
1887	January 31	April 22	83
1888	January 21	March 04	104
1889	February 18	March 30	41
1890	March 07	April 08	33
1891	March 01	April 10	41
1892	March 16	April 01	17
1893	January 28	April 07	70
1894	February 14	March 04	19
1895	February 02	April 18	76
1896	March 04	April 10	38
1897	March 03	April 03	32
1898	February 27	March 10	12
1899	February 01	April 17	73
1900	February 17	April 17	60
1901	February 14	April 14	60
1902	February 13	March 14	30
1904	January 25	April 25	91
1905	February 01	March 30	58
1906	March 17	March 22	6
1907	February 09	March 23	43
1908	March 17	March 22	6
1909	February 08	March 05	57
1910	February 17	March 20	32
1912	February 04	April 15	71
1913	February 116	March 26	39
1914	February 04	April 15	71
1915	February 01	April 09	68
1916	March 01	April 10	41
1917	February 05	April 20	75
1918	February 07	April 07	60
1920	February 13	March 28	44
1922	February 19	April 07	48
1923	February 05	April 28	83

1924	February 10	April 13	83
1925	January 28	March 24	85
1926	February 09	April 29	80
1927	January 26	March 17	51
1928	February 20	March 23	32
1929	February 01	April 23	54
1930	January 31	April 05	65
1933	March 23	April 07	16
1934	February 06	April 19	73
1935	February 22	April 17	55
1936	January 31	April 10	70
1937	February 21	April 12	51
1938	February 12	March 20	37
1939	February 26	April 18	52
1941	February 28	March 31	32
1942	February 06	March 21	44
1943	February 16	April 12	56
1944	March 19	March 24	6
1945	February 04	March 17	42
1946	February 27	March 14	18
1947	February 10	April 06	56
1948	January 31	April 04	64
1950	March 09	April 18	41
1951	February 01	March 30	58
1952	February 16	April 01	45
1956	February 28	March 03	6
1957	March 04	March 16	13
1958	February 11	March 04	53
1959	February 01	April 15	74
1960	February 28	April 11	44
1961	February 01	March 27	55
1962	February 09	April 15	71
1963	January 27	April 03	67
1965	February 23	April 20	57
1966	February 19	March 16	26
1967	February 07	March 31	53
1968	February 12	March 28	45
1969	February 15	April 07	52
1970	February 14	April 08	54
1971	February 02	April 21	79
1972	February 09	April 18	69
1973	February 28	March 4	5
1977	January 21	March 29	68
1978	February 13	April 10	57
1979	February 06	April 12	66
1980	February 10	April 07	57

1981	February 05	February 24	20
1982	February 04	March 31	56
1984	February 07	April 26	79
1985	February 12	March 27	44
1986	February 11	March 28	46
1989	March 07	March 28	22
1993	February 20	April 06	46
1994	January 30	April 09	70
1996	February 03	April 19	76
2003	February 15	March 29	42

*Records compiled by Traverse City Area Chamber of Commerce.
Thanks to Pat Hobson, manager of Operations
and Customer Service.*

TORNADOES IN NORTHERN MICHIGAN

Michigan is located on the northeast fringe of the Midwest tornado belt. The cold water of Lake Michigan in the spring and early summer may protect Michigan from some tornado activity.

Between 1950-87 Michigan averaged 15 tornadoes each year. During the same period northern Michigan averaged between 1 and 5 tornadoes a year, depending on location.

County	Tornadoes per year (avg.)
Crawford	5
Roscommon	5
Missaukee	5
Wexford	5
Mason	4
Osceola	4
Emmet	4
Grand Traverse	4
Leelanau	3
Clare	3
Benzie	3
Kalkaska	3
Otsego	2
Charlevoix	2
Antrim	2
Lake	1
Manistee	1

*Michigan Department of Agriculture, Climatology Program,
Michigan State University*

Five bad tornadoes

April 3, 1956: Started in Manistee County, and roared north through Benzie, Grand Traverse and Leelanau counties. Two fatalities, 24 injured and a quarter million dollars in property damage.

June 26, 1969: Touchdown about 15 miles southwest of Traverse City. One home and three barns destroyed. Sixteen other buildings badly damaged. No fatalities or injuries.

April 19, 1975: Fourteen people injured when a tornado touched down near Frederic in Crawford County. Eight trailers destroyed, and 16 buildings damaged.

July 5, 1994: Five homes damaged and 1,000 trees destroyed as a tornado touched down in Beaver Creek Township of Crawford County.

July 3, 1999: One tornado tracked from Montmorency County through Alcona County and into Oscoda County, where it left 80 homes and businesses damaged or destroyed in the community of Comins. $1.75 million in damage, two injuries, no fatalities.

Winds

Highest recorded wind gusts at the Mackinac Bridge:
128 mph on May 9th, 2003 and 117 mph on September 10th, 2001.

LAKE MICHIGAN

Lake Michigan's influence on life in northern Michigan is tremendous. The two largest industries in the north – agriculture and tourism – are reliant on weather, which is largely determined by Lake Michigan. It has been at the center of the northern Michigan economy dating back to the 17th century fur-trading days. French traders and Native Americans paddling handmade canoes and conducted commerce along trade routes that skipped from island to island to shoreline trading posts.

When the supply of fur became unreliable men turned to the water and found what seemed to be an endless supply of whitefish and trout. They could feed their families, and engage in trade, or both. The fishing industry created more jobs for boatbuilders, coopers, netmakers, and even salesmen, but the fish supply wasn't endless.

By the 1830's traffic on Lake Michigan was picking up as steamships from the east were able to enter the Great Lakes via the newly opened Erie Canal. These steamers needed a healthy diet of logs to burn, and sharp entrepreneurs set up fueling stations on the heavily wooded Manitou, Fox and Beaver Islands.

The steamships were soon enlisted to transport lumber from Michigan's inland forests to Chicago and other Lake Michigan ports. Between 1870 and 1900 Michigan led the nation in lumber production. Eventually city dwellers relied on the Lake Michigan steamships to bring them up north to the fresh air and waterfront cottages.

Today giant freighters and sleek cruise ships have replaced the cumbersome sidewheelers and wind-dependent schooners. They share the water with charter fishing boats, cross-lake ferries, yachts and recreational watercraft. The Lake Michigan shoreline is dotted with deluxe vacation homes and quaint cottages, second homes designed for a life of leisure, not work.

Lake Michigan cools the warm air in the summer before it reaches the shore, and in the winter, it heats up the blasts of frigid wind from the northwest. It creates a perfect climate for growing fruit along the shore, boaters love it, and the views can't be beat.

Several groups monitor the health of Lake Michigan on a daily basis. They watch for everything from foreign invaders – exotic species that arrive in the ballast water of international freighters – playing havoc with the Lake's ecosystem, to other states and countries that want to divert fresh water from Lake Michigan for their usage.

For more information on environmental issues effecting Lake Michigan contact:

The Tip of the Mitt
Watershed Council
www.watershedcouncil.org

Lake Michigan Federation
www.lakemichigan.org

Inland Seas Education
Association
www.schoolship.org

LAKE MICHIGAN
STATISTICS

Lake Michigan-Depth
Average depth: 279 ft.
Deepest point: 923 ft.
(2nd deepest Great Lake)

Lake Superior   1,333 ft.
Lake Michigan   923 ft.
Lake Ontario   802 ft.
Lake Huron   725 ft.
Lake Erie   212 ft.

The deepest points of Lake Michigan lie about 20 to 30 miles off the shore of Manistee and Benzie counties.

The deepest point between the islands and the mainland is about 200 feet.

The depth reaches 600 feet just south of the Beaver Island archipelago.

Lake Michigan - Area
Surface area: 22,278
(including Green Bay)

Other Great Lakes (sq. miles)
Lake Superior   31,700
Lake Huron   22,973
Lake Michigan   22,278
Lake Erie   9,906
Lake Ontario   7,340

Lake Michigan is 317 miles long and 118 miles wide.

Lake Michigan is the third largest Great Lake and the sixth largest freshwater lake in the world.

Technically Lake Michigan and Lake Huron are one lake connected by the Straits of Mackinac. As one lake with a surface area of over 45,000 square miles, it is the largest freshwater lake in the world.

Lake Michigan-Volume
Total volume: 1,180 cubic miles

Other Great Lakes (cubic miles)
Lake Superior   2,934
Lake Michigan   1,180
Lake Huron   850
Lake Ontario   393
Lake Erie   116

Major water sources of Lake Michigan
Fox River- Green Bay,

Wisconsin
Grand River - Grand Haven,
Michigan
Kalamazoo River –
Saugatuck, Michigan
Lake Michigan flows into
Lake Huron, which drains
into Lake St. Clair

Shoreline
Total miles of shoreline: 1,638

Shoreline miles-by county:
Ludington to Mackinaw City
(including islands)

Leelanau	151
Charlevoix	102
Emmet	75
Grand Traverse	56
Mason	28
Antrim	27
Manistee	25
Benzie	25

Total: 489

States that border Lake
Michigan: Michigan, Illinois,
Indiana, Wisconsin

Lake Michigan is the only
Great Lake entirely inside the
United States.

Water level
Average: 579 ft. above
sea level

The water level of Lake
Michigan fluctuates slightly
on a daily basis. The changes
are more measurable from
season-to-season and year-to-
year. The water level is generally lowest in the winter

when precipitation, in the
form of snow, remains piled
up on land, instead of running off into the lake, and
drier air increases evaporation. In the summer water
levels rise after snow and ice
run off into the lake.

Changes in water level are
due primarily to weather.
High precipitation amounts
mean high levels. Drier air
means less water is evaporated.
Lower average temperatures
also slow down evaporation.

Lake levels affect property
values, shipping, recreation,
and the environment. During
high water levels in the mid
1980's some shoreline home-
owners watched as their
beach disappeared and in
some cases, or their homes
crumble into the advancing
lake. The high water levels led
to increased shoreline erosion
and damage from flooding.

Low water levels can force
shippers to limit the amount
of cargo on Great Lakes
freighters, some marinas
become nearly inoperable,
and pristine sandy beaches,
can be replaced by a weed-
filled swamp.

**Modern day high water
record:** 582.35 ft. above
sea level   October, 1986

**Modern day low water
record:** 576.05 ft. above
sea level   March, 1964

Formerly known as: Grand Lac, by Samuel de Champlain, Governor of New France (Quebec).

Lake of the Stinking Water

Lake of the Puants (French called Winnebago Indians as Puans)

Lac St. Joseph by Allouez.

Lac des Illinois on 1679 map.

Indian name for the lake was Lake Michi gami.

DUNES

The world's largest fresh-water dunes line the eastern shore of Lake Michigan. The largest, highest and best known are those in the Sleeping Bear Dunes National Lakeshore in Leelanau and Benzie counties. To the south, in Ludington, lies the Nordhouse Dunes Wilderness Area. Both are federally managed and protected from development. Leelanau, Benzie and Mason have the most acres of protected dunes in northern Michigan.

Legislatively protected sand dunes

County	Acres of dunes
Leelanau	10,971
Benzie	6,619
Mason	6,640
Emmet	3,794
Charlevoix	2,144
Antrim	656
Manistee	588

How they were formed
During the Lake Nipissing phase, about 4,000 years ago, Lake Michigan was as high as 640 feet above sea level, about 60 feet higher than today. During that time a good part of the shoreline counties were underwater. Some of the inland lakes near the shoreline, such as Hamlin Lake and Crystal Lake, were once bays.

Over time river currents carried sand out to the Lake Michigan shore, which built up into large sand bars. Over the centuries that followed, the waters receded, the westerly winds whipped the sand against the shoreline ridge, and the dunes were born.

There are two kinds of dunes. The Sleeping Bear Dunes are perched dunes made up of sand and other material sitting atop a shoreline ridge. Beach dunes form at the water's edge and are made up mostly of wind-shipped sand. The wind continues to change the character of the dunes.
The National Park Service at Sleeping Bear report the popular Dune Climb has moved

Sleeping Bear Dunes (photo courtesy of Leelanau Historical Society)

about 4 feet per year.

The shifting sands have completely buried forests and telephone poles, and in 1931 forced the Coast Guard to move its station from Sleeping Bear Point to Glen Haven.

Vanishing Dunes

Sand dunes do disappear. Portions of some have slid into Lake Michigan, while others have been completely excavated and shipped off to glass factories.

The Pinnacle Sleeping Bear Dunes (photo courtesy of G.T. Pioneer & Historical Society)

Glass companies mined two dunes in Manistee County, nicknamed "Creeping Joe," and "Maggie Thorpe," and used their sand to make car molds, windshields and other glass products.

"Creeping Joe" was mined in the early part of the 20th century, while work on the Maggie Thorpe dune started in the 1930's. By the 1970's what once was a massive shoreline dune had been turned into a manmade lake. (Lake Michigan Federation)

Warning sign from Empire Bluffs (author photo)

There are at least three accounts of dune landslides – massive portions of the dunes sliding from their perch into Lake Michigan.

In December of 1914 about 20 acres of dunes near Sleeping Bear Point in

Leelanau County disappeared into the lake, falling from a height of 100 feet. It happened again in about the same location in March of 1971. Another 20 acres dropped into the water, this time, according to the National Oceanic and Atmospheric Administration (NOAA), leaving a huge hole in the bottom of the lake. Once again in February of 1995, near Sleeping Bear Point, more than 35 million cubic feet of sand washed into Lake Michigan. About 1,600 feet of beach shoreline was lost in this coastal landslide. Two years later scientists from the U.S. Geological Survey discovered debris

from the slide two miles from shore, including trees that had been growing on the bluff.

The Michigan Sand Dune Protection and Management Act was passed in 1976 following public outcry over sand mining in Manistee County. The law toughened regulations, but did not ban mining along the lakeshore.

Sleeping Bear Dunes National Lakeshore

"Be it enacted by the Senate and House of Representatives of the United States of America in Congress assembled, That (a) the Congress finds that certain outstanding natural features, including forests, beaches, dune formations and ancient glacial phenomena, exist along the mainland shore of Lake Michigan and on certain nearby islands..., and that such features ought to be preserved in their natural setting and protected from developments and uses which would destroy the scenic beauty and natural character of the area." H.R. 18776, October 21, 1970, Public Law 91-479

The idea to create a National Park around the Sleeping Bear Dunes began in 1958 with a federal survey of important shorelines. In 1959 the Sleeping Bear region was included in a Senate bill creating ten shoreline recreation areas. The original size was to be 26,000 acres, but that was soon bumped up to 77,000 acres, which would have taken out three holes from the private Crystal Downs golf course.
In the early 1960's Interior Secretary Stewart Udall, said the Sleeping Bear property should be increased to over 92,000 acres and include North Manitou Island and Sugarloaf Mountain. That

plan was withdrawn after Leelanau and Benzie County residents voiced their strong opposition.

Property owners in the target area formed associations to fight what they perceived as a federal land grab. Many had concerns they weren't receiving a fair price for their property, and others worried about condemnation. A bitter divide formed between the National Park Service and some of the locals. It took nearly ten years for the federal government to acquire over 1,400 privately owned parcels.

Up until 1963 the plan was referred to as the Sleeping Bear National Seashore, but common sense emerged and it was changed to National Lakeshore.

Senator Phil Hart was the driving force behind the idea, and today the Park's Visitor Center is named after him.

Before the federal effort to preserve the lakeshore, the State of Michigan had begun to acquire property.

In 1920, D.H. Day, pioneer lumberman and tourism promoter, donated 32 acres of Lake Michigan shoreline near Glen Haven for the D.H. Day State Park.

In 1923 the 180-acre Benzie State Park was created near the mouth of the Platte River. In 1931 the State added 1,545

Young canoeist on the Platte River in the National Lakeshore (photo courtesy of Travel Michigan)

acres of shoreline dunes from the federal government to form the Sleeping Bear Dunes State Park.

The Sleeping Bear Dunes National Lakeshore includes over 71,000 acres, including the dunes, two islands, 20 inland lakes, seven major watersheds, and forests.

There are 89 families that own property, mostly water-front, in the National Park.

The lone private business in the Park is Riverside Canoe on the Platte River in Honor.

Acres in Leelanau County: 56,621
Acres in Benzie County: 15,307

Shoreline: 68 total miles
35 miles (mainland)
33 miles (islands)

Max. Height: 460 ft. above Lake Michigan. Actual dunes are about 150 feet sitting atop a 300 ft. moraine on the shoreline.

Nordhouse Dunes

The Nordhouse Dunes Wilderness Area was created by the Michigan Wilderness Act of 1987.

Shoreline: 7,300 feet

Max Height: 140 ft. above Lake Michigan

The Nordhouse Dunes make up nearly a mile and a half of undeveloped shoreline in Mason County. They're part of the Manistee National Forest, and the only federally designated Wilderness Area on the Lower Peninsula mainland.

Approximately 11 miles of trails snake through the Wilderness Area which includes patches of pines and hardwoods. The dunes area is home for deer, coyote, fox, raccoon and porcupine, along with many varieties of birds. The Nordhouse Dunes Wilderness Area is located between the Lake Michigan Recreation Area to the north, and the Ludington State Park to the south.

Nordhouse Dunes (photo courtesy of Laura Jolly)

The Coastal Campaign

The largest privately owned property on Lake Michigan is now under the protection of the Grand Traverse Regional Land Conservancy. CMS Energy is selling over 6,000 acres of shoreline property in Manistee and Benzie counties, once destined to become a pumped storage power plant like the one in Ludington. The Conservancy is raising the $31 million dollar purchase price through grants from private foundations, including Mott and W.K. Kellogg, along with private contributions. The Coastal Campaign project will cover nearly 6,300 acres of forest, farmland, dunes, and three miles of shoreline.

LIGHTHOUSES

There are 25 lighthouses scattered between the islands and shoreline of northern Lake Michigan.

Lighthouse	Location	County	Height(ft.)
Ludington North	Ludington Break wall	Mason	57
Big Sable	8.5 miles N. of Ludington	Mason	112
Old Manistee Main	Near 5th Ave. Beach	Manistee	tower is gone
Manistee North	North Pier head	Manistee	39
Frankfort North	Break wall	Benzie	67
Point Betsie	5 miles N. of Frankfort	Benzie	37
Manning Memorial	Empire	Leelanau	55
South Manitou	SE tip of island	Leelanau	100
North Manitou	Shoal halfway between island and Pyramid Pt.	Leelanau	60
S. Fox Island	Southern tip of island	Leelanau	60
Grand Traverse	Cat Head Point	Leelanau	50
Old Mission	Tip of Old Mission Peninsula	Grand Traverse	41
Petoskey Pierhead	End of west pier	Emmet	44
Little Traverse	Harbor Pt.	Emmet	72
S. Fox Island	Southern tip of island	Leelanau	60

Skilagalee	S. of Waugoshance Pt	Emmet	58
Beaver Island	S. end of island	Charlevoix	41
St. James Harbor	Beaver Island	Charlevoix	41
Squaw Island	N. of Beaver Island	Charlevoix	N/A
Lansing Shoal	N. of Squaw Island	Mackinac	69
Gray's Reef	24 miles W. of Mac Bridge	Emmet	82
White Shoal	20 miles W. of Mac Bridge	Emmet	121
Waugoshance	17 miles W. of Mac Bridge	Emmet	76
McGulpin Pt.	3 miles W. of Mac Bridge	Emmet	25 est

Pt. Betsie Light (photo courtesy of Leelanau Historical Society)

Lighthouse	County	Established
Waugoshance Light	Emmet	1832* (lightship)
S.Manitou Light	Leelanau	1839*
Skillagalee Light	Emmet	1850 (Ile Aux Galets)
Beaver Head Light	Charlevoix	1851
Waugoshance Lighthouse	Emmet	1851
St. James Light	Charlevoix	1852
Grand Traverse Light	Leelanau	1852
Point Betsie Light	Benzie	1858
Big Sable Point	Mason	1867
S. Fox Island	Leelanau	1868*
McGulpins Point Light	Emmet	1869
Old Mission Point	Grand Traverse	1870
Ludington N. Breakwater	Mason	1871
S Manitou Lighthouse	Leelanau	1872
St. Helena Light	Emmet	1873
Frankfort N. Breakwater	Benzie	1873
Manistee N. Pierhead	Manistee	1873
Little Traverse Light	Emmet	1884 (Harbor Point)
Charlevoix South Pier	Charlevoix	1885*
Grays Reef Light	Emmet	1891 (light ship)
White Shoal Light	Emmet	1891 (light ship)
Squaw Island Light	Charlevoix	1892
Mackinac Point Light	Emmet	1892
Lansing Shoal	Mackinac	1900 (light ship)
White Shoal Lighthouse	Emmet	1910
Charlevoix South Pier	Charlevoix	1914
Lansing Shoals	Mackinac	1928
S. Fox Island Light	Leelanau	1934
N. Manitou Shoal Light	Leelanau	1935
Grays Reef Lighthouse	Emmet	1936
Manning Lighthouse	Leelanau	1991

*later replaced

Manistee Breakwall at sunset (photo courtesy of Travel Michigan)

North Manitou Shoal (photo courtesy of Travel Michigan)

The Waugoshance Lightship put in place in 1832 was the first on the Great Lakes.

The Waugoshance Light built in 1852 was decommissioned in 1910. Some of the light keepers believe it is haunted by the ghost of John Herman, former light keeper, who disappeared, presumably drowned, while on duty in 1894. The light was later used by the military as a World War II bombing target.

White Shoal is the only light on the Great Lakes with a candy cane paint job.

Point Betsie is the second most photographed lighthouse in the country, according to the Friends of Point Betsie Lighthouse. (**www.pointbetsie.org**)

Point Betsie, automated in 1983, was the last manned lighthouse on the eastern shore of Lake Michigan.

The Manning Light in Leelanau County was built to honor longtime Empire resident, Robert H. Manning, who always wanted a light on shore to guide him upon return from fishing trips. The light is not functional. The North Manitou Shoal was the last manned offshore light station on the Great Lakes. It was automated in 1980. Ile Aux Galets means island of pebbles in French.

Further reading…

Great Lakes Lighthouses: American and Canadian, Wes Oleszewski, copyright 1998, Avery Color Studios, Inc.

The Northern Lights: Lighthouses of the Upper Great Lakes, Charles K. Hyde, copyright 1986, Michigan Natural Resources Magazine, Lansing, MI

White Shoal Lighthouse (photo courtesy of State Archives of Michigan)

Frankfort North Light – 1914 (photo courtesy of U.S. Coast Guard Historian's Office)

BEACHES

There are hundreds of miles of beach and dunes open to the public between Ludington and the Straits of Mackinac. Beach locations range from those in downtown areas just feet from the main road, to those that are only reachable after a healthy hike through the woods. There is no system for ranking the quality of beaches, but some have appeared on "best of" lists.

In 2001 voting readers of Triple A Michigan's *Michigan Living* magazine voted Ludington Beach in Ludington as best in the state. Traverse City State Park beach was third and Frankfort Beach in Benzie County was fifth in the voting.

In 2002, Stephen Leatherman, aka Dr. Beach, who publishes an annual list of America's best salt-water beaches, visited Great Lakes beaches for the first time.

In a *Detroit News* article he said Lake Michigan beaches had "incredibly clear" water and was impressed with the wide beaches of "pretty, white and fine sand." Of the sand dunes he said, "...they're monsters. We don't have any that big on the East Coast. They're amazing, really."

Although he didn't include any of the Lake Michigan beaches in his annual list he singled out Ludington State Park beaches and Frankfort Beach.

Some of the criteria Dr. Beach uses in evaluation beaches include: sand quality, water clarity and temperature, cleanliness, number of sunny days, and safety record.

Leatherman, who runs the Laboratory for Coastal Research at Florida International University in Miami, started the Healthy Beaches Campaign (www.ihrc.fiu.edu/nhbc/) that aims to strike a balance between promoting the recreational value of beaches and the need to maintain environmental quality and safety.

Certified Healthy Beaches
Recognized Healthy Beaches

Glen Haven,	(Leelanau)
Frankfort Beach	(Benzie)
Platte Pointe	(Benzie)
Platte River Point	(Benzie)
Petoskey State Park	(Emmet)
North Bar	(Leelanau)
Glen Haven	(Leelanau)
Ludington State Park	(Mason)
Stearns Beach	(Mason)

Recognized healthy beaches can become Certified if the entities in charge choose to join the program and report conditions every year. One of the main factors in Healthy Beach status is water quality.

Bays, Harbors, and Coves

After Green Bay in Wisconsin, Grand Traverse Bay is the largest bay on the Great Lakes. In northern Michigan Grand Traverse and Little Traverse are the largest and most recognizable bays, but there are dozens more on the map.

Platte Bay	Benzie
Sleeping Bear Bay	Leelanau
Good Harbor Bay	Leelanau
Christmas Cove	Leelanau
Cat Head Bay	Leelanau
Hall Bay	Leelanau
Northport Bay	Leelanau
Ingalls Bay	Leelanau
Omena Bay	Leelanau
Suttons Bay	Leelanau
West Grand Traverse	Grand Traverse
East Grand Traverse	Grand Traverse
Bowers Harbor	Grand Traverse
Old Mission Harbor	Grand Traverse
Bell's Bay	Charlevoix
Greens Bay	Charlevoix (Beaver Island)
Mt. Pisgah Bay	Charlevoix (Beaver Island)
St. James Harbor	Charlevoix (Beaver Island)
Little Sandy Bay	Charlevoix (Beaver Island)
Cable Bay	Charlevoix (Beaver Island)
High Island Bay	Charlevoix (High Island)
Garden Island Harbor	Charlevoix (Garden Island)
Ninneegoes Bay	Charlevoix (Garden Island)
Bomways Bay	Charlevoix (Garden Island)
Jensen Harbor	Charlevoix (Garden Island)
Larse Harbor	Charlevoix (Garden Island)
Sturgeon Bay	Charlevoix (Garden Island)
Monatou Bay	Charlevoix (Garden Island)
Northcutt Bay	Charlevoix (Garden Island)
Fisherman Bay	Charlevoix (Hog Island)
Little Traverse Bay	Emmet
Sturgeon Bay	Emmet
Big Stone Bay	Emmet
Cecil Bay	Emmet
Trails End Bay	Emmet

Harbor Springs is the deepest natural harbor on the Great Lakes.

Water Clarity

The Inland Seas Education Association measures the clarity, or transparency, of the water in West Grand Traverse Bay using a Secchi disk. The eight-inch diameter disk is lowered into the water until it can no longer be seen. That depth is marked and recorded on a regular basis. The data can be used to compare water transparency over different periods whether on a day-to-day basis, or a season-to-season basis. Below are the readings taken during spring over a 15-year period.

Year	Feet
1989	6.4
1990	8.2
1991	8.3
1992	6.8
1993	7
1994	7.3
1995	8.6
1996	8.5
1997	10
1998	10.3
1999	10.5
2000	9.8
2001	9.2
2002	11
2003	13.9
2004	12.5

Students and volunteer instructors, as part of the Inland Seas Education Association's Great Lakes Schoolship Programs, took all readings.

Inland Seas Education Association
www.schoolship.org

For further reading on Lake Michigan:

Atlas of Michigan, edited by Lawrence M. Sommers, Department of Geography, Michigan State University, copyright 1977 Michigan State University Press, Wm. B. Eerdmans Publishing Co.

Sleeping Bear Yesterday and Today, by George Weeks, copyright 2005 George Weeks, University of Michigan Press and Petoskey Publishing

The Living Great Lakes: Searching for the Heart of the Inland Seas, by Jerry Dennis, copyright 2003 Jerry Dennis, Thomas Dunne Books, St. Martin's Press

A Nationalized Lakeshore: The Creation and Administration of Sleeping Bear Dunes National Lakeshore, by Theodore J. Karamanski, copyright 2000, National Park Service, Department of the Interior

Inland Seas Education Boat (photo courtesy of Inland Seas Education Association)

THE LAKE MICHIGAN ISLANDS

On a clear day with good binoculars you can see a few islands from the
mainland shore. With a detailed map, or better yet, a decent boat, you'll see many
more. The islands off Lake Michigan's northeastern shore number over two
dozen. Some are barely large enough to host a picnic, and can disappear
altogether when the lake level rises. Most of the small islands lie within an
archipelago anchored by Beaver Island, the largest in Lake Michigan.

Upper Lake Michigan Islands (by size)

Island	Sq. Miles	Acres	Shoreline (miles)	County
Beaver	58.4	37,385	41.6	Charlevoix
N. Manitou	20.4	13,056	20.6	Leelanau
S. Manitou	7.9	5,030	12.6	Leelanau
*Garden	7.8	4,914	20.7	Charlevoix
*High	5.8	3,692	12.5	Charlevoix
S. Fox	5.4	3,392	11.8	Leelanau
*Hog	3.3	2,075	16.0	Charlevoix
N. Fox	1.4	894	5.5	Leelanau
*Gull	.4	270	3.4	Charlevoix
Temperence	.37	235	6.2	Emmet
Waugoshance	.35	225	4.4	Emmet
Power	.32	205	2.8	Gr. Traverse
*Whiskey	.2	129	2.0	Charlevoix
*Trout	.2	115	1.8	Charlevoix
*Squaw	.1	75	1.6	Charlevoix
*Hat	.025	16	.6	Charlevoix
Fisherman's	.016	10	.7	Charlevoix
Bellow (Gull)	.01	7	.4	Leelanau
*Grape				Charlevoix
*Tim's				Charlevoix
*Shoe	.005	3.2	.3	Charlevoix
*Pismire	.004	2.5	.3	Charlevoix
Skillagalee				Emmet
Bassett	.003	1.9	.2	Gr. Traverse

Beaver Island archipelago

First Evidence of Man on the Islands

Archaeologists believe ancient Indians set up seasonal fishing villages on
some of the larger islands. The earliest artifacts include a large copper awl
dating back to 3,000 B.C., found on North Manitou Island, and spear points and
flint chips from 2,500 B.C. discovered on Beaver Island.

Artifacts found on Garden Island are dated to approximately 1,000 B.C.

Burial mounds discovered in 1875 suggest that prehistoric Indians operated a trading post on Beaver Island as early as 1500 to 1700 B.C.

There is evidence suggesting that Ojibwa tribes lived, at least during the warmer months, on Beaver Island in the mid 1700's.

First Europeans

In *The Journal of Beaver Island History: Volume One,* Terry Hart writes that there are geological indications that there might have been a European settlement on Beaver Island in the early 1600's, shortly after Champlain arrived in Canada.

It's likely that French voyageurs and fur trappers traveling between Mackinac and Wisconsin stopped for a breather on some of the Beaver Islands, and there's a good chance, but no evidence, that they trapped beaver there as early as the mid 17th century.

The first record of European man on Beaver Island is the 1832 visit by Father Friedrich Baraga, who paddled across the lake from his mission at L'Arbre Croche (Cross Village) to spread The Word. Baraga wrote that he received

a warm greeting from Indians living on the island in "eight pitiable huts of tree bark."

By the early 1840's a New York company had opened a fishing station on Beaver Island, and Mr. Alva Cable of Ohio, and his nephew, James, built a dock, a home, and opened a store. At that time they reported there were a few white men living on the island.

By the mid 1830's, on South Manitou Island William Burton was busy chopping down trees and setting up a dock for passing steamers.

Although there's no evidence of the operation until 1847, Nicholas Pickard probably started his wood station on North Manitou in the early 1840's. He built a dock on the west side of the island to accommodate passing steamers in need of fuel and food.

Some of the earliest residents of South Fox Island include John and Mary Snell who had a home there in the early 1840's, during which time Mr. Snell was surveying the island.

The first European settler on Power Island in West Grand Traverse Bay may have been McKinley Wilson, a Scottish immigrant who planted and grew corn on the island in the early 1850's. *(An Island in Grand Traverse Bay,* copyright

N. Manitou baseball team (photo courtesy of G.T. Pioneer & Historical Society)

Smith & Hull store in the island town of Crescent (photo courtesy of G.T. Pioneer & Historical Society)

East side dock on N. Manitou Island – 1908 (photo courtesy of Leelanau Historical Society)

1992, Kathleen Craker Firestone)

Island Ghost Towns

Ailsworth: A lumber town on the west side of N. Manitou Island with a peak population of about 200 in the 1860's. Named after George Aylsworth who owned the island's west side dock. For some unknown reason the name was misspelled. The town was abandoned by 1873 after the dock closed. Descendants of the Aylsworth family still live in Leelanau County.

North Manitou Village: Silas Boardman, a banking executive from Chicago, envisioned an island getaway for those in need of fresh air and relaxation. In the 1880's he moved his family to North Manitou where he built a home and began farming. In the next decade he carved out ten lots and sold them for $75 each to friends and family, calling the enclave North Manitou Village. Some of the

homes are still standing and remain in private ownership on what is now referred to as Cottage Row.

Crescent City: Largest town in N. Manitou history with a population over 200, located at the site of the ghost town, Ailsworth. The town included a new and bigger dock, a new high-capacity sawmill and railroad, a school, church, and even a baseball team. During that time most of the mature trees in the forest around the town were harvested. When there was none left, the mill closed, and the town ceased to be.

Success: Toward the end of the lumber boom on the mainland, some businessmen set up operations for a short time on some of the islands. In 1913 there were enough men working and living on Garden Island that a Post Office was opened in the general store. The name given to this small island community was Success; however, the Post Office closed after one

year, and the lumber operation didn't last much longer.

BEAVER ISLAND
(www.beaverisland.org)

Named after: The animal. One story claims the island's shape resembles a sprawled out Beaver. The other version: lots of beaver on the island in the mid 1700's when it was named.

Previously known as: Kitchi Miniss, the Ojibway word for "large island." Amikiminis, another Ojibway word meaning "presence of beavers." Isles du Castor, or Castor Island, used by early French mapmakers, meaning "island of beavers."

Later it was called **Great Beaver,** or **Big Beaver** to distinguish its size compared to the neighboring islands. Sometimes referred to as the "Emerald Isle."

Size: 58.4 square miles

Shoreline: 41.6 square miles

Distance from mainland: 32 miles from Charlevoix via the S-shaped path of the Ferry, or 32 miles by plane. Beaver Island is the most remote inhabited island in the Great Lakes.

Population: 550 year round. Between 1,500 – 2,000 seasonal.

Township and County: About 75% of the island lies in Peaine Township, the largest in Charlevoix County. The northern quarter of the island is in St. James Township.

Access: Beaver Island Boat Co. has two ferries, the *Emerald Isle* and the *Beaver Islander* that dock on Round Lake in Charlevoix. (See Transportation) Ferry service runs mid-April through late December. An adult round trip ticket is $35.00; with car, it's $61.00 one-way. Trip takes a little over two hours.

Island Airways offers year-round daily flights from Charlevoix Airport to the island. Round trip tickets are $79.00 for the 15 minute flight.

Then: Native Americans were the first to inhabit Beaver Island, probably in small fishing camps by the late 1600's. In 1832, Father Baraga, the Catholic priest who had taught Christianity to Indians at L'arbre Croche (present day Cross Village), became the first known European to land on the island.

In the 1840's more Europeans arrived on Beaver to set up

Harbor at Beaver Island (photo courtesy of Beaver Island Chamber of Commerce)

Emerald Isle Ferry (photo courtesy of Beaver Island Boat Co.)

logging and fishing operations. The Native Americans began moving away to nearby Garden and High islands. In 1850, a settlement of approximately 100 was recorded near Whiskey Pt, the site of a busy trading post.

The 1850's were turbulent times on Beaver Island. Competition for fishing territory was heating up as King Strang and his growing Mormon following moved in. (see box) Beaver Island with its deep harbor, thick woods, and plentiful fish supply was overtaking Mackinac Island as the economic powerhouse of the region. The Mormons were full participants in the growing economy, but were gradually driving away those who arrived before them.

After Strang's assassination in 1856, the Mormons were driven from the island. The Gentiles, many of them Irish immigrants, returned to the island, and were joined by others from County Donegal in Ireland. The fishing industry flourished, becoming the largest supplier of fresh water fish in the country by 1880. At that time the island population was up to 881.

By the 1890's the seemingly endless supply of fish nearly ended. The population dropped as the fishing industry suffered. Farming, boat building, and small logging operations were the staple of the island economy until large scale lumber operations arrived. The Beaver Island Lumber Company built a mill, docks and a railroad into the woods. The mill produced shingles and boards for the Chicago market, and created over 100 new jobs on the island.

The resort and tourism industry started in the early years of the new century. Salesmen in Chicago found buyers for beachfront lots and unsurveyed inland parcels, and the island was promoted as a tourist destination.

By the 1940's the year round population had dropped to about 200. Many residents left as the commercial fishing industry fizzled. In the 1970's tourism increased and the population began to rebound.

King Strang
America's Only King

Jesse James Strang, who preferred to be called James Jesse Strang, arrived on Beaver Island in 1847, and within less than ten years would be elected to the state legislature, crowned king of an island community numbering almost a thousand residents, and assassinated by two of his former followers. It is one of the most fascinating and bizarre chapters in Great Lakes history.

In 1847, Strang was scouting a new location for his small Mormon following from Voree, Wisconsin. He claimed to be God's handpicked successor to Joseph Smith, the assassinated Mormon leader. With Smith gone, the church split into several factions: most members followed Brigham Young west to Utah, while a few hundred followed Strang from Nauvoo, Illinois to Wisconsin. Strang claimed, in 1846, to have a vision from God describing Beaver Island, although it's likely Strang had already seen the island during a previous journey to Buffalo, New York.

King Strang (photo courtesy of Beaver Island Historical Society)

Strang saw many advantages to Beaver Island: it was sparsely populated; had a seemingly endless supply of lumber that could be used for building, wood burning, and for sale to passing steamer ships; the island had fertile ground for crops, a beautiful protected harbor, and there was now resident land agent. So the migration of Mormons from Wisconsin to Beaver Island began in 1847 with Strang and four families. By the end of 1850 there were 355 Mormons living on the island with 128 non-Mormons, mostly fishermen and families.

At this time Beaver Island was growing in importance over Mackinac Island, which had been the economic center of the region for nearly a century. With the diminishing fur trade the region's economy shifted to fishing, which favored Beaver Island. As Strang and his followers became the majority, the non-Mormons, or Gentiles, accused them of muscling in on their fishing territory and stealing their nets and boats. Eventually the Gentiles, some frightened, some disgruntled over the $10 head tax and other measures imposed by Strang, moved away. They made new homes – some on the neighboring islands, some on Mackinac Island or on the mainland.

Resentment towards Strang grew as he renamed the island's lakes and roads, and used the land as he wished – felling trees for buildings, and as fuel sold to passing steamer ships. He published *The Northern Islander,* the first newspaper in northern Michigan. In it he wrote articles about white traders who watered down whiskey they traded to Indians in exchange for fresh fish. This added to the resentment, but not as much as his change of heart on the issue of polygamy.

For years Strang had denounced the Mormon tradition of polygamy, but that changed in 1849 when he secretly wed Elvira Fields, an 18-year old schoolteacher. She was forced to masquerade as Strang's nephew for nearly a year. When Strang's wife of 13 years, Mary Perce, learned of his marriage she moved back to Wisconsin. Strang took three more wives, including two 19-year old cousins, and fathered a total of 14 children.

In 1850, on a stage built by followers inside a wooden tabernacle, Strang had himself crowned king of the island. About 235 people attended the ceremony in which a paper crown was placed on Strang's head and the crowd shouted, "Long live James, King in Zion!" He had successfully created the only monarchy on U.S. soil. Amazingly, most of the land used for homes and farms had never been purchased from the government. Many of the "kingdom's" residents were squatters, although Strang had purchased some of the best for himself, at least 100 acres.

A few months after his coronation, Strang was arrested and brought to Mackinac Island where he faced charges of threatening the lives of two followers. Strang, who was a lawyer before his Mormon career, quickly outwitted the local judge, and was set free. Tensions grew between Mormons and Gentiles that winter with accusations of thievery, vandalism and general thuggery coming from both sides. Newspapers in Detroit, Chicago, and Cleveland were covering the story of the king on Beaver Island.

On April 30, 1851 President Millard Fillmore ordered the Navy battleship Michigan to Beaver Island to arrest Strang and 30 other Mormons charged with counterfeiting and trespassing on federal land. They were taken to Detroit, where Strang successfully argued during his closing statement that he was being prosecuted for religious reasons. He and the other Mormons were found not guilty, and returned to Beaver Island.

The talented orator managed to win a seat in the State Legislature in 1852. He received the entire Mormon vote, which was enough to make him the new representative of the sprawling Newaygo District. As a state legislator, Strang was able to extend his control beyond Beaver Island. He ushered through a law that changed Emmet County boundary lines to include all of the Beaver Islands, Emmet County, Charlevoix County and Cheboygan County. St. James became the new county seat, controlled by Mormons.

There was some resentment of Strang's power grab, and in 1855 the legislature passed a law that separated the Beaver Islands from Emmet County. In doing so they created the county of Manitou, made up of the Beaver, Fox and Manitou islands.

On June 16, 1856, after finishing dinner with his four wives, King Strang was told the Navy ship *Michigan* had arrived and the captain had requested a word with Strang. As he walked toward the dock two disgruntled followers, Thomas Bedford and Alexander Wentworth, ambushed him from behind. They shot him several times and pistol-whipped him before they ran aboard the Navy ship seeking protection.

The wounded king remained on the island for 12 days before he was shipped back to Wisconsin where he died on July 9th. Meanwhile the murderers were taken to Mackinac Island where the sheriff of Emmet County freed them.

On July 5th, less than three weeks after the assassination, boatloads of angry, drunken Gentiles arrived at Beaver Island and began rounding up the Mormon families at gunpoint. Without their belongings they were pushed onto steamers waiting in the harbor and shipped to Chicago and other ports. The entire Mormon community was captured and kicked off the island within a few days. Michigan historian, Byron M. Cutcheon, called July 5th, 1856 "the most disgraceful day in Michigan history."

Reminders of the Mormon era are evident today in place names given by Strang like the town of St. James, King's Highway, Mt. Pisgah, and Lake Geneserath. Strang's contribution to history include the first newspaper in northern Michigan, *The Northern Islander* in 1850; his inventory of flora and fauna, *Some Remarks on the Natural History of Beaver Islands, Michigan* was published by the Smithsonian Institute, and his account of the Beaver Island years, *Ancient and Modern Michilimackinac* is still used by researchers and writers.

Beaver Island Light School (photo courtesy of Beaver Island Chamber of Commerce)

Beaver Island Ferry (photo courtesy of Terry Phipps)

Today: Although about 16 times as large as Mackinac Island, Beaver Island supports roughly the same year-round population--about 550. Most of the residents live in the harbor side town of St. James, at the northeastern tip of the island. There are some homes situated on the shores of a few of the island's inland lakes and more new cabins pop up in the woods every year. Like Mackinac, Beaver Island's main industry is tourism, although the number one provider of year-round jobs is the construction industry, followed by local government.

Education: The only school is Beaver Island Community School with a staff of nine teachers, and annual enrollment that's never topped 97 students.

Since 1975 Charlevoix Public Schools have owned the Beaver Island Lighthouse, which is used for Alternative Education classes. Students aged 16-21 who have dropped out, or are in danger of not graduating, spend several weeks helping to restore the lighthouse and attached quarters. In addition, their academic schedule runs seven days a week.

Law Enforcement: There is a full-time deputy from the Charlevoix County Sheriff's Department assigned to the island, and in the summer when the population triples, a part-time deputy is added. They respond mostly to petty crimes and complaints such as speeding, drunk driving, and vandalism.

There is no jail on the island, so petty criminals have to sit in the deputy's office while they're being processed. More serious criminals or suspects are flown to the county jail on the mainland.

Religion: Residents and visitors looking for a church have three choices. The oldest is Holy Cross Catholic Church, founded in 1860 by Father Baraga. Half of the original church building was moved from its original location, about two miles from town, to its present location overlooking St. James Harbor where it serves the mostly Catholic island population. There is also a Holy Cross Parish Hall built in 1908 that is used for weddings, school events, and other community gatherings.

The St. James Episcopal Mission church was built in 1954. A visiting Episcopal minister is flown to the island to lead services once a month in the winter. There is a resident priest during the summer months.
The Beaver Island Christian Church is non-denominational.

Lodging: There are 5 hotels and motels on the island, along with two Bed & Breakfasts. There are also a number of private homes and cottages for rent. For more information check the Chamber of Commerce website: www.beaverisland.org Phone: (231) 448 –2505

Busiest weekend: It's hard to find a room on the island during Homecoming Weekend in August. Residents play host to friends and family as former island dwellers are invited back for the weekend celebration.

Tourist hotspots: The main attraction of the island is its natural beauty -- magnificent dunes and some of the most pristine beachfront on the Great Lakes. Hikers and bikers enjoy the many wooded trails, some of which lead to inland lakes. Tourists can rent kayaks, or take charter boat ride, passing by some of the outer islands. Horseback riding and eco-tours are also popular. In St. James there are three museums popular with tourists: the Marine Museum, Mormon Print Shop Museum and the Toy Museum and Store.

Forty percent of the island is State land.

Lakes: Barney's Lake, Egg Lake, Font Lake, Fox Lake, Lake Geneserath, Green's Lake, Lake Maria, Miller's Marsh and Round Lake.

Famous visitors and residents: Nationally syndicated political writer David Broder writes at least one of his columns from Beaver Island every August. He and his wife Anne own the island home where her mother was born.

Other celebrity visitors to the island include newsman Walter Cronkite, actors Mel Gibson and Tim Allen, and Madonna. She and her husband, Guy Ritchie, were guests at the luxurious Deerwood Inn during the summer of 2003.

NORTH MANITOU ISLAND
(www.nps.gov/slbe/NMI.htm)

Named after: The Great Indian spirit, Manitou. Chippewa and Ottawa Indians believed The Great Manitou was a spirit floating on a raft with many animals.

Previously known as: One of the Manitou's

Size: 20.4 square miles, 7 miles long and 4 mile wide

Shoreline: 20.6 miles

Distance from mainland: 11 miles from Leland, 6.5 miles to Pyramid Pt.

Manitou Island Ferry (photo courtesy of G.T. Pioneer & Historical Society)

N. Manitou Lifesaving Station –1900 (photo courtesy of G.T. Pioneer and Historical Society)

Early N. Manitou cottage – 1915 (photo courtesy of Leelanau Historical Society)

Population: Uninhabited.

Township and County: Leland Township, Leelanau County

Access: A 50-minute ride aboard a Manitou Island Transit Co. ferry from Leland.

Then: N. Manitou started as a fuel station for the growing number of wood-hungry steam ships traveling between Chicago and Buffalo in the 1840's. By 1860 the island population included 180 Native Americans and 270 new arrivals, many of them immigrants from Europe and Scandinavia. They farmed, chopped wood, worked in the sawmill, or on one of the island's two docks.

The west side dock, where the village of Ailsworth came to be, closed in the early 1870's, and the island lost many residents. In 1877 the U.S. Lifesaving Service built the first of its three Manitou Passage stations on N. Manitou. By 1880 the population had dwindled to 71.

Commercial fruit farming began in the 1890's with the planting of thousands of apple, pear, apricot and cherry trees. After harvest the fruit could be shipped immediately to Chicago. In 1896 the N. Manitou Lighthouse was built at the southern end of the island.

In the years leading up to the turn of the century passenger ship traffic increased, bringing the leisure classes from Midwestern cities to the beauty of northern Michigan, including North Manitou Island. A Chicago banker built a vacation home and sold neighboring lots for $75 each to friends and family. North Manitou Village, or "Cottage Row," as it was known, consisted of about six homes, some servant's quarters, and a hotel.

In the early 1900's the abandoned village of Ailsworth came back to life after a Traverse City firm bought thousands of acres of forest, built a new dock and sawmill, and a railroad. The new village, Crescent City, even had a schoolhouse. The population in 1910 was 215, but the town fizzled in 1917 when lumbering operations shut down.

In 1926, William Angell, the former President of Continental Motors Company, began buying large tracts of land. He brought in deer to open the island up to hunting, and by 1937 the herd had multiplied to the point that there wasn't enough natural food for them on the island. A hunt was held that year with 18 deer harvested. Hunters bagged 41 the following year, and in 1944 the total reached 256. The island became part of the Sleeping Bear Dunes National Lakeshore in 1970, and the annual deer hunt continues to this day.

Fact: At one time there were two schoolhouses on N. Manitou. One school, built in 1906, operated until 1941, with never more than 25 students at one time.

Now: All but 27 acres are designated as wilderness. The island is popular with backpackers, hikers and campers. Attractions include the ruins of old homesteads, farms and other buildings, old cemeteries, dunes and Lake Manitou.

Highest point on the island is 421 feet above the Lake Michigan surface.

An annual fall deer hunt, by permit only, has been held since 1985.

In 1998, the North Manitou Island Lifesaving Station built in 1854 was designated as a National Historic Landmark.

Lakes: Lake Manitou and Tamarack Lake

SOUTH MANITOU ISLAND
(www.nps.gov/slbe/ SMI_page.htm)

Named after: The Great Indian spirit, Manitou. Chippewa and Ottawa Indians believed The Great Manitou was a spirit floating on a raft with many animals.

Previously known as: One of the Manitou's

Size: 7.9 square miles

Shoreline: 12. 6 miles

Distance from mainland: 15 miles to Leland, 7.5 miles to Pyramid Pt.

Population: Uninhabited

Township and County: Glen Arbor Township, Leelanau County.

Access: A 90-minute ride aboard a Manitou Island Transit Co. ferry from Leland.

North Manitou Light (photo courtesy of Leelanau Historical Society)

South Manitou Lighthouse – 1858 (photo courtesy of G.T. Pioneer & Historical Society)

Early schoolhouse on S. Manitou Island (photo courtesy of G.T. Pioneer & Historical Society)

Then: William Burton was the first person to capitalize on South Manitou's strategic location on the new super waterway that developed with the opening of the Erie Canal in 1825. Newly built steam-powered ships became the trucks and buses of the Great Lakes delivering goods and passengers between the East Coast and Chicago. Burton saw that S. Manitou was ideally situated to serve the refueling needs of the growing number of wood burning steamships. He opened a wooding station on the island's east side in 1835. By the end of the decade a lighthouse was built on the southern tip of the island. It was replaced, 18 years later, with a taller structure.

Immigrants from Germany and other European countries found work on "Burton's Wharf" which included a general store, a blacksmith shop, and a small railway for transporting lumber. By the 1870's, over a dozen families made their living on S. Manitou working the docks, chopping wood, or farming. Much of their produce was sold at market in Chicago, as up to 100 ships a day sailed through the Manitou Passage.

Business at the wood station began to slow in the 1880's as the newer ships were fueled by coal instead of wood. On the mainland the lumber industry offered plenty of jobs, and the shipping industry now had competition from the railroad.

After the turn of the century most island residents were involved in farming. They raised cattle in addition to vegetable and fruit crops. In 1902, the U.S. Lifesaving Station opened, bringing a few new residents and several new buildings. By 1910 there were two new lumber operations on the island processing what was left of the forests into cedar shingles and other wood products. In 1913 the mills closed for good.

In the 1920's one island farmer, George Conrad, nephew of one of the island's early settlers, developed Rosen Rye, a new strain of rye that brought international acclaim to the island. Later the Michelite Bean was developed, which won more international recognition from the agriculture community.

In the 1950's one island native, Fred Burdick, attempted to market the island as a resort. He built a few cabins and airstrip and called it Manitou Haven Resort. The project never caught on, and eventually came to a halt when the Federal Government announced it would include the Manitous in the new National Park.

Now: Popular with hikers and campers because of the numerous and well-marked trails, which lead past old farms, barns, cottages, through a stand of virgin Cedar trees and to the top of a 300 foot high dune over-looking Lake Michigan. Visitors enjoy guided tours, including a walk up to the top of the 100-foot high lighthouse, the old Coast Guard Station, and historic exhibits in the old Post Office, now the official Visitor's Center.

Fact: The oldest living Cedar tree known to man is found in "The Valley of the Giants," a stand of Cedars left untouched by loggers in the 19th and 20th century. With 528 gowth rings it pre-dates Columbus.

Fact: The Postal Service oper-ated an office on S. Manitou between 1879 and 1928.

Lakes: Florence Lake

GARDEN ISLAND

Named after: Native American word for Garden, which probably referred to corn and squash grown on the island by early Indians.

Previously known as: Miniss Kitigan, Ojibway for Garden Island. For a while in the 19th century it was referred to as Little Beaver Island.

Size: 7.8 square miles

Distance from: About two miles north of Beaver Island. 17 miles south of Naubinway in the Upper Peninsula.

Shoreline: 20.7 miles

Population: There are no year-round or seasonal resi-dents on Garden Island.

Township and County: St. James Township, Charlevoix County.

Access: By charter boat from Beaver Island, or private watercraft.

Then: Garden Island once supported a Native American fishing village, a small farm-ing community and a lumber town.

In the 1830's, Native Americans, including Chief Peaine, began moving to Garden Island where they fished, farmed and traded with white settlers on Beaver Island. At one point it's esti-mated that nearly 200 Native Americans lived on the Island. During King Strang's time in the 1850's the Mormons ran a school on Garden Island. The last year-

Giant Old Growth Cedar Tree on S. Manitou Island (photo courtesy of Manitou Island Transit Co.)

round resident was a Native American – Peter Monatou – who died in 1947 and is buried in the Native American cemetery on the island's west side. Historians believe there are at least 3,000 Native American gravesites on the island.

The first European settler is believed to be James Morey, who was rescued by Garden Island Indians after he shipwrecked on Whiskey Island.

Several Danish families made their homes on the island in the latter half of the 19th century. They farmed, built comfortable homes, a church and schoolhouse, and developed a reputation as quality boat builders. There is some evidence of their craftsmanship today in the ruins of some of these structures.

Between 1910 and 1920 there were several short-lived lumber operations on the island, some of which manufactured wooden boxes, rail ties and fence posts. The last year-round white residents died on the island in the 1930's. There is a Homesteader's Cemetery on the north side of the island with about 30 graves.

Now: Garden Island is part of the Beaver Islands Wildlife area. The island, with its trails, and historic ruins is popular with hikers, backpackers, hunters and recreational boaters. Followers of the Native American natural-

ist, Keewaydinoquay, still gather on the north shore during summer to teach and practice a traditional, environmentally conscientious way of life.

HIGH ISLAND

Named after: The highest vantage point in the Beaver Islands is at the summit of the Top O'The World Trail, 240 feet above the surface of Lake Michigan.

Size: 5.8 square miles. About four miles long and two miles wide

Shoreline: 12.5 miles

Distance from: 4 miles west of Beaver Island, 9 miles southwest of Garden Island, 2 miles south of Trout Island, 7 miles east of Gull Island

Population: Uninhabited

Township and County: St. James Township, Charlevoix County

Access: By charter boat from Beaver Island, or private watercraft. There is a landing strip, but it is not maintained, and is unsafe to use.

Then: Native Americans began settling on High Island in the 1830's, moving away from the European traders setting up shop on Beaver Island. They farmed, fished, and traded with Beaver Islander's. The Indian population on High Island topped out in the late 1800's at about 100. In the 1890's Franciscans built a church, The Assumption of Our Lady, on the island. Some followers of King Strang moved to High Island in the 1850's.

The busiest period in the island's history was the early 1900's when members of "King Ben's" House of David ran a logging operation. Ben Purnell and his followers in the Israelite House of David had established a permanent settlement in Benton Harbor. The Israelites did not drink or use tobacco. They did not shave and sported beards to their waist. They were vegetarians and grew most of what they ate. The Israelites were also known for their talent in and love of the game of baseball.

In 1912 the Israelites set up a logging operation at an abandoned lumber camp on High Island. They ran a large sawmill, shingle mill, blacksmith shop, and potato farm. A school was built as the population topped out at about 150 Israelites and 100 Indians around 1920.

The House of David disbanded in the mid 1920's shortly after "King Ben" was charged with sexual misconduct toward some of the females in his church.

After the last Native Americans left High Island in the 1940's, wild horses roamed the island. A horse trader that heard about this thought High Island would be the perfect place to raise wild horses for the rodeo. With concerns of animal cruelty in the press and negative public opinion, the landowners ordered the horses removed.

Now: High Island has been called one of the most beautiful islands on the Great Lakes and is designated as a State Natural Area. Hikers enjoy the west side with its high-perched dunes and sandy plateaus that mark previous lake levels. The island supports a number of threatened and endangered plant and bird species.

Lakes: Lake Maria

SOUTH FOX ISLAND

Named after: The animal

Previously known as: Thomas Island, on an 1839 government map. The Odawa and Ojibwa Indians called them Wau-goosh-e-min-iss, or "the fox, their islands." James Jesse Strang, who ruled

Logs stacked on High Island dock built by members of House of David (photo courtesy of Beaver Island Historical Society)

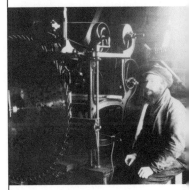

House of David sawmill on High Island (photo courtesy of Beaver Island Historical Society)

South Fox from above (photo courtesy of Mirada Ranch)

Beaver Island in the 1850's, called South Fox, "Patmos Island." Some people called it Big Fox Island.

Size: 5.4 square miles

Shoreline: 11.8 miles

Distance from mainland: 16.5 miles from Cathead Pt. at the tip of the Leelanau Peninsula. 4 miles south of N. Fox Island.

Population: N/A

Access: By private watercraft or airplane

Township and County: Leelanau Township, Leelanau County

Then: South Fox is the most remote – 16.5 miles from the mainland – of the northern Michigan islands. This may be one reason it remained sparsely populated through its history, compared to the Beaver or Manitou islands. A few rugged families and individuals,

attracted by the never-ending supply of fish, settled in the 1840's and 1850's.

A small lumber operation, including a sawmill and wood dock for passing steamers, was established in the 1860's. In 1867 the lighthouse was built on the southern tip of the island. It was replaced in 1934, and manned year round through 1958, when it went automatic.

One lumber operation or another was active on the island through the 1930's. In 1954, Sterling Nickerson & Sons of Kingsley built a new sawmill that produced 15,000 board feet of lumber a day. In 1959, Sterling Nickerson Jr. drowned when the ship he used to transport lumber to Wisconsin was lost at sea. The timbered land was sold in 1965.

In 1962, the Nickerson's brought 17 deer to the island – some came from the zoo in Traverse City and a park in

Baldwin. In the late 60's new owners set up a hunting lodge, and with the DNR, arranged for a deer hunt. By this time the deer population had grown to the point of concern. 382 deer were taken in the 1970 hunt.

In 1973, the owners--Lynn Dillin and wife Virginia, were killed when their small plane crashed during a foggy landing attempt on the island airstrip.

Three men from Hart purchased the land, which consisted of about 2/3rd's of the island, from the Dillin estate. They sold it a few years later to what turned out to be three Flint area men involved in a drug trafficking ring. The land reverted back to the Hart men when the drug suspects fell behind on payments. In the early 1980's, one of the three owners from Hart, Stanley Riley, was killed on his way to the island when the small plane he was in crashed near Adrian.

In 1983 an Army Chinook helicopter crashed on the island, killing all six crew aboard.

Now: David Johnson, a developer whose projects include Bay Harbor just South of Petoskey, owns two thirds of the island. Johnson bought it in 1989.

HOG ISLAND

Size: 3.3 square miles

Shoreline: 16 miles

Distance from Garden Island: Four miles east of Garden Island

Population: People-zero. Snakes-numerous!

Access: Private watercraft

Township and County: St. James Township, Charlevoix County

Then: A low-lying, swampy island difficult to access because of the rocky shores. There is no evidence of settlement on the island. A hut observed on the island by researchers in 1938 was probably built by a fisherman as seasonal shelter. The *Beaver Islander* describes an early 1970's logging operation that lasted less than a year. Some 20 miles of roads were built, a small channel was dredged and the take was 180,000 board feet of lumber.

Today: An official State Natural Area described as one of the least disturbed in the Beaver Island archipelago and home to threatened bird and plant species. Inland is heavily forested, including some old growth hardwoods.

NORTH FOX ISLAND

Named after: The animal

Previously known as: The Odawa and Ojibwa Indians called them Wau-goosh-e-min-iss, or "the fox, their islands." Labeled as Pierce Island on 1839 government map. James Jesse Strang, who ruled Beaver Island in the 1850's, called North Fox, Paros Island. Some folks called it Little Fox Island.

Distance from mainland: 4 miles from South Fox, 8 miles from Beaver Island

Size: 1.4 square miles About 2 miles long and 1 mile wide

Shoreline: 5.5 miles

Access: Private watercraft

Township and County: Leelanau Township, Leelanau County

Then: There has been very little human activity on North Fox. The 1860 census indicates a population of 9, three families drawn by the fishing opportunities. By 1870 the fishing families were gone.

In 1959, Frank Shelden, a geologist and land developer from Detroit, bought North Fox Island. He had a home and airstrip built and an-nounced plans to market the island as a resort for fellow pilots. However, in 1976, when charges of criminal sexual conduct were brought against Shelden, and State Police alleged that he was connected to a national child pornography ring involving underage boys, he vanished. Shelden was on the board of Brother Paul's Nature Camp for Boys--advertised as a health island getaway for boys.

Dreams of building a world-class resort fell through in the early 90's due to public opposition. Partners including Mark Conner of Beaver Island and Paul Nine, who developed the Grand Traverse Resort, envisioned an island paradise to include an 18-hole golf course, two marinas, an airport and 612 home sites.

After several years of battling with opponents they sold to another developer, David Johnson, whose projects include Bay Harbor Resort near Petoskey.

Today: The island is owned by the State DNR, purchased from David Johnson for $2.2 million dollars in 2000. (Johnson bought the island for $1.3 million in 1994.)

POWER ISLAND

Named after: Eugene and Sadye Power whose $270,000 gift put the island into public owner-ship forever.

Previously known as: According to *"An Island in Grand Traverse Bay,"* by Kathleen Craker Firestone, the island had many identi-ties since 1850, when it was known as Island Number 10. After that it was known as Eagle or Hawk Island until the Federal Government officially tagged it as Harbor Island, although the locals called it Hog Island. It became Marion Island in 1872, named after the new owner's daughter. Henry Ford, the auto pioneer, bought it in 1917, and it was known as Ford Island until 1959. After that it was known as Rennie Island after the new owner, Pete Rennie of Traverse City.

Distance from mainland: 6.5 miles north of downtown Traverse City. 1 mile from Bowers Harbor

Size: 205 acres

Shoreline: 2.8 miles

Access: Private watercraft

Township and County: Peninsula Township, Grand Traverse County

The 205-acre uninhabited Power Island off the shore of Traverse City (photo courtesy of Fred and Tina Tank)

Then: Despite its convenient location to Traverse City, there has never been a major settlement, logging operation, or resort development on the island. In the early 1850's McKinley Wilson planted corn and lived on the island for a few years. A Chicago businessman had hopes of turning the island into a yachting resort, but nothing ever developed. Nothing much happened during Henry Ford's domain, although he did entertain his friends, Thomas Edison and Harvey Firestone, on the island.

In the early 20th century a dancehall and pavilion built on the smaller Bassett Island attracted boatloads of visitors. The pavilion was torn down in 1934. A logging operation established in the mid 1940's lasted about two years.

In 1967, nine deer from the Traverse City Zoo were added to the small herd already on the island. Private deer hunts were held in the

Visitors to the Marion Island dance hall arrived by steamship at this dock, actually connected to the adjoining Bassett Island. (photo cour-tesy of GT Pioneer & Historical Society)

Power Island is a popular destination in West Bay for recreational boaters. (photo courtesy of Fred and Tina Tank)

early 70's, but the herd continued to grow. Wildlife managers decided it was best if there was no deer population. Public deer hunts in 1976 and 1977 apparently accomplished that goal.

The last individual to own the island, Pete Rennie, drowned in 1965. Apparently, the propeller-driven boat sled that he used to travel over the frozen bay had engine problems. It's presumed he fell through the ice while walking toward his island.

Now: The island remains in its natural state. Caretaker Fred Tank lives with his family in a cabin on the island part of the year. It's a popular meeting spot for pleasure boaters who drop anchor near the shore, some wading inland to enjoy the many trails. The island is owned by Grand Traverse County and is protected from development in perpetuity.

Caretaker's lodge on Power Island (photo courtesy of Fred and Tina Tank)

BASSETT ISLAND

Named after: Dick Bassett, the first documented owner of the island

Previously known as: Squaw Island, The Haunted Island, Fisherman's Island

Distance from mainland: 6.5 miles north of downtown Traverse City. 1 mile from Bower's Harbor

Size: Less than two acres at times of low lake level. Completely submerged at high water periods.

Shoreline: 0.2 mile

Access: Private watercraft, or by foot from Power Island

Then: Water levels on West Grand Traverse Bay were low enough in the late 1800's that Bassett Island was considered separate from Marion Island (now Power Island), even though it was literally a stone's throw away.

Sometime between the mid 1860's and 1880 Dick Bassett, a Civil War veteran, made himself at home on the tiny island. He built a home, some outbuildings, and a dock. He also planted a garden and fished. The locals considered him a mysterious hermit.

In 1901 Bassett sold the island to a steam ship company which built a two-story dance pavilion and dining room in 1906. Although it lasted only a few years, it was a popular destination for locals and early tourists. The pavilion was torn down in 1934.

In 1917, Henry Ford bought both islands, and since then they've gone by one name, and are considered one island.

Now: Officially part of Power Island. If water levels are low the island is visible and open to hikers.

GULL ISLAND

Named after: The thousands of herring gulls that nest there.

Previously known as: Bellow Island–it's official name. Trout Island, Bell Island, Fish Island and Fisher Island

Distance from mainland:
Size: 4 acres
Shoreline: 3.4 miles

Access: Private watercraft

Township and County: Leelanau Township, Leelanau County

Then: A couple from Ionia, Elizabeth Boyer Bell and her husband, became the first owners of Gull Island in 1853. Three local families owned the island at different times, but it remained undisturbed, but for the nesting gulls, until 1910 when Lee Ustick purchased it.

The Harvard professor hired Byron Woolsey to build a summer home out of local timber and stones. The Ustick family rarely visited their island getaway, which was an open invitation to vandals and the native gulls. Eventually the home deteriorated and collapsed, although the two stone chimneys remain standing, and visible from the mainland shore.

Retired Great Lakes Captain, Herbert Yost, bought the island in 1960, passed it on

Looking at Bassett Island from Power Island (photo courtesy of Fred and Tina Tank)

Gull Island

to his daughters, who sold it to the Leelanau Conservancy in 1994.

Today: Gull Island is the southernmost herring gull colony in Lake Michigan, and one of the top sites in the Great Lakes for avian research. The Leelanau Conservancy estimates there are nearly 2,000 active herring gull nests and 100 active cormorant nests on the island. The conservancy's goal is to keep the island as a bird sanctuary.

SMALLER ISLANDS

Tiny Hat Island was once used by the military as a bombing range during World War II.

Two of the smallest islands near Beaver, Pismire and Shoe islands, have been designated as Michigan Island Wilderness Areas. They are uninhabited and used for nesting by herring gulls, ring bill gulls, double-crested cormorants, great blue herons and Caspian terns.

Squaw Island, north of Beaver Island, is home to an abandoned lighthouse. The red brick house and tower were built in 1892.

Further reading:

Exploring North Manitou, South Manitou, High and Garden Islands of the Lake Michigan Archipelago, by Robert H. Ruchhoft, copyright 1991 Robert H. Ruchhoft, The Pucelle Press, Cincinnati, Ohio

The Fox Islands North and South, by Kathleen Craker Firestone, copyright 1996 by Kathleen Craker Firestone, published by Kathleen Craker Firestone

An Island in Grand Traverse Bay, by Kathleen Craker Firestone, copyright 1992, published by Kathleen Craker Firestone
South Manitou Island: From Pioneer Community to National Park, by Myron H. Vent, copyright 1973, Publishing Center for Cultural Resources, New York City

The Journal of Beaver Island History Volume I 1976: Essays on the History of Beaver Island, copyright 1981 Beaver Island Historical Society, Beaver Island Bicentennial Committee

The Journal of Beaver Island History Volume 3 1988: Essays on the History of Beaver Island, copyright 1988 Beaver Island Historical Society, Beaver Island Bicentennial Committee

*The Living Great Lakes:
Searching For the Heart of
the Inland Seas,* by Jerry
Dennis, copyright 2003 Jerry
Dennis, Thomas Dunne
Books, St. Martin's Press

Island Life in Lake Michigan,
by Robert T. Hatt, copyright
1948 Cranbrook Institute of
Science, Cranbrook Press,
Bloomfield Hills, Michigan

*Assassination of a Michigan
King,* copyright 1988, 1997
by Roger Van Noord,
University of Michigan Press,
Ann Arbor, Michigan

*King Strang: A Brief
Biography of the Mormon
King Who Ruled Beaver
Island -and Five Wives – in
the 1850's,* copyright 1971 by
Robert P. Weeks, The Five
Wives Press, Ann Arbor,
Michigan

INLAND LAKES

Top Twenty Largest Inland Lakes in Michgan

	Lake	Sq. miles	County
1	Houghton Lake	31.3	Roscommon
2	Torch Lake	29.4	Antrim
3	Lake Charlevoix	27.0	Charlevoix
4	Burt Lake	26.8	Cheboygan
5	Mullet Lake	26.0	Cheboygan
6	Lake Gogebic	20.9	Gogebic
7	Black Lake	15.8	Cheboygan
8	Manistique	15.8	Mackinac/Luce
9	Crystal Lake	15.8	Benzie
10	Portage Lake	15.1	Houghton
11	Higgins Lake	15.0	Roscommon
12	Fletcher Pond	14.0	Alpena
13	Hubbard Lake	13.8	Alcona
14	Lake Leelanau	13.0	Leelanau
15	Indian Lake	12.5	Schoolcraft
16	Elk Lake	12.1	Antrim
17	Michigamme Res.	11.3	Iron
18	Glen Lake	9.8	Leelanau
19	Grand Lake	8.8	Presque Isle
20	Long Lake	8.8	Alpena

(photo courtesy Terry Phipps)

Largest Inland Lakes in northern Michigan

	Lake	Sq. miles	County
1	Hougton Lake	31.3	Roscommon
2	Torch Lake	29.4	Antrim
3	Lake Charlevoix	27.0	Charlevoix
4	Burt Lake	26.8	Cheboygan
5	Mullett Lake	26.0	Cheboygan
6	Crystal Lake	15.2	Benzie
7	Higgins Lake	15.0	Roscommon
8	Lake Leelanau	13.0	Leelanau
9	Elk Lake	12.1	Antrim
10	Glen Lake	9.8	Leelanau
11	Hamlin Lake	7.8	Mason
12	Walloon Lake	6.75	Charlevoix/Emmet
13	Long Lake	4.47	Grand Traverse
14	Lake Mitchell	4.03	Wexford
15	Skegemog Lake	4.0	Kalkaska/Antrim/ and Grand Traverse
16	Big Platte Lake	3.9	Benzie
17	Lake St. Helen	3.73	Roscommon
18	Crooked Lake	3.6	Emmet
19	Portage Lake	3.3	Manistee
20	Green Lake	3.13	Grand Traverse
21	Otsego Lake	3.08	Otsego
22	Duck Lake	3.02	Grand Traverse
23	Lake Margrethe	3.0	Crawford
24	Paradise (Carp) Lake	2.97	Emmet
25	Lake Missaukee	2.94	Missaukee

*Torch Lake
(photo courtesy
Terry Phipps)*

Did You Happen To See the Most Beautiful Lake in the World?

The claim by many tourism promoters and proud locals that National Geographic has ranked a few northern Michigan lakes as "the most beautiful in the world" is nothing more than urban legend, or perhaps rural legend.

Several hotels around Higgins Lake claim it is the "Sixth Most Beautiful Lake in the World."

Torch Lake has been identified as the 2nd and 3rd most beautiful. One of these claims specifically cites Torch as #3 behind Lake Geneva in Switzerland and Lake Louise in Canada, as ranked by National Geographic.

There is confusion around Glen Lake. It's been promoted as "one of the top five most beautiful lakes," and as the 2nd most beautiful, the third most beautiful, and the seventh most beautiful.

Officials with National Geographic, the magazine and the Society, say they have never ranked the world's most beautiful lakes, and have not proclaimed any titles upon any lakes in northern Michigan.

The myth dates back at least into the 1930's when

a representative of National Geographic, while visiting the Glen Lake area, denied that it was ever ranked as one of the five most beautiful in the world by his organization. According to a National Park Service publication, he disputed the validity of the statement, but did agree, "I have never seen a lake more beautiful."

So perhaps tourism promoters around Glen Lake would be more accurate with a sign such as this: "Welcome to Glen Lake, the Most Beautiful Lake* in the World!"

*Individual opinion from former employee of National Geographic

INLAND LAKES BY COUNTY

Antrim County

Lakes with over 50 acres surface area: 20

Combined acres of natural and artificial lakes and ponds: 30,277

Most of the lake action is on the county's east side with Torch and Elk Lakes appearing as fingers on the same hand as East and West Grand Traverse Bay.

Torch Lake is the longest lake in the state at 19 miles. It's also the second largest inland lake in Michigan and the

(photo courtesy Terry Phipps)

largest in water volume. Over forty miles of shoreline features some of the most expensive waterfront property in Michigan and hundreds of luxury lakefront "cottages."

Boaters love the Chain of Lakes, an inland waterway connecting at least twelve lakes.

Largest lakes Antrim County

Lake	Sq. Miles	Deepest Point
*Torch Lake	29.4	315 ft.
†Elk Lake	12.1	192 ft.
††Lake Skegemog	4.0	29 ft.
Lake Bellaire	2.8	95 ft.
Intermediate Lake	2.4	66 ft.

*2nd largest inland lake in Michigan. Deepest lake in Michigan.
†16th largest lake in Michigan.
††Also lies in Grand Traverse and Kalkaska counties.

Chain of Lakes

One of the great boating adventures in northern Michigan is the Chain of Lakes. Starting in Elk Lake at Elk Rapids, travel south to enter Lake Skegemog, then turn north into the Torch River.

Along the three-mile no-wake float you're likely to do a lot of waving to the friendly oncoming boaters and cottage residents along the banks. You'll emerge at the southern point of Torch Lake and, if it's a typical summer day, be surrounded by dozens of boaters who have dropped anchor for some socializing on the sand bar.

From there its north along the eastern shore of Torch to the Clam River which takes you to the rest of the Lower Chain of Lakes: Clam Lake, Lake Bellaire, and Intermediate Lake.

The Upper Chain O' Lakes includes six narrow and smaller lakes. Starting at the town of Central Lake you'll enter Hanley Lake, then on to Benway Lake, Wilson Lake, Ellsworth Lake, St. Clair Lake and Six Mile Lake.

Benzie County

Lakes with over 50 acres surface area: 7

Combined acres of natural and artificial lakes and ponds: 17,884

The big lakes are on the west side near the Lake Michigan shoreline, while a series of smaller lakes, such as Lake Ann, are in the northeast quadrant of the county near the population center of Traverse City.

Crystal Lake is the largest and deepest lake in the coun-

Boating is popular recreation in northern Michigan (photo courtesy Terry Phipps)

ty and the ninth largest in the State. It is the largest of the 14 Crystal Lakes in Michigan.

Largest lakes Benzie County

Lake	Sq. Miles (acres)	Deepest Point
*Crystal Lake	15.7	140 ft.
Big Platte Lake	3.9	72 ft.
Little Platte Lake	1.25	8 ft.
Lake Ann	.82 (527)	75 ft.
Lower Herring Lake	.70 (450)	60 ft.
Upper Herring Lake	.70 (450)	45 ft.

*9th largest lake in Michigan

Charlevoix County

Lakes with over 50 acres surface area: 15

Combined acres of natural and artificial lakes and ponds: 23,415

Largest lakes Charlevoix County

Lake	Sq. Miles (acres)	Deepest Point
*Lake Charlevoix	27	122 ft.
†Walloon Lake	6.75	40 ft.

Lake Geneserath	.76 (489)	50 ft.
Thumb Lake	.76 (484)	135 ft.
Deer Lake	.69 (443)	22 ft.

*3rd largest lake in Michigan.
†Lies partially in Emmet County.

Clare County

Lakes with over 50 acres surface area: 18

Combined acres of natural and artificial lakes and ponds: 5,716

Largest lakes Clare County

Lake	Sq. Miles (acres)	Deepest Point
Eight Pt. Lake	.60 (387)	25 ft.
Crooked Lake	.41 (264)	73 ft.
Big Mud Lake	.34 (217)	5 ft.
Long Lake	.33 (210)	76 ft.

Crawford County

Lakes with over 50 acres surface area: 8

Combined acres of natural and artificial lakes and ponds: 2,948

One of many pristine lakes in northern Michigan (photo courtesy Terry Phipps)

Largest lakes
Crawford County

Lake	Sq. Miles (acres)	Deepest Point
Lake Margrethe	3.0	65 ft.
K.P. Lake	.17 (110)	25 ft.
Shellenbarger Lake	.17 (109)	109 ft.
Shupac Lake	.17 (107)	90 ft.

Emmet County

Lakes with over 50 acres surface area: 8

Combined acres of natural and artificial lakes and ponds: 10,412

Largest lakes
Emmet County

Lake	Sq. Miles (acres)	Deepest Point
†Walloon Lake	6.75	40 ft.
Crooked Lake	3.6	61 ft.
Paradise (Carp) Lake	2.97	17 ft.
Pickerel	1.69	80 ft.
Wycamp Lake	1.0	7 ft.
Lark's (Round) Lake	.95 (605)	9 ft.
French Farm Lake	.91 (585)	10 ft.

†Lies partially in Charlevoix County.

Grand Traverse

Lakes with over 50 acres surface area: 16

Combined acres of natural and artificial lakes and ponds: 17,846

Largest lakes
Grand Traverse

Lake	Sq. Miles (acres)	Deepest Point
Long Lake	4.47	80 ft.
Green Lake	3.13	100 ft.
Duck Lake	3.02	96 ft.
Fife Lake	.96 (616)	55 ft.
Silver Lake	.94 (600)	96 ft.
Spider Lake	.72 (459)	36 ft.

Islands in Long Lake: Olson (Long) Island and Fox Island are privately owned. Picnic, South and Brush islands are owned by conservancies or a foundation.

Kalkaska County

Lakes with over 50 acres surface area: 16

Combined acres of natural and artificial lakes and ponds: 5,931

Summer fun

Largest lakes
Kalkaska County

Lake	Sq. Miles (acres)	Deepest Point
*Lake Skegemog	4.0	29 ft.
Manistee Lake	1.32	15 ft.
Bear Lake	.49 (316)	60 ft.
Big Twin Lake	.48 (307)	76 ft.
Crawford Lake	.25 (160)	8 ft.
Starvation Lake	.20 (125)	47 ft.

Lake Skegemog was originally named Round Lake.

Lake County

Lakes with over 50 acres suface area: 18

Combined acres of natural and artificial lakes and ponds:

Largest lakes
Lake County

Lake	Sq. Miles (acres)	Deepest Point
Big Star Lake	1.43	25 ft.
Wolf Lake	.65 (418)	13 ft.
Big Bass Lake	.45 (290)	40 ft.
Idlewild Lake	.16 (105)	22 ft.

Leelanau County

Lakes with over 50 acres surface area: 12

Combined acres of natural and artificial lakes and ponds: 17,541

Largest lakes
Leelanau County

Lake	Sq. Miles (acres)	Deepest Point
*Lake Leelanau	13	121 ft.
†Glen Lake	9.8	125 ft.
(Big Glen)	7.6	125 ft.
(Little Glen)	2.2	13 ft.
Lime Lake	1.05	67 ft.
Little Traverse	1.0	60 ft.
Cedar Lake	.41 (262)	46 ft.
School Lake	.27 (175)	6 ft.

*14th largest lake in Michigan
†18th largest lake in Michigan

Glen Lake was once named Bear Lake. Lake Leelanau was originally Carp Lake.

Manistee County

Lakes with over 50 acres surface area: 7

Combined acres of natural and artificial lakes and ponds: 8,248

Largest lakes
Manistee County

Lake	Sq. Miles (acres)	Deepest Point
Portage Lake	3.30	60 ft.
Bear Lake	2.73	22 ft.
Tippy Dam Pond	1.91	50 ft.
Manistee Lake	1.45	50 ft.
Pine Lake	.25 (158)	50 ft.

Mason County

Lakes with over 50 acres surface area: 13

Combined acres of natural and artificial lakes and ponds: 9,711

Largest lakes
Mason County

Lake	Sq. Miles (acres)	Deepest Point
Hamlin Lake	7.8	78 ft.
Round Lake	.89 (571)	10 ft.
Pere Marquette	.87 (554)	46 ft.
Bass Lake	.82 (524)	NA

Missaukee County

Lakes with over 50 acres surface area: 7

Combined acres of natural and artificial lakes and ponds: 4,565

Largest lakes
Missaukee County

Lake	Sq. Miles (acres)	Deepest Point
Lake Missaukee	2.94	27 ft.
Crooked Lake	.78 (500)	12 ft.
Lake Sapphire	.41 (264)	8 ft.
Grass Lake	.20 (126)	4 ft.

Osceola County

Lakes with over 50 acres surface area: 9

Combined acres of natural and artificial lakes and ponds: 3,482

Largest lakes
Osceola County

Lake	Sq. Miles (acres)	Deepest Point
Rose Lake	.58 (370)	33 ft.
Big Lake	.34 (218)	85 ft.
Hicks Lake	.24 (155)	33 ft.
Sunrise Lake	.19 (120)	68 ft.

(photo courtesy Terry Phipps)

Otsego County

Lakes with over 50 acres surface area: 17

Combined acres of natural and artificial lakes and ponds: 7,281

Largest lakes Otsego County

Lake	Sq. Miles (acres)	Deepest Point
Otsego Lake	3.08	23 ft.
Big Bear Lake	.55 (350)	36 ft.
Big Bradford Lake	.36 (228)	102 ft.
Lake Tecon	NA	NA
Lake Manuka	.25 (163)	27 ft.

Roscommon County

Lakes with over 50 acres surface area: 5

Combined acres of natural and artificial lakes and ponds: 39,132

(photo courtesy Terry Phipps)

Largest lakes Roscommon County

Lake	Sq. Miles (acres)	Deepest Point
*Houghton Lake	31.3	21 ft.
†Higgins Lake	15	135 ft.
Lake St. Helen	3.73	25 ft.
Dead Stream Flooding	1.54	NA
Marl Lake	.37	4 ft.
Backus Lake Flooding	NA	
Robinson Creek Flooding	NA	

Largest lake in Michigan.
†11th largest lake in Michigan.

Wexford County

Lakes with over 50 acres surface area: 9

Combined acres of natural and artificial lakes and ponds: 6,788

Largest lakes Wexford County

Lake	Sq. Miles (acres)	Deepest Point
Lake Mitchell	4.03	22 ft.
Hodenpyl Dam Pond	2.63	70 ft.
Lake Cadillac	1.80	27 ft.
Long Lake	.30 (190)	8 ft.
Pleasant Lake	.18 (112)	10 ft.

Cadillac contains the largest lake entirely within its city limits of any city in the United States. Lake Cadillac is entirely within the city limits while Lake Mitchell is only partially within the city limits.

The two lakes are now almost exactly equal in size but in the 19th century one was much larger than the other and they were known as Big Clam Lake and Little Clam Lake. In 1873 a small stream running between the two was dug into the Clam Lake Canal to drain some of Big Clam into Little Clam. Cadillac's canal was featured on Ripley's Believe It or Not in the 1970's because in the winter the canal freezes before the lakes and then when the lakes freeze, the canal thaws and remains unfrozen all winter long. Every year multiple snowmobiles and, unfortunately, lives are lost as snowmobilers try to run the length of the canal, from one frozen lake to the other across the open water, on their snowmobiles.

(photo courtesy Terry Phipps)

WATERFRONT PARCELS

County	Lake	Waterfront parcels
Roscommon	Houghton Lake	2,000
Roscommon	Higgins Lake	1,068
Mason	Hamlin Lake	800
Wexford	Lake Mitchell	646
Wexford	Lake Cadillac	171
Benzie	Crystal Lake	1,613
Leelanau	Glen Lake (Big and Little)	652
Manistee	Bear Lake	381
Manistee	Portage Lake	346
Crawford	Lake Margrethe	215
Emmet	Crooked Lake	569
Antrim	Torch Lake	1,563
Antrim	Elk Lake	563

WATER CLARITY
(2003 Cooperative Lakes Monitoring Program – DEQ)

Volunteers from waterfront property owner associations take readings for water clarity, or transparency. The Department of Environmental Quality provides training and manages the program.

Transparency is measured by lowering a Secchi disk into the water until it cannot be seen from the surface. The black and white disk is eight inches in diameter and hangs at the end of a measuring tape. A short distance of visibility indicates there are suspended particles, such as algae cells, in the water. This is likely the result of nutrients such as fertilizer runoff from the shore. The readings below list the minimum and maximum depths that the Secchi disk was visible over several tests.

The TSI is the Trophic State Index, which is used to compare water clarity, chlorophyll and total phosphorus. These give a reading of the lakes productivity on a scale of 0 to 100. Higher levels of productivity, the amount of plant and animal life that can be produced in the lake, can indicate higher levels of weed growth and algae, and mucky bottom sediments.

Lake	County	Readings	Min.	Max.	TSI
Lake Ann	Benzie	19	10	29	34
Arbutus 1	Gr. Traverse	19	10	13	41
Arbutus 2	Gr. Traverse	19	12	28	36
Arbutus 3	Gr. Traverse	19	11	22	38
Arbutus 4	Gr. Traverse	19	10	21	38
Arbutus 5	Gr. Traverse	19	10	17	41
Silver Lake	Gr. Traverse	19	14.5	42.5	31
Spider 1	Gr. Traverse	17	11	33	35
Spider 2	Gr. Traverse	17	11	29	36
Spider 3	Gr. Traverse	17	9	27	36
Long Lake	Gr. Traverse	19	20	55	28
Stone Ledge Lake	Wexford	15	7	13	45
Pleasant Lake 1	Wexford	17	4.3	6.5	53
Lake Margrethe	Crawford	19	12	30	36
Lake Leelanau*(north)*	Leelanau	14	10	33	34
Lake Leelanau*(south)*	Leelanau	13	5.6	26	38
Arnold Lake	Clare	16	14	25	35
Shingle Lake	Clare	18	9	15	43
Lily Lake	Clare	16	7	9	47
Windover Lake	Clare	9	11	24	36
Austin Lake	Osceola	18	8	13.5	42
Big Lake	Osceola	19	11.5	31	35
Wells Lake	Osceola	19	12	20	37
Big Bradford Lake	Otsego	7	15	19	
Ranger Lake	Otsego	12	15	20	36
Viking Lake	Otsego	19	10	14	41
Sapphire Lake	Missaukee	14	7.5	8	48
Big Platte Lake	Benzie	19	9	23	39
Crystal Lake	Benzie	6	19	30	
Blue Lake	Mason	12	19	32.5	29
Upper Hamlin Lake	Mason	16	6	13	44
Lower Hamlin Lake	Mason	16	9	16	40
Bear Lake	Manistee	13	7.5	12	44
Bear Lake 1	Kalkaska	11	27	48.5	26
Bear Lake 2	Kalkaska	11	26.5	49.5	26
Starvation Lake	Kalkaska	9	18	25.7	32
Cub Lake	Kalkaska	18	16	23	34

MERCURY POLLUTION

The Michigan Environmental Council, in late 2003, issued a list of the Top 10 worst mercury-polluted lakes in Michigan. Their findings are based on analysis of fish tissue from the lakes. The only northern lower Michigan lake on the list is Todd Lake in Osceola County, which ranked ninth.

In September of 2004 the U.S. Environmental Protection Agency listed ten northern Michigan lakes with higher-than-recommended mercury levels. The average levels of mercury found in fish from those lakes were higher than .23 parts per million. At that level the EPA recommends pregnant women and children limit their consumption of fish from those lakes. The ten lakes on the EPA list are:

Burt Lake	Lake Paradise
Crooked Lake	Mullet Lake
Ellsworth Lake	Pickerel Lake
Intermediate Lake	Torch Lake
Lake Geneserath	Walloon Lake

Mercury pollution is caused primarily by coal-burning power plants. Other sources are the burning of hazardous and medical waste, production of chlorine, and some natural occurrence.

RIVERS AND STREAMS
MOST RIVERS AND STREAMS BY COUNTY

County	Miles of rivers and streams/State rank	Main river(s)
Clare	331 / 39	Tobacco, Muskegon
Osceola	301 / 47	Muskegon, Hersey
Kalkaska	284 / 52	Pine Manistee,
Manistee	276 / 53	Rapid Boardman Manistee, Bear Creek,
Antrim	264 / 56	Pine Jordan
Wexford	254 / 58	Intermediate Manistee,
Lake	250 / 59	Pine, Clam Pine, Pere Marquette.
Mason	238 / 61	Little Manistee Pere Marquette, Big Sable

Charlevoix	215 / 66	Boyne, Jordan
Missaukee	209 / 67	Clam, Muskegon
Crawford	204 / 69	Au Sable, Manistee
Roscommon	204 / 69	Au Sable, Muskegon Tittabawassee
Otsego	191 / 70	Sturgeon,Pigeon Au Sable
Grand Traverse	168 / 72	Boardman
Benzie	104 / 74	Platte, Betsie
Emmet	98 / 75	Maple, Crooked Bear, Carp Lake
Leelanau	58 / 76	Crystal

THE RIVERS

AuSable River

Length: 157 miles (main stream)
Counties: Otsego, Crawford, Oscoda, Alcona, Iosco
Source: Lake Tecon in Otsego County
Drains into: Lake Huron
Designations: Blue Ribbon Trout Stream (129 miles)
                      Michigan Natural River

Betsie River

Length: 52 miles mainstream (93 miles including all streams)
Counties: Grand Traverse, Benzie, Manistee
Source: Green Lake, Interlochen
Drains into: Betsie Bay, Lake Michigan
Designations: Michigan Natural River

Boardman River

Length: 49 miles (130 miles including all streams)
Counties: Kalkaska, Grand Traverse

(photo courtesy Terry Phipps)

Source: North Branch from Mahan Swamp near the town of Kalkaska
South Branch from streams near town of South Boardman
Drains into: West Grand Traverse Bay
Designations: Blue Ribbon Trout Stream (36 miles)
              Michigan Natural River

Jordan River

Length: 33 miles mainstream
Counties: Charlevoix, Antrim
Source: Small creeks north of Mancelona
Drains into: Lake Charlevoix
Designations: Blue Ribbon Trout Stream (9 miles)
              Michigan Natural River

Manistee River

Length: 232 miles
Counties: Antrim, Otsego, Crawford, Kalkaska, Missaukee, Wexford, Manistee
Source: Cedar swamp near Alba in Antrim County
Drains into: Lake Michigan
Designations: Blue Ribbon Trout Stream (35 miles)
              National Wild and Scenic River (26 miles)
              Michigan Natural River

Pere Marquette

Length: 66 miles mainstream (149 miles including all streams)
Counties: Lake, Mason
Source: Four main branches: Big South Branch (41 miles), Little South
Branch (13 miles), Middle Branch (17 miles) and Baldwin River (12 miles)
Drains into: Pere Marquette Lake
Designations: Blue Ribbon Trout Stream (39 miles)
              National Wild and Scenic River (66 miles)
              Michigan Natural River

Pine River

Also known as: South Branch of the Manistee River
Length: 57 miles
Counties: Wexford, Osceola, Lake, Manistee
Sources: Negro Creek, Spalding Creek, Rose Lake Creek
Drains into: Tippy Dam Pond, Manistee County
Designations: Blue Ribbon Trout Stream
              National Wild and Scenic River (26 miles)
              Michigan Natural River

Pigeon River
Length: 42 miles
Counties: Otsego and Cheboygan
Sources: Headwaters a few miles northeast of Gaylord
Drains into: Mullett Lake
Designations: Blue Ribbon Trout Stream
              Michigan Natural River

(photo courtesy Terry Phipps)

Platte River
Length: 30 miles
Counties: Benzie
Source: Lake Ann
Drains into: Lake Michigan
Designations: Blue Ribbon Trout Stream (6 miles)

Sturgeon River
Length: 40 miles
Counties: Otsego and Cheboygan
Source: Hoffman Lake (Charlevoix County), and stream just north of Gaylord
Drains into: Burt Lake
The Sturgeon drops about 14 feet per mile, making it the swiftest river in Michigan's Lower Peninsula.

BLUE RIBBON TROUT STREAMS

Of Michigan's 12,500 miles of classified trout streams, 868 miles are considered Blue Ribbon Trout Streams. The DNR definition of a Blue Ribbon Trout Stream: It must be one of Michigan's best trout streams, be able to support excellent stocks of wild resident trout; have the physical characteristics to permit fly casting, but be shallow enough to wade; produce diverse insect life and good fly hatches, have earned a reputation for providing an excellent (quality) trout fishing experience, and have excellent water quality.

Most of the Blue Ribbon Trout Streams flow through northern Michigan.

STREAM AND COUNTY	MILES
AuSable (Main Branch) / Crawford	79
AuSable (North Branch) / Crawford and Otsego	24
AuSable (South Branch) / Crawford and Roscommon	19
AuSable (East Branch) / Crawford	7
Baldwin Creek / Lake	12

Bear Creek / Manistee	15
Big Creek (West and East Branch) / Crawford	13
Boardman River / Grand Traverse and Kalkaska	36
Boyne River / Charlevoix	4
Cedar River / Antrim	4
Cedar River / Clare	3.5
Clam River / Missaukee	19
Jordan River / Antrim	9
Little Manistee River / Mason and Lake	31
Manistee River / Kalkaska and Crawford	4
Maple River / Emmet	4
Pere Marquette River / Mason and Lake	39
Pigeon River / Cheboygan and Otsego	31
Pine River / Manistee, Lake and Osceola	57
Platte River / Benzie	6
Big Sable River / Mason and Lake	12
Sturgeon River / Cheboygan and Otsego	21

NATIONAL WILD AND SCENIC RIVERS

Congress created the National Wild and Scenic River designation in 1968 to protect rivers from further damming, diverting and degradation. The goal of the designation is to preserve the natural character of the river. Michigan has 625 miles of National Wild and Scenic Rivers that possess "remarkable scenic, recreational, geologic, fish and wildlife, historic, cultural or other similar values."

WILD AND SCENIC RIVER / SECTION /CLASSIFICATION	MILES
Bear Creek / From Coates Highway to confluence with the Manistee River / Scenic / Designated 3/3/92	6.5
Manistee River / From boat ramp south of Tippy Dam to M-55 Bridge Recreational / Designated 3/3/92	26
Pere Marquette River / downstream from the Middle and Little South Branches to U.S. 31 / Scenic / Designated 11/10/78	66
Pine River / Starting at Lincoln Bridge / Scenic Designated 3/3/92	26

MICHIGAN NATURAL RIVERS

Before Michigan became a state her rivers supplied natives and early settlers with the essentials for survival: food in the form of abundant fish, and transportation, via handmade canoes.

Later the rivers became nature's conveyor belts for the lumber industry, which floated logs from the interior woods to sawmill stations on the Lake Michigan shore. Dams were built and the natural force of water was harnessed to provide electric power for the mills.

In the 20th century industry expanded in Michigan, and so did the dumping of waste into rivers. The role of northern Michigan rivers became one of recreation– fishing, camping, and canoeing. In some areas erosion of riverbanks began as shoreline vegetation was cut to make room for cottages.

The Natural Rivers program was designed to prevent further damage and to pro- mote preservation of natural, healthy rivers. Local and State governments work to design a management plan in the designated Natural River areas. Zoning laws are the primary tool used for protecting "fish, wildlife, scenic beauth, floodplain, ecologic, historic and recreational values of the river and adjoining lands."

Michigan Natural Rivers and Tributaries in Northern Michigan

Au Sable River

<u>Alcona County</u>
Blockhouse Creek

<u>Crawford County</u>
Big Creek (including East Branch, Middle Branch and West Branch)
Bradford Creek
East Branch Au Sable River
Kolka Creek
North Branch Au Sable River
South Branch Au Sable River

<u>Montmorency County</u>
Middle Branch Big Creek

<u>Oscoda County</u>
Beaver Creek
Big Creek, Big Creek Township (including East Branch and West Branch)
Blockhouse Creek
Comins Creek

(photo courtesy Terry Phipps)

East Branch Big Creek,
Greenwood Township
Glennie Creek
Loud Creek
Middle Branch Big Creek,
Greenwood Township
Nine Mile Creek
Perry Creek
Sohn Creek
Wolf Creek

Otsego County
Chub Creek
Kolka Creek
North Branch Au Sable River
Turtle Creek
West Branch Big Creek

Roscommon County
Beaver Creek
Douglas Creek
East Creek
Hudson Creek
Robinson Creek
South Branch Au Sable River
South Creek
Thayer Creek

Betsie River
Mainstream: Benzie and
Manistee counties

Benzie County
Little Betsie River
Dair Creek

Boardman River
Mainstream: Grand Traverse
County

Grand Traverse County
Bancroft Creek
Beitner Creek
Carpenter Creek
East Creek
Jackson Creek

Jaxson Creel
North Branch Boardman
River
Parker Creek
South Branch Boardman
River
Swainston Creek
Twenty Two Creek

Kalkaska County
Crofton Creek
Failing Creek
North Branch Boardman
River
South Branch Boardman
River
Taylor Creek

Jordan River
Mainstream: Antrim and
Charlevoix counties
Tributaries: All tributaries
entering the mainstream
upstream (south) of Rogers
Bridge, Charlevoix County,
T32N, R7W, Section 26/35

*In 1972, the Jordan was the first
river in Michigan designated as
a natural wild and scenic river.*

Pere Marquette River
Mainstream: Lake and
Mason counties

Lake County
Baldwin River
Blood Creek
Bray Creek
Cole Creek, including North
Branch and South Branch
Danaher Creek
Kinney Creek
Leverentz Creek
Little South Branch Pere
Marquette River

Middle Branch Pere
Marquette River
Sandborn Creek
Sweetwater Creek

Mason County
Big South Branch Pere
Marquette River
Carr Creek
Swan Creek
Weldon Creek

Newaygo County
Big South Branch Pere
Marquette River
Cedar Creek
Little South Branch Pere
Marquette River
McDuffee Creek
Pease Creek

Oceana County
Big South Branch Pere
Marquette River
Ruby Creek
Pigeon River
Mainstream: Otsego and
Cheboygan counties
Tributaries: All tributaries in
both counties upstream
(south) of M-68, Cheboygan
County

Pine River
Mainstream: Osceola, Lake,
Wexford and Manistee
counties

Wexford County
North Branch of the Pine
River
Spalding Creek
Fairchild Creek
Poplar Creek
Dowling Creek
Hoxey Creek

Unnamed stream with
sources in sections 27 and
34, South Branch Twp.
Yates Creek

Osceola County
North Branch of the Pine River
Sixteen Creek
Fairchild Creek
Unnamed stream with source
at dam in section 8 of
Burdell Twp.
East Branch of the Pine River
Rose Lake outlet
Emery Lake outlet
Edgetts Creek
Diamond Lake outlets
Unnamed stream with source
in section 20, Sherman Twp.
Sprague Creek
Beaver Creek
Little Beaver Creek
Coe Creek
Dyer Creek
Lake County
Unnamed stream with source
in section 14, Ellsworth Twp.
Coe Creek
Sellars Creek
Unnamed stream with source
in section 20, Dover Twp.
Unnamed stream with source
in section 19, Dover Twp.
Unnamed stream with source
in section 24, Newkirk Twp.
Silver Creek including all
perennial tributaries
Unnamed stream with source
in section 13, Newkirk Twp.
Unnamed stream with source
in section 11, Newkirk Twp.
Unnamed stream with source
in section 7, Dover Twp.
Unnamed stream with source
in section 1, Newkirk Twp.
Poplar Creek

Upper Manistee River
Mainstream: Antrim, Otsego, Crawford, Kalkaska and Missaukee counties

Antrim County
All headwater streams
Otsego County
Frenchman's Creek
Crawford County
Lost Lake Outlet
Unnamed stream, section 30, Frederic Twp. (T28N, R4W)
Goose Creek
Portage Creek, including all perennial tributaries

Kalkaska County
Unnamed stream with source in section 13, Blue Lake Twp.
Goose Creek
Portage Creek, including all perennial tributaries
Clear Creek
Black Creek, including all perennial tributaries
Dempsey Creek
Big Devil Creek
Big Cannon Creek
North Branch of the Manistee River, including all perennial tributaries
Willow Creek
Pierson Creek
Maple Creek
Little Cannon Creek
Silver Creek
Waterhole Creek, including all tributaries
Babcock Creek
Filer Creek
Nelson Creek
Spring Creek
Bourne Creek
Ham Creek
Haynes Creek
Fisher Creek

Missaukee County
Silver Creek
Filer Creek
Ham Creek
Gravy Creek
Hopkins Creek
Fisher Creek

(photo courtesy Terry Phipps)

NUMBER OF WATER ACRES BY COUNTY

With the exception of Roscommon County, those counties bordering Lake Michigan contain the most water as their boundary lines extend into the big lake. Roscommon, while inland, is home to some of the largest inland lakes in the State, including the largest, Houghton Lake.

County	Water acres
Roscommon	33,280
Antrim	28,480
Charlevoix	23,552
Grand Traverse	17,792
Benzie	16,960
Leelanau	16,000
Emmet	10,560
Mason	10,496
Manistee	9,600
Wexford	6,912
Otsego	6,720
Missaukee	4,800
Kalkaska	4,736
Lake	3,968
Clare	3,904
Crawford	2,944
Osceola	2,560

WETLAND ACREAGE IN NORTHERN MICHIGAN

County	Wetlands (sq. miles)	% of total county land
Antrim	56.66	11.9
Benzie	53.58	16.7
Charlevoix	105.23	25.2
Emmet	91.55	19.6
Grand Traverse	68.58	14.7
Kalkaska	78.92	14.1
Leelanau	42.83	12.3
Manistee	114.85	21.1
Missaukee	139.56	24.6
Wexford	130.91	23.2

Northwest Michigan Council of Governments from COG SWAMP Data

THE WOODS

Forest Land

County	Acres of forest (public and private)
Lake	315,200
Crawford	308,100
Wexford	281,700
Kalkaska	271,100
Roscommon	258,000
Manistee	253,300
Clare	245,500
Otsego	239,600
Missaukee	237,900
Emmet	208,100
Antrim	189,700
Osceola	185,600
Grand Traverse	175,800
Mason	172,700
Charlevoix	172,200
Benzie	146,600
Leelanau	126,900

Source: Michigan State University Tourism Resource Center

Percentage of forested land by county

81-90%	71-80%	61-70%	51-60%
Lake	Benzie	Antrim	Leelanau
Crawford	Kalkaska	Charlevoix	Osceola
	Manistee	Clare	Mason
	Otsego	Emmet	
	Roscommon	Missaukee	
	Wexford		

% of land owned by DNR by county (northern Michigan)

County	Total acres	DNR-owned acres	DNR %
Roscommon	338,315	202,817	59.95
Crawford	359,845	178,231	49.53
Kalkaska	359,669	158,873	44.17
Benzie	204,192	62,196	30.46
Otsego	334,272	98,460	29.46
Missaukee	363,289	104,329	28.72
Emmet	300,855	76,432	25.41
Grand Traverse	299,27	68,186	22.78
Charlevoix	266,224	58,474	21.96
Lake	365,393	61,205	16.75
Wexford	366,675	54,240	14.79
Antrim	305,558	44,840	14.67
Clare	364,756	53,376	14.63
Manistee	350,101	24,271	6.93
Osceola	367,337	19,345	5.27
Leelanau	220,233	8,430	3.83
Mason	315,526	6,616	2.10

In Michigan 12.51% of land is owned by the DNR.

Payments in Lieu of Taxes (PILT)

Since much of the land in northern Michigan is owned by the State of Michigan, local units of government lose out on collecting property taxes. Instead, they receive, from the State DNR, Payments in Lieu of Taxes. The amount paid out depends on when the State became owner of the land. On property obtained before 1933 the State pays out $2.00 and acre. On land the State obtained after 1933, the payment is based on the assessed value of the property.

Roscommon County receives the highest amount of Payments in Lieu of Taxes as it also has the most DNR-owned land. However, the amount of land owned by the DNR is not always in direct relation to the payments made to individual counties.

For instance, while almost 60% of land in Roscommon County is owned by the DNR, it receives an annual PILT of $524,00. While in Oakland County only 5% of the land is owned by the DNR, yet it receives an annual PILT check for $1,168,673. The apparent inequity is due to the difference in land values and the time the DNR came into ownership of the property.

PILT made to northern Michigan counties in 2002

County	PILT received	DNR-owned acreage	% of total county acreage
Roscommon	$524,001	202,817	59.95
Kalkaska	$478,569	158,873	44.17
Crawford	$453,651	178,231	49.53
Grand Traverse	$353,470	68,186	22.78
Emmet	$340,233	76,432	25.41
Missaukee	$287,865	104,329	28.72
Otsego	$270,117	98,460	29.46
Wexford	$258,072	54,240	14.79
Charlevoix	$212,729	58,474	21.96
Lake	$163,619	61,205	16.75
Benzie	$163,061	62,196	30.46
Antrim	$159,035	44,840	14.67
Mason	$149,865	6,616	2.10
Clare	$135,425	53,376	14.63
Leelanau	$133,751	8,430	3.83
Manistee	$81,810	24,271	6.93
Osceola	$78,592	19,345	5.27

State Forests in Northern Michigan

Au Sable State Forest   780,000 acres
Includes Mason Tract along Au Sable River
Crawford, Roscommon, Oscoda, Ogemaw, Clare, Gladwin,
Arenac, Iosco

Mackinaw State Forest   6,660,000 acres
Includes islands in Lake Michigan and Huron
Antrim, Otsego, Montmorency, Charlevoix, Cheboygan,
Emmet, Presque Isle

Pere Marquette State Forest   529,000 acres
Mason, Lake, Osceola, Manistee, Wexford, Missaukee,
Leelanau, Benzie, GT, Kalkaska,

TALLEST TREES

Height (feet)	Variety	County/town
121	Eastern Hemlock	Emmet/Cross Village
113	N. White Cedar	Leelanau/S. Manitou Island
100	White Ash	Antrim/Elk Rapids
98	American Beech	Manistee/Onekema
90	Rock Elm	Gr. Traverse/Traverse City
89	Giant Sequoia	Manistee/Manistee
89	Eastern Tamarack	Lake/Luther
86	White Poplar	Charlevoix/Charlevoix
83	Sweetgum	Gr.Traverse/Traverse City
81	English Oak	Benzie/Benzonia

STATE CHAMPION TREES

Variety	Circumference (inches)	Height (feet)	Crown (feet)	Location
Apricot	123	54	63	Leelanau County
White Ash	243	100	61	Elk Rapids
American Beech	193	98	106	Onekema
European White Birch	158	78	71	Greilickville
*Mountain Paper Birch	112	67	80	Sleeping Bear Dunes
*Northern White Cedar	216	113	42	S. Manitou Island
American Chestnut	208	64	80	Old Mission Peninsula
Red Osier Dogwood	10	17	20	Frankfort
*Roundleaf Dogwood	11	40	16	Leland
Common Elderberry	14	26	18	Cedar
Rock Elm	203	90	81	Traverse City
Fringetree	24	18	25	**Traverse City
Eastern Hemlock	164	121	62	Cross Village
*Eastern Hophornbeam	115	74	111	Grand Traverse
Hophornbeam Ironwood	115	47	50	Grand Traverse
Ground Juniper	17	18	8	Sleeping Bear Dunes
Leatherwood	13	11	8	Sleeping Bear Dunes, Empire
Norway Maple	173	80	75	Empire
Sugar Maple	225	78	80	Manistee
European Mountain Ash	56	32	25	Grand Traverse
English Oak	155	81	76	Benzonia
Austrian Pine	119	73	59	**Traverse City
*White Poplar	239	86	126	Charlevoix
Smooth Serviceberry	69	42	44	Maple City
Giant Sequoia	151	89	30	Manistee
Sweetgum	68	83	70	**Traverse City
Eastern Tamarack	109	89	64	Luther
Bebbs Willow	36	31	18	Maple City
Black Willow	400	76	92	**Traverse City
Corkscrew Willow	66	73	44	Northport
*Meadow Willow	13	34	18	Leelanau
*Purple Osier Willow	15	37	49	Omena
Shining Willow	130	74	81	**Traverse City

Source: Global ReLeaf of Michigan (globalreleaf.org)
Also listed on National Register of Big Trees by American Forests-dot-com
**Grounds of former State Hospital in Traverse City*

Champion Tree Project

He's been on the Today Show, featured in dozens of newspapers including *USA Today, New York Times, Readers Digest,* and *Washington Post.* Politicians, professors, and scientists seek him out, as do foreign governments, but he is not rich or famous. He is David Milarch, tree farmer.

Milarch and his sons, Jared and Jake, founded the Champion Tree Project in 1996 at their tree nursery in Copemish, after discovering that very old trees could be cloned. Until then the scientific world said it couldn't be done. Once the Milarch's proved it could be they was an onslaught of interest and media coverage.

Highlights

- Cloned the world's oldest tree, a 4,768-year-old bristle cone pine in the mountains of California.

- Cloned the 13 remaining trees planted by President George Washington at Mt. Vernon. Milarch is planting the clones on the grounds of the Edsel and Eleanor Ford House in Grosse Point Shores.

- Milarch planted one of the Mt. Vernon clones on the grounds of the U.S. Capitol on Arbor Day, 2003.

- Has planted champion trees at the Pentagon and the Calvary Cemetery in New York to memorialize victims of the September 11th terrorist attacks.

- The Champion Tree Project has teamed up with the National Tree Trust to produce and market champion tree clones. Among the potential customers: golf courses, corporate headquarters, and municipalities that want to create Living Libraries of America's greatest trees. Proceeds from the endeavor will go to supporting the mission to clone all of the USA's champion trees, and to create living museums of trees in urban areas.

On the web: **www.championtreeproject.org**

ENDANGERED SPECIES

ANTRIM

Endangered	Threatened	Of Special Concern
	Red-shouldered Hawk	Northern Goshawk
	Common Loon	Eastern flat-shorl
	Bald Eagle	Grizzled Skipper
	Calypso or Fairy-slipper	Eastern Massasauga
	Pitcher's Thistle	Spike-lip Crater
	Ginseng	Ram's Head Lady's
	Pine-drops	Slipper
	Lake Huron Tansy	
	Lake Huron Locust	

BENZIE

Endangered	Threatened	Of Special Concern
Piping Plover	Cut-leaved Water-parsnip	Woodland Vole
Prairie Warbler	Prairie Moonwort	Spittlebug
Migrant Loggerhead Shrike	Fascicled Broom-rape	Douglas Stenelmis
Michigan Monkey-flower	Osprey	Riffle Beetle
	Calypso or Fairy-slipper	Eastern Box Turtle
	Pitcher's Thistle	Northern Goshawk
	Common Loon	Wood Turtle
	Bald Eagle	
	Lake Huron Locust	
	Red-shouldered Hawk	

CHARLEVOIX

Endangered	Threatened	Of Special Concern
Piping Plover	Pumpelly's Brome Grass	Woodland Vole
Michigan Monkey-flower	Fascicled Broom-rape	Climbing Fumitory
	Osprey	American Bittern
	Limestone Oak Fern	Beauty Sedge
	Dwarf Lake Iris	English Sundew
	Hill's Pondweed	Dune Cutworm
	Seaside Crowfoot	Common Moorhen
	American Shore-grass	Houghton's
		Goldenrod

Aweme Borer
Butterwort
Torrey's Bulrush
Stitchwort

Deepwater Pondsnail
Caspian Tern
Common Tern

CLARE

Endangered	Threatened	Of Special Concern
Kirtland's Warbler	Red-shouldered Hawk	Northern Goshawk
Migrant Loggerhead Shrike	Common Loon	Elktoe
	Bald Eagle	Slippershell Mussel
	Ginseng	Secretive Locust
	Osprey	Hill's Thistle
		Blanding's Turtle
		Wood Turtle
		Woodland Vole
		Round Pigtoe
		Red-legged Spittlebug
		Eastern Box Turtle

CRAWFORD

Endangered	Threatened	Of Special Concern
American Chestnut	Prairie or Pale Agoseris	Northern Goshawk
Kirtland's Warbler	Dusted Skipper	Slippershell Mussel
	Red-shouldered Hawk	Secretive Locust
	Calypso or Fairy-slipper	Boreal Brachionyncha
	False-violet	Boreal Brachionyncha
	Rough Fescue	Hill's Thistle
	Common Loon	Blanding's Turtle
	Bald Eagle	Wood Turtle
	Vasey's Rush	Henry's Elfin
	Ginseng	Northern Prostrate
	Osprey	Clubmoss
	Houghton's Goldenrod	Red-legged Spittlebug
	Fleshy Stitchwort	Alleghany or Sloe Plum
	New England Violet	Grizzled Skipper
		Clinton's Bulrush
		Eastern Massasauga
		Prairie Dropseed

EMMET

Endangered	Threatened	Of Special Concern
Round-leaved Orchis	Slough Grass	Beauty Sedge
Hungerford's Crawling	Pumpelly's Brome Grass	Ram's Head Lady's-
Water Beetle	Red-shouldered Hawk	Slipper
Piping Plover	Large Water-starwort	English Sundew
Migrant Loggerhead Shrike	Calypso or Fairy-slipper	Blanding's Turtle
Michigan Monkey-flower	Pitcher's Thistle	Early Hairstreak
King Rail	False-violet	Woodland Vole
	Common Loon	Butterwort
	Limestone Oak Fern	Sprague's Pygarctia
	Bald Eagle	Grizzled Skipper
	Dwarf Lake Iris	Torrey's Bulrush
	Osprey	Eastern Massasauga
	Hill's Pondweed	Douglas Stenelmis
	Spotted Pondweed	Riffle Beetle
	Pine-drops	
	Houghton's Goldenrod	
	Common Tern	
	Lake Huron Tansy	
	Lake Huron Locust	
	Blunt-lobed Woodsia	

GRAND TRAVERSE

Endangered	Threatened	Of Special Concern
Migrant Loggerhead Shrike	Red-shouldered Hawk	Northern Goshawk
King Rail	Pitcher's Thistle	Pussy-toes
	Common Loon	Hill's Thistle
	Bald Eagle	Ram's Head Lady's-
	Osprey	Slipper
	Pine-drops	Wood Turtle
	Lake Huron Tansy	Eastern Massasauga
		Ebony Boghaunter

KALKASKA

Endangered	Threatened	Of Special Concern
Kirtland's Warbler	Dusted Skipper	Northern Goshawk
	Red-shouldered Hawk	American Bittern

Spotted Turtle
Common Loon
Bald Eagle
Whorled Pogonia
Vasey's Rush
Canada Rice-grass
Osprey
Hill's Pondweed
Houghton's Goldenrod
New England Violet

Blanding's Turtle
Wood Turtle
Eastern Flat-whorl
Red-legged Spittlebug
Clinton's Bulrush
Eastern Massasauga
Prairie Dropseed

LAKE

Endangered	Threatened	Of Special Concern
	Dusted Skipper	Northern Goshawk
	Red-shouldered Hawk	Hill's Thistle
	Spotted Turtle	Engelmann's Spike-rush
	Persius Duskywing	Black-fruited Spike-rush
	Common Loon	Blanding's Turtle
	Bald Eagle	Wood Turtle
	Ottoe Skipper	Dwarf-bulrush
	Frosted Elfin	Alleghany or Sloe Plum
	Great Plains Spittlebug	Tall Beak-rush
	Karner Blue	Tooth-cup
	Bog Bluegrass	Eastern Massasauga
		Douglas Stenelmis
		Riffle Beetle
		Eastern Box Turtle

LEELANAU

Endangered	Threatened	Of Special Concern
Piping Plover	Walking Fern	Blanchard's Cricket
Prairie Warbler	Green Spleenwort	Frog
Peregrine Falcon	Cut-leaved Water-parsnip	Walking Furnitory
	Prairie Moonwort	Beauty Sedge
	Pumpelly's Brome Grass	Ram's Head Lady's-
	Calypso or Fairy-slipper	Slipper
	Broad-leaved Sedge	Fir Clubmoss
	Pitcher's Thistle	Furrowed Flax
	Showy Orchis	Woodland Vole
	Common Loon	Pugnose Shiner

	Bald Eagle	Eastern Box Turtle
	Fascicled Broom-rape	
	Ginseng	
	Pine-drops	
	Deepwater Pondsnail	
	Lake Huron Tansy	
	Lake Huron Locust	
	Three-birds Orchid	

MANISTEE

Endangered	Threatened	Of Special Concern
Migrant Loggerhead Shrike	Lake Sturgeon	Cooper's Hawk
Indiana Bat or Indiana	Red-shouldered Hawk	Northern Goshawk
Myotis	Pitcher's Thistle	Northern Harrier
	Cisco or Lake Herring	Hill's Thistle
	Trumpeter Swan	Cerulean Warbler
	Common Loon	Blanding's Turtle
	Bald Eagle	Wood Turtle
	Fascicled Broom-rape	Dwarf –bulrush
	Ginseng	Woodland Vole
	Osprey	Pugnose Shiner
	Lake Huron Locust	Brown Walker
	Wild rice	Alleghany or Sloe Plum
		Eastern Massasauga
		Eastern Box Turtle

MASON

Endangered	Threatened	Of Special Concern
Northern Goshawk	Lake Cress	Northern Goshawk
Prairie Warbler	Dusted Skipper	Northern Harrier
	Cut-leaved Water-parsnip	Hill's Thistle
	Red-shouldered Hawk	Ram's Head Lady's-Slipper
	Pitcher's Thistle	Cerulean Warbler
	Spotted Turtle	Engelmann's Spike-rush
	Persius Duskywing	Blanding's Turtle
	Common Loon	Wood Turtle
	Bald Eagle	Dwarf-bulrush
	Short-fruited Rush	Alleghany or Sloe Plum
	Vasey's Rush	Tall Beak-rush

Great Plains Spittlebug
Karner Blue
Fascicled Broom-rape
Ginseng
Lake Huron Locust

Tooth-cut
Eastern Massasauga
Eastern Box Turtle

MISSAUKEE

Endangered

Short-eared Owl
Kirtland's Warbler
Migrant Loggerhead Shrike

Threatened

Dusted Skipper
Red-shouldered Hawk
Common Loon
Bald Eagle
River Redhorse
Osprey
Hill's Pondweed

Of Special Concern

Elktoe
Slippershell Mussel
Secretive Locust
Wood Turtle
Eastern Flat-whorl
Round Pigtoe
Eastern Massasauga
Rainbow

OSCEOLA

Endangered

Short-eared owl
Migrant Loggerhead Shrike

Threatened

Common Loon
Osprey

Of Special Concern

Elktoe
Slippershell Mussel
Grasshopper Sparrow
Blanding's Turtle
Wood turtle
Round Pigtoe

OTSEGO

Endangered

Kirtland's Warbler

Threatened

Prairie or Pale Agoseris
Dusted Skipper
Goblin Moonwort
Red-shouldered Hawk
Rough Fescue
Common Loon
Bald Eagle
Hill's Pondweed
Yellow Pitcher-plant

Of Special Concern

Northern Goshawk
Secretive Locust
Spike-lip Crater
Boreal Brachionyncha
Hill's Thistle
Ram's Head Lady's-Slipper
Wood Turtle
Doll's Merolonche

Three-horned Moth
Blazing Star Borer
Red-legged Spittlebug
Alleghany or Sloe
Grizzled Skipper

ROSCOMMON

Endangered	Threatened	Of Special Concern
Kirtland's Warbler	Red-shouldered Hawk	Elktoe
King Rail	Calypso or Fairy-slipper	Slippershell Mussel
	Spotted Turtle	Secretive Locust
	Yellow Rail	Boreal Brachionyncha
	Rough Fescue	Black Tern
	Common Loon	Hill's Thistle
	Bald Eagle	Ram's Head Lady's-Slipper
	Least Bittern	Blanding's Turtle
	Osprey	Common Moorhen
	Deepwater Pondsnail	Wood Turtle
		Doll's Merolonche
		Alleghany or Sloe Plum
		Rainbow

WEXFORD

Endangered	Threatened	Of Special Concern
Kirtland's Warbler	Red-shouldered Hawk	Cooper's Hawk
	Common Loon	Northern Goshawk
	Bald Eagle	Slippershell Mussel
	Virginia Bluebells	Northern Harrier
	Ginseng	Hill's Thistle
	Osprey	Wood Turtle
		Grizzled Skipper
		Eastern Box Turtle

Eagles in Northern Michigan

Every January the DNR conducts a two-week eagle survey. Residents are asked to report any sightings of eagles: location, size, number, etc.

Over the past 20 years the number of sightings has grown from 4 in 1979 to over 400 in 2001.

*Winter eagle sightings in *northern Michigan.*

Year	Eagle sightings
1979	4
1980	7
1981	12
1982	10
1983	14
1984	11
1985	5
1986	N/A
1987	13
1988	39
1989	39
1990	24
1991	41
1992	N/A
1993	N/A
1994	N/A
1995	117
1996	182
1997	400
1998	258
1999	315
2000	301
2001	443
2002	322

Alcona, Alpena, Antrim, Arenac, Benzie, Charlevoix, Cheboygan, Clare, Crawford, Emmet, Gladwin, Grand Traverse, Iosco, Kalkaska, Lake, Leelanau, Manistee, Mason, Missaukee, Montmorency, Ogemaw, Osceola, Oscoda, Otsego, Presque Isle, Roscommon, and Wexford counties.

Cougars in northern Michigan

The official line from the state DNR is that cougars disappeared from the state in the early years of the last century. Some reports say the last cougar was killed in 1906 near Sault Ste. Marie. However, the reports of cougar sightings never ended.

The Michigan Wildlife Habitat Foundation says a scat analysis done in 2000 confirmed the presence of two cougars in the northern Lower Peninsula, and five in the U.P. They also claim plaster impressions of paw prints taken from the Mesick area of Wexford County and from Tower in Cheboygan County are those of cougars.

The Michigan Wildlife Conservancy says DNA evidence confirmed the presence of cougars in Emmet, Roscommon, Alcona, and Presque Isle counties. Members of the study team actually saw cougars during their work in Benzie and Roscommon counties.

In 2002, after a livestock attack in Kalkaska County, the state DNR said that may have been the work of a cougar or some other large, feral cat.

In 2003, after several sightings by its own staff and volunteers, the National Park Service posted signs stating, "You are a Visitor in Cougar Habitat," at trailheads in the park. The cougar is on the Michigan Endangered Species list, and cannot be harmed unless posing a threat to livestock or humans.

The DNR says there isn't enough evidence to prove that cougars live in Michigan. The department has said some sightings may have been escaped pets, or other animals mistaken as bobcats.

In October of 2004, National Park Service researchers from Sleeping Bear Dunes and Pictured Rocks began a one year study which they hope will prove the existence of cougars in northern Michigan. They're using motion-sensitive video cameras and other advanced technology.

Cougar evidence in northern lower Michigan

Mesick	Wexford County	paw prints confirmed by Michigan Wildlife Conservancy
Tower	Cheboygan County	paw prints confirmed by Michigan Wildlife Conservancy
Sleeping Bear	Benzie County	visual sighting by Michigan Wildlife Conservancy staff
Emmet and Roscommon counties		DNA evidence confirms scat is from cougars
Sleeping Bear Benzie and Leelanau counties		National Park staff and volunteers and visitors report cougar sightings and tracks since 1970's. Several reports of cougar cubs alone and with adult

Appearance

Size: 80 to 200 pounds; 7 to 9 feet from nose to tip of tail

Appearance: Usually tan or brown with a very long tail

Other Names: Mountain lion, puma, panther, catamount

Behavior: Cougars are usually solitary, except for mothers with young.

Territory: Males mark out a territory of 10 to 20 miles. Females usually settle near their mothers.

Turf: Young males may travel over 200 miles in search of their own territories.

Food: Main source of food is the white-tailed deer although cougars will dine on beaver, rabbits, birds, porcupines, coyotes, bobcats, and other smaller animals, and occasionally even fish and frogs.

For more information: **www.miwildlife.org**

Wolves cross the Straits

The first evidence of gray wolves from the U.P. came in October of 2004 when one was shot and killed near Rogers City. A trapper thought it was a coyote, but discovered it was wearing a radio collar. The DNR collared a 70-pound female wolf near Engadine the previous November. The wolf probably wandered across the frozen Straits of Mackinac, and probably wasn't the only one.

Since then, more wolf tracks have been confirmed around Rogers City, and the DNR says it's unable to receive radio signals from another 20 collared wolves in the U.P. Members of the local Odawa Indians say they've tracked two packs of wolves near Rogers City and in Wilderness State Park in Emmet County.

There are over 300 wolves estimated to be living in the U.P. They are protected under the endangered species laws; however, due to the increasing wolf population, there's a good chance it will be taken off the list.

In early 2005 wildlife biologists began a wolf survey of the tip of the Lower Peninsula.

LAND

Total acreage by county

Six of the ten smallest counties in the state are in northern Michigan. Benzie County is the smallest followed by Leelanau at number two, Charlevoix is the fourth smallest, Emmet is 7th, Grand Traverse 8th, and Antrim is the ninth smallest county in Michigan.

County	Sq. miles/acres Total	Sq. miles/acres Land	Sq. miles/acres Water
Roscommon	580 / 371,264	528 / 337,984	52 / 33,280
Wexford	577 / 368,960	566 / 362,048	11 / 6,912
Clare	576 / 368,704	570 / 364,800	6 / 3,904
Lake	574 / 367,360	568 / 363,392	6 / 3,968
Osceola	573 / 366,528	569 / 363,968	4 / 2,560
Missaukee	572 / 366,336	565 / 361,536	8 / 4,800
Kalkaska	570 / 365,056	563 / 360,320	7 / 4,736
Crawford	563 / 360,576	559 / 357,632	5 / 2,944
Manistee	558 / 357,056	543 / 347,456	15 / 9,600
Otsego	526 / 336,704	516 / 329,984	11 / 6,720
Antrim	525 / 335,808	480 / 307,328	45 / 28,480
Mason	511 / 326,976	494 / 316,480	17 / 10,496
Gr. Traverse	494 / 316,160	466 / 298,368	28 / 17,792
Emmet	484 / 310,016	468 / 299,456	17 / 10,560
Charlevoix	458 / 292,992	421 / 269,440	37 / 23,552
Leelanau	366 / 234,496	341 / 218,496	25 / 16,000
Benzie	348 / 223,168	322 / 206,208	27 / 16,960

Source: Michigan State University Tourism Resource Center

POPULATION DENSITY (2000)

County	Land area (sq. miles)	Persons per sq. mile
Michigan	56,804	175
Grand Traverse	465	167
Emmet	468	67.2
Charlevoix	421	62.6
Leelanau	341	60.6
Mason	494	57.1
Clare	570	55.1
Wexford	565	53.9
Benzie	322	49.8
Roscommon	565	48.8
Antrim	480	48.5
Otsego	516	45.3
Manistee	543	45.1
Osceola	569	41.0
Kalkaska	563	29.5
Crawford	559	25.6
Missaukee	565	25.5
Lake	568	20.0

HIGHEST POINTS IN LOWER PENINSULA

County	location	above sea level	state rank
Wexford	Briar Hill/Harrietta	1,706	7th
Crawford	Cote Dame Marie	1,524	11th
Kalkaska	Cleary Hill/Fletcher	1,476	17th
Oscoda	Mt. Tom/Mio	1,462	20th
Montmorency	Comstock Hills	1,449	21st
Otsego	Redner Hill/KP Lake	1,424	23rd
Crawford	Bald Hill/Luzerne	1,404	24th
Kalkaska	Falk Hill/Cote Dame Marie	1,403	25th
Kalkaska	Waldo Hill/Fletcher	1,394	27th
Missaukee	Allen Hill/Stittsville	1,378	29th

HIGHEST POINT, BY COUNTY

Wexford	Briar Hill/Harrietta	1,706
Crawford	Cote Dame Marie	1,524
Kalkaska	Cleary Hill/Fletcher	1,476
Otsego	Redner Hill/KP Lake	1,424
Missaukee	Allen Hill/Stittsville	1,378
Roscommon	Emery Hill/Prudenville	1,366
Emmet	Emmet Hgts/Harbor Springs	1,316
Charlevoix	Richardson Hill/Boyne City	1,079
Benzie	North Hills/Thompsonville	1,073
Leelanau	Sleeping Bear/Empire	1,044
Grand Traverse	Mcrea Hill/Grawn	933

No other counties included above 583 ft.
www.AmericasRoof.com

CONSERVANCIES

These nonprofit groups work to keep important undeveloped areas wild and, in some cases, to return developed ones to a more pristine state. Their partners are willing property owners who frequently get income tax, property tax and sometimes estate tax benefits in return.

Of Michigan's 43 land conservancies, just a handful existed before 1980. The real boom came during the 1990s, when 20 new conservancies formed. Conservancies run on donations, dues and endowments -- some directed by volunteers, others with paid staffs.

Acres preserved by Conservancies

Little Traverse Conservancy	23,197
Grand Traverse Regional Conservancy	16,785+
Leelanau Conservancy	4,500
Headwaters Land Conservancy	3,467
Cadillac Area Land Conservancy	675

Little Traverse Conservancy (www.landtrust.org)

Counties: Charlevoix, Cheboygan, Chippewa, Emmet and Mackinac

Established: 1972 – Northern Michigan's first regional land conservancy

Acres preserved: 23,767

Miles of water frontage: 70+

Projects: 345

Conservation Easement/Purchase of Development Rights   projects: 143

Acres: 10,317   **Value:** $24,435,231

Nature Preserves projects: 156

Acres: 7,971   **Value:** $34,793,523

Transfer/Assist projects: 46

Acres: 4,908   **Value:** $25,111,026

Total value of land: $84,339,780

The Little Traverse Conservancy is northern Michigan's largest membership-supported organization with 4,092 members.

Leelanau Conservancy (www.theconservancy.com)

Counties: Leelanau County

Established: 1988

Acres preserved: 4,500

Through conservation easements or Purchase of Development Rights the conservancy has preserved 2,424 acres (79 separate projects).

21 other projects have become Natural Areas, preserves, or parks. Of those, 10 are open to the public, 11 are open only through guided tours.

Largest parcel: 340 acre Houdek Dunes site near Leland

Miles of Lake Michigan shoreline preserved: 3

Inland lakes shoreline miles preserved: 6

Holdings include: Kehl Lake Natural Area with 180 acres around Kehl Lake at the tip of the peninsula; Cedar River Natural Area with 120 acres of untouched wetlands accessible only by canoe or kayak; Whaleback Natural Area – 40 acres of hardwoods leading to the top of a towering dune with panoramic views of Lake Michigan; Belanger Creek Preserve – 68 acres with 2,800 feet of stream frontage and lots of wildlife; Hall Beach on Lake Michigan in Leland; Nedows Bay Park on Lake Leelanau, and Gull Island in Northport Bay.

Grand Traverse Regional Land Conservancy (www.gtrlc.org)

Coverage area: Antrim, Benzie, Grand Traverse, Kalkaska and Manistee counties.

Established: 1991

Acres preserved: over 16,785 acres

The conservancy has negotiated 118 Conservation Easements and created 28 nature preserves.

Largest parcel owned: 240-acre Bauer/Polaczyk Nature Preserve-Antrim County

Largest parcel Conservancy helped preserve: 565 acre Camp Sakakawea, the Crooked Tree Girl Scout Camp in Grand Traverse County. Property is owned by Rotary Camps and Services. GT Regional Land Conservancy holds a conservation easement on the land.

Miles of lake frontage: 49.26

Total value of land preserved by GTRLC: $34,331,238.00

In 2003 the GTRLC embarked on its Coastal Campaign to preserve 6,320 acres along Lake Michigan. The land includes more than three miles of shoreline between Elberta and Arcadia, and a mix of forest and farmland. It is the Conservancy's largest project to date, and the largest farmland preservation project in the Midwest. The Coastal Campaign seeks to raise $30 million for the project over several years.

Headwaters Land Conservancy (www.headwatersconservancy.org)

Counties: Otsego, Crawford, Roscommon, Presque Isle, Montmorency, Oscoda, Ogemaw, Arenac, Alpena, Alcona, and Iosco

Established: 1993

Acres preserved: 3,467 total

Within Otsego, Crawford and Roscommon: 828

Largest property: 737 acre Tote Road Club, a family hunt club in Oscoda County. Tote Road Lake and Dollar Lake both lie with in the property which includes 8,000 feet of lake frontage and 4,000 feet on a tributary of Marsh Creek.

Cadillac Area Land Conservancy (www.netonecom.net/~cavb/CALC.htm)

Counties: Wexford, Missaukee, Lake and Osceola

Acres preserved: 675

OTHER LANDS

Grass River Natural Area (www.grassriver.org)

Location: near Alden in Antrim County

Acres: 1,160

Land: Wetlands, cedar forests and wildlife habitat along the Grass River, abutting Clam Lake and Lake Bellaire

Features: Offers miles of marked hiking trails, bird watching and wildflower programs, organized hikes and year round classes. Trails for wheelchairs and visually impaired.

Owner: Purchased in 1972 through private donations and continued memberships

Access: Driveway is on Alden Highway, half mile west of Comfort Rd.

University of Michigan Biological Station

Location: On Douglas Lake near Levering in Emmet County

Acres: approximately 10,000 (all open to public)

Land: Extensive pine forests, northern hardwoods, conifer swamps, fields and meadows, pine plains, all types of wetlands, and rivers and streams

Features: Approximately 150 buildings including: a 250-seat auditorium, 24,000 square foot lakeside laboratory, 2,000 square foot greenhouse, 70 one-room cabins, 30 larger cabins, a 14-room residence hall, and dining hall for up to 275 people.

Serves as a major instructional and research center for students and scientists from around the world.

Year round staff of fifteen: administrative, technical and maintenance

Owner: University of Michigan since 1909

Operated by University's College of Literature, Science and the Arts

Access: County Rd. 64, six miles east of Pellston

POPULATION
& HOUSING

POPULATION

Populations Peaks

For most of the 20th century the population of northern Michigan has been rebounding from its peak during the lumber boom.   In the 1870's the railroad expanded into the northern forests and opened the door to a 50-year economic boom that saw populations double within twenty years. As the country grew and expanded westward, the demand for lumber jumped. There was no shortage of entrepreneurs ready to exploit the northern forests, and plenty of willing workers looking for a steady paycheck.

By the 1910's the unimaginable was being realized. Lumber barons and lumber-jacks discovered there was indeed a limited supply of trees. Lumber companies moved or folded, lumber camps closed, and lumber towns struggled to survive, or became ghost towns.

Manistee County has never completely recovered from its all-time high population of 27,856, achieved in 1900. It took most of the northern counties 60 to 80 years to regain the population once enjoyed during the early years of the 20th century.

A few counties, Clare, Grand Traverse, Emmet and Otsego sustained minor popu-lation loss after the lumber boom, and went on to enjoy relatively steady growth through the present day.   There is evidence of a population boom in Otsego and Kalkaska counties after oil and gas were discovered. Kalkaska County's popula-tion doubled between 1970 and 1980, while Otsego doubled between 1960 and 1980.

	1860	1870	1880	1890	1900	1910	1920
Antrim	179	1,985	5,237	10,413	16,568	19,965	11,543
Benzie		2,184	3,433	5,237	9,685	10,638	6,947
Charlevoix		1,724	5,115	9,686	13,956	19,157	15,788
Clare		366	4,187	7,558	2,943	9,240	8,250
Crawford			1,159	2,962	8,360	3,934	4,049
Emmet	1,149	1,211	6,639	8,756	15,931	18,560	15,639
Gr. Traverse	1,286	4,443	8,422	13,355	20,479	23,784	19,518
Kalkaska		424	2,937	5,160	7,133	8,097	5,577
Lake		548	3,233	6,505	4,957	4,939	4,437
Leelanau		4,576	6,253	7,944	10,556	10,608	9,061
Manistee	975	6,074	12,532	24,230	27,856	26,688	20,899
Manitou	1,042	891	1,334	860			
Mason	831	3,263	10,665	16,385	18,885	21,832	19,831
Missaukee		130	1,553	5,048	9,308	10,606	9,004
Osceola	27	2,093	10,777	14,630	17,859	17,889	15,221
Otsego			1,974	4,272	6,175	6,552	6,043
Roscommon			1,459	2,033	1,787	2,274	2,032
Wexford		650	6,815	11,278	16,845	20,769	18,207
Michigan	749,113	1,184,059	1,636,937	2,093,889	2,420,982	2,810,173	3,668,412

1930	1940	1950	1960	1970	1980	1990	2000	
9,979	10,964	10,721	10,373	12,612	16,194	18,185	23,110	Antrim
6,587	7,800	8,306	7,834	8,593	11,205	12,200	15,998	Benzie
11,981	13,031	13,475	13,421	16,541	19,907	21,468	26,090	Charlevoix
7,032	9,163	10,253	11,647	16,695	23,822	24,952	31,252	Clare
3,097	3,765	4,151	4,971	6,482	9,465	12,260	14,273	Crawford
15,109	15,791	16,534	15,904	18,331	22,992	25,040	31,437	Emmet
20,011	23,390	28,598	33,490	39,175	54,899	64,273	77,654	Grand Traverse
3,799	5,159	4,597	4,382	5,272	10,952	13,497	16,571	Kalkaska
4,066	4,798	5,257	5,338	5,661	7,711	8,583	11,333	Lake
8,206	8,436	8,647	9,321	10,872	14,077	16,527	21,119	Leelanau
17,409	18,450	18,524	19,042	20,094	23,019	21,265	24,527	Manistee
18,756	19,378	20,474	21,929	22,612	26,365	25,537	28,274	Mason
6,992	8,034	7,458	6,784	7,126	10,009	12,147	14,478	Missaukee
12,806	13,309	13,797	13,595	14,838	18,928	20,146	23,197	Osceola
5,554	5,827	6,435	7,545	10,422	14,993	17,957	23,301	Otsego
2,055	3,668	5,916	7,200	9,892	16,374	19,776	25,469	Roscommon
16,827	17,976	18,628	18,466	19,717	25,102	26,360	30,484	Wexford
4,842,325	5,256,106	6,371,766	7,823,194	8,881,826	9,262,078	9,295,297	9,938,444	Michigan

POPULATION PROJECTIONS

County	2000 Population	2006 Projection	2025 Projection
Antrim	23,110	26,200	26,419
Benzie	15,998	18,300	20,652
Charlevoix	26,090	28,900	32,405
Clare	31,252	35,100	39,973
Crawford	14,273	15,600	16,749
Emmet	31,437	35,300	40,453
Grand Traverse	77,654	85,900	94,921
Kalkaska	16,571	18,500	20,522
Lake	11,333	12,800	15,609
Leelanau	21,119	24,000	27,058

Manistee	24,527	26,100	28,800
Mason	28,274	29,900	31,921
Missaukee	14,478	15,900	17,652
Osceola	23,197	25,000	26,996
Otsego	23,301	26,700	30,699
Roscommon	25,469	28,900	32,933
Wexford	30,484	33,000	35,970
Total	438,567	486,100	539,732

HIGHEST PERCENTAGE OF SENIOR CITIZENS – BY COUNTY

County	Citizens over 65 (%)	under 18 (%)	under 5 (%)
Roscommon	23.8	20.0	4.3
Lake	19.7	21.9	5.2
Manistee	18.1	22.6	5.3
Antrim	17.5	24.4	5.7
Benzie	17.5	23.4	5.9
Leelanau	17.4	24.4	5.1
Clare	17.3	24.4	5.8
Mason	16.8	24.2	5.4
Crawford	16.6	24.5	5.4
Charlevoix	14.9	25.9	6.5
Missaukee	14.8	27.1	6.4
Emmet	14.3	25.3	6.2
Osceola	14.2	27.1	6.2
Wexford	14.0	26.8	6.4
Otsego	13.7	26.8	6.2
Kalkaska	13.7	23.6	6.4
Grand Traverse	13.1	25.4	6.1
Michigan	12.3	6.1	6.8

U.S. Census Bureau (2000)

LARGEST TOWNS IN NORTHERN MICHIGAN

Town	2002 est. population	2000 population	%Change	County
1. Traverse City	14,319	14,532	-0.4	Grand Traverse
2. Cadillac	10,034	10,000	+0.3	Wexford
3. Ludington	8,434	8,357	+0.9	Mason
4. Manistee	6,379	6,586	-3.1	Manistee
5. Petoskey	6,169	6,080	1.5	Emmet
6. Houghton Lake	NA	3,749		Roscommon
7. Gaylord	3,741	3,681	+1.6	Otsego
8. Boyne City	3,369	3,503	-3.9	Charlevoix
9. Clare	3,165	3,173	+0.8	Clare
10. Charlevoix	2,858	2,994	-4.5	Charlevoix
11. St. Helen	NA	2,993		Roscommon
12. East Jordan	2,416	2,507	-3.6	Charlevoix
13. Reed City	2,419	2,430	-0.5	Osceola
14. Kalkaska	2,249	2,226	+0.2	Kalkaska
15. Harrison	2,111	2,108	+0.1	Clare
16. Grayling	1,970	1,952	+0.9	Crawford
17. Evart	1,724	1,738	-0.8	Osceola
18. Prudenville	NA	1,737		Roscommon
19. Elk Rapids	1,721	1,700	+1.2	Antrim
20. Harbor Springs	1,568	1,567	+0.1	Emmet
21. Frankfort	1,506	1,513	-0.5	Benzie

LARGEST TOWNSHIPS (POPULATION)

Township	Population (2002)	County
Garfield	15,358	Grand Traverse
East Bay	10,001	Grand Traverse
Long Lake	7,718	Grand Traverse
Grayling	6,822	Crawford
Blair	6,695	Grand Traverse
Bagley	5,958	Otsego
Denton	5,783	Roscommon
Bear Creek	5,652	Emmet
Peninsula	5,305	Grand Traverse
Green Lake	5,196	Grand Traverse
Hayes	4,937	Clare
Kalkaska	4,920	Kalkaska
Paradise	4,420	Grand Traverse
Acme	4,366	Grand Traverse
Mancelona	4,363	Antrim
Elmwood	4,325	Leelanau
Roscommon	4,300	Roscommon
Richfield	4,191	Roscommon
Manistee	3,938	Manistee
Surrey	3,581	Clare

MEDIAN AGE - OLDEST BY TOWN/COUNTY

1. Northport	50.2	Leelanau
2. Frankfort	49.3	Benzie
3. Alden	49.3	Antrim (Tie)
4. Empire	49.1	Leelanau
5. Beulah	48.8	Benzie
6. Greilickville	48.1	Leelanau
7. St. Helens	47.6	Roscommon
8. Suttons Bay	47.2	Leelanau
9. Mackinac City	44.7	Emmet
10. Houghton Lake	44.2	Roscommon

MEDIAN AGE – YOUNGEST BY TOWN/COUNTY

1. Kingsley	28.3	Grand Traverse
2. Pellston	31.2	Emmet
3. Buckley	31.3	Wexford
4. Mesick	31.5	Wexford
5. E. Jordan	32.7	Charlevoix
6. Alanson	32.8	Emmet
7. Ellsworth	33.1	Antrim
8. Copemish	33.3	Manistee
9. Mancelona	33.4	Antrim
10. Hersey	33.6	Osceola

THROUGH THE YEARS: FEWER MARRIAGES

Some of the fastest growing counties of the 1990's were in northern Michigan, yet the instance of marriage hardly kept pace. As populations jumped by 15, 20, 25, even 30%, the increase in the number of weddings was in the single digit range, with a few exceptions.

Leelanau County experienced a 67% increase in the number of weddings. One possible explanation: with its picturesque waterfront resorts and inns, Leelanau County, like Mackinac Island, may be a wedding destination site. (Mackinac Island lies in Mackinac County which leads the state with 39.8 marriages per 1,000 people.)

The numbers suggest fewer people are getting married, or that the number of weddings is far from keeping pace with the population growth. Consider that many new residents who move to the north, are retired, and already married. Many young people move away from their northern homes to start careers and families elsewhere.

County	No. of Marriages 1992	No. of Marriages 2002	Change	Population Change 1990-2000
Antrim	176	184	+ 5%	+27.1%
Benzie	135	121	-10%	+31.1%
Charlevoix	234	203	-13%	+21.5%
Clare	214	232	+8%	+25.2%
Crawford	96	101	+ 5%	+16.4%
Emmet	292	291	flat	+25.5%
Grand Traverse	671	708	+11%	+20.8%
Kalkaska	117	129	+10%	22.8%
Lake	81	60	-19%	32%
Leelanau	95	159	+67%	27.8%
Manistee	176	151	-13%	15.3%

Mason	227	232	+ 2%	10.7%
Missaukee	88	109	+24%	19.2%
Osceola	173	211	+22%	15.1%
Otsego	186	196	+ 5%	29.8%
Roscommon	150	152	+ 1%	28.8%
Wexford	263	250	- 5%	15.6%
Totals	**3,374**	**3,489**	**+3.4%**	

Michigan Department of Community Health
U.S. Census Bureau

MOST MARRIAGE MINDED – COUNTIES RANKED (2002)

County	No. of Marriages	Persons Married per 1,000 People
Grand Traverse	708	17.4
Emmet	291	18.0 (highest in Lower Peninsula)
Wexford	250	16.2
Clare	232	14.6
Mason	232	16.1
Osceola	211	18.0 (highest in Lower Peninsula)
Charlevoix	203	15.4
Otsego	196	16.2
Antrim	184	15.5
Leelanau	159	14.6
Roscommon	152	11.8
Manistee	151	12.0

Kalkaska	129	15.1
Benzie	121	14.4
Missaukee	109	14.6
Crawford	101	13.7
Lake	60	10.3
Michigan	65,104	13.0

DIVORCE (2002)

County	No. of Divorces	No. of Persons Divorced per 1,000
Grand Traverse	415	10.2
Wexford	169	11.0
Mason	153	10.6
Emmet	148	9.2
Clare	140	8.8
Otsego	133	11.0
Charlevoix	120	9.1
Antrim	105	8.8
Roscommon	99	7.7
Manistee	89	7.1
Benzie	86	10.2
Osceola	80	6.8
Kalkaska	78	9.2
Leelanau	73	6.7
Missaukee	71	9.5
Crawford	56	7.6
Lake	31	5.3
Michigan	37,804	7.5

HOUSING

County	Owner Occupied	Median Value ($)	Renter Occupied	Median Rent ($)
Antrim	5,209	110,000	1,281	460
Benzie	3,639	107,400	856	486
Charlevoix	5,532	112,700	1,817	470
Clare	6,532	70,500	2,079	397
Crawford	3,387	79,500	940	453
Emmet	6,349	131,500	2,975	513
Grand Traverse	17,669	130,400	6,654	614
Kalkaska	3,109	85,100	885	468
Lake	1,888	61,300	738	387
Leelanau	5,008	165,400	1,138	565
Manistee	5,311	77,400	1,754	424
Mason	5,940	81,500	2,379	425
Missaukee	2,340	78,700	798	460
Osceola	3,574	70,000	1,517	409
Otsego	5,067	102,500	1,557	540
Roscommon	7,724	78,900	1,580	420
Wexford	5,688	79,900	2,352	451
Michigan	2,269,175	115,600	976,313	546

Bureau of the Census 2000

VACATION HOME OWNERSHIP

Housing units that are classified as vacant for seasonal, recreational, or occasional use make up a class that is often referred to as "vacation" homes. These may be large summer estates on Long Island, time-sharing condos in Fort Lauderdale, or simple fishing cabins in northern Michigan. Analysts often use this category to estimate the number of second homes in a given area.

Michigan is tied with Hawaii and Wyoming for 10th in percentage of homes classified as vacation homes.

County	All Housing	Vacation Homes
Michigan	4,234,279	234,371
Grand Traverse	34,842	2,983
Emmet	18,554	5,130
Charlevoix	15,370	4,409
Antrim	15,090	5,183
Kalkaska	10,822	3,773
Crawford	10,042	4,104
Otsego	13,375	3,828
Roscommon	23,109	11,223
Clare	22,229	8,714
Missaukee	8,621	2,875
Lake	13,498	8,312
Osceola	12,853	3,430
Wexford	14,872	2,240
Manistee	14,272	3,569
Mason	16,063	3,843
Benzie	10,312	3,223
Leelanau	13,297	4,167

from the U.S. Census Bureau

WATERFRONT REAL ESTATE

For a textbook lesson on supply and demand one only has to study the northern Michigan waterfront real estate market. The best properties were bought for a few hundred dollars in the late 19th century, and some of them have never been sold, just passed on from one generation to the next. Some of the most desirable lake frontage will probably never come on the market, offered first to family and neighbors, who are glad to add to their holdings and maintain a tidy generational privacy.

Jack Lane, a realtor and native of Traverse City, likes to say the whole world is coming to his hometown. He's seen his client base stretch beyond metro Detroit, Chicago and northern Indiana, into Florida, Texas, New York, California, and other states. His theory is that Traverse City has these five key elements going for it: natural beauty, first class medical facilities, a healthy arts and culture scene, jet air service, and a crime-free climate. Lane hosts "Ask the Realtor" on WTCM AM-580 every Saturday morning, where he frequently quotes recent water front sales figures.

He sees Big Glen Lake as the most valuable water front up north stating it's at the point that, "if you have to ask how much it is, you can't afford it." He says prices have gone up steadily with the last boom coming during the NASDAQ bubble in the late 1990's.

Ken Schmidt of Coldwell Banker Schmidt Realtors in Traverse City is also a native – he and his brother Fred run the real estate business founded by their grandfather in 1927. Schmidt observed another recent boom in water front real estate after the 1987 National Governor's Conference which was about the same time that the Grand Traverse Resort expanded and the first year-round jet air service came to Traverse City. He too sees a pattern of 2nd homebuyers coming from around the country back to northern Michigan where they have some kind of connection; some may have camped here as kids, or vacationed with their families. Schmidt says no matter where their careers have taken them, they want to build a vacation home back in northwestern Michigan.

Another recent effect on the price of vacation property up north is the internet, which Schmidt says allows people from all over the world to constantly search for that perfect lakefront property. Waterfront property values

preciate 5-8% a year on
erage, but Schmidt says
ere have been some pretty
g spikes in the late 80's,
d late 90's driven by the
gh demand and dwindling
pply of top-quality water-
nt.

e price range for lake-
nt property in northern
ichigan can range from
,500 to $15,000 per foot
waterfront property. That
n mean a 100 foot lot sells
between $150,000 and
,500,000. Some of the fac-
rs that affect the sale price
clude:

cation - generally the clos-
to town the higher the
ce
ivacy – the more distance
tween neighbors and the
ad the higher the price
ach quality – sandy brings
igher price than rocky
ews – sunset, sunrise,
ldlife, etc can all affect
price
istance between house and
ore. If you have to climb
wn or up to the beach, the
ce will probably be lower
an a flat parcel
ke – larger lakes and those
th access to other lakes are
ore desirable
se of access – close to high-
y and/or airport is a plus
reage – more land means
gher price, and
e House! — large, newer
mes with top-notch ameni-
s add a lot to the property,

while some older, smaller
homes may be a liability to a
seller if the buyer has to pay
for a tear down.

The following information is
provided by local realtors and
is current as of spring 2004.
More information can be
found on the listed websites.

TRAVERSE CITY

Ken Schmidt
Coldwell Banker Schmidt
Realtors
www.cbschmidt.com

The premier waterfront in
Traverse City is on West Bay
at the base of the peninsula
where the range is between
$7,500 - $9,000 per foot.
These lots provide sunset
views, sandy beach, and are
in town, or conveniently
close to it.

The Deepwater Point section
of East Bay provides privacy
and convenience to town.
The range is $7,000 - $9,000
per foot. Elsewhere, frontage
on East or West Bay near or
in Traverse City runs $4,500-
$6,000, depending on the fac-
tors listed above.

LEELANAU COUNTY

Glen Lake/Lake Michigan
Mark Carlson Coldwell
Banker Schmidt Realtors
www.markecarlson.com

Some of the most expensive inland lake frontage in northern Michigan sits on Big Glen Lake. Demand is high, and supply is low, as very few properties become available. Sellers demand and receive over $10,000 per foot on Big Glen.

Little Glen Lake lot prices are not as high, falling in the $250,000-$600,000 range. There are more wetland areas around Little Glen, which diminishes the values slightly. The same price range applies to frontage on S. Lake Leelanau, Lime Lake and Little Traverse Lake.

Waterfront lots on Lake Michigan near Glen Arbor and Leland demand the highest prices, usually over $10,000 per foot, and up to $13,000 per foot with a sandy beach and good western view. Property in the Indiana Woods section between Lake Michigan and N. Lake Leelanau "would be off the charts if something became available."

Some of the exclusive enclaves in the area include: Strom High in Empire, Deer Trail west of Glen Arbor, Leland Woods, Birchwood Shores, Omigisi and Gills Pier north of Leland.

NORTHPORT AND SUTTONS BAY

Judy Levin Coldwell Banker Schmidt Realtors
www.judylevin.com

There's a lot of lake frontage at the tip of the Leelanau Peninsula, including Lake Michigan with sunrise and sunset views, and N. Lake Leelanau. The most expensive, and desirable properties are on Lake Michigan north of Northport, and on the northern end of Lake Leelanau. The gated community of Northport Point, which includes a private golf club, rarely has a property come on the market. Only one transaction has taken place since 1985, and that was a home that sold for $1,000,000 in the year 2000.

Another exclusive area north of Northport is known as Magic Carpet where a parcel with 175 feet of frontage recently sold for $1.2 million, or over $6,850 per foot.

Property along the West Grand Traverse Bay between Northport and Traverse City can range between $1,150 - $4,600 per foot.

Transactions in the year 2004 include:
 A 4,000 sq. foot home with 82 feet on Big Glen Lake that sold for nearly $14,000 per foot.

95 feet on Lake Michigan near Glen Arbor with a 2,000 square foot home for $13,000 per foot.

A 2,600 foot home with 100 feet on Glen Lake in Glen Arbor sold for $12,300 per foot.

2,600 square foot home with 117 feet on N. Lake Leelanau in Leland sold for $11,500 per foot.

160 feet on Lake Michigan at the Leland Harbor with a 1,475 square foot home sold for $10,000 per foot.

295 feet on N. Lake Leelanau with 4 BR, 7 bath, 5,000 square foot home sold for $9,322 per foot.

TORCH LAKE

Lynne Delling Coldwell Banker Schmidt Realtors www.lynnedelling.com

Recent sales prices of homes have ranged from $595,00 to $2,650,000 based on variables such as amount of waterfrontage, quality of beach, the size, age and quality of the house, depth and overall size of lot, sunset or sunrise views, and convenience to highway or resorts.

About 70-80% of the new homes built since 1990 have gone up on the west side that parallels US 31, providing convenient access to Traverse City, Elk Rapids and Charlevoix, and quicker commutes to the airport. The land boom around Torch and other lakes started in the late 80's, and at that time much of the west side was undeveloped.

The most desirable stretch on Torch is on the east side between Alden to the south and Old State Rd. (624) that leads into Central Lake, on the north. Benefits include sunset views, deeper and flatter lots, and cooler breezes. The east side is further from US 31, but close to Shanty Creek Resort.

The price range for a buildable lot on Torch Lake with at least 100 feet of water front and a 350 foot deep lot runs between $500-625,000 on average. The price is closer to $800,000 if the lot includes a sandy beach, is relatively flat, wooded with large mature trees, extra deep, and affords privacy from neighboring properties. Recent sales examples (both on the east side): an open lot with few trees and rocky shoreline - $570,000. The wooded lot, about 1,000 feet deep, with sandy beach - $750,000.

Existing home prices vary based on size, age, and location. Home styles can range from a small 100-year old family cottage to a modern 5,000 square foot home with all the luxuries. The range is generally $595,000 - $2,650,000.

Most homes bought and built are 2nd homes, and the average buyer is getting younger. Couples between 35-45 with kids are becoming more common than the 45-60 year old boomers who used to make up most of the segment. Most are from downstate and Illinois, Indiana and Ohio. Some of the 2nd home buyers are from western states, but usually have ties to northern Michigan.

BENZIE COUNTY

Matt Case, GRI
Coldwell Banker Schmidt
Realtors
www.2cases.com

CRYSTAL LAKE

Waterfront property on Crystal Lake, based on recent sales, ranges from $5,800 to over $10,000 per foot. Examples: A five-bedroom home with 106 feet of frontage went for $650,000, while a rustic cabin on 35 feet of water sold for $375,000. Of three vacant buildable lot transactions in 2004 the average price paid was $5,492 per foot.

With its deep lots separating M-22 (Pilgrim Highway) from the beachfront homes the west side is the most desirable stretch on Crystal Lake. Rare is the instance that a home or lot comes up for sale; usually they are passed on or sold to family or friends without ever being listed.   Another prestigious stretch is along South Shore Drive along the south side. Many of the homes in these two areas have been in the same family for several generations.

One of the original developments on Crystal Lake, the Congregational Summer Assembly, is located at the southwest corner of the lake. Properties in the private association rarely, if ever, go on the market.

Interest in Crystal Lake property comes mostly from families, empty nesters and retirees. Geographically, interest is strongest from the Detroit area and other Midwestern cities: Chicago, St. Louis, and more recently, the Toledo area.

LAKE MICHIGAN

With a varying terrain that makes access difficult, plus limitations from Dunes legislation available Lake Michigan properties are scarce. The most desirable stretches are from the west side of Crystal Lake up through Crystal Downs and to the edge of the National Lakeshore. Low bluffs are most valuable as they provide easier access to the water, and are aren't as difficult to build on as high bluffs. Crystal Downs, while exclusive, is not entirely private. It is possible to buy property within Crystal Downs without belonging to the association.

Recent sales include a 1950's cottage in Crystal Downs with 150 feet of frontage on a low bluff. Sale price: $1,000,000, or $6,666 per foot.

A two acre lot with a 2,000 square foot, 3 BR home and 106 feet of frontage sold for $900,000, or $8,490 per foot. Buyers tore down the home and built new.

A lot with 225 feet of frontage, but perched on a high bluff, sold for $480,000, or $2,133 per foot. Access was challenging, and view limited.

Interested buyers seem to be mostly from out of state, and older as younger families looking for waterfront focus on inland lakes, which offer better recreation opportunities.

CHARLEVOIX

Don Toffolo Coldwell Banker Schmidt Realtors
www.dontoffolo.com

Vacant building lots on Lake Charlevoix, based on 2003

and 2004 sales, run $3,000 - $5,000 per foot. In the past twenty years many multi-million dollar homes have been built, several above the $7,000,000 mark. Those properties close in to the town of Charlevoix are among the most desirable and expensive, such as those found around Oyster Bay, Evergreen (near Castle Farms), Chula Vista on the North Arm near Whiting Park, the west side of the South Arm, and the stretch between Young State Park and Oyster Bay on the North Arm.

Frontage on Lake Michigan ranges between $2,000 per foot up to $6,000 per foot close to Charlevoix.

Best waterfront bargains are found around Boyne City and East Jordan where a road runs between the home and beach. Owners enjoy the view, private frontage, and lower priced property in exchange for having to cross a road to get to the beach.

EMMET COUNTY

Joe Blachy Coldwell Banker Schmidt Realtors
www.petoskeyresorthomes.com

Joe says when someone calls and says "I have $500,000 to spend...I want to buy a nice little 3 BR, 2 bath house on a nice lake..." I tell them, "you should have called five or ten years ago! Waterfront land and homes in northern Michigan are the best investment, especially in the past 5-10 years." Many of the in-demand properties have appreciated 50% in the past 5-7 years.

Supply and demand is in play, especially on Walloon Lake, one of the most desirable in Michigan. In 2004, a 100-foot building site sold for $1,000,000, or $10,000 per foot. Another lot, with 107 feet of frontage on Walloon went for $1,295,000, or $12,102 per foot.

Besides Walloon Lake the hot properties lie within long-established private associations such as Harbor Point and Wequetonsing, where properties rarely go on the market, instead passed on from generation to generation. Any waterfront close to Petoskey or Harbor Springs will bring a premium price and properties on nearby Mullet, and Burt Lake are in demand.

ROSCOMMON COUNTY

Kerry Hollingshead
Real Estate One
www.reomich.com/
higginslake/

Prices on Houghton Lake,

Michigan's largest inland lake, range between $2,000 and $4,000 per foot. In 2005, a 7 acre site with 600 feet of frontage owned by the Mallory Ignitions family sold for $2.4 million, or $4,000 per foot.

The most desirable stretches are along the west side, Long Point Drive on the small peninsula and on Old Trail on the northeast side. About 80% of the buyers are 2nd homebuyers.

On Higgins Lake the average price per foot is about $6,000. Home sales range between $650,000 and $1.5 million. In 2004, a 63 foot lot with 2,300 square foot home and 2-car garage was sold for $675,000, or $10,714 per foot. The most prestigious addresses are on the Gold Coast, upper west side, and the private Sunrise Heights.

MASON COUNTY

Michael Banninga
Century 21 Bayshore
www.Ludingtonwaterfront.com

The premium waterfront in Mason County, on Lake Michigan, is in short supply and high demand. Buyers will find beautiful sandy beaches between Big Point and Little Point Sable light-houses. With building restrictions from Dunes legislation, or challenging terrain, there are limited properties on the market. Based on recent sales the range is $4,500 - $6,000 per foot for a vacant lot. Average sales price, based on the most recent activity, is $540,000.

Buyers are looking for lots on low bluffs that can be built on, with access to utilities, and unobstructed views. Most buyers are coming from Chicago, Detroit, and other areas within a 4-5 hour drive of Ludington. Many have either vacationed in the area before, or visited friends' homes in the area.

The most exclusive stretch along Lake Michigan is the long-established Epworth enclave, a private association which owns all of the land and homes, and leases them to members. Leasing rights are usually passed on within the same family.

There are three other private associations, but properties from within do become available on the open market.

On Hamlin Lake the typical lot will sell for $2,000 per foot.

OLD REAL ESTATE ADS

From the Traverse City Record Eagle, *July of 1975...*

ON THE JEWELED SETTING OF GLEN LAKE a unique century summer home with 200' water frontage and lakefront cottage for extra family and guests.... All the summer living you can use for $65,000 (!!!)

WEST BAY ON TIP OF OLD MISSION PENINSULA 200+ft. frontage. Unique home in a beautiful wooded setting... 4 bedrooms, 2 baths, 2 fireplaces, 2,000 sq. ft.... $89,500 (!!!)

NEW LISTING on Peninsula Drive. 118' on West Bay near Braemar Estates. Plan your new home today. Invest in this lovely lot. $17,900 (!!!)

WEST BAY sand beach, Peninsula Drive, 5 bedrooms, fireplace, 2 car garage, rental apartments and 35 x 40' metal storage building, $65,000. (!!!)

OMENA bayfront, 150' sand beach, 3 bedrooms, $50,000. (!!!)

From the Leelanau Enterprise, *June of 1975...*

LAKE MICHIGAN wooded 300 feet. 700 ft deep, south fo Fill's Pier Rd. in Roaring Brook area. $170 per foot. Scarce!

NORTHPORT, 60 x 234 lot, bay frontage, Cherry Home Subdivision, $10,000.

NE side of LAKE LEELANAU, 10.1 surveyed acres with private access to lake. $58,000

LAKEFRONT HOME, upper Lake Leelanau, 107 ft. frontage, 4 BR, 2.5 bath, att. Garage, $59,500

160 FT. OF LAKE LEELANAU, S. of Leland, $175 per foot.

From The Torch, *May of 1975...*

ATTRACTIVE COTTAGE ON TORCH LAKE, 2BR, scr. Porch, Super Sandy beach, nice trees, $33,500

From the Charlevoix Courier, *June of 1957...*

ROUND LAKE, 40', good dock, small home, $8,500

LAKE CHARLEVOIX
SUMMER COTTAGE, 2BR, fireplace, boat & motor, furnished, deep lot, 66' frontage, $6,800

From the Benzie Patriot, *June 1955...*

CRYSTAL LAKE, BEULAH, 4 BR, 2 ba, on N. Shore 3 miles from Beulah, $13,500

...from 1953

FINE LAKE FRONTAGE *(Crystal and Lake Michigan)* from $2.65 to $45 per foot

...from 1952

SUMMER HOME SITES, Crystal Lake North, East, and South shores, $20 - $40 per foot

LAKE MICHIGAN WATERFRONT REAL ESTATE

County	Number of parcels on Lake Michigan (including bays)
Antrim	869
Manistee	540
Mason	N/A
Benzie	230
Leelanau	1,400+
Grand Traverse	N/A
Emmet	1,482

COUNTIES
& TOWNS

COUNTIES AND TOWNS

ANTRIM COUNTY
COUNTY SEAT: BELLAIRE

203 E. Cayuga
Bellaire, MI 49615
(231) 533-6320
www.antrimcounty.org

Formed: As Meegisee *(also listed as Meguzee)* County in 1840

Named after: In 1843 the county was renamed after County Antrim, Ireland. As one story goes, Tulie O'Malley, a State Senator around that time, wanted to honor the early Irish settlers who helped build the railroad. He attached an amendment to an appropriations bill that renamed four counties after counties in Ireland, and one county after the Irish patriot, Robert Emmet.

Due to a spelling error, before it became Antrim, it was officially on the books as Antim County.

First settler: In 1846, Andrew C. Wadsworth, a surveyor from Connecticut, arrived in Elk Rapids. Taking in the rich pine forests and the river that flowed into the big lake, he saw potential for a better life. Wadsworth built a cabin near the mouth of the Elk Rapids River, and went back for his wife and children a year later. By 1851, he had built a sawmill on the river and plotted the town of Elk Rapids.

Land area: 476.9 sq. miles (8th smallest county in Michigan)

Water area: 125.0 sq. mi.   **Elevation:** 621 ft. (Ellsworth)

Population: 24,094 (July 2003)   **State rank:** 61
23,110 (2000)
18,185 (1990)

Population growth since 1990: 32.5%   **State rank:** 7

Townships	2002 Population
Banks	1,838
Central Lake	2,278
Chestonia	569

Custer	1,048
Echo	928
Elk Rapids	2,764
Forest Home	1,865
Helena	888
Jordan	915
Kearney	1,828
Mancelona	4,363
Milton	2,100
Star	811
Torch Lake	1,168
Warner	406

Ethnicity in Antrim County:
- White (96.2%)
- American Indian (1.7%)
- Hispanic (1.2%)
- Two or more (1.2%)

Antrim County is has 25 miles of shoreline on East Grand Traverse Bay, is home to two of the state's largest lakes (Torch and Elk), and includes the 100-mile long Chain O' Lakes.

BELLAIRE 49615

Named after: The pure, fresh air. Mr. Ambrose E. Palmer sold his land to the county because officials wanted a location more centered than Elk Rapids for the county seat. Palmer is credited with naming the town Bellaire in 1879.

Once known as: Keno

Slogan: "Welcome to Bellaire, You'll Love It...," "Village for All Seasons"

Incorporated as village: 1891

Land area: 1.8 square miles

Population: (U.S. Census Bureau)
- 1,164   2000
- 1,152   2002 *(estimate)*

Males: 565 (48.5%)
Females: 599 (51.5%)

Median resident age: 37.5
years

Ethnicity in Bellaire:
• White (95.2%)
• Hispanic (2.2%)
• Two or more (1.8%)
• American Indian (1.1%)

Ancestries:
• German (26.5%)
• English (19.2%)
• Irish (13.9%)
• United States (9.6%)
• French (5.2%)
• Dutch (4.2%)

Median household income:
$32,243 *(year 2000)*
Median house value: $90,400
(year 2000)

**Industries providing
employment:**
• Manufacturing (19.0%)
• Arts, entertainment, recreation, accommodation and
  food services (18.1%)
• Educational, health and
  social services (17.6%)
• Retail trade (13.3%)

Known for: Shanty Creek
Resort. The resort is a major
year round employer with its
Arnold Palmer and Tom
Weiskopf-designed golf courses, downhill ski slopes and
cross country ski trails.

White Pine Stampede, a 25
and 50 kiliometer point-to-
point race draws nearly one
thousand cross country skiers
to the resort every February.
The *Grand Victorian Bed and*

Breakfast, built in 1895, was
placed on the National
Register of Historic Places by
the United States Department
of Interior.

Antrim County Courthouse is
listed on the National
Register of Historic Places.

ELK RAPIDS 49629

Named after: The elk horns
found at the mouth of the
Elk River in 1858, by the
first settler, Abraham
Wadsworth

Once known as: Stevens
*(Original name given by
Wadsworth)*

First settler: Abraham
Wadsworth arrived from
Connecticut in 1846. After
building a cabin near the site
of the current Town Hall, he
went back east for his wife.
In 1851 he built the first
sawmill in the county, and
platted the village by 1852.

Incorporated as village: 1900

Slogan: "Proud of our Past"
"Working Together for a
Better Tomorrow"

Land area: 1.7 square miles

Population: (U.S. Census
Bureau)
• 1,700   2000
• 1,721   2002 *(estimate)*

Males: 826 (48.6%)
Females: 874 (51.4%)

Median resident age:
43.4 years

Ethnicity in Elk Rapids:
• White (95.7%)
• Hispanic (2.1%)
• American Indian (1.2%)
• Two or more (0.8%)
• Other (0.6%)

Ancestries:
• German (28.8%)
• English (20.4%)
• Irish (15.6%)
• French (7.3%)
• Polish (5.9%)
• Dutch (5.4%)

Median household income:
$31,382 (year 2000)
Median house value:
$136,900 (year 2000)

**Industries providing
employment:**
• Educational, health and
social services (19.8%)
• Arts, entertainment, recreation, accommodation and
food services (16.8%)
• Retail trade (15.9%)
• Manufacturing (15.1%)

Known for: *Grace Memorial
Harbor,* expanded and up-dated
in 1999, has 220 slips, making
it one of the larger marinas
on Grand Traverse Bay.

The *Chain O' Lakes* starts in
Elk Lake on the east side of
Elk Rapids.

The annual Harbor Days celebration, known for one of
the best fireworks shows in
the north, is held the first
weekend of August.

The *giant swan* outside the
Chamber of Commerce building on US 31 has become a
visual symbol for the town.
In 1864 Dexter & Noble
built saw mills, a lumber
yard, grist mill and a boat
dock on Lake Michigan. The
charcoal blast furnace turned
out 24 tons of pig iron per
day and employees in Elk
Rapids numbered 365. There
were seven churches and
seven saloons. By 1910 the
hardwoods had been logged
off and the industry died out.

A cement plant was erected in
1890 and later moved to
Petoskey. Population sank to
684 during the Depression in
1930. Today Elk Rapids
remains a peaceful picturesque village with an appeal
to tourists and residents alike.

MANCELONA 49659

Named after: Mancelona
Andress, youngest daughter
of the town's founder, Perry
Andress

Once known as: Tiptown;
Mancelona Andress' nick-
name was Tip.

First settler: Perry Andress
and family arrived in 1869.

He farmed and built the town's first hotel. The family moved to Petoskey seven years later. Mancelona's grave is in the Greenwood Cemetery in Petoskey.

Slogan: "Land for All Seasons – Land for All Reasons"

Incorporated as village: 1889

Land area: 1.0 square miles

Population: (U.S. Census Bureau)
• 1,408   2000
• 1,405   2002*(estimate)*

Males: 663 (47.1%)
Females: 745 (52.9%)

Median resident age: 33.4 years

Ethnicity in Mancelona:
• White (94.2%)
• American Indian (2.3%)
• Hispanic (2.2%)
• Two or more (1.9%)
• Other (0.7%)

Ancestries:
• German (26.6%)
• Irish (15.9%)
• English (15.2%)
• French (8.7%)
• United States (8.7%
• Polish (5.8%)

Median household income: $29,583 (year 2000)
Median house value: $59,500 (year 2000)

Industries providing employment:
• Manufacturing (26.3%)
• Educational, health and social services (17.5%)
• Arts, entertainment, recreation, accommodation and food services (16.3%)
• Retail trade (12.5%)

Known for: Each February nearly 1,000 skiers line up in back of the high school for the start of the White Pine Stampede, a 25 and 50-kilometer point-to-point cross country race to Bellaire.

Mancelona Bass Festival held first weekend of June since 1955. Features a Grand Parade, Rolling Pin Toss, Banana Split Eating Contest and a Bass Fishing Contest!

ELLSWORTH 49729

Named after: Colonel Ephraim Elmer Ellsworth, the first Union soldier killed in the Civil War; the first postmaster of Ellsworth, Lewis DeLine, served with Ellsworth.

First settler: Erwine Dean and August Davis in 1881

Incorporated as village: 1938

Land area: 0.7 square miles

Population: (U.S. Census Bureau)
• 483   2000

- 475   2002*(estimate)*
Males: 237 (49.1%)
Females: 246 (50.9%)

Median resident age:
33.1 years

Ethnicity in Ellsworth:
- White (96.5%)
- Two or more (1.9%)
- Hispanic (1.0%)
- Other (1.0%)
- American Indian (0.8%)

Ancestries:
- Dutch (35.4%)
- German (22.4%)
- English (6.8%)
- Irish (5.8%)
- Polish (3.7%)
- French (3.7%)

Median household income:
$38,125 (year 2000)
Median house value: $84,700
(year 2000)

**Industries providing
employment:**
- Manufacturing (24.4%)
- Educational, health and
  social services (21.0%)
- Arts, entertainment, recreation, accommodation and
  food services (15.1%)

Known for: Two of the best
restaurants in Michigan are
located less than a mile apart
in this small town.
Tapawingo, owned by Pete
Peterson, has received national acclaim from food publications including *Gourmet* and
Food and Wine. Peterson
started his career as a chef
down the road at *The Rowe
Inn,* under the ownership of
Wes Westhaven since 1972.
It also appears regularly at
the top of critic's lists for its
cuisine and wine list. "The
Rowe" also launched the
career of Jim Milman who
opened Hattie's in Suttons
Bay, and Hanna Bistro in
Traverse City.

CENTRAL LAKE 49622

Named after: Its location at
central point of the upper
Chain of Lakes

First settler: Robert Clow in
the spring of 1866. The town
was established in 1871 by
James Wadsworth, the son
of the first European settler in
Antrim County. The young
Wadsworth built a sawmill
and opened a store on
Intermediate Lake.

Platted: 1883

Incorporated as village: 1895

Slogan: "Sailing to a better
tomorrow, today."

Land area: 1.0 square miles

Population: (U.S. Census
Bureau)
- 990   2000
- 1,011   2002 *(estimate)*

Males: 494 (49.9%)
Females: 496 (50.1%)

Median resident age:
38.7 years

Ethnicity in Central Lake:
- White (97.2%)
- American Indian (2.4%)
- Two or more (0.8%)
- Hispanic (0.5%)

Ancestries:
- German (20.9%)
- Irish (16.0%)
- English (11.7%)
- United States (7.4%)
- Polish (7.3%)
- Dutch (6.5%)

Median household income:
$38,173 (year 2000)
Median house value: $77,000
(year 2000)

Industries providing employment:
- Manufacturing (33.0%)
- Educational, health and social services (16.2%)
- Construction (11.1%)

Known for: Ellsworth is located on the north end of Ellsworth Lake on the upper Chain O' Lakes.

ATWOOD 49729
(Banks Twp.)

Named after: unknown

Nickname: Atwood the Adorable

Located in northernmost section of Antrim County on US 31 between Eastport and Charlevoix. Atwood was a lumber town settled in the 1860's, that saw the arrival of many Dutch settlers in the 1880's. Like many a northern Michigan lumber town, it's vitality faded along with the mature forests.

Known for: Birthplace of author, Rex Beach, a contemporary of Zane Grey and Jack London in the early 1900's. Over two dozen of his books were made into movies, including "The Spoilers," which was filmed four times.

Rex Beach Rd. intersects US 31 north of Atwood and leads to the Lake Michigan shore. Many visitors assume the name of the beach is Rex, and are unaware of his significance.

ALDEN 49612
(Helena Township)

Named after: William Alden Smith, a local railroad official, in the 1880's; Smith went on to become the first salaried state game warden in the country and served as a U.S. Representative and Senator.

Once known as: Noble, probably after the Elk Rapids pioneer, Henry Noble. From 1869 to 1882 the town was known as Spencer Creek, sharing the name of the stream that runs through town and into Torch Lake.

Slogan: "Where Neighbors Care"

Population: (U.S. Census Bureau)
- 1980   781
- 1990   837
- 2000   878

Males: 448 (51%)
Females: 430 (49%)

Median age: 49.3 (2000)

Ethnicity in Alden:
- White (97.2%)
- Black (0.1%)
- Native American (0.9%)
- Hispanic (0.3%)
- Asian/Hawaiian/Pacific Islander (.5%)
- Two or more (1.4%)

Median household income: (1999) $40,096

Today: Alden's location on the southeast end of Torch Lake, about 20 minutes from TC, makes it a popular summer resort town. It houses several seasonal shops, and has a public access to Torch Lake.

ALBA 49611
(Star Township)

Named after: Alba Haywood, a local entertainer in the 1880's

Once known as: Cascade; in 1876 it became a flag station on the Grand Rapids and Indiana Railroad.

Platted as village: 1878

Population: (U.S. Census Bureau)
- 1980   453
- 1990   575
- 2000   745

Males: 371 (49.8%)
Females: 374 (50.2%)

Median age: 38.2

Ethnicity in Alba:
- White (97.7%)
- Black (0.0%)
- Native American (1.2%)
- Hispanic (0.9%)
- Asian/Hawaiian/Pacific Islander (0.0%)
- Two or more (0.8%)

Median household income: $37,500 (1999)

Today: Alba lies at the crossroads of US 131 and C-42, a few miles north of Mancelona, and 15 miles west of Gaylord. Alba is popular with snowmobilers as it connects to hundreds of miles of trails throughout the Jordan Valley region.

EASTPORT 49627

Named: In 1873 it was named Eastport as it was on the eastern shore of Grand Traverse Bay across from Northport.

The village later moved to the northern point of Torch Lake.

Once known as: Wilson, between 1872 and 1873

First settler: Lumberman, Murdock Andres, arrived in 1863.

KEWADIN 49648

Named: After local Indian Chief, Ke-way-din, who is said to have been over 100 years old when he died and was buried in 1884.

Once known as: Indian Town

First settler: Charles Avery acquired land patents in 1856.

TORCH LAKE
(Torch Lake Township)

Named after: The Lake, which was named for the torches the Indians used for night fishing.

Once known as: Waswagonlink, the Indian word for "lake of torches"

Named Brownstown after the first settler, Captain John W. Brown

First settler: Captain Brown arrived in 1858

Population: 1,159

Median age: 52

BENZIE COUNTY
County seat: Beulah

PO Box 398
Beulah, MI 49617
(231) 882-9671

Formed: in 1863 as part of Leelanau County; 1869- separated from Leelanau

Named after: The French called it "Aux Bec Scies." The Indians said "Un-Zig-A-Zee-Bee." Roughly interpreted, it means "River of the Sawbill (duck)," and eventually it evolved to Betsie, which is the name that stuck for the river and the bay. Other variations such as Benzie and Benzonia were used to name the county and the first settlement.

First settler: In 1858, Congregational minister, Charles E. Bailey, moved from New York after reading a newspaper article about the Grand Traverse region. With family and friends he settle near Crystal Lake, established a mission, and the region's first college, Grand Traverse College.

Land area: 321.3 sq. mi. (Michigan' smallest county)
Water area: 538.3 sq. mi.

Elevation: 600 ft. (Frankfort)

Population:
17,078 (July 2003)
State rank: 68
15,998 (2000)
12,200 (1990)

Population growth since 1990: 40%
State rank: 2

Median age: 41

Townships	2002 Population
Almira	16,818
Benzonia	2,936
Blaine	523
Colfax	669
Crystal Lake	994
Gilmore	875
Homestead	2,202
Inland	1,728
Joyfield	850
Lake	661
Platte	400
Weldon	559
Frankfort (city)	1,506

Ethnicity in Benzie County:
• White (95.4%)
• American Indian (2.4%)
• Hispanic (1.5%)
• Two or more (1.2%)

Industries providing employment:
• Educational, health and social services (19.2%)
• Manufacturing (14.9%)
• Retail trade (14.6%)
• Construction (12.2%)
• Arts, entertainment, recreation, accommodation and food services (11.1%)

BENZONIA 49616

Named after: From the Greek word meaning "good place to live."

First settler: In 1858, Congregational minister, Charles E. Bailey, moved from New York after reading a newspaper article about the Grand Traverse region. With family and friends he settle near Crystal Lake, established a mission, and the region's first college, Grand Traverse College.

Incorporated as Village: 1891

Land area: 1.1 square miles

Population: (U.S. Census Bureau)
• 519   2000
• 483   2002 *(estimate)*

Males: 260 (50.1%)
Females: 259 (49.9%)

Median resident age: 39.7 years

Ethnicity in Benzonia:
• White (91.9%)
• American Indian (4.4%)
• Hispanic (2.9%)
• Two or more (1.5%)
• Other (1.0%)

Ancestries:
• German (27.4%)
• English (15.6%)
• Irish (8.3%)
• French (6.7%)

- Italian (5.0%)
- Norwegian (4.0%)

Median household income:
$28,650 (year 2000)
Median house value: $88,000
(year 2000)

Industries providing employment:
- Manufacturing (19.1%)
- Retail trade (18.1%)
- Educational, health and social services (15.6%)
- Arts, entertainment, recreation, accommodation and food services (12.1%)

Known for: Home of Pulitzer Prize-winning author Bruce Catton

First college in northern Michigan: Grand Traverse College, established in 1863 in Benzonia

Home of Gwen Frostic

Largest historical society in Michigan

BEULAH 49617

Named after: A passage from the Bible. Reverend Charles Bailey, founder of the neighboring town of Benzonia, probably viewed a surveyor's blunder as a divine act when naming Beulah. In 1873 a canal was dug between Crystal Lake and the Betsie River so that, in theory, Lake Michigan steamboats could service the inland lake. However, because Crystal Lake was at a higher elevation, the water level dropped about 10 feet, which left the beautiful sandy beach that exists today. Rev. Bailey may have seen this as a divine act, hence the biblically-inspired name from Isaiah 62.4: "You shall no more be termed Forsaken and your land shall no more be termed Desolate; but you shall be called My Delight is in Her, and your land Beulah, that is Married."

Once known as: Crystal City and Beulah Vista Resort

First Settler: Rev. Charles Bailey who settled Benzonia, the village up the road

Platted: 1890

Incorporated as a Village: 1932

Land area: 0.5 square miles

Population: (U.S. Census Bureau)
- 363   2000

Males: 166 (45.7%)
Females: 197 (54.3%)

Median resident age: 48.8 years

Ethnicity in Beulah:
- White (97.2%)
- Hispanic (1.7%)
- American Indian (0.8%)
- Other (0.6%)

Ancestries:
- German (28.9%)
- English (16.0%)
- Irish (14.9%)
- Polish (6.9%)
- United States (6.6%)
- Scottish (6.1%)

Median household income: $31,250 (year 2000)
Median house value: $94,700 (year 2000)

Industries providing employment:
- Educational,health and social services (28.6%)
- Retail trade (14.3%)
- Arts, entertainment, recreation, accommodation and food services (12.6%)
- Manufacturing (10.9%)

Known for: The Cherry Hut Restaurant, Betsie River Trail – 23 miles to Frankfort, Beulah Beach on Cyrstal Lake

ELBERTA 49628

Named after: A peach variety once plentiful in the region; in 1911, citizens changed the name to reflect the local peach-growing industry. One too many crop-killing frosts brought an end to the peach industry.
Once known as: Frankfort City, or South Town, in the 1860's; changed to South Frankfort in 1872

First settler: John Greenwood in 1855

Platted: 1866 by George M. Cartwright, the "Father of Elberta"

Land area: 0.7 square miles

Population: (U.S. Census Bureau)
- 457   2000
- 457   2002 *(estimate)*

Males: 224 (49.0%)
Females: 233 (51.0%)

Median resident age: 36.5 years

Ethnicity in Elberta:
- White (95.2%)
- American Indian (3.3%)
- Two or more (2.2%)
- Hispanic (0.9%)
- Black (0.7%)

Ancestries:
- German (31.3%)
- Irish (16.2%)
- English (13.1%)
- French (5.3%)
- United States (4.8%)
- Polish (4.6%)

Median household income: $28,403 (year 2000)
Median house value: $72,800 (year 2000)

Industries providing employment:
- Educational, health and social services (26.8%)
- Manufacturing (20.7%)
- Arts, entertainment, recreation, accommodation and food services (14.6%)

FRANKFORT 49635

Named after: Either the city in Germany, or an early cabin; Walter Romig's *Michigan Place Names* states that a former resident suggested the name because the town reminded him of Frankfort, Germany. In Tom BeVier's *Images of Benzie County,* he relates the story of an early settler named Frank Martin. During one of those early, cold winters, Martin and friends built a wind barrier out of brush and logs outside their cabin, which they called Frank's Fort.

First settler: Joseph Oliver in 1850

Slogan: "Always in Season"

Land area: 1.4 square miles

Population: (U.S. Census Bureau)
- 1,513   2000
- 1,506   2002 *(estimate)*

Males: 664 (43.9%)
Females: 849 (56.1%)

Median resident age:
49.3 years

Ethnicity in Frankfort:
- White (94.4%)
- American Indian (2.9%)
- Hispanic (1.8%)
- Two or more (1.1%)

Ancestries:
- German (23.9%)
- English (17.8%)
- Irish (11.4%)
- Norwegian (10.3%)
- French (6.7%)
- United States (4.0%)

Median household income:
$33,821 (year 2000)
Median house value:
$101,900 (year 2000)

Industries providing employment:
- Educational, health and social services (25.2%)
- Arts, entertainment, recreation, accommodation and food services (12.1%)
- Retail trade (11.7%)
- Manufacturing (10.9%)
- Construction (10.6%)

Known for: History of car ferries, location on Betsie Bay, marina, Lake Michigan beach, lighthouse, Crystal Downs golf course, hang gliding.

HONOR   49640

Named after: The daughter of an early businessman. Joseph A. Gifford, of the London-based Guelph Patent Cask Company, chose to open a plant in the area based on its seemingly endless supply of hardwood trees. The company, which manufactured large wooden casks for beverages, set up shop in 1895. Gifford named the town Honor in honor of his one-year old daughter, Honor!

First settler: Joseph A. Gifford in 1895

Slogan: "Coho Capital"

Incorporated as a Village: 1914

Land area: 0.6 square miles

Population: (U.S. Census Bureau)
- 299   2000
- 302   2002 *(estimate)*

Males: 150 (50.2%)
Females: 149 (49.8%)

Median resident age: 38.5 years

Ethnicity in Honor:
- White (85.6%)
- American Indian (8.0%)
- Two or more (4.0%)
- Hispanic (3.3%)
- Other (3.0%)
- Korean (0.7%)

Ancestries:
- Irish (18.4%)
- German (16.7%)
- French (13.7%)
- English (10.4%)
- Norwegian (8.4%)
- Polish (6.4%)

Median household income: $32,917 (year 2000)
Median house value: $70,000 (year 2000)

Industries providing employment:
- Arts, entertainment, recreation, accommodation and food services (18.8%)
- Educational, health and social services (14.8%)
- Public administration (14.1%)
- Retail trade (13.3%)
- Manufacturing (11.7%)

Known for: First county seat during the lumber boom years of 1908 – 1916, National Coho Festival held each August, fishing on the Platte River, Platte River Fish Hatchery, the state's largest, where millions of Coho and Chinook salmon are released each year.

LAKE ANN 49650 (L.A.)

Named after: The lake, which was named after the wife of the first settler.

First settler: A.P. Wheelock in 1862

Slogan or Nickname: "Little L.A."

Incorporated as Village: 1892

Land area: 0.4 square miles

Population: (U.S. Census Bureau)
- 276   2000
- 278   2002*(estimate)*

Males: 132 (47.8%)
Females: 144 (52.2%)

Median resident age: 42.3 years

Ethnicity in Lake Ann:
- White (96.7%)
- Hispanic (1.8%)
- American Indian (1.1%)
- Two or more (1.1%)

Ancestries:
- German (33.3%)
- English (23.6%)
- French Canadian (9.8%)
- Scottish (7.6%)
- Polish (6.9%)
- Scotch-Irish (6.2%)

Median household income:
$42,917 (year 2000)
Median house value:
$129,200 (year 2000)

Industries providing employment:
- Retail trade (21.0%)
- Educational, health and social services (16.7%)
- Arts, entertainment, recreation, accommodation and food services (13.6%)
- Manufacturing (10.5%)

Known for: Fire almost wiped out this former lumber town in 1897, 1914 and 1918. Was the smallest incorporated village in the state as recently as 1998.
The Lake Ann Grocery, where the sign over the counter reads, "If we don't have it, you don't need it."

THOMPSONVILLE 49683 (T-VILLE)

Named after: Sumner Thompson owner of Thompson Lumber Company

Once known as: Beecher's Side; some of the investors in Thompson Lumber were descendants of the famous nineteenth century Presbyterian minister, Henry Ward Beecher. The locals referred to the east side of town, where Thompson Lumber was located, as "Beecher's Side."

During the lumber boom Thompsonville boosters referred to their town as "The Biggest Little Town in Michigan," and "the best lighted city in the United States," after the town received its first electric company in 1895.

Land area: 1.0 square miles

Population: (U.S. Census Bureau)
457   2000
463   2002(*estimate*)

Males: 230 (50.3%)
Females: 227 (49.7%)

Median resident age:
34.9 years

Ethnicity in Thompsonville:
- White (95.8%)
- American Indian (2.4%)
- Other (1.1%)

Ancestries:
- German (29.5%)
- English (17.1%)
- Dutch (11.8%)
- Irish (11.8%)
- United States (9.0%)
- French (5.9%)

Median household income: $29,125 (year 2000)
Median house value: $55,000 (year 2000)

Industries providing employment:
• Manufacturing (31.2%)
• Arts, entertainment, recreation, accommodation and food services (19.4%)
• Construction (11.0%)

Known for: Crystal Mountain Resort, Midwest's #1 Ski Resort (*Ski Magazine,* 2005) During the lumber boom years Thompsonville was at the crossroads of two railroads and home to several lumber companies, a chemical plant, two hotels, three saloons, its own newspaper, a school, and an opera house. Its population peaked at the turn of the century at about 1,500.

CHARLEVOIX COUNTY COUNTY SEAT: CHARLEVOIX

203 Antrim Street
Charlevoix, MI 49720
(231)-547-7200
1-800-548-9157
www.charlevoixcounty.org

Formed: Boundary lines drawn in 1840 when it was named Keskkauko County; renamed Charlevoix in 1843

Named after: Pierre Francois-Xavier de Charlevoix, Jesuit missionary and explorer, arrived onshore in 1721 during his search for a northwest passage.

First settler: Medad Thompson who came to Charlevoix with his wife, Phoebe, in 1854. They built a home and began to farm land near the present day Railroad Depot Museum.

John S. Dixon built a permanent home in 1854, and later added a large dock. He became the town's first president in 1879.

Land area: 416.8 sq. mi.

Water area: 973.9 sq. mi.

Elevation: 669 ft. (Charlevoix)

Population:
26,712 (July 2003)
State rank: 56
26,090 (2000)
21,468 (1990)

Population growth since 1990: 24.4%
State rank: 18

Townships	2002 Population
Bay	1,084
Boyne Valley	1,276
Chandler	291
Charlevoix	1,722
Evangeline	788
Eveline	1,585
Hayes	1,961
Hudson	687

Marion	1,552
Melrose	1,440
Norwood	746
Peaine	275
St. James	324
South Arm	1,904
Wilson	2,108
Boyne City	3,369
Charlevoix (city)	2,858
East Jordan (city)	2,416

Ethnicity in Charlevoix County:
- White (95.8%)
- American Indian (2.4%)
- Two or more (1.2%)
- Hispanic (1.0%)

Industries providing employment:
- Manufacturing (21.0%)
- Educational, health and social services (20.2%)
- Retail trade (11.8%)
- Construction (10.8%)
- Arts, entertainment, recreation, accommodation and food services (10.5%)

Description: Resort town, former lumber area, Beaver Island, large lake, Hemingway country.

CHARLEVOIX 49720

Named after: French Jesuit explorer, and missionary, Pierre Francois-Xavier de Charlevoix who stopped at the foot of the Pine River in 1721 while searching for the great Northwest Passage to the Pacific.

Once known as: Pine River by early settlers starting in the 1850's.

First settler: Medad Thompson who came to Charlevoix with his wife, Phoebe, in 1854. They built a home and began to farm land near the present day Railroad Depot Museum.

John S. Dixon built a permanent home in 1854, and later added a large dock. He became the town's first president in 1879.

Incorporated as Village: 1879

Incorporated as City: 1905

Slogan: "Charlevoix the Beautiful"
"A City on Three Lakes"

Land area: 2.0 square miles

Population: (U.S. Census Bureau)
- 2,994   2000
  9th largest in northern Michigan
- 2,858   2002 (estimate)

Males: 1,407 (47.0%)
Females: 1,587 (53.0%)

Median resident age: 40.8 years
Ethnicity in Charlevoix:
- White (94.5%)
- American Indian (3.5%)
- Two or more (1.3%)
- Hispanic (1.2%)

Ancestries:
- German (17.8%)
- English (15.8%)
- Irish (15.5%)
- United States (8.4%)
- Dutch (8.4%)
- Polish (7.4%)

Median household income:
$35,284 (year 2000)
Median house value:
$113,400 (year 2000)

Industries providing employment:
- Educational, health and social services (20.7%)
- Retail trade (17.5%)
- Manufacturing (15.8%)
- Arts, entertainment, recreation, accommodation and food services (10.4%)

The earliest settlers came for the fish in the early 1850's, or were chased from their settlements on Beaver Island by the followers of King Strang. The fishermen on the mainland had it out with the Mormons of Beaver Island in "the Battle of Pine River" in 1853. Although the fishermen chased the Strangites back to Beaver Island, several moved on to less volatile fishing grounds.

BOYNE CITY 49712

Named after: The Boyne River. John Miller, one of the early settlers, named it after a river in Ireland.

Once known as: Boyne until it was renamed Boyne City in 1904.

First settlers: John Dixon and John Miller arrived with their families in 1856. Miller's wife, Harriet, was said to be a "spiritualist" who dreamed about a cabin on a bear-shaped lake. The New York couple's search for that mystical lake brought them to Pine Lake (Lake Charlevoix), which hardly resembles a bear!

First hotel: The Pine Lake House, built in 1879 by A. J. Hall.

Incorporated as Village: 1885

Slogan: "Home town feel...small town appeal"

Land area: 3.9 square miles
Population: (U.S. Census Bureau)
- 3,503   2000
  7th largest in northern Michigan
- 3,369   2002 (*estimate*)

Males: 1,710 (48.8%)
Females: 1,793 (51.2%)

Median resident age: 37.9 years

Ethnicity in Boyne City:
- White (96.6%)
- American Indian (2.1%)
- Two or more (1.2%)
- Hispanic (0.7%)

Ancestries:
- German (23.6%)
- English (15.0%)
- Irish (13.2%)
- United States (8.9%)
- Polish (8.3%)
- French (6.5%)

Median household income:
$35,819 (year 2000)
Median house value:
$94,200 (year 2000)

Industries providing employment:
- Manufacturing (23.4%)
- Educational, health and social services (22.4%)
- Arts, entertainment, recreation, accommodation and food services (12.9%)
- Retail trade (11.4%)
- Construction (10.0%)

EAST JORDAN 49727

Named after: Its location on the east bank of the Jordan River.

Early settlers: William Fletcher Empey was a timber spotter for a Toledo company. He built a home on the eastern shore of Pine Lake's (Lake Charlevoix) southern arm in 1874. Later that year he opened the first general store, and became the town's first postmaster in 1877.

Incorporated as a Village: 1887

Slogan: "Where River, Lake, and Friendly People Meet" "Swan City" "Discover East Jordan...One Season at a Time"

Land area: 3.1 square miles

Population: (U.S. Census Bureau)
- 2,507   2000
- 2,410   2002 *(estimate)*

Males: 1,218 (48.6%)
Females: 1,289 (51.4%)

Median resident age: 32.7 years

Ethnicity in East Jordan:
- White (93.6%)
- American Indian (3.4%)
- Two or more (2.6%)
- Hispanic (1.6%)
- Other (0.8%)

Ancestries:
- German (19.5%)
- Irish (15.6%)
- English (12.2%)
- United States (8.9%)
- Polish (6.3%)
- French (5.1%)

Median household income:
$35,924 (year 2000)
Median house value:
$76,000 (year 2000)

Industries providing employment:
- Manufacturing (36.6%)
- Educational, health and social services (18.5%)
- Retail trade (12.1%)

BOYNE FALLS 49713

Named after: The waterfalls on the nearby Boyne River, which was named after a river in Ireland.

Early settlers: When the GR & I Railroad arrived in 1874 the town's history began. Mr. A. D. Carpenter built the first store in town, and the first post office opened that year.

Incorporated as Village: 1893

Land area: 0.5 square miles

Population: (U.S. Census Bureau)
- 370   2000
- 360   2002 *(estimate)*

Males: 182 (49.2%)
Females: 188 (50.8%)

Median resident age: 34.0 years

Ethnicity in Boyne Falls:
- White (97.6%)
- American Indian (1.9%)
- Two or more (0.5%)

Ancestries:
- Polish (20.5%)
- German (17.8%)
- English (7.6%)
- Irish (7.6%)
- Italian (7.6%)
- Scottish (6.2%)

Median household income: $32,143 (year 2000)
Median house value: $74,700 (year 2000)

Industries providing employment:
- Retail trade (22.4%)
- Manufacturing (19.0%)
- Educational, health and social services (16.1%)
- Arts, entertainment, recreation, accommodation and food services (12.6%)
- Construction (11.5%)

HORTON BAY

Named after: Samuel Horton of Toledo, Ohio. In 1869, Captain Horton and family bound for Grand Rapids aboard the *Rover*, ran into high winds and took refuge on Lake Charlevoix. They remained there, waiting for the winds to die down, for several days, and finally chose to settle at what is now Horton Bay.

Once known as: Horton's Bay from 1879 to 1894.

First settler: Samuel Horton in 1843.

Slogan: "City on the Bay"

Population: 49

Known for: Hemingway connection. Ernie's old fishing haunts, married here, mentioned in several Nick Adam's stories, the General Store, 4th of July Parade in the heart of the financial district.

CLARE COUNTY
COUNTY SEAT:
HARRISON

Formed: In 1840 as Kaykakee (Pigeon Hawk) after a chief who had signed the Treaty of 1826

Named after: In 1843 it was named after County Clare in Ireland. As one story goes, Tulie O'Malley, a State Senator around that time, wanted to honor the early Irish settlers who helped build the railroad. He attached an amendment to an appropriations bill that renamed four counties after counties in Ireland, and one county after the Irish patriot, Robert Emmet.

First settler: The first pioneer family in the area was that of Civil War veteran, William Crawford, who homesteaded in Grant Township. A community grew there around a sawmill and was named Crawfordville, which was later renamed Dover.

Land area: 566.8 sq. mi.

Water area: 8.4 sq. mi.

Elevation: 841 ft. (Clare)

Population:
31,589 (July 2003)
State rank: 47
31,252 (2000)
24,952 (1990)

Population growth since 1990: 26.6%
State rank: 15

Townships   2002 Population

Township	Population
Arthur	683
Franklin	825
Freeman	1,170
Frost	1,177
Garfield	1,992
Grant	3,073
Greenwood	1,081
Hamilton	2,003
Hatton	946
Hayes	4,937
Lincoln	1,826
Redding	539
Sheridan	1,620
Summerfield	462
Surrey	3,581
Winterfield	495
Clare (city)	3,165
Harrison (city)	2,111

Ethnicity in Clare County:
• White (96.7%)
• American Indian (1.4%)
• Hispanic (1.1%)
• Two or more (1.0%)

Industries providing employment:
• Educational, health and social services (20.0%)
• Manufacturing (17.5%)
• Retail trade (14.4%)
• Arts, entertainment, recreation, accommodation and food services (11.6%)

Known for: Welcome center on US 27, where the North begins, fishing, hunting and outdoor sports.

CLARE 48617

Named after: the County

First settler: The first settler's arrived with the lumber boom and railroad. In 1871 the Pere Marquette Railroad built a station at Clare.

Incorporated as a Village: 1879

Incorporated as a City: 1891

Slogan: "Up North Begins Here"

Land area: 3.1 square miles

Population: (U.S. Census Bureau)
• 3,173   2000
• 3,209   2002 *(estimate)*

Males: 1,391 (43.8%)
Females: 1,782 (56.2%)

Median resident age: 37.2 years

Ethnicity in Clare:
• White (96.3%)
• Hispanic (1.6%)
• American Indian (1.3%)
• Two or more (0.9%)

Ancestries:
• German (28.1%)
• English (18.2%)
• Irish (14.6%)
• French (7.7%)
• Dutch (5.2%)
• United States (5.0%)

Median household income: $27,299 (year 2000)

Median house value: $78,500 (year 2000)

Industries providing employment:
• Educational, health and social services (27.6%)
• Retail trade (17.3%)
• Arts, entertainment, recreation, accommodation and food services (13.9%)
• Manufacturing (13.7%)

Known for: Largest city in the county, Doherty Hotel, Irish Festival in March, Amish, fishing and hunting, Welcome Center.

HARRISON 48625

Named after: William Henry Harrison, the ninth President, and the first to die in office. Harrison served one month of his term in 1841 before succumbing to pneumonia.

Incorporated as a village: 1875

Incorporated as a city: 1891

Slogan: "20 Lakes in 20 Minutes"

Land area: 3.7 square miles

Population: (U.S. Census Bureau)
• 2,108   2000
• 2,111   2002 *(estimate)*

Males: 1,019 (48.3%)
Females: 1,089 (51.7%)

Median resident age:
39.1 years

Ethnicity in Harrison:
• White (93.9%)
• Black (2.0%)
• American Indian (1.8%)
• Hispanic (1.5%)
• Two or more (1.4%)
• Asian (0.6%)

Ancestries:
• German (19.5%)
• English (12.4%)
• Irish (11.2%)
• United States (9.3%)
• Polish (5.3%)
• French (4.9%)

Median household income:
$26,392 (year 2000)
Median house value:
$82,100 (year 2000)

Industries providing employment:
• Educational, health and social services (22.2%)
• Retail trade (15.3%)
• Arts, entertainment, recreation, accommodation and food services (12.3%)
• Manufacturing (11.4%)

Known for: Harrison is the county seat for Clare County

FARWELL 48622

Named after: Samuel Farwell, father-in-law of the superintendent of the railroad being built from Ludington to Saginaw.

Early settlers: Edmund Hall, John Van Riper and George L. Hitchcock credited as founders in 1870. Platted by Josiah Littlefield in 1872.

Incorporated as a village: 1879

Land area: 1.4 square miles

Population: (U.S. Census Bureau)
• 855   2000
• 864   2002 *(estimate)*

Males: 388 (45.4%)
Females: 467 (54.6%)

Median resident age:
39.5 years

Ethnicity in Farwell:
• White (96.8%)
• American Indian (1.8%)
• Two or more (0.7%)
• Black (0.6%)

Ancestries:
• German (17.7%)
• Irish (14.9%)
• United States (14.6%)
• English (9.7%)
• French (5.8%)
• Scottish (4.1%)

Median household income:
$24,583 (year 2000)
Median house value:
$63,300 (year 2000)

Industries providing employment:
- Educational, health and social services (25.7%)
- Manufacturing (24.6%)
- Arts, entertainment, recreation, accommodation and food services (15.1%)

Known for: Served as the first county seat from 1871 to 1879.

CRAWFORD COUNTY
COUNTY SEAT:
GRAYLING

200 W Michigan Avenue
Grayling, MI 49738
www.crawfordco.org

Formed: In 1840 from part of Mackinac County and unorganized territory; was named Shawano County until 1843.

Named after: William Harris Crawford, Secretary of War and Treasurer for Presdient James Monroe. Ran for President in 1824.

First settler: Michael Sloat Hartwick in the 1860's.

Land area: 572.7 sq. mi.

Water area: 26.5 sq. mi.

Elevation: 1,137 ft. (Grayling)

Population:
14,808 (July 2003)
State rank: 70

17,243 (2000)
12,260 (1990)

Population growth since 1990: 20.8%
State rank: 22

Townships   2002 Population

Beaver Creek	1,520
Frederic	1,438
Grayling	6,822
Lovells	589
Maple Forest	513
South Branch	1,882
Grayling (city)	1,970

Ethnicity in Crawford County:
- White (96.8%)
- Black (1.4%)
- Hispanic (0.7%)
- Two or more (0.7%)

Industries providing employment:
- Manufacturing (22.8%)
- Educational, health and social services (19.2%)
- Retail trade (12.5%)

GRAYLING 49738
AND 49739

Named after: The grayling, a trout that once thrived in the Au Sable River that runs through town. The native fish disappeared from the local waters around 1915 due to the destruction of its habitat by the lumber industry.

Once known as: AuSable and Forest. When the railroad

arrived it was called Jackson, Crawford Station, or just Crawford. In the lumber days it was known as Milltown.

Platted: 1874, by Jackson, Lansing & Saginaw Railroad

Incorporated as Village: 1903

Incorporated as City: 1935

Slogan:" The Heart of the North"

Land area: 2.0 square miles

Population: (U.S. Census Bureau)
- 1,952   2000
- 1,970   2002 *(estimate)*

Males: 858 (44.0%)
Females: 1,094 (56.0%)

Median resident age: 39.5 years

Ethnicity in Grayling:
- White (95.7%)
- Hispanic (1.5%)
- American Indian (1.3%)
- Two or more (0.8%)
- Asian Indian (0.7%)
- Black (0.5%)

Ancestries:
- German (21.2%)
- English (12.8%)
- Irish (11.8%)
- United States (7.1%)
- French (6.9%)
- Polish (5.5%)

Median household income: $24,250 (year 2000)

Median house value: $62,400 (year 2000)

Industries providing employment:
- Educational, health and social services (22.7%)
- Retail trade (17.2%)
- Arts, entertainment, recreation, accommodation and food services (16.8%)

Known for:
Camp Grayling, the largest military installation east of the Mississippi River, and home of the National Guard. Grayling has a rich lumber history, producing more white pine than any other area of the country during the boom days of the late 19th century.

Fly fishing and canoeing on the AuSable River running east and the Manistee River running west.

The Fly Factory, the first fly shop and guide service on the AuSable River.

AuSable River Canoe Marathon, the richest canoe marathon in North America running from Grayling to Oscoda (end of July).

Home of the state's first winter sports area. In 1921 the town offered skiing, ski-jumping, skating and "The World's Fastest Toboggans." They ran on ice-covered steel tracks and hit speeds of 60 – 100 miles-per-hour. Grayling also hosted a Winter Carnival event featuring elaborate thrones carved out of ice.

FREDERIC 49733

Named after: Frederic Barker, an early settler

Once known as: Forest, Frederickville

First settler: Probably Federic Barker in the early 1870's

Slogan: Snowmobile Capital of Northern Michigan

Population:
1,287   (1990)
(Frederic Township)

Frederic caters to snowmobilers and cross-country skiers in the winter. It's located at a major junction and offers food, fuel and repairs to snowmobilers.

Forbush Corner offers miles of cross-country ski trails and boasts of having the largest fleet of Nordic-only grooming equipment in the Midwest.

EMMET COUNTY
COUNTY SEAT:
PETOSKEY

200 Division Street
Petoskey MI 49770
(231) 348-1702
http://www.co.emmet.mi.us/

Formed: In 1840 from part of Mackinac County; was named Tonegadana County until 1843.

Named after: Irish patriot, Robert Emmet, who at 24 years of age was hung for leading a rebellion against the British.

First settler: French soldiers built fort at Mackinaw City in 1715. At that time Ottawa and Ojibwe had seasonal camps. Indians had well-established settlements between Harbor Springs and Cross Village in 1840, when county boundaries were marked off.

Land area: 467.8 sq. mi.

Water area: 414.4 sq. mi.
Elevation: 786 ft. (Petoskey)

Population:
32,741 (July 2003)
State rank: 46
31,437 (2000)
25,040 (1990)

Population growth since 1990: 30.8%
State rank: 10

Townships	2002 Population
Bear Creek	5,652
Bliss	629
Carp Lake	837
Center	538
Cross Village	301
Friendship	885
Littlefield	2,843
Little Traverse	2,444

McKinley	1,340
Maple River	1,297
Pleasantview	834
Readmond	518
Resort	2,510
Springvale	1,798
Wawatam	712
West Traverse	1,454
Harbor Springs (city)	1,568
Petoskey (city)	6,169

Ethnicity in Emmet County:
- White (93.8%)
- American Indian (4.1%)
- Two or more (1.5%)
- Hispanic (0.9%)

Industries providing employment:
- Educational, health and social services (22.7%)
- Retail trade (15.3%)
- Arts, entertainment, recreation, accommodation and food services (12.8%)
- Construction (10.6%)

PETOSKEY   49770

Named after: Chippewa Chief Petosega (the rising sun), who owned most of the land that makes up the town.

Once known as: Bear River until 1873, and as Porter's Village-named after Rev. Andrew Porter, founder of an Indian Presbyterian mission in 1852.

Incorporated as Village: 1879

Incorporated as City: 1896

Slogan: "Land of the Million Dollar Sunsets"

Land area: 5.0 square miles

Population: (U.S. Census Bureau)
- 6,080   2000
- 6,169   2002 *(estimate)*

Males: 2,805 (46.1%)
Females: 3,275 (53.9%)

Median resident age: 38.7 years

Ethnicity in Petoskey:
- White (93.6%)
- American Indian (3.9%)
- Two or more (1.3%)
- Hispanic (1.2%)

Ancestries:
- German (23.7%)
- English (14.8%)
- Irish (14.8%)
- Polish (9.5%)
- United States (5.2%)
- French (5.0%)

Median household income: $33,657 (year 2000)
Median house value: $120,700 (year 2000)

Industries providing employment:
- Educational, health and social services (26.9%)
- Retail trade (18.5%)
- Arts, entertainment, recreation, accommodation and food services (14.4%)

Known for: Gaslight Shopping District, Winter Sports Park, Bay Harbor and Bay View communities, Perry Davis Hotel, Festival on the Bay, Nat'l Trust for Historic Preservation named Petoskey to its 11 most Endangered Places list in 1996, Same organization named Stafford's Perry Davis to its list of America's Historic Hotels.

HARBOR SPRINGS   49740

Named after: Its natural harbor, the deepest in Michigan, and the many springs in the area

Once known as: Bayfield, and as L'Arbre Croche, or Crooked Tree by French Jesuits starting in 1742 (after the large crooked tree that marked the Ottawa Indians village)Named Little Traverse in 1862 after the French name for the crossing of the bay.

Incorporated as Village: 1881

Incorporated as City: 1932

Settled: Originally by Ottawa Indians

Land area: 1.3 square miles

Population: (U.S. Census Bureau)
• 1,567   2000
• 1,568   2002 (*estimate*)

Males: 704 (44.9%)
Females: 863 (55.1%)

Median resident age: 46.6 years

Ethnicity in Harbor Springs:
• White (91.4%)
• American Indian (7.6%)
• Two or more 2.0%)
• Hispanic (0.6%)

Ancestries:
• German (18.0%)
• English (16.8%)
• Irish (14.6%)
• French (7.6%)
• Polish (7.0%)
• United States (6.4%)

Median household income: $35,341 (year 2000)
Median house value: $151,600 (year 2000)

Industries providing employment:
• Educational, health and social services (19.4%)
• Arts, entertainment, recreation, accommodation and food services (16.2%)
• Retail trade (11.6%)
• Construction (10.8%)
• Professional, scientific, management, administrative, and waste management services (10.6%)

Known for: The deepest natural harbor on the Great Lakes

M-119 Scenic drive, "Tunnel of Trees"

Old money resort town
First golf course in
northern Michigan
Bowling on Main Street
on April Fool's Day.

Boyne Highlands and
Nub's Nob Ski resorts

MACKINAW CITY   49701

Named after:
Michilimackinac, the fort
built there by the French in
1712. Originally the name
Mackinac was used to
describe the entire Straits
region. Mackinaw is the
French spelling.

Once known as: Mackinac
until 1934 when it was
lengthened to Mackinaw City

Incorporated as a village:
1882

Slogan: "Michigan's Favorite
Vacation Getaway"

Land area: 3.4 square miles

Population: (U.S. Census
Bureau)
- 859   2000
- 853   2002 *(estimate)*

Males: 402 (46.8%)
Females: 457 (53.2%)

Median resident age:
44.7 years

Ethnicity in Mackinaw City:
- White (92.3%)
- American Indian (6.4%)
- Two or more (2.2%)
- Hispanic (0.8%)

Ancestries:
- German (23.3%)
- Irish (16.5%)
- English (10.1%)
- French (9.1%)
- Polish (7.7%)
- United States (5.2%)

Median household income:
$37,031 (year 2000)
Median house value:
$119,100 (year 2000)

**Industries providing
employment:**
- Educational, health and
  social services (20.3%)
- Arts, entertainment, recreation, accommodation and
  food services (18.4%)
- Retail trade (14.9%)
- Public administration
  (11.1%)

Known for:
Located in Emmet and
Cheboygan counties

Colonial Michilimackinac

South end of the Mackinac
Bridge, and the Labor Day
Bridge Walk

Historic Mill Creek

Mackinac Bridge Museum

Mackinaw Mush Sled Dog
Race in February

ALANSON   49706

Named after: Alanson Howard, son of the President of the Grand Rapids & Indiana Railroad.

Once known as: Hinman

First settled: 1875

Incorporated as a village: 1905

Land area: 1.0 square miles

Population: (U.S. Census Bureau)
- 785   2000
- 800   2002 *(estimate)*

Males: 384 (48.9%)
Females: 401 (51.1%)

Median resident age: 32.8 years

Ethnicity in Alanson:
- White (88.8%)
- American Indian (8.2%)
- Two or more (3.3%)
- Hispanic (1.0%)
- Black (0.9%)
- Other (0.5%)

Ancestries:
- German (22.4%)
- Irish (13.5%)
- English (12.2%)
- United States (9.6%)
- Polish (7.5%)
- French (5.9%)

Median household income: $33,125 (year 2000)

Median house value: $82,400 (year 2000)

Industries providing employment:
- Educational, health and social services (19.2%)
- Arts, entertainment, recreation, accommodation and food services (16.2%)
- Retail trade (14.9%)
- Manufacturing (13.8%)
- Construction (11.0%)

Known for: World's shortest swing bridge. When it was built, over the Crooked River, in the 1950's it was a hand-cranked bridge.

Location on the Crooked River.

PELLSTON   49769

Named after: William Pells, who bought land and re-sold it to settlers starting in 1876.

Incorporated as a village: 1907

Slogan: "The Icebox of the Nation"

Land area: 1.9 square miles

Population: (U.S. Census Bureau)
- 771   2000
- 785   2002 *(estimate)*

Males: 383 (49.7%)
Females: 388 (50.3%)

Median resident age:
31.2 years

Ethnicity in Pellston:
• White (89.5%)
• American Indian (8.6%)
• Two or more (2.7%)
• Hispanic (0.8%)
• Black (0.6%)

Ancestries:
• German (17.1%)
• Irish (12.7%)
• English (9.6%)
• French (7.4%)
• United States (6.7%)
• French Canadian (4.8%)

Median household income:
$37,292 (year 2000)
Median house value:
$71,600 (year 2000)

Industries providing employment:
• Manufacturing (19.1%)
• Arts, entertainment, recreation, accommodation and food services (15.6%)
• Retail trade (14.4%)
• Construction (13.8%)
• Educational, health and social services (11.3%)

Known for: Pellston Regional Airport

Mentioned frequently as having the coldest temperatures in the nation

U of M Biological Station on Douglas Lake

CROSS VILLAGE   49723

Named after: The large crosserected by early Jesuit missionaries in the 1700's.

Once known as:
Anamiewatigoing, a Native American word meaning At The Tree of Prayer, or Cross. Known as Old *L'Arbre Croche* by the French to differentiate from New L'Arbre Croche (Harbor Springs). Called *LaCroix* (The Cross) until 1875 when it was changed to Cross Village.

Slogan or Nickname:
"Land of the Cross, Land of the Crooked Tree."

GRAND TRAVERSE COUNTY
COUNTY SEAT: TRAVERSE CITY

400 Boardman Ave
Traverse City, MI 49684
(231)-922-4700
www.grandtraverse.org

Formed: In 1851 from part of Omeena County

Named after: La Grand Traverse, what the French voyageurs called the shortcut across the bay from Charlevoix County to the tip of the Leelanau Peninsula.

First settler: Presbyterian missionary, Peter Dougherty, arrived at Old Mission in

1839 to teach the Protestant religion to Native Americans in the region.

Population:
82,011 (July 2003)
State rank: 24
77,654 (2000)
64,273 (1990)

Population growth since 1990: 27.6%
State rank: 13

Townships 2002 Population

Township	Population
Acme	4,366
Blair	6,695
East Bay	10,001
Fife Lake	2,390
Garfield	15,358
Grant	1,039
Green Lake	5,196
Long Lake	7,718
Mayfield	1,390
Paradise	4,420
Peninsula	5,305
Union	495
Whitewater	2,571
Traverse City	14,319

Land area: 465.1 sq. mi.

Water area: 136.1 sq. mi.

Elevation: 599 ft.
(Traverse City)

Ethnicity in Grand Traverse County:
• White (95.6%)
• American Indian (1.5%)
• Hispanic (1.5%)
• Two or more (1.1%)
• Other (0.5%)

Industries providing employment:
• Educational, health and social services (22.0%)
• Retail trade (14.9%)
• Manufacturing (12.1%)
• Arts, entertainment, recreation, accommodation and food services (10.7%)

TRAVERSE CITY 49684, 49686 AND 49696

Named after: Grand Traverse Bay, which comes from La Grande Traverse, the name given to the bay by French voyageurs in 1847.

Once known as: Wequetong, or "head of the bay," until renamed Traverse City in 1854 by Albert Lay, one of the town's founding fathers.

Slogan: "Cherry Capitol of the World"

Land area: 8.4 square miles

Population: (U.S. Census Bureau)
• 14,532   2000
• 14,468   2002 *(estimate)*

Males: 6,902 (47.5%)
Females: 7,630 (52.5%)

Median resident age:
38.1 years

Ethnicity in Traverse City:
• White (95.0%)
• Hispanic (1.7%)
• American Indian (1.7%)

- Two or more (1.4%)
- Black (0.7%)

Ancestries:
- German (25.8%)
- Irish (16.5%)
- English (16.0%)
- Polish (8.9%)
- French (5.5%)
- Dutch (4.7%)

Median household income:
$37,330 (year 2000)
Median house value:
$124,600 (year 2000)

Industries providing employment:
- Educational, health and social services (23.8%)
- Retail trade (15.7%)
- Arts, entertainment, recreation, accommodation and food services (13.0%)

FIFE LAKE   49633

Named after the lake, which is named after William H. Fife, a state highway commissioner from Acme. Originally two towns, Fife Lake and North Fife Lake; they were combined and incorporated as one village in 1889.

Land area: 0.7 square miles

Population: (U.S. Census Bureau)
- 466   2000
- 467   2002 (estimate)

Males: 231 (49.6%)
Females: 235 (50.4%)

Median resident age:
34.6 years

Ethnicity in Fife Lake:
- White (90.6%)
- American Indian (7.9%)
- Two or more (5.4%)
- Black (0.6%)

Ancestries:
- German (24.9%)
- United States (18.7%)
- English (13.9%)
- Irish (12.2%)
- Scottish (7.7%)
- French (5.6%)

Median household income:
$32,361 (year 2000)
Median house value:
$74,500 (year 2000)

Industries providing employment:
- Retail trade (16.5%)
- Manufacturing (16.1%)
- Educational, health and social services (13.3%)
- Construction (11.6%)

KINGSLEY   49649

Named after one of the town's first settlers, Judson W. Kingsley, who arrived in the early 1870's. The town was named Paradise, after the township it's located in, from 1876 to 1883, at which point it was renamed Kingsley.

Land area: 1.1 square miles

Population: (U.S. Census Bureau)
• 1,469   2000
• 1,510   2002 (estimate)

Males: 688 (46.8%)
Females: 781 (53.2%)

Median resident age:
28.3 years

Ethnicity in Kingsley:
• White (96.2%)
• Hispanic (1.8%)
• American Indian (1.5%)
• Two or more (0.9%)
• Other (0.7%)

Ancestries:
• German (28.6%)
• English (11.3%)
• Irish (10.3%)
• Dutch (5.9%)
• Polish (5.7%)
• United States (4.5%)

Median household income:
$32,614 (year 2000)
Median house value:
$100,300 (year 2000)

Industries providing employment:
• Manufacturing (20.3%)
• Educational, health and social services (17.3%)
• Retail trade (17.0%)
• Arts, entertainment, recreation, accommodation and food services (10.1%)

INTERLOCHEN   49643

Named after: Its location between (interlocking) Duck and Green lakes. Another version handed down by locals is that it was named after the railroad interlocking switch that controlled the tracks where the Manistee & Northeastern and Pere Marquette crossed. Historians won't verify either version.

Once known as: Wylie. The town of Wylie formed in the late 1880's by a cooperage company. It went out of business around 1915, after the supply of trees ran out. Part of Wylie overlapped with what is now Interlochen. Platted in 1890 by Edwin Benedict, Alexander Lamberg and their wives. It was a busy lumber and railroad town until about 1915 when there were no more big trees left.

Today Interlochen is best known as the home for the internationally acclaimed Interlochen Center for the Arts, a year round high school dedicated to arts, and a summer arts camp attracting the most talented young people from around the world. The Interlochen State Park is across the street and features a stand of virgin pines.

WILLIAMSBURG   49690

Named after: Unknown

Once known as: Mill Creek after the stream, then Dunbar after the first postmaster; renamed Williamsburgh in 1869, shortened to Williamsburg in 1894.

ACME   49610

Named after: Unknown

First settler: L.S. Hoxsie arrived in the 1850's from Lenawee County. He platted the community and sold homesites. In 1864, he built a sawmill on Acme creek, and eventually the town supported two woolen mills and a shingle mill. By the 1890's most of the trees had been cut down, which led to the closing of the mills and the community's first office.

Today Acme is home to northern Michigan's largest resort, the impressive VASA trail system, and probably the region's next shopping center.

As of early 2005 Meijer has announced intentions to build a super store on M-72, next to a proposed retail-residential village development.

Population:
4,332 (Acme township)

OLD MISSION   49673

Once known as: Grand Traverse from 1839-52 when Rev. Peter Dougherty and native Indians were settled here. In 1852 they moved across the bay and called their new settlement the New Mission. At that time Grand Traverse became Old Mission.

KALKASKA COUNTY
COUNTY SEAT:
KALKASKA

605 North Birch Street
Kalkaska, MI 49646
Phone: 231-258-3300

Formed: In1840 from part of Mackinac County. Was named Wabassee County, after Indian chief, until 1843. Was attached to Grand Traverse County and Antrim County before being organized as Kalkaska County in 1871.

Named after: Kalkaska is a Chippewa word of unknown meaning. Some believe it means "flat land," while others claim it means "burned over land."

First settler: William Copeland settled near Barker Creek in 1855.

Slogan or Nickname: "Space to Grow" (vandals once spray-painted the word "marijuana" under the slogan posted at the western entrance to town).

Land area: 465.1 sq. mi.

Water area: 136.1 sq. mi.

Elevation: 1,013 (Kalkaska)

Population:
17,177 (July 2003)
State rank: 67
16,571 (2000)
13,497 (1990

**Population growth
since 1990:** 27.3%
State rank: 14

Townships   2002 Population

Townships	2002 Population
Bear Lake	770
Blue Lake	435
Boardman	1,420
Clearwater	2,429
Coldsprings	1,486
Excelsior	889
Garfield	836
Kalkaska	4,920
Oliver	280
Orange	1,220
Rapid River	1,045
Springfield	1,313

**Ethnicity in Grand Kalkaska
County:**
• White (95.6%)
• American Indian (1.5%)
• Hispanic (1.5%)
• Two or more (1.1%)
• Other (0.5%)

**Industries providing
employment:**
• Educational, health and
  social services (22.0%)
• Retail trade (14.9%)
• Manufacturing (12.1%)
• Arts,entertainment, recreation,accommodation and
food services (10.7%)

KALKASKA   49646

Named after: Chippewa word
of unknown meaning; first
spelled Kalcaska.

Slogan or Nickname:
"Trout Capital," or "Home
of the National Trout Festival"

Platted: by Albert A. Abbott
in early 1870's

Incorporated as Village:
1887

Land area: 2.5 square miles

Population: (U.S. Census
Bureau)
• 2,226   2000
• 2,249   2002 *(estimate)*

Males: 1,044 (46.9%)
Females: 1,182 (53.1%)

Median resident age:
35.3 years

Ethnicity in Kalkaska:
• White (95.7%)
• American Indian (1.6%)
• Two or more (1.2%)
• Hispanic (0.9%)
• Black (0.7%)

Ancestries:
• German (24.2%)
• Irish (15.5%)
• English (11.6%)
• French (6.9%)
• Polish (5.0%)

- Dutch (4.5%)

Median household income:
$27,891 (year 2000)
Median house value:
$72,700 (year 2000)

Industries providing employment:
- Manufacturing (24.5%)
- Arts, entertainment, recreation, accommodation and food services (13.7%)
- Retail trade (10.8%)
- Educational, health and social services (10.8%)

Mr. A.A. Abbot of Decatur, Michigan purchased 1,000 wooded acres and built a sawmill on the Boardman River in 1872. In 1873, Lizzie Farnham became the first teacher in the town's first school, which opened inside a private home. The first church, built by Congregationalists, opened that year, and the first newspaper was published in 1874.

RAPID CITY   49676

Named after: Its setting on the Rapid River

Once known as: Van Buren after early land owners

Platted: In 1892 by Charles and Carrie Van Buren

Chicago & Western Railroad (Pere Marquette) arrived in 1891

SOUTH BOARDMAN
49680

Named after: Its setting on the south branch of the Boardman River

Once known as: Boardman

Early settler: Hamilton Stone built railroad depot and hotel in mid 1870's.

LAKE COUNTY
COUNTY SEAT: BALDWIN

800 Tenth Street
Baldwin, MI 49304
Phone: 231-745-4641

Formed: In 1840 as part of Mackinac County; was named Aischum County until 1843

Land area: 567.4 sq. mi.

Water area: 7.2 sq. mi.

Elevation: 838 ft. (Baldwin)

Population:
11,795 (July 2003)
State rank: 73
11,333 (2000)
8,583 (1990)

Population increase since 1990: 37.4%
State rank: 3

Townships	2002 Population
Chase	1,211
Cherry Valley	378

Dover	339
Eden	386
Elk	899
Ellsworth	835
Lake	851
Newkirk	735
Peacock	450
Pinora	665
Pleasant Plains	1,538
Sauble	327
Sweetwater	245
Webber	2,046
Yates	718

Ethnicity in Lake County:
- White (83.9%)
- Black (11.2%)
- Two or more (2.4%)
- American Indian (2.3%)
- Hispanic (1.7%)
- Other (0.6%)

Industries providing employment:
- Manufacturing (23.3%)
- Educational, health and social services (15.3%)
- Retail trade (13.0%)

BALDWIN   49304

Named after: Henry Baldwin, governor of Michigan in 1872

Once known as: Hannibal, after an early settler; changed to Baldwin City in 1872, and finally to Baldwin in 1875.

Early settlers: Mr. Hannibal whom the town was named after in the early 1870's, and Isaac Grant who owned the first store in the area.

Incorporated as Village: 1887

Land area: 1.3 square miles

Population: (U.S. Census Bureau)
- 1,107   2000
- 1,111   2002 *(estimate)*

Males: 588 (53.1%)
Females: 519 (46.9%)

Median resident age: 35.1 years

Ethnicity in Baldwin:
- White (58.4%)
- Black (34.3%)
- Two or more (4.2%)
- American Indian (3.7%)
- Hispanic (2.7%)

Ancestries:
- German (12.7%)
- Dutch (7.0%)
- Irish (6.1%)
- English (4.6%)
- United States (3.9%)
- French (2.3%)

Median household income: $15,550 (year 2000)
Median house value: $39,700 (year 2000)

Industries providing employment:
- Educational, health and social services (26.3%)
- Retail trade (18.3%),
- Manufacturing (13.8%)
- Public administration (12.8%)

LUTHER   49656

Named after: B.T. Luther, a partner in an early sawmill

Once known as: Wilson

Land area: 0.9 square miles

Population: (U.S. Census Bureau)
• 339   2000

Males: 171 (50.4%)
Females: 168 (49.6%)

Median resident age: 39.9 years

Ethnicity in Luther:
• White (90.3%)
• American Indian (5.6%)
• Hispanic (3.2%)
• Two or more (2.9%)
• Black (0.6%)

Ancestries:
• Irish (15.6%)
• German (14.7%)
• United States (8.8%)
• French (7.4%)
• Polish (6.5%)
• Dutch (5.6%)

Median household income: $24,583 (year 2000)
Median house value: $35,000 (year 2000)

Industries providing employment:
• Manufacturing (30.6%)
• Construction (12.9%)
• Retail trade (11.3%)

IDLEWILD   49642

Named after: One of the area lakes

Slogan or Nickname: "A Historic Community" or "The Black Eden of Michigan"

Early settlers: In 1912 there were two year round settlers. In 1915 three real estate investors bought and platted much of the town. They wanted to build a resort community for middle and upper class African-Americans. Lots were sold, primarily to African-Americans, for $35 each. The lakeside town became a well known summer resort for black families around the Midwest.

Listed on the National Register of Historic Places

LEELANAU COUNTY
COUNTY SEAT: LELAND

301 E. Cedar St.
Leland, MI   49654
www.leelanaucounty.com

Formed: In 1840 from part of Mackinac County

Named after: One of the many counties named by Indian agent, Henry Schoolcraft. Said to be an Indian word meaning "Delight of Life." He spelled it originally as "Leelinau." It was changed to Leelanau, but somebody in Lansing misread the "u" as a "w," and so it was "Leelanaw" until 1896. Some believe the name is not from an Indian language, but more likely from French using the word lee, meaning the side that is sheltered from the wind, although much of Leelanau County is anything but sheltered from the wind.

First settler: Probably William Burton who set up a wooding station on S. Manitou Island in the mid 1830's. First settler on mainland Leelanau County was John LaRue in 1848. He settled near Glen Arbor at the mouth of the Crystal River after spending less than a year on S. Manitou.

Land area: 348.5 sq. mi.

Water area: 2183.9 sq. mi.

Elevation: 619 ft. (Empire)

Population:
21,860 (July 2003)
State rank: 63
21,119 (2000)
16,527 (1990)

Population growth since 1990: 32.3%
State rank: 8

Median age: 42.6

Townships	2002 Population
Bingham	2,481
Centerville	1,144
Cleveland	1,083
Elmwood	4,325
Empire	1,126
Glen Arbor	802
Kasson	1,667
Leelanau	2,197
Leland	2,091
Solon	1,605
Suttons Bay	3,052
Traverse City (city)	149

Ethnicity in Leelanau County:
• White (92.0%)
• American Indian (4.2%)
• Hispanic (3.3%)
• Other (1.3%)
• Two or more (1.0%)

Industries providing employment:
• Educational, health and social services (22.3%)
• Arts, entertainment, recreation, accommodation and food services (11.7%)
• Construction (11.5%)
• Retail trade (11.3%)

LELAND   49654

Named after: "Lee" meaning the quarter toward which the wind blows

Slogan or Nickname: "Fishtown"

First settler: Antoine Manseau in 1853

Population:
2,033   (2000)

Males: 1,005
Females: 1,028

Average age: 42.6

Ethnicity in Leland:
• White (93.9%)
• Hispanic (6.1%)
• Black or African
  American (0.7%)
• American Indian (0.6%)
• Asian (0.2%)

NORTHPORT   49670

Named after: Its location at
the northern point of the
Leelanau peninsula

Once known as:
Waukazooville, after Chief
Waukazoo and the Waukazoo
Indians.

Slogan or Nickname: "The
Whole Point of the Leelanau
Peninsula"

First settlers: In 1849,
Reverend George N. Smith,
schooner captain, James J.
McLaughlin and his brother-
in-law, William Case, built a
log home just south of the
village limits. Arriving on the
heels of the trio were 40-50
Indian families who named
the village after their Chief
Waukazoo.

Northport served as the first
County Seat from 1863-1882

Platted: In 1852 by Joseph
Dame

Land area: 1.7 square miles

Population: (U.S. Census
Bureau)
• 648   2000
• 652   2002 (estimate)

Males: 301 (46.5%)
Females: 347 (53.5%)

Median resident age:
50.2 years (highest in
northern Michigan)

Ethnicity in Northport:
• White Non-Hispanic
  (93.2%)
• Hispanic (3.5%)
• American Indian (2.3%)
• Two or more (0.8%)

Ancestries:
• German (23.0%)
• English (18.4%)
• Irish (15.1%)
• Norwegian (9.6%)
• French (5.7%)
• Polish (5.2%)

Median household income:
$40,368 (year 2000)
Median house value:
$136,200 (year 2000)

Industries providing
employment:
• Educational, health and
  social services (20.8%)
• Arts, entertainment, recreation, accommodation and
  food services (12.3%)
• Construction (11.9%)

- Manufacturing (11.5%)
- Retail trade (10.8%)

SUTTONS BAY   49682

Named after: Harry Sutton, who owned the land upon which the village was established

Once known as: Suttonsburg upon its founding in 1854. Renamed Pleasant City in 1860 by Rev. A. Herbstrit, who wanted to build a National University on the bay. He was not able to raise the money, and the town was renamed Suttons Bay.

First settler: Harry Sutton who, in the mid 1850' established a wooding station for passing steamers.

Land area: 1.1 square miles

Population: (U.S. Census Bureau)
- 589   2000
- 591   2002 *(estimate)*

Males: 283 (48.0%)
Females: 306 (52.0%)

Median resident age: 47.2 years

Ethnicity in Suttons Bay:
- White (95.6%)
- Hispanic (2.7%)
- American Indian (1.4%)
- Other (1.0%)

Ancestries:
- German (24.4%)
- English (14.8%)
- Irish (10.7%)
- Norwegian (9.2%)
- Polish (7.3%)
- Czech (5.9%)

Median household income: $44,063 (year 2000)
Median house value: $144,200 (year 2000)

Industries providing employment:
- Educational, health and social services (17.4%)
- Retail trade (14.9%)
- Professional, scientific, management, administrative, and waste management services (13.9%)

EMPIRE   49630

Named after: The *Empire*, a schooner that became ice-bound in the town harbor in the winter of 1863. Local residents used the boat as a school.

Incorporated as Village: 1895

Land area: 1.2 square miles

Population: (U.S. Census Bureau)
- 378   2000
- 380   2002 *(estimate)*

Males: 184 (48.7%)
Females: 194 (51.3%)

Median resident age:
49.1 years
Ethnicity in Empire:
- White (98.9%)
- American Indian (0.8%)
- Two or more (0.5%)

Ancestries:
- German (25.7%)
- English (22.2%)
- Irish (21.7%)
- French (7.1%)
- Polish (6.6%)
- Czech (5.0%)

Median household income:
$39,722 (year 2000)
Median house value:
$129,700 (year 2000)

Industries providing employment:
- Arts, entertainment, recreation, accommodation and food services (18.6%)
- Educational, health and social services (16.5%)
- Construction (14.4%)
- Retail trade (12.4%)

In the late 1800's, Empire was a lumber boomtown supporting a large sawmill, two large docks, a railroad, two churches, a newspaper and a population numbering over 1,000 persons. The big Empire Lumber Co. mill burned down in 1903, but was re-built only to burn down again in 1916, at which time most available timber had already been harvested.

GREILICKVILLE   49684

Named after: Godfrey Greilick and his three sons who built a sawmill on West Bay in the 1880's.

Once known as: Norrisville, after the brothers Norris, Seth and Albert, who were the first settlers in 1875, and operated a grist mill and brick yard. Many buildings in downtown Traverse City and on the grounds of the old State Hospital were built with bricks from the Greilickville plant.

Land area: 4.5 square miles

Population: (U.S. Census Bureau)
- 1,415   2000

Males: 671 (47.4%)
Females: 744 (52.6%)

Median resident age:
48.1 years

Ethnicity in Greilickville:
- White (97.6%)
- American Indian (1.0%)
- Two or more (0.8%)
- Black (0.6%)
- Hispanic (0.6%)

Ancestries:
- German (37.1%)
- Irish (21.1%)
- English (19.0%)
- Polish (9.6%)
- French (8.2%)
- Norwegian (4.2%)

Median household income:
$48,269 (year 2000)

Median house value:
$136,100 (year 2000)

Industries providing employment:
• Educational, health and social services (30.7%)
• Arts, entertainment, recreation, accommodation and food services (13.0%)
• Retail trade (12.1%)
• Manufacturing (10.1%)

LAKE LEELANAU   49653

Named after: The lake that narrows through the town

Once known as: Le Naro after the narrow segment that splits the large lake in half. Also known as Provemont, derived, perhaps, from the word improvement.

Early settler: A. DeBelloy arrived in 1867 looking for oil, but instead found a deep artesian well. The mineral water was promoted as having healing qualities, which was a big draw, attracting many visitors who came to full their jugs with the magical water.

OMENA   49674

Named after: The Indian word, O-me-nah, meaning "Is it so?" According to local lore Rev. Peter Dougherty,

when addressed by local Indians, would respond with O-me-nah? Is it so? However, there is scant evidence to prove this. Other possible origins of the word Omena according to Amanda Holmes in her book, *Omena: A Place in Time* (copyright 2003, Omena Historical Society): it may mean "beautiful gift," or "one who helps others."

Once known as: New Mission, named by Rev. Peter Dougherty, who in 1850 moved his original mission across the bay from the peninsula that ran north of Traverse City. The move created Old Mission on the peninsula, and New Mission, which would eventually become Omena.

Dougherty sometimes referred to the settlement as Grove Hill.

Services have been held every Sunday since Dougherty and the Indians built the Presbyterian Church in 1858. A painting of the village by Dougherty's daughter hangs in the church.

PESHAWBESTOWN   49682

Named after: Chief Peshaba, head of the local Ottawa tribe in the late 1800's

Once known as: Eagletown, as early as the mid 1850's

Early settlers: A band of Ottawa Indians from Cross Village and Father Angelus Van Praemel, a Catholic priest, established the village in 1852. The 12.5-acre village is within the Grand Traverse Band of Ottawa and Chippewa reservation.

GLEN ARBOR   49636

Named after: A thick vine of grapes in the treetops inspired Harriet Fisher, wife of one of the town's first settlers, to name the area Glen Arbor.

First settlers: The "Three Johns," John LaRue, John Fisher and John Dorsey; LaRue arrived first in 1848.

MAPLE CITY   49664

Named after: The abundant maple forest which surrounded the town in the 1800's

Once known as: Peg Town, after the factory that produced wooden shoe pegs used by shoemakers before nails were available.

First settler: Kasson Freeman surveyed the village in 1865

CEDAR   49621

Named after: The tree that once dominated its landscape

Once known as: Cedar City

Nickname: "Sausage Capital," after Pleva's Meats, the anchor store of downtown Cedar! Cedar native, Ray Pleva, started working in the family meat market at nine years old. He sold the store to a relative in 2002. (See Inventors in Business chapter).

"The Community That Cares"

At one time referred to as Little Poland, after the large Polish population. Many Cedar-area farms were started by Poles who arrived in the county in the late 1800's.

First settler: Benjamin Boughey in mid 1880's

MANISTEE COUNTY
COUNTY SEAT:
MANISTEE

415 Third Street
Manistee, MI 49660
(231) 723-3331
www.manisteecounty.net

Formed: In 1840 from part of Mackinac County

Named after: Indian word meaning "spirit of the woods," in reference to the sound of the wind blowing through the forest.

First settlers: The Stronach family, John, Joseph and Adam, built a sawmill in

1841 near the present town of Manistee.

Land area: 543.6 sq. mi.

Water area: 737.2 sq. mi.
Population:
25,317 (July 2003)
State rank: 58
24,527 (2000)
21,265 (1990)

Population growth since 1990: 19.1%
State rank: 26

Townships 2002 Population

Township	Population
Arcadia	660
Bear Lake	1,739
Brown	689
Cleon	922
Dickson	1,006
Filer	2,328
Manistee	3,938
Maple Grove	1,313
Marilla	390
Norman	1,718
Onekema	1,595
Pleasanton	875
Springdale	732
Stronach	798
Manistee (city)	6,379

Ethnicity in Manistee County:
- White (92.9%)
- Hispanic (2.6%)
- American Indian (2.2%)
- Black (1.6%)
- Two or more (1.5%)
- Other (1.0%)

Industries providing employment:
- Educational, health and social services (20.2%)
- Manufacturing (18.8%)
- Arts, entertainment, recreation, accommodation and food services (13.1%)
- Retail trade (12.1%)

MANISTEE 49660

Named after: The county and river

Early settlers: John Stronach and sons built first sawmill in 1840. In 1831 a settler intending to begin lumber operations built a cabin, but since it was on an Indian reservation he was thrown off.

Incorporated as City: 1869

Land area: 3.3 square miles

Population: (U.S. Census Bureau)
- 6,586   2000
- 6,379   2002 *(estimate)*

Males: 3,062 (46.5%)
Females: 3,524 (53.5%)

Median resident age: 40.4 years

Ethnicity in Manistee:
- White (93.9%)
- American Indian (2.5%)
- Hispanic (2.2%)
- Two or more (1.9%)
- Other (1.0%)

Ancestries:
- German (26.9%)
- Polish (22.8%)
- Irish (11.3%)
- English (9.4%)

- Swedish (5.9%)
- French (5.8%)

Median household income:
$30,351 (year 2000)
Median house value:
$66,500 (year 2000)

Industries providing employment:
- Educational, health and social services (21.5%)
- Manufacturing (16.4%)
- Arts, entertainment, recreation, accommodation and food services (16.0%)
- Retail trade (13.2%)

BEAR LAKE   49614

Named after: The lake

First settler: Russell Smith in 1863

Platted: In 1874 by George and David Hopkins

Incorporated as Village: 1893

Land area: 0.3 square miles

Population: (U.S. Census Bureau)
- 318   2000
- 322   2002 (estimate)

Males: 160 (50.3%)
Females: 158 (49.7%)

Median resident age: 39.2 years

Ethnicity in Bear Lake:
- White (90.9%)
- Hispanic (4.7%)
- American Indian (3.5%)
- Asian (2.5%)
- Two or more (1.6%)

Ancestries:
- German (24.8%)
- English (22.6%)
- Irish (7.5%)
- French (6.6%)
- Polish (6.0%)
- Norwegian (4.4%)

Median household income:
$31,389 (year 2000)
Median house value:
$71,300 (year 2000)

Industries providing employment:
- Arts, entertainment, recreation, accommodation and food services (25.0%)
- Educational, health and social services (20.6%)
- Manufacturing (16.2%)

ONEKEMA   49675

Named after: Oneka-ma-engk was the original name for Portage Lake, which the town is situated on.

Once known as: Portage, but changed because there was already a post office in Michigan named Portage.

Early settlers: Stronach family built a sawmill on the creek between Portage Lake and Lake Michigan in 1845.

Land area: 0.6 square miles

Population: (U.S. Census Bureau)
• 647   2000
• 653   2002 *(estimate)*

Males: 346 (53.5%)
Females: 301 (46.5%)

Median resident age: 38.9 years

Ethnicity in Onekama:
• White (76.8%)
• Hispanic (21.8%)
• Other (13.1%)
• American Indian (1.1%)
• Two or more (1.1%)

Ancestries:
• German (16.4%)
• Irish (10.7%)
• English (10.2%)
• French (5.9%)
• Swedish (5.7%)
• United States (5.1%)

Median household income: $29,091 (year 2000)
Median house value: $82,700 (year 2000)

Industries providing employment:
• Educational, health and social services (23.2%)
• Agriculture, forestry, fishing and hunting, and mining (12.9%)
• Manufacturing (12.1%)

KALEVA   49645

Named after: Kalevala, an epic work of music and poetry in Finland.

Once known as: Manistee Crossing, and then just Crossing to signify the crossing of the Pere Marquette and Manistee & Northeastern railroads.

Early settlers: Jacob Saari and John Haksluto to found a Finnish settlement.

Land area: 1.1 square miles

Population: (U.S. Census Bureau)
• 509   2000
• 487   2002 *(estimate)*

Males: 244 (47.9%)
Females: 265 (52.1%)

Median resident age: 36.1 years

Ethnicity in Kaleva:
• White (91.7%)
• Hispanic (3.9%)
• American Indian (3.1%)
• Two or more (1.6%)
• Other (1.4%)

Ancestries:
• German (23.0%)
• Irish (12.0%)
• English (8.6%)
• United States (7.1%)
• Polish (6.1%)
• French (5.7%)

Median household income: $30,714 (year 2000)
Median house value: $52,900 (year 2000)

Industries providing employment:
- Manufacturing (17.4%)
- Arts, entertainment, recreation, accommodation and food services (16.4%)
- Retail trade (15.0%)

Home of the famous Bottle House

COPEMISH   49625

Named after: Indian word for "big beech," as it is believed that some Indian leaders held council under a large beech tree here.

First settlers: Buckley and Douglas Lumber Co. set up lumber operations in 1883.

Platted: 1889

Incorporated as Village: 1891

Land area: 0.9 square miles

Population: (U.S. Census Bureau)
- 232   2000
- 235   2002 *(estimate)*

Males: 113 (48.7%)
Females: 119 (51.3%)

Median resident age: 33.3 years

Ethnicity in Copemish:
- White (89.7%)
- American Indian (6.9%)
- Hispanic (3.4%)
- Two or more (3.4%)

Ancestries:
- United States (26.3%)
- German (21.1%)
- Irish (9.5%)
- Polish (9.1%)
- Swedish (7.3%)
- English (6.0%)

Industries providing employment:
- Manufacturing (28.8%)
- Construction (16.9%)
- Educational, health and social services (11.0%)
- Arts, entertainment, recreation, accommodation and food services (10.2%)

EASTLAKE   49626

Named after: Its location on east shore of Manistee Lake.

Early settlers: Lumberman, Louis Sands, built a mill here in 1870.

Incorporated as Village: 1912

Land area: 1.2 square miles

Population: (U.S. Census Bureau)
- 441   2000
- 593   2002 *(estimate)*

Males: 211 (47.8%)
Females: 230 (52.2%)

Median resident age: 42.2 years

Ethnicity in Eastlake:
- White (91.4%)

- American Indian (5.4%)
- Hispanic (2.5%)
- Other (1.1%)
- Two or more (0.9%)

Ancestries:
- Polish (24.3%)
- German (19.0%)
- Irish (9.8%)
- French (7.7%)
- English (6.8%)
- Swedish (5.4%)

Median household income:
$31,750 (year 2000)
Median house value:
$59,800 (year 2000)

Industries providing employment:
- Manufacturing (25.0%)
- Arts, entertainment, recreation, accommodation and food services (20.5%)
- Educational, health and social services (17.3%)

BRETHREN   49619

Named after: German Baptist Brethren Church

First settler: Samuel S. Thorpe in 1900 with the German Baptist Brethren colony.

MASON COUNTY COUNTY SEAT: LUDINGTON

304 East Ludington Avenue
Ludington, MI 49431
Phone: 231-843-8202

Formed: In 1840 from part of Ottawa and Oceana Counties; was named Notipekagon County until 1843.

Named after: Steven T. Mason, Michigan's first governor
First settler: (Aaron) Burr Caswell, in 1847, moved his family from Illinois to the mouth of the Pere Marquette River. In 1849 he built the first frame house in the county, which now stands in White Pine Village. He was the county's first probate judge, first fish inspector, first coroner, first surveyor, and the first county seat was established in his home in 1855.

Land area: 495.2 sq. mi.

Water area: 746.7 sq. mi.

Elevation:
584 ft.(Ludington)
678 (Scottville)

Population:
28,685 (July 2003)
State rank: 50
28,274 (2000)
25,537 (1990)

Population growth since 1990: 12.3%
State rank: 42

Townships 2002 Population

Township	Population
Amber	2,100
Branch	1,210
Custer	1,341
Eden	574

Free Soil	845
Grant	889
Hamlin	3,244
Logan	344
Meade	297
Pere Marquette	2,308
Riverton	1,368
Sheridan	996
Sherman	1,126
Summit	1,036
Victory	1,493
Ludington (city)	8,434
Scottville (city)	1,274

Ethnicity in Mason County:
- White (94.0%)
- Hispanic (3.0%)
- American Indian (1.7%)
- Two or more (1.5%)
- Other (0.8%)
- Black (0.7%)

Industries providing employment:
- Manufacturing (22.3%)
- Educational, health and social services (21.2%)
- Retail trade (12.1%)

LUDINGTON   49431

Named after: James Ludington, major landowner who helped establish the lumber boomtown in the 1860's.

First settler: Burr Caswell and family built a home out of driftwood in 1847 and settled just south of current Ludington city limits. Ludington arrived in 1859 and began buying land for his timber operations.

Platted: 1867 by James Ludington

Incorporated as City: 1873
Population: (U.S. Census Bureau)
- 8,357   2000
- 8,434   2002 *(estimate)*

Land area: 3.4 square miles

Males: 3,838 (45.9%)
Females: 4,519 (54.1%)

Median resident age:
39.0 years

Ethnicity in Ludington:
- White (92.5%)
- Hispanic (4.2%)
- Two or more (1.8%)
- American Indian (1.7%)
- Other (1.1%)
- Black (1.0%)

Ancestries:
- German (27.7%)
- Irish (13.3%)
- English (11.3%)
- Polish (10.0%)
- Swedish (7.2%)
- French (5.2%)

Median household income:
$28,089 (year 2000)
Median house value:
$73,000 (year 2000)

Industries providing employment:
- Educational, health and social services (23.9%)
- Manufacturing (19.4%)
- Retail trade (13.6%)

SCOTTVILLE   49454

Named after: Hiram Scott, who owned an early sawmill and platted the village with Charles Blain. Although not documented, the story goes that the two men flipped a coin for naming rights, with Scott winning, and choosing the name, Scottville.

Once known as: Mason Center, because it was near the center of the county, and as Sweetland, after James Sweetland who built a sawmill in 1878, and sold it the next year to Hiram Scott.

Platted: In 1882 by Hiram Scott and Charles Blain

Incorporated as Village: 1889

Incorporated as City: 1907

Land area: 1.5 square miles

Population: (U.S. Census Bureau)
• 1,266   2000
• 1,274   2002 *(estimate)*

Males: 588 (46.4%)
Females: 678 (53.6%)

Median resident age: 36.2 years

Ethnicity in Scottville:
• White (91.9%)
• Hispanic (4.8%)
• Two or more (2.6%)
• American Indian (2.3%)
• Other (1.3%)
• Black (0.6%)

Ancestries:
• German (26.9%)
• Irish (11.9%)
• English (11.5%)
• Swedish (5.9%)
• French (5.1%)
• Dutch (4.4%)

Median household income: $27,750 (year 2000)
Median house value: $53,500 (year 2000)

Industries providing employment:
• Manufacturing (22.0%)
• Educational, health and social services (21.0%)
• Retail trade (13.3%)
• Arts, entertainment, recreation,accommodation and food services (12.9%)

Home of the world famous Scottville Clown Band!

CUSTER   49405

Named after: General George A. Custer

First settler: Railroad town founded in 1876

Platted: 1878 by Charles Rousssegui

Land area: 1.0 square miles

Population: (U.S. Census Bureau)
• 318   2000
• 321   2002 *(estimate)*

Males: 159 (50.0%)
Females: 159 (50.0%)

Median resident age:
37.3 years

Ethnicity in Custer:
• White (90.9%)
• American Indian (5.3%)
• Hispanic (3.5%)
• Other (3.5%)
• Two or more (3.1%)

Ancestries:
• German (25.5%)
• Irish (14.2%)
• English (7.5%)
• Dutch (6.0%)
• Italian (6.0%)
• United States (5.7%)

Median household income:
$29,444 (year 2000)
Median house value:
$65,600 (year 2000)

**Industries providing
employment:**
• Manufacturing (20.6%)
• Retail trade (15.3%)
• Construction (13.0%)
• Arts, entertainment, recre-
ation, accommodation and
food services (13.0%)

FREE SOIL   49411

Named after: The anti-slavery
political party formed in
Buffalo, New York in the
1850's. Named by Charles
Freeman, one of the early
settlers in this part of
Mason County.

Once known as: Free Soil
Mills when it was just a
lumber settlement.

Incorporated as Village:
1915

Land area: 1.03 sq. miles

Population:
177   (2000)

Apple and peach growing
replaced lumbering

MISSAUKEE COUNTY
COUNTY SEAT:
LAKE CITY

111 South Canal
PO Box 800
Lake City, MI 49651
(231) 839-4967
www.missaukee.org

Formed: In 1840 from
Mackinac County; attached
to Manistee and Wexford
County until 1871.

Named after: Local Indian
Chief Nesaukee

First settler: First survey of
the county was done in the
mid 1850's by W. L.
Coffinberry. First person to
build a permanent home was
W. Richardson in 1867.

Land area: 566.7 sq. mi.

Water area: 7.1 sq. mi.

Elevation:
1,260 ft. (Lake City)

Population:
15,189 (July 2003)
State rank: 69
4,478 (2000)
12,147 (1990)

**Population growth
since 1990:** 25%
State rank: 16

Townships   2002 Population

Township	Population
Aetna	513
Bloomfield	496
Butterfield	569
Caldwell	1,413
Clam Union	910
Enterprise	205
Forest	1,127
Holland	238
Lake	2,520
Norwich	679
Pioneer	479
Reeder	1,157
Richland	1,483
Riverside	1,084
West Branch	555
Lake City	930
McBain (city)	592

**Ethnicity in Missaukee
County:**
• White (96.9%)
• American Indian (1.3%)
• Two or more (1.2%)
• Hispanic (1.2%)

**Industries providing
employment:**
• Manufacturing (22.4%)
• Educational, health and
  social services (18.7%)
• Retail trade (12.8%)

LAKE CITY   49651

Named after: Its setting on
the eastern shore of Lake
Missaukee, once known as
Muskrat Lake.

Once known as: Reeder

First settler: Daniel Reeder in
1868

Incorporated as Village:
1889

Incorporated as City:
1932

Land area: 1.1 square miles

Population: (U.S. Census
Bureau)
• 923   2000
• 930   2002 *(estimate)*

Males: 437 (47.3%)
Females: 486 (52.7%)

Median resident age:
40.5 years

Ethnicity in Lake City:
• White (96.7%)
• Hispanic (1.6%)
• Other Asian (0.8%)
• American Indian (0.5%)
• Two or more (0.5%)

Ancestries:
• German (26.5%)
• English (16.6%)
• Irish (12.7%)
• Dutch (9.3%)
• United States (6.5%)
• French (6.1%)

Median household income:
$28,864 (year 2000)
Median house value:
$72,100 (year 2000)

Industries providing employment:
- Educational, health and social services (27.9%)
- Manufacturing (15.4%)
- Retail trade (15.4%)

MCBAIN   49657

Named after: Gillis McBain, first sheriff of Missaukee County.

Once known as: Owens until 1889

First settler: Gillis McBain in 1887. He was followed by several other Scotch-Irish loggers from Canada.

Incorporated as Village: 1893

Incorporated as City: 1907 (smallest city in the United States at that time).

Slogan or Nickname: "Join us in McBain - the place for business and family!"

Land area: 1.2 square miles

Population: (U.S. Census Bureau)
- 584   2000
- 592   2002 *(estimate)*

Males: 254 (43.5%)
Females: 330 (56.5%)

Median resident age:
39.9 years

Ethnicity in McBain:
- White (97.6%)
- Hispanic (1.2%)
- Black (0.9%)
- Two or more (0.5%)

Ancestries:
- Dutch (49.5%)
- German (13.5%)
- United States (7.0%)
- Irish (6.7%)
- English (6.3%)
- Polish (3.6%)

Median household income:
$35,156 (year 2000)
Median house value:
$69,500 (year 2000)

Industries providing employment:
- Educational, health and social services (30.8%)
- Manufacturing (19.5%)
- Retail trade (11.6%)

OSCEOLA COUNTY COUNTY SEAT: REED CITY

301 West Upton Avenue
Reed City, Michigan 49677
Phone: (231) 832-3261

Formed: In 1840 as Unwattin County, after an Ottawa Indian Chief

Named after: In 1843 the name was changed to Osceola after a Seminole Indian Chief from Florida.

First settler: The earliest residents settled on the river near present day Hersey. Nathan Hersey was probably the first to arrive in 1840. Delos A. Blodgett arrived around that time, eventually earning a fortune in the lumber business.

Land area: 566.0 sq. mi.

Water area: 7.1 sq. mi.

Elevation:
1,038 (Reed City)

Population:
23,509 (July 2003)
State rank: 62
23,197 (2000)
20,146 (1990)

Population growth since 1990: 16.7%
State rank: 34

Townships	2002 Population
Burdell	1,259
Cedar	417
Evart	1,528
Hartwick	639
Hersey	1,898
Highland	1,229
Le Roy	1,176
Lincoln	1,658
Marion	1,600
Middle Branch	875
Orient	819
Osceola	1,140
Richmond	1,714
Rose Lake	1,249
Sherman	1,103
Sylvan	1,053
Evart (city)	1,724
Reed City	2,419

Ethnicity in Osceola County:
• White (96.8%)
• American Indian (1.3%)
• Two or more (1.2%)
• Hispanic (1.0%)

Industries providing employment:
• Manufacturing (31.7%)
• Educational, health and social services (18.4%)
• Retail trade (11.6%)

REED CITY   49677

Named after: James M. Reed, one of the town's founding fathers

Once known as: Tunshla, and Todd's Slashings after the cutover land owned by another town father, Frederick Todd.

First settlers: Willis M. Slosson, Frederick Todd, William A. Hibgee and James M. Reed, arrived in late 1860's.

Incorporated as a village:
1872 (ruled invalid)
Re-incorporated 1875

Incorporated as a city: 1932

Slogan: "Crossroads City" (located at US 10 and US 131 crossing)

Land area: 1.9 square miles

Population: (U.S. Census Bureau)
2,430   2000
2,419   2002 *(estimate)*

Males: 1,111 (45.7%)
Females: 1,319 (54.3%)

Median resident age:
36.2 years

Ethnicity in Reed City:
• White (95.1%)
• Two or more (2.0%)
• American Indian (1.9%)
• Black (1.1%)
• Hispanic (0.9%)

Ancestries:
• German (29.3%)
• English (13.5%)
• Irish (11.2%)
• French (5.0%)
• United States (4.8%)
• Polish (4.4%)

Median household income:
$30,756 (year 2000)
Median house value:
$66,500 (year 2000)

Industries providing employment:
• Manufacturing (27.7%)
• Educational, health and social services (26.5%)
• Retail trade (13.3%)

EVART   49631

Named after: Civil War veteran Perry Oliver Everts. His name was misspelled at the first town meeting in 1870 as Evart, and the name stuck. Historians say organizers wanted to name the town after a Civil War veteran, and the town's first settler, Joseph Smith. However, they went with Everts because Smith was too common.

First settler: Joseph Smith arrived from England in 1857. In 1862 he joined the Union Army, returning to Evart after the Civil War.

Incorporated as village: 1872

Incorporated as city: 1938

Land area: 2.0 square miles

Population: (US Census Bureau)
1,738   2000
1,724   2002 *(estimate)*

Males: 782 (45.0%)
Females: 956 (55.0%)

Median resident age:
34.2 years

Ethnicity in Evart:
• White (96.2%)
• American Indian (1.7%)
• Two or more (1.4%)
• Hispanic (1.3%)
• Black (0.5%)

Ancestries:
• German (24.2%)
• Irish (14.3%)
• English (12.2%)
• United States (7.5%)

- Polish (6.0%)
- French (3.8%)

Median household income:
$23,348 (year 2000)
Median house value:
$59,300 (year 2000)

Industries providing employment:
- Manufacturing (36.1%)
- Educational, health and social services (16.0%)
- Arts, entertainment, recreation, accommodation and food services (12.7%)
- Retail trade (12.2%)

MARION 49665

Named after: Maryann Clarke, wife of Christopher Clarke, one of the town founders.

First settlers: Christopher Clarke and John Chadwick founded the town as a station on the Pere Marquette Railroad in late 1870's.

Incorporated as a village: 1889

Land area: 1.4 square miles

Population: (U.S. Census Bureau)
836   2000
840   2002 *(estimate)*

Males: 407 (48.7%)
Females: 429 (51.3%)

Median resident age: 35.9 years

Ethnicity in Marion:
- White (97.1%)
- American Indian (1.6%)
- Two or more (1.2%)
- Hispanic (1.0%)

Ancestries:
- English (13.9%)
- German (12.0%)
- United States (9.1%)
- Irish (9.1%)
- Dutch (4.5%)
- French (4.2%)

Median household income:
$26,467 (year 2000)
Median house value:
$55,200 (year 2000)

Industries providing employment:
- Manufacturing (24.9%)
- Educational, health and social services (21.1%)
- Retail trade (14.7%)
- Arts, entertainment, recreation, accommodation and food services (13.5%)

LEROY 49655

Named after: LeRoy Carr, a federal land agent in the area at the time of settlement.

First settlers: Several men with the Grand Rapids & Indiana Railroad, including the town's founder, James J. Blevins.

Incorporated as a village: 1883

Slogan:
"Year Round Playground"

Land area: 1.0 square miles

Population: (U.S. Census Bureau)
267   2000
264   2002 *(estimate)*

Males: 114 (42.7%)
Females: 153 (57.3%)

Median resident age:
35.3 years

Ethnicity in LeRoy:
• White (97.8%)
• American Indian (1.9%)
• Two or more (1.9%)

Ancestries:
• German (34.8%)
• Swedish (15.4%)
• English (9.4%)
• Irish (9.0%)
• United States (8.6%)
• French (7.1%)

Median household income:
$32,188 (year 2000)
Median house value:
$63,700 (year 2000)

Industries providing employment:
• Manufacturing (31.8%)
• Educational, health and
  social services (14.4%)

HERSEY   49639

Named after: Nathan Hersey, a fur trapper, believed to be the first white man to arrive in the county. He arrived in 1843, but didn't settle.

First settler: Delos A. Blodgett in 1851; he platted the village on part of his farm in 1869.

Incorporated as a village:
1875

Slogan: "It's Historic. It's Hospitable. It's Home!"

Land area: 1.1 square miles

Population: (U.S. Census Bureau)
374   2000
379   2002 *(estimate)*

Males: 192 (51.3%)
Females: 182 (48.7%)

Median resident age:
33.6 years

Ethnicity in Hersey:
• White (97.1%)
• Two or more (1.1%)
• Korean (0.8%)
• American Indian (0.8%)
• Hispanic (0.5%)

Ancestries:
• German (31.3%)
• English (12.3%)
• Irish (10.7%)
• United States (9.1%)
• Dutch (6.7%)
• Polish (4.5%)

Median household income:
$38,929 (year 2000)
Median house value:
$65,000 (year 2000)

Industries providing employment:
• Educational, health and

social services (34.5%)
- Manufacturing (28.2%)
- Retail trade (13.6%)

TUSTIN   49688

Named after: Dr. J.P. Tustin, a medical missionary for the Grand Rapids & Indiana Railroad. He went to Sweden to recruit laborers to help build the railroad.

Once known as: New Bleking

First settler: William J. Townsend in 1872

Incorporated as a village: 1893

Land area: 0.4 square miles

Population: (US Census Bureau)
237	2000
234	2002 *(estimate)*

Males: 111 (46.8%)
Females: 126 (53.2%)

Median resident age: 35.6 years

Ethnicity in Tustin:
- White (98.7%)
- Asian (1.3%)

Ancestries:
- German (20.7%)
- English (18.1%)
- Swedish (12.2%)
- Irish (9.7%)
- French (7.2%)
- Polish (6.8%)

Median household income: $29,063 (year 2000)
Median house value: $61,200 (year 2000)

Industries providing employment:
- Manufacturing (24.5%)
- Educational, health and social services (19.6%)
- Arts, entertainment, recreation, accommodation and food services (15.7%)
- Retail trade (11.8%)

OTSEGO COUNTY COUNTY SEAT: GAYLORD

225 West Main St.
Gaylord, MI 49735
Phone: (989) 731-7500

Formed: In 1840 as Okkado or Okkudo County; Okkado was an Indian word meaning sickly, or stomach pain.

Named after: Renamed in 1843 after Otsego County and Otsego Lake in New York. Otsego said to mean "clear water."

First settlers: Lumbermen arrived in 1868. The first settlement, founded in 1872 was Otsego Lake, also the first County seat.

Land area: 514.5 sq. mi.

Water area: 11.4 sq. mi.

Elevation: 1,349 ft. (Gaylord)

Population:
24,268 (July 2003)
State rank: 60
23,301 (2000)
17,957 (1990)

**Population growth
since 1990:** 35.1%
State rank: 4

Townships   2002 Population

Bagley	5,958
Charlton	1,410
Chester	1,351
Corwith	1,858
Dover	660
Elmira	1,670
Hayes	2,498
Livingston	2,414
Otsego Lake	2,595
Gaylord (city)	3,741

Ethnicity in Otsego County:
• White (97.0%)
• American Indian (1.5%)
• Two or more (1.2%)
• Hispanic (0.8%)

**Industries providing
employment:**
• Educational, health and
  social services (17.7%)
• Manufacturing (15.3%)
• Retail trade (14.2%)
• Arts, entertainment, recreation, accommodation and
  food services (11.4%)

In the late 19th century
Otsego County had a
large potato crop. Otsego
potatoes were known
across the country.

The Dayton Last Block
Works was once the largest
manufacturer of last blocks
(used in shoe making and ten-
pins for bowling) in the world.

Otsego County contains the
headwaters for the AuSable,
Black, Pigeon, Sturgeon and
Manistee Rivers.

Alpine Festival

GAYLORD   49735, 49734

Named after: Augustine
Smith Gaylord, attorney
for the Jackson, Lansing &
Saginaw Railroad that
arrived in 1874

Once known as: Barnes

First settlers: Dr. N.L.
Parmater, C.C. Mitchell and
William H. Smith

Incorporated as village: 1881

Named county seat: 1878

Incorporated as city: 1922

Slogan: "The Alpine Village"

Land area: 3.9 square miles

Population: (U.S. Census
Bureau)
• 3,681   2000
• 3,741   2002 (estimate)

Males: 1,629 (44.3%)
Females: 2,052 (55.7%)

Median resident age:
37.6 years

Ethnicity in Gaylord:
- White (95.3%)
- American Indian (2.0%)
- Hispanic (1.7%)
- Two or more (1.5%)

Ancestries:
- German (28.6%)
- Polish (19.4%)
- Irish (12.4%)
- English (10.9%)
- French Canadian (4.8%)
- Italian (4.1%)

Median household income:
$28,770 (year 2000)
Median house value:
$92,700 (year 2000)

Industries providing employment:
- Educational, health and social services (19.3%)
- Retail trade (17.4%)
- Arts, entertainment, recreation, accommodation and food services (14.7%)
- Manufacturing (13.1%)

VANDERBILT   48795

Named after: Cornelius Vanderbilt, the entrepreneur who made a fortune in shipping and railroads; was one of the... Grand Hotel on Mackinac Island.

First settler: Arrived in 1880 with the Michigan Central Railroad, owned by Cornelius Vanderbilt.

Incorporated as village: 1901

Slogan: "Gateway to the Pigeon River Country State Forest."

Land area: 1.1 square miles

Population: (U.S. Census Bureau)
- 587   2000
- 596   2002 *(estimate)*

Males: 291 (49.6%)
Females: 296 (50.4%)

Median resident age:
35.7 years

Ethnicity in Vanderbilt:
- White (97.8%)
- American Indian (2.0%)

Ancestries:
- German (24.4%)
- English (14.8%)
- Irish (14.8%)
- Polish (13.6%)
- United States (11.1%)
- French Canadian (4.3%)

Median household income:
$27,969 (year 2000)
Median house value:
$67,200 (year 2000)

Industries providing employment:
- Arts, entertainment, recreation, accommodation and food services (25.8%)
- Manufacturing (25.4%)
- Retail trade (13.7%)

JOHANNESBURG   49751

Named after: Johanna Hanson, sister of the president of the Johannesburg Manufacturing Company.

First settler: Probably Thorwald Hanson of the Johanesburg Manufacturing Company in 1901.

Population: (U.S. Census Bureau)
• 2,010   2000

Male: 1,035
Female: 975

Median age: 42.3

ROSCOMMON COUNTY
COUNTY SEAT:
ROSCOMMON

500 Lake St.
Roscommon, MI 48653-760
www.roscommoncounty.net

Formed: In 1840 as Mikenauk County, after an Ottawa Chief.

Named after: County Roscommon in Ireland; renamed in 1843, along with three other northern counties, after counties in Ireland.

First settler: George C. Robinson of Detroit in 1845

Land area: 521.4 sq. mi.

Water area: 58.4 sq. mi.

Elevation: 1,130 ft.
(Roscommon)

Population:
26,230   (July 2003)
State rank: 57
25,469   (2000)
19,776 (1990)

**Population growth
since 1990:** 32.6%
State rank: 6

Townships   2002 Population

Au Sable	396
Backus	369
Denton	5,783
Gerrish	3,119
Higgins	2,129
Lake	1,346
Lyon	1,483
Markey	2,415
Nester	287
Richfield	4,191
Roscommon (city)	4,300

Ethnicity in Roscommon County:
• White (97.4%)
• American Indian (1.1%)
• Hispanic (0.8%)
• Two or more (0.7%)

Industries providing employment:
• Educational, health and social services (21.2%)
• Retail trade (18.3%)
• Arts, entertainment,recreation, accommodation and food services (11.8%)
• Manufacturing (10.5%)

ROSCOMMON 48653

Named after: The county

Once known as: "The Robinson recorded plat"

First settler: George C. Robinson of Detroit founded the town in 1845.

Incorporated as a village: 1882

Named county seat: 1875

Land area: 1.6 square miles

Population: (U.S. Census Bureau)
• 1,133   2000
• 1,117   2002 *(estimate)*

Males: 523 (46.2%)
Females: 610 (53.8%)

Median resident age: 38.8 years

Ethnicity in Roscommon:
• White (95.9%)
• American Indian (1.8%)
• Two or more (1.5%)
• Black (1.2%)

Ancestries:
• German (24.1%)
• Irish (16.3%)
• French (9.0%)
• United States (8.2%)
• English (8.2%)
• Polish (7.2%)

Median household income: $28,229 (year 2000)

Median house value: $57,600 (year 2000)

Industries providing employment:
• Educational, health and social services (21.8%)
• Retail trade (18.6%)
• Arts, entertainment, recreation, accommodation and food services (16.2%)
• Manufacturing (12.1%)

HOUGHTON LAKE 48629

Named after: State geologist Douglass Houghton, who drowned in 1845 at the age of 36 in Lake Superior.

Once known as: Muskegon Lake, Red Lake, and Roscommon Lake, all prior to 1852.

First settler: Lumberman S.C. Hall in 1873

Slogan: "Your Four Seasons Getaway," "Home of Tip-Up Town USA"

Land area: 5.9 square miles

Population: (U.S. Census Bureau)
3,749   2000

Males: 1,773 (47.3%)
Females: 1,976 (52.7%)

Median resident age: 44.2 years

Ethnicity in Houghton Lake:
• White (97.3%)
• American Indian (1.2%)
• Hispanic (0.9%)
• Two or more (0.7%)

Ancestries:
• German (22.1%)
• English (18.0%)
• Irish (11.4%)
• Polish (8.2%)
• United States (6.9%)
• French (5.5%)

Median household income:
$27,443 (year 2000)
Median house value:
$71,800 (year 2000)

Industries providing employment:
• Educational, health and social services (23.2%)
• Retail trade (18.7%)
• Arts, entertainment,recreation, accommodation and food services (18.4%)

PRUDENVILLE   48651

Named after: The town's founder, John Pruden.

Once known as: Edna between 1876-1886

First settler: John Pruden in 1875

Land area: 2.8 square miles

Population: (U.S. Census Bureau)
• 1,737   2000

Males: 821 (47.3%)
Females: 916 (52.7%)

Median resident age:
51.8 years

Ethnicity in Prudenville:
• White (97.9%)
• American Indian (1.2%)
• Two or more (0.6%)
• Hispanic (0.5%)

Ancestries:
• German (24.9%)
• Irish (12.5%)
• Polish (11.8%)
• English (10.6%)
• United States (8.5%)
• Italian (6.0%)

Median household income:
$29,821 (year 2000)
Median house value:
$79,500 (year 2000)

Industries providing employment:
• Educational, health and social services (22.6%)
• Retail trade (21.5%)
• Arts, entertainment, recreation, accommodation and food services (17.3%)

ST. HELEN   48656

First settler: Founded in 1872 by the Henry L. Stevens & Co. Lumber Company

Land area: 5.0 square miles

Population: (U.S. Census Bureau)
• 2,993   2000

Males: 1,455 (48.6%)
Females: 1,538 (51.4%)
Median resident age:
47.6 years

Ethnicity in St. Helen:
- White(97.8%)
- American Indian (1.1%)
- Hispanic (0.8%)
- Two or more (0.6%)

Ancestries:
- German (25.5%)
- Irish (14.1%)
- English (10.4%)
- Polish (8.8%)
- French (7.8%)
- United States (5.4%)

Median household income:
$24,104 (year 2000)
Median house value:
$52,400 (year 2000)

Industries providing employment:
- Retail trade (19.6%)
- Educational, health and social services (16.4%)
- Manufacturing (15.1%)
- Arts, entertainment, recreation, accommodation and food services (11.3%)
- Construction (11.1%)

Charlton Heston spent several of his boyhood years in St. Helen, and still owns property in the area.

WEXFORD COUNTY
COUNTY SEAT:
CADILLAC

437 E. Division Street
Cadillac, Michigan 49601

(231) 779-9453
www.wexfordcounty.org
Formed: In 1840 as Kautawaubet County; at first it was thought that Kautawaubet was an Indian name, but it has no significance.

Named after: In 1843 the name was changed to Wexford, after County Wexford in Ireland. Although unconfirmed, a commonly circulated story is that a State lawmaker at the time wanted to honor the Irish immigrants who helped build the railroad, so he inserted, into an appropriations bill, Irish names for five counties in northern Michigan.

Land area: 565.5 sq. mi.

Water area: 10.3 sq. mi.

Elevation: 1,328 feet (Cadillac)

Population:
31,251 (July 2003)
State rank: 48
30,484 (2000)
26,360 (1990)

Population growth since 1990: 18.6%
State rank: 27

Townships 2002 Population

Township	Population
Antioch	830
Boon	692
Cedar Creek	1,515
Cherry Grove	2,322
Clam Lake	2,239
Colfax	779
Greenwood	559
Hanover	1,217

Haring	2,966
Henderson	194
Liberty	824
Selma	1,938
Slagle	586
South Branch	340
Springville	1,705
Wexford	825
Cadillac (city)	10,034
Manton (city)	1,212

Ethnicity in Wexford County:
- White (96.7%)
- American Indian (1.3%)
- Two or more (1.1%)
- Hispanic (1.0%)

Industries providing employment:
- Manufacturing (26.0%)
- Educational, health and social services (17.9%)
- Retail trade (14.0%)

CADILLAC   49601

Named after: Antoine de la Mothe Cadillac, founder of Detroit

Once known as: Clam Lake

First settler: Lumberman, George A. Mitchell, platted the town in 1872.

Incorporated as village of Clam Lake: 1875

Incorporated as City of Cadillac: 1877

Slogan:
"Chestnut Town U.S.A."
"City on the Lakes, Surrounded by Forests, United by Rivers, Connected with Trails."

Land area: 6.8 square miles

Population: (U.S. Census Bureau)
- 10,000   2000
- 10,034   2002 *(estimate)*

Males: 4,774 (47.7%)
Females: 5,226 (52.3%)

Median resident age:
35.6 years

Ethnicity in Cadillac:
- White 95.9%)
- American Indian (1.6%)
- Two or more (1.4%)
- Hispanic (1.2%)

Ancestries:
- German (22.1%)
- English (13.7%)
- Irish (11.2%)
- Dutch (8.9%)
- Polish (6.9%)
- Swedish (6.8%)

Median household income:
$29,899 (year 2000)
Median house value:
$72,500 (year 2000)

Industries providing employment:
- Manufacturing (26.4%)
- Educational, health and social services (19.5%)
- Retail trade (14.6%)
- Arts, entertainment, recreation, accommodation and food services (10.8%)

Cadillac contains the largest lake entirely within its city limits of any city in the United States. Lake Cadillac lies entirely within the limits of the City, while Lake Mitchell is partially within the city limits.

The canal connecting both lakes was once featured in Ripley's Believe It or Not because in the winter it freezes up before the lakes do, but once the lakes are frozen the canal thaws.

For unknown reasons Cadillac is one of the hot spots for Lou Gehrig's Disease, occuring at a rate of over 10 times the national average.

MESICK   49668

Named after: Howard Mesick, a sawmill operator who platted the village in 1890.

Once known as: The Gladiola Capital; in the 1940's and 50's Mesick was known for its numerous gladiolas, but that ended when a virus killed most of the flowers off.

First settlers: Howard and Eleanor Mesick built a cabin at the site of the present day Mesick Jr. High School. They were alone until 1901, when the railroad laid tracks through their property, at which point Mesick opened the first store in Mesick.

Incorporated as a village: 1901

Slogan: "The Mushroom Capital"

Land area: 1.1 square miles

Population: (U.S. Census Bureau)
• 447   2000
• 446   2002 (*estimate*)

Males: 226 (50.6%)
Females: 221 (49.4%)

Median resident age: 31.5 years

Ethnicity in Mesick:
• White (97.1%)
• Hispanic (1.6%)
• Black (0.7%)

Ancestries:
• German (14.8%)
• English (13.2%)
• French (7.4%)
• Polish (7.2%)
• Irish (6.5%)
• Dutch (4.3%)

Median household income: $24,375 (year 2000)
Median house value: $52,800 (year 2000)

Industries providing employment:
• Manufacturing (18.8%)
• Retail trade (16.0%)
• Educational, health and social services (13.9%)
• Arts, entertainment, recreation, accommodation and food services (11.1%)

MANTON   9663

Named after: George Manton, one of the town's first settlers

Once known as: Cedar Creek

First settlers: Three Irishmen, George Manton, Ezra Harger and William Meares, settled in 1872, about a year before the Grand Rapids and Indiana Railroad built a station in Manton.

Incorporated as village: 1877

Slogan: "The Irish City"

Land area: 1.6 square miles

Population: (U.S. Census Bureau)
- 1,221   2000
- 1,212   2002 *(estimate)*

Males: 580 (47.5%)
Females: 641 (52.5%)

Median resident age:
36.1 years

Ethnicity in Manton:
- White (96.9%)
- Two or more (1.4%)
- Hispanic (1.1%)
- American Indian (0.9%)

Ancestries:
- German (22.1%)
- English (13.5%)
- Irish (9.3%)
- United States (8.1%)
- Dutch (5.7%)
- French (4.8%)

Median household income: $27,339 (year 2000)
Median house value: $60,300 (year 2000)

Industries providing employment:
- Manufacturing (30.3%)
- Educational, health and social services (15.9%)
- Retail trade (15.0%)
- Arts, entertainment, recreation, accommodation and food services (11.4%)

BUCKLEY   49620

Named after: Buckley and Douglas Lumber Company

Once known as: New Wexford; it was located just a few miles from the now defunct town of Wexford.

First settler: Glen and Kate Brigham platted the village in 1905.

Incorporated as a village: 1907

Land area: 1.8 square miles

Population: (U.S. Census Bureau)
- 550   2000
- 549   2002 *(estimate)*

Males: 262 (47.6%)
Females: 288 (52.4%)

Median resident age:
31.3 years

Ethnicity in Buckley:
- White (91.3%)
- Hispanic (3.6%)
- American Indian (2.9%)
- Two or more (1.6%)
- Other (1.3%)
- Black (0.7%)

Ancestries:
- German (25.6%)
- Polish (12.5%)
- Irish (11.6%)
- French Canadian (7.8%)
- United States (6.9%)
- English (6.7%)

Median household income:
$36,667 (year 2000)
Median house value:
$81,600 (year 2000)

Industries providing employment:
- Retail trade (20.9%)
- Educational, health and social services (19.6%)
- Manufacturing (14.0%)
- Arts, entertainment, recreation, accommodation and food services (12.6%)

Michigan Place Names, by Walter Romig, L.H.D., copyright 1986 by Wayne State University, Wayne State University Press

BUSINESS

EMPLOYMENT

Workforce and Employment (2002)

County	Workforce	Employed	Unemployed	Unemployment Rate	(2003)
Grand Traverse	48,325	45,350	2,975	6.1%	(6.5%)
Emmet	19,475	17,875	1,600	8.3%	(8.3%)
Mason	15,400	13,975	1,450	9.3%	(12.5%)
Wexford	14,725	13,550	1,175	8.0%	(9.8%)
Charlevoix	13,950	12,900	1,050	7.6%	(8.8%)
Otsego	13,850	12,900	950	6.8%	(8.2%)
Leelanau	12,125	11,600	525	4.4%	(5.2%)
Clare	11,525	10,275	1,250	10.8%	(10.9%)
Manistee	11,475	10,525	950	8.2%	(9.3%)
Antrim	11,050	10,150	900	8.2%	(9.5%)
Osceola	10,650	9,775	850	8.0%	(8.6%)
Roscommon	8,825	8,000	825	9.3%	(9.8%)
Benzie	8,525	7,900	650	7.5%	(8.8%)
Kalkaska	8,150	7,500	650	8.1%	(9.5%)
Missaukee	6,775	6,275	500	7.3%	(8.0%)
Crawford	5,550	5,100	450	8.0%	(8.9%)
Lake	3,750	3,325	425	11.5%	(11.4%)
Total (region)	235,175	206,975	17,175	7.3%	
Michigan	5,062,000	4,720,000	342,000	6.8%	(7.3%)

UNEMPLOYMENT

Unemployment Rate

County	1999	2000	2001	2002	2003	2004
Leelanau	3.3%	2.8%	3.3%	4.3%	5.2%	4.4%
U.S.				5.8%	6.0%	5.5%
Grand Traverse	3.7%	3.7%	5.1%	5.8%	6.5%	6.1%
Otsego	4.6%	4.4%	6.2%	7.3%	8.2%	6.8%
MICHIGAN	3.8%	3.5%	5.3%	6.2%	7.3%	6.8%
Missaukee	5.8%	5.2%	8.0%	7.5%	8.0%	7.3%
Benzie	5.6%	5.2%	6.6%	7.4%	8.8%	7.5%
Charlevoix	.2%	5.1%	6.6%	7.6%	8.8%	7.6%
Osceola	5.7%	5.4%	8.2%	7.5%	8.6%	8.0%
Crawford	6.6%	5.8%	6.7%	8.1%	8.9%	8.0%
Wexford	6.7%	6.6%	10.3%	8.3%	9.8%	8.0%
Kalkaska	6.2%	5.7%	9.1%	8.9%	9.5%	8.1%
Manistee	6.1%	6.0%	7.0%	7.8%	9.3%	8.2%
Antrim	6.3%	5.3%	7.4%	7.8%	9.5%	8.2%
Emmet	7.0%	6.6%	7.0%	7.6%	8.3%	8.3%
Mason	6.2%	5.5%	11.2%	12.5%	12.5%	9.3%
Roscommon	7.6%	6.5%	7.6%	8.7%	9.8%	9.3%
Clare	.8%	6.6%	8.9%	9.3%	10.9%	10.8%
Lake	8.2%	6.9%	9.3%	9.7%	11.4%	11.5%

Michigan Department of Labor and Economic Growth

Top Employers by County

ANTRIM COUNTY

Company	Employees	Type
Club Corp. International, Bellaire (Shanty Creek)	650	Hotel/Motel
Great Lakes Packing, Kewadin	350	Cherry processing
DURA Automotive Systems, Mancelona	325	Parking brakes
Lamina Bronze Products, Bellaire	160	Hydraulic motors
Steel Tank & Fabricating Co., Mancelona	135	Pressure tanks
Antrim County Nursing Home, Bellaire	130	Health care
Mancelona Manufacturing	110	Automotive/Metal stampings
Texas Instruments, Cental Lake	100	Elec. motor protectors
Mancelona School District	83	Education
County of Antrim, Bellaire	70	Government
Elk Rapids Engineering	70	Sharpening machines

BENZIE COUNTY

Company	Employees	Type
Crystal Mt. Resort	300/*515	Resort
Conteinental Industries, Benzonia	200	Motor vehicle parts
Smeltzer Orchard, Frankfort	180	Frozen/dried fruits and veg.
County of Benzie, Beulah	112	Government
Benzie Nursing Facility, Frankfort	75	Health care
Hotel Frankfort, Frankfort	75	Hotel-dining
Graceland Products, Frankfort	70	Dried fruits
Graceland Fruit Co-op	70	Frozen/dried fruits and veg.
JST Corporation, Benzonia	50	Grocery stores
Production Industries, Inc., Frankfort	45	Metal conveyor chains

*seasonal high

CHARLEVOIX COUNTY

Company	Employees	Type
East Jordan Iron Works, Inc.	850	Iron castings, hydrants
Allied Signal, Inc., Boyne City	290	Precision control indicators
DURA Automotive, E. Jordan	230	Parking brakes, hinges
Charlevoix Area Hospital	200	Health care
Lexalite International Corp., Charlevoix	170	Safety lighting
LexaMar Corp., Boyne City	168	Plastic injection molding
Consumers Power Co.,	150	Utility
Harbor Industries, Inc., Charlevoix	130	Store display racks/fixtures
Medusa Cement Co., Charlevoix	130	Portland cement
Watchtower Tract Society, East Jordan	130	Religious organization
Hoskins Manufacturing, Char.	120	Industrial wire
Grandvue Medical Care, East Jordan	110	Health care
District Health Dept. #3, Charlevoix	100	County health

CLARE COUNTY

Company	Employees	Type
Mid-Michigan Regional Medical Center, Clare	290	Health care
Stage Right Corp., Clare	183	Portable stages
Renosol Corp., Farwell	180	Liquid vinyl and urethane
Clare Nursing Home	176	Health care
Martinrea Industries	150	
Mid-Michigan Community College, Harrison	125	Education
Dodge City Citizens Group, Harrison	100	Social services
Mellings Products Corp., Farwell	100	Oil filter assemblies
Doherty Operating Corp., Clare	90	Dining/Hotel
County of Clare	90	Government
Jay's Sporting Goods	80	Sporting goods

CRAWFORD COUNTY

Company	Employees	Type
Mercy Hospital	483	Health care
Crawford AuSable Schools	300	Education
Camp Grayling	214	Military
Weyerhauser	185	Wood products
Custom Forest Products	162	Window and door stock
County of Crawford	160	Government
State of Michigan	155	Government
Holiday Inn, Grayling	97	Hospitality
A.J.D. Forest Products	86	Lumber, pallets
Fick and Sons	85	Petroleum marketing
Stephan Wood Products	40	Truck parts
AuSable Woodworking, Frederick	38	Wood novelties

EMMET COUNTY

Company	Employees	Type
Northern Michigan Hospital, Petoskey	1,180	Health care
Little Traverse Band of Odawa Indians	656	Tribal government
Boyne U.S.A.	600	Ski and golf resort
Burns Clinic Medical Center, Petoskey	515	Health care
Continental Structural Plastic, Petoskey	200	Plastic fan parts, Child restraint seats
Glass Alternatives, Inc., Petoskey	160	Plastic injection molding
McLaughlin Co., Petoskey	150	Industrial fasteners
Control Engineering Co., Harbor Springs	150	Electrical enclosures
Manthei, Inc., Petoskey	140	Hardwood veneers
Northern Die Cast Corp., Harbor Springs	140	Castings
Circuit Controls Corp., Petoskey	137	Wiring devices
Petoskey Plastics, Inc.	130	Plastic seat protectors

GRAND TRAVERSE COUNTY

Company	Employees	Type
Munson Healthcare	4,000	Health care
Munson Medical Center	3,389	Health care
Traverse City Area Public Schools	2,085	Education
Grand Traverse Resort & Spa	1,000	Hospitality
Munson Home Health	700	Health care
Traverse City Education Association	670	Education union
Northwestern Michigan College	663	Education
Glen's Market	661	Groceries
Priority Health	650	Health maintenance
Sara Lee Bakery	620	Frozen Foods
Traverse Bay Area ISD	550	Education
Tower Automotive	500	Manufacturing
Grand Traverse County	500	Government
Coldwell Banker Schmidt Realtors	470	Real estate
Grand Traverse Pavillions	414	Nursing home
Great Wolf Lodge	400	Hospitality

KALKASKA COUNTY

Company	Employees	Type
Kalkaska Memorial Health Center	210	Health care
Kalkaska Public Schools	200	Education
Craft House Corp.	200	Machine shop
Well Tech	173	
Key Energy	134	
Alken-Ziegler	119	Manufacturing
Forest Area Schools	110	Education
Coding Products	95	
Wayne Wire Cloth Products	95	
Kalkaska County	90	Government

LAKE COUNTY

Company	Employees	Type
County of Lake, Baldwin	125	Government
Lake County Care Center	100	Health care
Baldwin Community Schools	100	Education
Houseman's Foods and Family Center, Baldwin	58	Variety store
Lake County Road Commission, Baldwin	40	Government
Peacock Industries, Inc.,	40	Machine systems
Baldwin Family Health Care	34	Health care
Austin Tube Products, Inc.,	30	Fabricated steel/alum.
Rothig Forest Products, Inc., Irons	28	Construction materials
Miller, Jerome Lumber Co., Baldwin	25	Logging and sawmill
Lake-Osceola State Bank	25	Bank

LEELANAU COUNTY

Company	Employees	Type
Grand Traverse Band of Ottawa Chippewa Indians	500	Tribal government
Suttons Bay Public Schools	140	Education
County of Leelanau	105	Government
Glen Lake Community Schools	99	Education
Easling Construction	87	Construction
Western Ave. Grill, Glen Arbor	55	Restaurant
National Park Service	50/*130	Gov./Tourism
Leland Public Schools	50	Education
Northport Lumber	42	Lumber
Homestead Resort	41/*192	Resort
Northport Schools	39	Education
Bluebird Restaurant	30/*105	Restaurant
Leelanau Fruit Collective	25/*125	Fruit processing

*seasonal high

MANISTEE COUNTY

Company	Employees	Type
Little River Casino	700	Gaming
Manistee Public Schools	450	Education
Oaks Correctional Facility	393	State prison
West Shore Medical Center	325	Health care
Packaging Corp. of America	300	Paper products
Little River Band of Ottawa Indians Tribal government	180	Tribal operations
Morton Salt (Rohm & Haas Co.)	175	Salt
Manistee City and County	150	Government
Scholle Custom Packaging	150	Bulk containers
Manistee County Medical Care	145	Extended care
Manistee-Benzie Community Mental Health	140	Mental health
K-Mart Corp.	130	Retail
Martin Marietta Magnesia Specialties, Inc.	120	Chemicals

MASON COUNTY

Company	Employees	Type
Memorial Medical Center of W. Michigan, Ludington	434	Health care
Whitehall Industries	275	Machining
Mason County Fruit Packers	250	Cherry, apple products
Mason County Central Schools District, Scottville	250	Education
Lake Michigan Carferry	250	Transportation
Harsco Track Technologies	249	Railroad equipment
Metalworks	219	Sheet metal fabricating
Ludington Area School	218	Education
Great Lakes Casting Corp., Ludington	200	Gray iron castings
Meijer	155	Retail
Wal-Mart	150	Retail
Dow Chemical Co., Ludington	140	Industrial chemicals
FloraCraft, Inc., Ludington	139	Styrofoam products
Oakview Medical Care, Ludington	134	Health care
House of Flavors Manufacturing	127	Ice cream products
Ludington Components/Haworth	123	Office furniture
County of Mason	107	Government
West Shore Community College	100	Education
Mason Lake ISD	100	Education

MISSAUKEE COUNTY

Company	Employees	Type
Lake City Forge, Inc.	185	Steel die forgings
McBain Public Schools	130	Education
Ciena Health Care Mgmt.	120	Health care
Autumnwood Nursing Home	105	Health care
Missaukee County, Lake City	100	Government
Biewer Sawmill, McBain	85	Sawmill, millwork
Foster's Supermarket	50	Grocery store
Northern Michigan Christian School, McBain	50	Education
Ebel's Supermarket, Falmouth	45	Grocery store
McDonald's	45	Restaurant
Pine Tech Inc.	30	Lumber products

OSCEOLA COUNTY

Company	Employees	Type
Collins & Aikman	800	Auto interiors
Yoplait USA, Reed City	400	Yogurt
Spectrum Health, Reed City	300	Health care
PPG Industries	250	Tempered glass
Reed City Area Public Schools	250	Education
Evart Public Schools	190	Education
Pine River Public Schools	185	Education
Liberty Dairy Co., Evart	160	Milk, cottage cheese, dips
County of Osceola	130	Government
Karftube, Inc., Reed City	125	Tube fabricating
Marion Schools	110	Education
Eagle Village	105	Employment training
Reed City Tool & Die	100	Tool & die
IMC Potash, Hersey	90	Crop nutrition products

OTSEGO COUNTY

Company	Employees	Type
Treetops Sylvan Resort	400/*550	Hotel/Resort
Gaylord Community Schools	361	Education
Otsego Memorial Hospital	285	Health care
Reptron Manufacturing	250	Electronic components
Cooper Standard Automotive	250	Auto weather stripping
Super Wal-Mart	248	Retail
Georgia Pacific	230	Lumber
Glen's Markets	155	Grocer
Tendercare Michigan, Inc., Gaylord	140	Health care
Diocese of Gaylord Schools	138	Education
Unipro Unlimited, Inc., Vanderbilt	125	Oil dipsticks/filter paper
Hidden Valley/Otsego Club, Gaylord	50/*150	Hotel/Resort
Industrial Air Technology	40	

*seasonal high

ROSCOMMON COUNTY

Company	Employees	Type
Lear Corp., Roscommon	300	Automotive stampings
Super Wal-Mart, Houghton Lake	200	Department store
Kirtland Community College, Roscommon	162	Education
ROOC, Inc., Roscommon	150	Sheltered workshop
International Health Care, Roscommon	100	Health care
Catts Realty Co. (Glen's), Houghton Lake	100	Grocery store
Glen's Market #5, Roscommon	65	Grocery store
Larken, Inc., Houghton Lake	65	Hotels-Motels
Gerrish-Higgins Schools, Roscommon	60	Education
Northern Supermarkets, Inc. (Carters), Houghton Lake	55	Grocery store

WEXFORD COUNTY

Company	Employees	Type
Avon Rubber and Plastics, Cadillac	800	Molded rubber products
Four-Winns, Inc., Cadillac	800	Fiberglass boats
Mercy Hospital, Cadillac	550	Health care
Hays Lemmerz	410	Exhaust manifolds
Michgan Rubber Products, Cadillac	400	Molded rubber products
Meijer, Inc., Cadillac	400	Department store
Rexair, Inc.	350	Vacuum cleaners
AAR Cadillac Manufacturing	325	Air cargo, pallets
FIAMM Technologies, Inc.,	250	Industrial air/ electric horns
Borg Warner Emmissions	200	Auto fans and blowers
Lakeview Lutheran Manor Cadillac	200	Health care
Northern Supermarkets, Inc., (Carters), Cadillac	140	Grocery store
County of Wexford	120	Government
City of Cadillac	100	Government

Jobs in the service and retail sector are most plentiful in all but two northern counties: Wexford and Osceola each have strong manufacturing bases.

Most Jobs – by Sector and County (2002)

Sector	No. of Jobs	Sector	No. of Jobs
ANTRIM		**BENZIE**	
Service	2,654	Service	2,588
Retail	1,758	Retail	1,329
Manufacturing	1,526	Construction	976
Government	1,392	Government	760
FIRE	989	Manufacturing	674
Construction	969	FIRE	644
CHARLEVOIX		**CLARE**	
Service	3,668	Service	3,614
Manufacturing	3,171	Retail	3,091

Retail	2,608	Government	1,725
Government	1,935	Manufacturing	1,381
Construction	1,621	Construction	1,246
FIRE	995	FIRE	1,142

CRAWFORD		EMMET	
Service	2,211	Service	7,513
Retail	1,252	Retail	4,493
Government	990	Construction	2,362
Manufacturing	880	Manufacturing	2,109
FIRE	511	Government	1,884
Construction	470	FIRE	1,592

GRAND TRAVERSE		KALKASKA	
Service	19,943	Service	1,011
Retail	13,233	Retail	937
Manufacturing	6,627	Manufacturing	919
Government	5,909	Government	860
Construction	5,295	Mining Industry	579
FIRE	4,719	Transportation Utilities	490

LAKE		LEELANAU	
Service	1,138	Service	3,707
Retail	697	Retail	1,615
Government	533	Construction	1,114
FIRE	292	Government	847
Construction	259	FIRE	744
Manufacturing	191	Farming	702

MANISTEE		MASON	
Service	3,210	Service	3,611
Retail	2,098	Retail	3,289
Manufacturing	1,718	Manufacturing	3,072
Government	1,694	Government	2,208
Construction	764	FIRE	929
FIRE	580	Construction	928

MISSAUKEE	
Service	1,089
Retail	876
Farming	693
Government	625
Manufacturing	614
Construction	423

OSCEOLA	
Manufacturing	3,348
Service	2,220
Retail	1,777
Government	1,395
Construction	776
Farming	683

OTSEGO	
Service	4,190
Retail	3,121
Manufacturing	2,011
Government	1,441
Construction	1,267
FIRE	817

ROSCOMMON	
Retail	3,076
Service	1,983
Government	1,599
Construction	794
FIRE	666
Manufacturing	353

WEXFORD	
Service	5,719
Manufacturing	5,514
Retail	4,091
Government	2,036
Transportation and Utilities	854
FIRE	816

FIRE = Finance, Insurance and Real Estate

Number of Service Jobs – by County (2002)

Gr. Traverse	19,943
Emmet	7,513
Wexford	5,719
Otsego	4,190
Leelanau	3,707
Charlevoix	3,668
Clare	3,614
Mason	3,611
Manistee	3,210
Antrim	2,654
Benzie	2,588
Osceola	2,220
Crawford	2,211
Roscommon	1,983
Lake	1,138
Missaukee	1,089
Kalkaska	1,011
17 county total	**70,069**

Number of Retail Trade Jobs – by County (2002)

Gr. Traverse	13,233
Emmet	4,493
Wexford	4,091
Mason	3,289
Otsego	3,121
Clare	3,091
Roscommon	3,076
Charlevoix	2,608
Manistee	2,098
Osceola	1,777
Antrim	1,758
Leelanau	1,615
Benzie	1,329
Crawford	1,252
Kalkaska	937
Missaukee	876
Lake	697
17 county total	**49,341**

Number of Manufacturing Jobs – by County (2002)

Gr. Traverse	6,627
Wexford	5,514
Osceola	3,348
Charlevoix	3,171
Mason	3,072
Emmet	2,109
Otsego	2,011
Manistee	1,718
Antrim	1,526
Clare	1,381
Kalkaska	919
Crawford	880
Benzie	674
Missaukee	614
Leelanau	353
Roscommon	353
Lake	191
17 county total	34,461

Health Care Jobs and Wages ($) – by County

Grand Traverse	6,880	359,379,248
Emmet	2,357	124,512,866
Wexford	1,547	61,272,971
Otsego	1,222	51,436,727
Mason	999	47,344,878
Manistee	935	38,357,409
Charlevoix	912	32,657,750
Clare	899	30,908,268
Crawford	816	33,505,126
Osceola	730	24,126,921
Roscommon	567	20,027,284
Kalkaska	446	16,696,172
Benzie	363	21,975,577
Lake	335	13,368,319
Leelanau	324	15,105,709
Antrim	128	6,364,250
Missaukee	113	3,268,953

Partnership for Michigan's Health   www.economicimpact.org

Number of Government and Government Enterprise Jobs – by County (2002)

County	Total No. of gov't jobs	Federal Civilian	Federal Military	State & local govt. jobs
Gr. Traverse	5,909	566	277	5,066
Mason	2,208	114	71	1,532
Wexford	2,036	159	59	1,818
Charlevoix	1,935	80	59	1,739
Emmet	1,884	120	58	1,706
Clare	1,725	95	59	1,571
Manistee	1,694	110	52	1,532
Roscommon	1,599	60	46	1,493
Otsego	1,441	230	46	1,165
Osceola	1,395	83	44	1,268
Antrim	1,392	76	43	1,273
Crawford	990	168	28	794
Kalkaska	860	46	31	783
Leelanau	847	142	38	667
Benzie	760	38	43	679
Missaukee	625	38	28	559
Lake	533	63	21	449
17 county total	27,833	2,188	1,003	24,094

Number of Construction Jobs – by County (2002)

Gr. Traverse	5,295
Emmet	2,362
Charlevoix	1,621
Otsego	1,267
Clare	1,246
Leelanau	1,114
Benzie	976
Antrim	969
Mason	928
Roscommon	794
Osceola	776
Manistee	764
Wexford	757
Crawford	470
Kalkaska	453
Missaukee	423
Lake	259
17 county total	20,474

Number of Finance, Insurance and Real Estate (FIRE) Jobs – by County (2002)

Gr. Traverse	4,719
Emmet	1,592
Clare	1,142
Charelvoix	995
Antrim	989
Mason	929
Otsego	817
Wexford	816
Leelanau	744
Roscommon	666
Benzie	644
Manistee	580
Crawford	511
Osceola	396
Lake	292
Kalkaska	275
Missaukee	253
17 county total	**15,544**

Number of Transportation and Public Utility Jobs – by County (2002)

Gr. Traverse	2,249
Wexford	854
Emmet	588
Mason	544
Charlevoix	534
Otsego	502
Kalkaska	490
Manistee	441
Clare	426
Osceola	354
Roscommon	271
Missaukee	212
Antrim	180
Crawford	135
Benzie	94
Lake	0
Leelanau	0
17 county total	**7,874**

Number of Farm Jobs – by County (2002)

Leelanau	702
Missaukee	693
Osceola	683
Mason	673
Gr. Traverse	584
Clare	451
Manistee	448
Antrim	381
Wexford	317
Emmet	279
Charlevoix	229
Benzie	188
Kalkaska	185
Otsego	176
Lake	144
Roscommon	39
Crawford	0
17 county region	**6,172**

Number of Non-farm Jobs – by County (2002)

Gr. Traverse	61,566 (26%)
Emmet	21,623 (9%)
Wexford	20,564 (8.6%)
Otsego	15,149 (6%)
Mason	15,066 (6%)
Charlevoix	14,848 (6%)
Clare	13,081 (5.5%)
Manistee	11,103 (4.6%)
Osceola	10,648 (4.4%)
Antrim	10,009 (4.2%)
Leelanau	9,116 (3.8%)
Roscommon	9,089 (3.8%)
Benzie	7,331 (3%)
Crawford	6,735 (2.8%)
Kalkaska	5,753 (2.4%)
Missaukee	4,436 (1.8%)
Lake	3,268 (1.4%)
17 county total	**239,385**

WAGES AND INCOME

Average Wage per Job – by County (2003)

County	Avg. annual wage	State rank
Michigan	$38,135	---
Osceola	$34,966	13
Charlevoix	$31,241	27
Grand Traverse	$30,514	30
Kalkaska	$29,946	33
Emmet	$29,162	37
Wexford	$28,659	45
Manistee	$28,330	47
Otsego	$27,926	49
Mason	$27,541	51
Crawford	$25,786	59
Leelanau	$25,860	63
Clare	$25,380	65
Lake	$25,118	66
Missaukee	$24,623	70
Benzie	$24,213	71
Antrim	$24,176	72

U.S. Bureau of Labor Statistics

Median Household Income – by County (2002)

County	Median household income	% of state median household income
Leelanau	48,083	108.5
Michigan	44,315	100.0
Grand Traverse	43,311	98.0
United States	42,409	
Emmet	41,756	94.2
Otsego	41,580	93.8
Charlevoix	41,143	92.8
Benzie	38,587	87.1
Antrim	38,371	86.6
Wexford	35,338	79.7
Mason	34,836	78.6

Kalkaska	34,457	77.8
Missaukee	34,402	77.6
Osceola	34.164	77.1
Manistee	34,031	76.8
Crawford	32,612	73.6
Roscommon	29,376	66.3
Clare	29,150	65.8
Lake	26,173	59.1

Wage Estimates – Major Occupations – by Market

Market	Employment	Hourly wage	Average annual
Detroit	1,976,540	$20.43	$42,500
Ann Arbor	277,200	$18.85	$39,206
Michigan	4,310,420	$18.57	$38,619
Flint	162,700	$18.35	$38,175
Lansing	199,200	$18.09	$37,628
Grand Rapids/Muskegon/ Holland	533,880	$17.26	$35,901
Saginaw	165,720	$17.26	$35,901
Kalamazoo/Battle Creek	196,960	$17.22	$35,818
Benton Harbor	63,450	$16.59	$34,497
Northwest Lower	126,270	$15.18	$31,575
Northeast Lower	74,340	$13.77	$28,649

Michigan Dept. of Labor and Economic Growth

Where the Workers Live

Have you ever wondered where all those other drivers are
headed? Most are on their way to or from jobs in the same
county in which they live. But for many the commute runs
across several county lines, as indicated in the table below.

Where the jobs are: Antrim
Where the workers live

Antrim	5,671
Kalkaska	1,112
Grand Traverse	937
Charlevoix	244
Otsego	116
Leelanau	66
Wayne	39
Wexford	34

Where the jobs are: Benzie
Where the workers live

Benzie	3,691
Manistee	459
Grand Traverse	242
Leelanau	60
Wexford	43
Barry	34

Where the jobs are: Charlevoix
Where the workers live

Charlevoix	8,665
Antrim	1,347
Emmet	794
Otsego	147
Cheboygan	89
Kalkaska	45
Grand Traverse	36

Where the jobs are: Clare
Where the workers live

Clare	6,535
Isabella	936
Midland	220
Gladwin	325
Osceola	92
Roscommon	88

Where the jobs are: Crawford
Where the workers live

Crawford	3,694
Roscommon	634
Otsego	185
Kalkaska	126
Grand Traverse	44
Montmorency	43
Ogema	36

Where the jobs are: Emmet
Where the workers live

Emmet	13,001
Charlevoix	2,183
Cheboygan	1,580
Antrim	165
Otsego	118
Presque Isle	104
Mackinac	99

Where the jobs are: Grand Traverse
Where the workers live

Grand Traverse	34,862
Leelanau	4,182
Benzie	2,550
Wexford	1,333
Antrim	1,285
Manistee	494
Missaukee	185
Charlevoix	102

Roscommon	67
Oakland	67

Where the jobs are: Kalkaska
Where the workers live

Kalkaska	3,478
Grand Traverse	554
Antrim	395
Missaukee	92
Wexford	52

Where the jobs are: Lake
Where the workers live

Lake	1,619
Newaygo	172
Osceola	153
Mason	128
Manistee	70

Where the jobs are: Leelanau
Where the workers live

Leelanau	5,090
Grand Traverse	1,113
Benzie	288
Wexford	22
Manistee	20

Where the jobs are: Manistee
Where the workers live

Manistee	7,988
Mason	788
Benzie	230
Lake	149
Grand Traverse	131
Wexford	128

Where the jobs are: Mason
Where the workers live

Mason	10,494
Oceana	541
Lake	196
Muskegon	71
Ottawa	46

Where the jobs are: Missaukee
Where the workers live

Missaukee	2,707
Wexford	281
Osceola	243
Roscommon	100
Clare	52

Where the jobs are: Osceola
Where the workers live

Osceola	5,952
Mecosta	896
Lake	742
Clare	461
Wexford	273
Newaygo	153
Missaukee	138
Isabella	117

Where the jobs are: Otsego
Where the workers live

Otsego	9,274
Crawford	694
Montmorency	517
Antrim	439
Cheboygan	375
Charlevoix	199
Emmet	126
Grand Traverse	96

Where the jobs are: Roscommon
Where the workers live

Roscommon	6,140
Crawford	807
Ogemaw	226
Missaukee	215
Clare	118
Gladwin	60

Where the jobs are: Wexford
Where the workers live

Wexford	10,898
Missaukee	2,478
Osceola	1,624
Grand Traverse	357
Lake	303
Manistee	227
Clare	192
Mecosta	90

U.S. Census, 2000

AGRICULTURE

Agriculture is the second-largest industry in Michigan contributing $37 billion a year to the state economy. Over 500,000 residents make their living in the agriculture and food processing industries.

There is great variety with over 125 commodities, making Michigan second to California in agricultural diversity. Michigan is the leading state for 11 commodities including tart cherries, Niagara grapes, blueberries, strawberries, cucumbers, dry beans and several flowering plants.

The Grand Traverse region leads the country in tart cherry production, and northern Michigan is one of the leading producers of other fruits such as sweet cherries, apples and grapes. Fruit growing is confined mainly to the counties along the Lake Michigan shoreline. Further inland, away from the water, livestock operations flourish in Missaukee and Otsego counties where agriculture is a key component to the local economy. In some parts of northern Michigan, such as Crawford and Roscommon counties, the forest is so thick that hardly any farms exist.

The number of farms, and size of farms, in northern Michigan is slowly decreasing. One reason is the demand for new housing and commercial development. As farmers approach retirement age, the temptation to sell to land developers intensifies, especially if the next generation is not interested in continuing farm operations.

Several conservancy groups are working to preserve farmland by using programs like purchase of development rights (PDR), which pays a farm owner in to give up any future rights to develop the land. More than 40% of the state's total farmland is in some form of preservation agreement.

In 1994 Peninsula Township, in Grand Traverse County, gained national attention when voters approved a 1.25 mil property tax increase to buy development rights from farmers.

MOST FARMS BY COUNTY

County	No. of Farms (2002)	(1997)	Change
Osceola	591	578	up 2%
Grand Traverse	489	485	up 1%
Mason	478	475	up 1%
Leelanau	429	420	up 2%
Clare	414	421	down 2%
Missaukee	412	377	up 9%
Wexford	395	298	up 33%
Antrim	382	301	up 27%
Manistee	315	330	down 5%
Charlevoix	299	230	up 30%
Emmet	274	248	up 10%
Benzie	181	165	up 10%
Kalkaska	175	162	up 8%
Lake	173	153	up 13%
Otsego	170	160	up 6%
Crawford	47	35	up 34%
Roscommon	46	45	up 2%
Total farms:	**4,485**	**4,883**	**down 8%**

U.S. Department of Agriculture, National Agricultural Statistics Service

MOST FARMLAND ACRES BY COUNTY

County	Acres (2002)	Acres (1997)	Change
Osceola	115,922	115,888	up slightly
Missaukee	97,792	94,026	up 4%
Mason	79, 621	83,256	down 4%
Clare	64, 365	67,542	down 5%
Antrim	63,428	59,120	up 7%
Leelanau	62,406	66,569	down 6%
Grand Traverse	62,268	66,997	down 7%
Manistee	46,442	51,758	down 10%
Wexford	45, 852	47,842	down 4%
Emmet	43,665	44,037	down 1%
Charlevoix	38,799	35,597	up 9%
Otsego	34, 585	36,075	down 6%
Kalkaska	24,104	23,129	up 4%
Lake	23,378	26,383	down 11%
Benzie	23,055	24,608	down 6%
Roscommon	7,394	4,664	up 59%
Crawford	6,308	3,722	up 69%
Total farmland acres	**839, 384**	**808, 153**	**up 4%**

U.S. Department of Agriculture, National Agricultural Statistics Service

TOTAL ACRES IN FARMS: 1900 – 1950

Agriculture in northern Michigan peaked in 1920, relative to the number of acres being farmed. Several counties had population numbers that wouldn't be seen again until the end of the century. The growth fueled in the late 1800's by the arrival of the railroad and beginning of the lumber boom, reversed as the forests disappeared.

By 1920, much of the forest had been cut over leaving behind thousands of acres of stumps and burned out landscape. Lumber companies promoted the land as a good farming opportunity and sold it cheap to hopeful families. However, the soil was damaged, and many desperate families left northern Michigan, forfeiting their land to the State. The number of acres being farmed has declined slowly and steadily ever since.

Many families were unable to make a go of farming the cutover land in the 1920's and 30's, and were unable to sell it. The State wound up in possession of large tracts of land, and that explains why the State (DNR) owns so much land in northern Michigan.

County	1900	1920	1930	1950
Osceola	187,664	259,130	251,398	243,700
Clare	82,236	186,581	144,042	141,804
Mason	131,162	183,428	155,149	164,928
Grand Traverse	148,649	170,188	136,064	142,969
Missaukee	101,414	168,710	162,019	171,750
Leelanau	142,858	165,399	132,823	121,484
Antrim	120,285	153,729	141,662	153,627
Manistee	114,636	147,569	129,672	123,771
Wexford	106,554	146,712	127,206	140,844
Charlevoix	104,930	134,723	105,199	122,967
Emmet	101,701	125,218	106,010	120,527
Benzie	67,814	89,414	72,560	69,872

Lake	60,421	88,438	80,217	70,453
Kalkaska	56,892	86,868	72,636	88,105
Crawford	29,248	50,884	18,448	11,306
Otsego	47,605	73,961	60,765	89,150
Roscommon	23,201	51,349	28,342	16,939
Michigan	17,561,698	19,032,961	17,118,951	17,269,992

GeoStat Center, University of Virginia Library

AVERAGE SIZED FARM, BY COUNTY

County	2002 Avg. size-acres	1997 Avg. size-acres	Change
Missaukee	237	249	-5%
Otsego	203	229	-11%
Osceola	196	200	-2%
Mason	167	175	-5%
Antrim	166	196	-15%
Roscommon	161	104	+55%
Emmet	159	178	-11%
Clare	155	160	-3%
Manistee	147	157	-6%
Leelanau	145	158	-8%
Kalkaska	138	143	-3%
Lake	135	172	-22%
Crawford	134	106	+26%

Charlevoix	130	155	-16%
Benzie	127	149	-15%
Grand Traverse	127	138	-8%
Wexford	161	116	+28%

U.S. Department of Agriculture, National Agricultural Statistics Service

MARKET VALUE OF AGRICULTURE PRODUCTS SOLD

County	2002	State Rank	1997	Change
Missaukee	39,545,000	(37)	35,660,000	+11%
Mason	24,955,000	(42)	24,353,000	+2%
Osceola	19,185,000	(47)	19,501,000	-2%
Leelanau	15,988,000	(48)	30,602,000	-48%
Antrim	15,854,000	(49)	17,497,000	-9%
Clare	11,560,000	(52)	13,091,000	-12%
Grand Traverse	11,366,000	(53)	18,791,000	-40%
Wexford	9,520,000	(56)	8,990,000	+6%
Manistee	8,031,000	(58)	9,594,000	-16%
Emmet	5,867,000	(60)	5,666,000	+4%
Kalkaska	5,636,000	(62)	5,493,000	+3%
Otsego	4,736,000	(64)	3,775,000	+25%
Benzie	4,222,000	(65)	6,744,000	-37%
Charlevoix	3,991,000	(66)	4,328,000	-8%
Lake	2,117,000	(76)	2,181,000	-3%

Roscommon		NA	554,000	NA
Crawford	149,000	(82)	131,000	+14%
Total	182,722,000		206,951,000	-13%

Market Value: Top Livestock Producers

The market value of livestock versus crops is higher in six northern Michigan counties: Missaukee, Osceola, Clare, Emmet, Charlevoix and Lake.

County	Livestock	Crops	Total sales
Missaukee	$28,833,000	$10,712,000	$39,545,000
Osceola	$14,589,000	$4,596,000	$19,501,000
Clare	$9,478,000	$2,082,000	$11,560,000
Mason	$8,409,000	$16,546,000	$24,353,000
Antrim	$4,786,000	$11,068,000	$15,854,000
Grand Traverse	$3,813,000	$7,553,000	$11,366,000
Leelanau	$3,460,000	$12,528,000	$15,988,000
Wexford	$3,151,000	$6,369,000	$9,520,000
Emmet	$3,016,000	$2,851,000	$5,867,000
Charlevoix	$2,153,000	$1,839,000	$3,991,000
Otsego	$1,298,000	$3,437,000	$4,736,000
Manistee	$1,133,000	$6,897,000	$8,031,000
Lake	$1,129,000	$987,000	$2,117,000
Benzie	$879,000	$3,342,000	$4,222,000
Kalkaska	$720,000	$4,915,000	$5,636,000

Roscommon	NA	$450,000	$554,000
Crawford	NA	NA	$149,000

CHRISTMAS TREES (CUT)

County	Acres	Rank State	Rank National
Missaukee	9,427	1	6
Wexford	5,927	2	8
Osceola	2,583	6	27
Manistee	2,546	7	28
Kalkaska	1,684	9	42
Antrim	1,266	11	64

Helsel's North Country Farms in Lake City, The Christmas Tree Capital (courtesy of Helsel's North Country Farms)

Christmas Trees (2002)

Michigan is one of the leading Christmas tree producers in the country, with over a third of the cut trees coming from the northern part of the State. Nationally, Michigan ranks third in trees harvested, 2nd in acres of Christmas trees, and 3rd in number of Christmas tree farms.

Trees harvested		Acres of Christmas trees		Christmas tree farms	
Oregon	6,466,551	Oregon	67,804	Pennsylvania	2,164
N. Carolina	2,915,507	Michigan	60,520	Oregon	2,024
Michigan	2,380,173			Michigan	1,978

Nationally, Missaukee County ranks sixth in the number of trees harvested. In Michigan, Missaukee County dominates the market with more farms, more acres and far more trees cut than any other county.

Many of the tree farms were not planted until the 1960's and 70's, when it was discovered they grew well in the sandy soil. With so many farms located in and around Lake City, it's known as "The Christmas Tree Capital of the Nation."

In 1984, the Nation's Christmas Tree came from the Dutchman Tree Farm in Lake City. After winning a national competition, the owners presented their 20-foot spruce to President Reagan in Washington D.C.

Nationally there are about 500,000 acres of land devoted to Christmas trees. 25 to 30 million Christmas trees are sold in the U.S. each year. Average height at time of sale is between 6-7 feet. Average growing time is seven years.

County	No. of farms	Acres in production	Trees cut
Missaukee	73	9,427	654,011
Wexford	61	5,927	365,184
Osceola	51	2,583	89,382
Manistee	35	2,546	98,909
Kalkaska	36	1,684	44,091
Antrim	35	1,266	33,296
Mason	33	1,065	21,280

Grand Traverse	32	948	31,440
Leelanau	34	693	9,726
Benzie	14	643	19,431
Otsego	7	363	2,257
Lake	13	303	2,783
Charlevoix	17	254	362
Clare	13	208	N/A
Emmet	7	117	1,135
Total (Northwest)	461	28,027	1,373,287
% of State	20%	37%	37%
Michigan	1,798	60,520	2,380,173

2002 Census of Agriculture
U.S. Department of Agriculture, National Agricultural Statistics Service
National Christmas Tree Association

How Northern Michigan Counties Rank

State rank	Tart cherries	Grapes	Asparagus	Hay	Snap Beans
1	Leelanau	Berrien	Oceana	Sanilac	St. Joseph
2	Oceana	Van Buren	Mason	Huron	Kalamazoo
3	Gr. Traverse	Cass	Van Buren	Isabella	Montcalm
4	Antrim	Kalamazoo	Manistee	Osceola	Branch
5	Mason	Gr. Traverse	Berrien	Barry	Mason

Commercial Fruit Growing (2000)

Between 1997 and 2000 fruit-producing acreage dropped by 11% in Michigan. However Northwest Michigan continues as a major producer of cherries. Of all the sweet cherry orchards in the state, 90% are in northwest Michigan, and of all tart cherry orchards in the state, 60% are in the northwest region.

The wine producing industry has experienced steady growth, but represents only 4% of the grape growing acreage in the state.

For apples, 15% of the state's orchards are in northwest Michigan.

Leelanau County ranked third in the state for total fruit producing acreage.

Leading Fruit Producers

County	Acres	Rank State	Rank National
Tart Cherries			
Leelanau	9,064	1	1
Grand Traverse	4,051	3	3
Antrim	2,901	4	4
Benzie	1,415	7	10
Manistee	892	9	13
Sweet Cherries			
Leelanau	4,600	1	6
Grand Traverse	1,999	2	12
Apples			
Leelanau	2,066	8	37
Manistee	1,203	11	53
Benzie	1,084	12	57

Land in Orchards

County	Acres (2002)	Acres (1997)
Leelanau	16,305	17,941
Grand Traverse	7,670	9,741
Mason	5,198	5,135
Antrim	4,761	4,754
Benzie	2,941	3,270
Manistee	2,497	3,809
Charlevoix	540	809
Emmet	41	62
Clare	34	35
Wexford	24	63
Otsego	15	16
Osceola	12	56
Missaukee	-	18
Lake	-	23

U.S. Department of Agriculture, National Agricultural Statistics Service

		Cherries				
County	Commercial operations	Apples	Tart	Sweet	Grapes	Peaches
Antrim	44	660	2,080	810		
Benzie	39	930	1,200	270		
Grand Traverse	124	900	4,100	1,800	255	
Leelanau	184	2,000	8,100	4,150	275	50
Manistee	43	1,150	850	250		95
Charlevoix, Cheboygan, Emmet	17	60	170			
Mason	36	1,650	1,800	530	330	

Fruit Growing Operations by County (Acres)

CHERRIES

Northwest Michigan has been a major producer of cherries for nearly a century. Traverse City is known as the "Cherry Capital of the World," and hosts the annual National Cherry Festival every July.

Most cherry growing is done along the Lake Michigan shoreline between Manistee County and Antrim County. The lake breezes cool the orchards in the summer time and warm the arctic wind in the wintertime. It's a perfect climate for growing fruit, especially cherries.

Rev. Peter Doughtery planted the first cherry trees in 1852 on Old Mission peninsula where in 1839 he became the first European to settle among the natives near Traverse City.

The first commercial tart cherry orchard was planted in 1893 on the Ridgewood Farm, which was located at the site where Dougherty planted his first cherry trees.

Northwest Michigan produces 120 - 150 million pounds of tart cherries annually, about half of the state's crop. Michigan is number one, producing 75% of the nation's tart cherry crop.

Growers in northern Michigan, produce about 50 million pounds of sweet cherries, about 80% of the state's total. As a state, Michigan provides about 20% of the country's sweet cherry crop.

Sweet Cherry Production -statewide

Record high: 37,500 tons   1978
Record low: 500 tons   1945

Tart Cherry Production – statewide

Record high: 380 million lbs.   1964
Record low: 15 million lbs.   2002

Tart Cherries growing north of Northport (Author photo)

The number of farms growing sweet or tart cherries has decreased since 1991, however the total acreage devoted to cherry-growing has increased.

SWEET CHERRIES

County	Farms 1991	1994	1997	2000	2002	Acres 1991	1994	1997	2000	2002
Antrim	39	34	34	27	34	950	880	920	810	978
Benzie and Charlevoix	31	22	24	23	36	360	350	340	290	436
Gr. Traverse	108	98	100	89	97	2,060	1,750	1,850	1,800	1,999
Leelanau	151	145	150	137	136	3,800	3,750	4,050	4,150	4,608
Manistee	25	26	22	19	15	300	270	290	250	276
Mason	27	25	24	21	20	500	480	490	530	542
Total (Northwest)	381	350	354	316	338	7,970	7,480	7,940	7,850	8,839
% State total	37%	38%	39%	39%	33%	47%	47%	47%	47%	46%
Michigan	635	565	545	500	690	9.050	8,500	8,900	8,700	10,082

TART CHERRIES

County	Farms 1991	1994	1997	2000	2002	Acres 1991	1994	1997	2000	2002
Antrim	46	42	38	35	38	2,610	2,600	2,350	2,250	2,901
Benzie	36	29	27	26	25	1,260	1,300	1,250	1,200	1,415
Gr. Traverse	117	115	105	97	96	4,700	4,600	4,450	4,100	4,051
Leelanau	172	164	151	143	143	7,700	7,700	7,850	8,100	9,064
Manistee	39	32	25	26	20	1,580	1,200	1,100	850	892
Mason	31	30	27	24	26	1,960	1,920	1,860	1,800	2,227
Total (Northwest)	441	412	373	351	348	19,810	19,320	18,860	18,300	20,550
% State total	32%	33%	34%	36%	32%	34%	34%	36%	37%	38%
Michigan	935	845	705	615	735	38,200	36,000	33,500	30,800	34,386

APPLES

The number of apple growers has increased since 1991, but the total acreage devoted to apples has gone down. The only county showing an increase in apple orchard acreage was Mason County.

County	Farms 1991	1994	1997	2000	2002	Acres 1991	1994	1997	2000	2002
Antrim	37	36	33	29	40	850	750	800	720	664
Benzie	31	32	30	26	30	1,200	1,250	1,250	930	1,084
Gr. Traverse	69	65	66	54	63	1,150	1,100	1,100	900	936
Leelanau	74	78	77	67	77	2,200	2,250	2,400	2,000	2,066
Manistee	39	39	34	29	31	2,100	2,050	1,850	1,150	1,203
Mason	36	36	36	28	43	1,500	1,500	1,700	1,640	1,773
Charlevoix					23					198
Other					24					56

Total (Northwest)	286	286	276	233	331	9,000	8,900	9,100	7,350	7,980
% State total	16%	16%	17%	17%	16%	13%	13%	14%	13%	13%
Michigan	1,500	1,450	1,300	1,100	1,750	59,000	59,000	58,000	47,500	55,539

PEACHES

County	Farms					Acres				
	1991	1994	1997	2000	2002	1991	1994	1997	2000	2002
Leelanau	25	26	15	12	30	85	50	45	50	78
Manistee	21	20	17	15	18	190	170	125	95	105
Mason	20	17	17	14	22	300	250	250	330	428
Gr. Traverse				29						66
Other	40	37	31	27	30	135	80	80	65	49
Total (Northwest)	106	100	80	68	100	710	550	500	560	726
%-State total	13%	14%	14%	13%	12%	8%	7%	8%	9%	10%
State	705	600	515	460	732	8,300	6,800	6,000	5,700	6,326

The town of Elberta in Benzie County is named after the Elberta peach – at one time the most popular variety in the region. The first peach trees were planted in Benzie County in 1866. A variety developed locally was named after the town of Frankfort. Eventually one too many crop was destroyed by frost leading to the demise of the peach industry in Benzie County.

GRAPE GROWERS

With the growing success of northern Michigan's wine industry comes demand for more land – from current growers and newcomers. Land price are going up as a result: from $2,000 to $4,000 an acre a few years ago to as much as $20,000 an acre today. Northern Michigan's wine industry is concentrated on the Leelanau Peninsula and Old Mission Peninsula, but some observers believe it will inevitably expand into neighboring counties such as Benzie and Antrim.

According to the 2003 Michigan Fruit Survey conducted by the USDA National Agricultural Statistics Service, there are 465 grape farms in Michigan, about 14% of them in northern Michigan. About 13% of the land used for growing grapes is in northern Michigan. Acres of Niagaras rose 15% to 3,450, and acres of wine grapes rose 26% to 1,500.

Number of grape farms

County	1997	2000	2003	Change from 1997
Grand Traverse	8	20	34	+52%
Leelanau	15	20	26	+57%
Northwest total	40	43	67	+60%
Michigan	500	450	465	-7%

Acres of grapes

County	1997	2000	2003	Change from 1997
Grand Traverse	210	255	395	+53%
Leelanau	200	275	325	+61%
Northwest total	440	550	740	+60%
Michigan	12,500	13,500	14,400	+15%

Boskydel - First commercial vineyard in northern Michigan

In 1970, Bernie Rink planted his first grapes on his Lake Leelanau property. His sons claim it was "Field of Dreams" in reverse, as the vineyard replaced their ballfield. In 1975, Rink opened the first bonded winecellar on the Leelanau Peninsula, and became the first in northern Michigan to sell estate-bottled wine.
(In 1974, Chateau Grand Traverse opened as the first northern Michigan vineyard, but did not use estate grapes in its first year of production.)

Many of the regions winemakers have learned from Rink's experiments, and compared notes while opening and growing their own vineyards.

Rink has chosen to keep his winemaking operation manageable by not expanding beyond the original 25 acres of grapes. He produces eight different wines from six grape varieties. He does not enter wine competitions, and stopped advertising years ago. Explaining why he's not a member of the Leelanau Peninsula Vintners, Rink says, "if you're on the wine trail, you get a lot of foot traffic." The pioneer vintner produces about 7,000 gallons of wine each year, most of which sells to repeat customers through his wine-tasting room.

Rink says his best-selling wine is the De Chaunac, a dry red, called "the best of its kind in the country," by the American Wine Review.

On the web: www.boskydel.com

LEELANAU PENINSULA VINTNERS
(www.lpwines.com)

Bel Lago Vineyard and Winery

Black Star Farms

Chateau Fontaine

Chateau de Leelanau Vineyard and Winery

Ciccone Vineyard and Winery

Gill's Pier Vineyard & Winery

Good Harbor Vineyards

L. Mawby

Leelanau Wine Cellars

Shady Lane Cellars

Willow Vineyard

BEL LAGO VINEYARD AND WINERY

(www.bellago.com)
6530 S. Lake Shore Dr.
Cedar, MI 49621 (231) 228-4800

Acres of grapes: 30

Varieties: 14 production, 80 test varieties

First planting: 1987

Varieties of wine: 20

Top seller: Leelanau Primavera, a semi-dry blend

Awards and recognition:
2001 Chardonnay, Gold Medal and Best of Class,
Michigan State Fair
1997 BRUT Sparkling Wine, Gold and Best of Show,
Michigan State Fair
2002 Gewurztraminer, Gold Medals at
Riverside International Competition and
International Tasters Guiild.
California Wine writer, Dan Berger, called the
2002 Bel Lago Gewurztraminer
*"one of the best American-made Gewurtraminers
I have ever tasted."*

Winemaker: Charles E. Edson, Ph.D
Winemaker: Chrish Parrish, Asst.

Cases sold per year: 3,000

Owners: Charles Edson and Amy Iezzoni

BLACK STAR FARMS

(www.blackstarfarms.com)
10844 E. Revold Rd.
Suttons Bay, Michigan 49682
231-271-4970

Acres of grapes: 50

Varieties: 8

First planting: 1994

Varieties of wine: 22

Top seller: Late Harvest Reisling

Awards and recognition:
Arcturos Cabernet Franc,
Double Gold, 2005 Great Lakes
Great Wine
Arcturos Pinot Gris,
Gold, 2005 Tasters Guild
International Wine Judging
Spirit of Cherry,
Beverage Tasting Institute,
Exceptional
A Capella Reiling Ice Wine,
Double Gold, 2004
Tasters Guild International
Wine Judging

The Inn, Black Star Farms
(courtesy Black Star Farms)

Winemaker: Lee Lutes

Cases sold per year: 10,000

Owners: Kerm Campbell, Donald Coe, Lee Lutes

CHATEAU FONTAINE
(www.chateaufontaine.com)
2290 S. French Rd.
Lake Leelanau, Michigan 49653 (231) 256-0000

Acres of grapes: 23

Varieties: 6

First planting: 1990

Varieties of wine: 10

Top seller: Pinot Gris

Awards and recognition:
2001 Riesling, Double Gold Medal at

International Tasters Guild
2001 Chardonnay, Gold Medal at International Tasters Guild
2002 Chardonnay, Gold Medal at Michigan State Fair
Winemaker: Bruce Simpson

Cases sold per year: 3,000

Owners: Dan and Lucie Matthies

CHATEAU DE LEELANAU VINEYARD & WINERY
(www.chateaudeleelanau.com)
5048 S.W. Bayshore Dr.
Suttons Bay, MI 49682   (231) 271-8888

Acres of grapes: 28

Varieties: 6

First planting: 1990

Varieties of wine: 16

Top seller: SelectHarvest Reisling 2001

Awards and recognition:
2000 Andante, Gold Medal and Best of Show in
Sparkling Wine at 2003 Michigan State Fair

Winemaker: John Fletcher and Vera Klokocka

Cases sold per year: 3,500

Owners: Dr. Roberta Kurtz

CICCONE VINEYARD & WINERY
(www.cicconevineyards.com)
10343 East Hilltop Road
Suttons Bay, MI 49682   (231) 271-5553

Acres of grapes: 16

Varieties: 14

First planting: 1995

Varieties of wine: 4

Top seller: Dolcetto

Awards and recognition:
2002 Gewurztraminer, Gold Medal, 2004 Great Lakes
Wine Judging
Gold Medal, Tasters Guild International
2002 Dolcetto, Gold Medal, 2004 Great Lakes
Wine Judging

Winemaker: Silvio T. Ciccone

Cases sold per year: 2,500

Owners: Silvio and Joan Ciccone

GILL'S PIER VINEYARD & WINERY
5620 N. Manitou Trail
Northport, MI 49670   (231) 256-7003

Acres of grapes: 4

Varieties: 4

First planting: 2003

Varieties of wine: 5
(grapes sourced from Old Mission vineyards)

Top seller: Cheerio Cherry and Icebox Apple

Awards and recognition:
2002 Riesling, Best of Class for Semi-dry wines
Michigan State Fair
Cheerio Cherry, Gold Medal Tasters Guild International

Winemaker: Bryan Ulbrich

GOOD HARBOR VINEYARDS
(www.goodharbor.com)
Route 1, Box 888
Lake Leelanau, MI   (231) 256-7165

Acres of grapes: 46 in production.
20 planted in Spring 2005

Varieties: 7

First planting: 1978

Varieties of wine: 12

Top sellers: Fishtown White, Tillium,
Harbor Red, and Cherry

Awards and recognition:
Over 955 of wine produced have won Gold, Silver or
Bronze medals at the Michigan State Fair or Tasters Guild
International wine judging

Winemaker: Bruce Simpson

Cases sold per year: 20,000

Owners: Bruce Simpson

L.MAWBY
(www.lmawby.com)
4519 S. Elm Valley Rd
Suttons Bay, MI 49682 (231) 271-3522

Acres of grapes: 13

Varieties: 10

First planting: 1973

Varieties of wine: 10 *(all sparkling)*

Top seller: SEX Brut Rose Sparkling Wine

*Larry Mawby during
the busy harvest time
(Courtesy L. Mawby)*

Awards and recognition:
Has won Best in Sparkling Wine Category at Michigan State Fair several times and in the Eastern International Competition. *Wine Enthusiast* magazine ranks L. Mawby in Top 15 sparkling wine producers in N. America.

Winemaker: Larry Mawby

Cases sold per year: 4,000

Owner: Larry Mawby

Winter harvest scene at L. Mawby vineyards in Leelanau County (photo courtesy of L. Mawby)

LEELANAU CELLARS
(www.leelanaucellars.com)
12693 E. Tatch Road (C.R. 626)
Omena, MI   49674   (231) 386-5201

Acres of grapes: 30

Varieties: 11

First planting: 1977

Varieties of wine: 30

Top seller: Late Harvest Reisling

Awards and recognition:
2003 Pinot Grigio, Double Gold Medal, 2004 Great Lakes Wine Competition and Gold/Best of Class at the 2004 Pacific Rim International Wine Competition

Winemaker: Sean Walters

Cases sold per year: 45,000

Owners: Michael & Robert Jacobson

SHADY LANE CELLARS
(www.shadylanecellars.com)
9580 Shady Lane
Suttons Bay, MI 49686   (231) 947-8865

Acres of grapes: 30

Varieties: 4

First planting: 1989

Varieties of wine: 14

Top seller: Serenity White *(house blend)*

Awards and recognition:
'95 Blanc de Blancs – Best of Show at Michigan
State Fair *(Sparkling)*
Semi-dry Reisling, Gold Medal – Michigan State Fair

Winemaker: Adam Satchwell

Cases sold per year: 4,500

Owners: Joe O'Donnell and Bill Stouten

WILLOW VINEYARD
10702 East Hilltop Rd.
Suttons Bay, MI 49682   (231) 271-4810

Acres of grapes: 8

Varieties: 3

First planting: 1992

Varieties of wine: 4

Top seller: Pinot Gris

Awards and recognition:
Pinot Gris, Gold Medal at Michigan State Fair
Invited to Jefferson Cup two years in a row:

Won American Merit Award for Pinot Gris and Chardonnay

Winemaker: John Crampton

Cases sold per year: 1,100

Owners: John and Jo Crampton

Willow Vineyard is Michigan's smallest commercial vineyard.

RAFTSHOL VINEYARDS
1865 N. W. Bayshore Dr.
Suttons Bay, MI 49682 (231) 271-5650

Acres of grapes: 15

Varieties: 6

First planting: 1985

Varieties of wine: 9

Top seller: Raftshol Red

Awards and recognition:
2000 Pinot Noir, Gold Medal and Best of Show *(Red Wine),*
Michigan State Fair

Winemaker: David Gruber

Cases sold per year: 1,000

Owners: Warren Raftshol

WINERIES OF OLD MISSION PENINSULA
(www.wineriesofoldmission.com)

Bowers Harbor Vineyards
Chateau Chantal
Chateau Grand Traverse
Peninsula Cellars

View from Chateau Grand Traverse Vineyards over West Bay (Edward O'Keefe III)

CHATEAU GRAND TRAVERSE
(www.cgtwines.com)
12239 Center Rd.
Traverse City, MI 49686   (231) 223-7355

Acres of grapes: 70

First planting: 1974

Varieties of grapes: 10

Varieties of wine: 32

Best seller: Late Harvest Riesling and Semi dry Riesling

Awards and Recognition:
The **2002 Late Harvest Riesling** won the following:
Double Gold Medal, 2003 San Francisco International Wine Competition
Double Gold Medal, 2003 International Eastern Wine Competition
2002 Semidry Riesling, Chairman's Award, Los Angeles County Fair
2003 Dry Johannisburg Riesling, Gold Medal, San Francisco International Wine Competition
Best of Show-White Wine recognition at Michigan State Fair for **2001 Whole Cluster Riesling Wine** and **Johannisberg Riesling Ice Wine**

Wine Maker: Bernd Croissant

Cases sold per year: 43,500
(2nd largest volume Michigan winery)

Owners: Edward O'Keefe Sr., Edward O'Keefe III, Sean O'Keefe

Chateau Grand Traverse was the first vineyard in northern Michigan, opening in 1974.

CHATEAU CHANTAL
(www.chateauchantal.com)
1500 Rue de Vin
Traverse City, MI 49686   (800) 969-4009

Acres of grapes: 92

First planting: 1986

Varieties of grapes: 7

Varieties of wine: 20

Best seller: Nice Red *(fruity, semi-sweet blend)*

Awards and recognition:
Gold Medals at 2004 Taster's Guild International Wine
Competition for: **Cerise** *(cherry port-style wine)*, **Celebrate!**
(sparkling wine), and **Trio** *(dry red blend)*.

Winemaker: Mark Johnson

BOWERS HARBOR VINEYARDS
(www.bowersharbor.com)

Acres of grapes: 24

First planting: 1990

Varieties of grapes: 8

Varieties of wine: 6-8

Best seller: Riesling and Pinot Grigio

Awards and recognition:
2002 - **2896 Langley** *(Merlot-Cabernet Franc blend)*,
Best of Show - Michigan State Fair

Winemaker: Cornell Olivier, Bernd Croissant, Bryan Ulbrich

Cases sold per year: 6,000

Owners: Jack and Linda Stegenga

PENINSULA CELLARS
(www.peninsulacellars.com)
11480 Center Rd. (M-37)
Traverse City, MI 49686   (231) 933-9787

Acres of grapes: 19

First planting: 1991

Varieties: 9

Varieties of wine: 18, plus some custom wines

Top seller: Riesling

Awards and recognition:
Best White Wine, 2003 International Eastern
Wine Competition
World Riesling Cup, 2003 World Riesling Championships
Best White Wine, 2003 San Francisco International Wine
Competition

Winemaker: Bryan Ulbrich

Cases sold per year: 5,500

Owners: David and Joan Kroupa

NEW WINERIES

Ten years ago there were 12 wineries in Michigan. Today there are over forty with nearly half in northern Michigan. At least three new wineries, under development on old farms, were scheduled to open in spring of 2005.

Brys Estate Vineyard and Winery, owned by former Detroiters, Eileen and Walter Brys, is located on an old cherry farm on the Old Mission Peninsula. They have 20 acres of vines planted, and have hired winemaker, Cornel Olivier – a former intern at Chateau Grand Traverse, with plans of a fall 2005 harvest.

On the Leelanau Peninsula, **Idisor's Choice Winery,** near Cedar, is owned by David Stanton of Jackson, Michigan. 18 acres are planted on the 131-acre farm. First bottles of wine should be produced in 2005. Winemaker is Dough Matthias from Chateau Fontaine.

<u>French Valley Vineyards</u> is on a 75-acre former farm near Lake Leelanau. The husband and wife team of Pam Leonard and Stephen Kozelko will have 12 acres planted by summer of 2005. Charles Edson of nearby Bel Lago handles the winemaking.

CENTENNIAL FARMS

County	Number	Oldest farm	Location
Antrim	23	1864	Jolliffe Rd., Banks Twp.
First owner: John Jolliffe		Current owner: John and Phyllis Elzinga	
Benzie	17	1864	Benzie Blvd., Beulah
First owner: Emory Madison Wellman		Current owner: Arnie Wellman	
		1864	1163 S. Marshall, Beulah
First owner: Ann Marshall		Current owner: Otto and Shirley Edinger	
Charlevoix	18	1857	Beaver Island
First owner: John Bonner		Current owner: Patrick and Rose Bonner	
Clare	8	1870	8360. S. Athey Rd., Clare
First owner: Joseph and Esther Schunk		Current owner: Robert and Fern Williams	

County	Number	Oldest farm	Location
Crawford	2	1887	Co. Rd. 612, Frederic
First owner: Eli Forbush		Current owner: David Forbush	
Emmet	12	1874	US 131 S., Petoskey
First owner: John Coveyou		Current owner: Lawrence and Elsie Fettig	
Gr. Traverse	52	1854	Old Mission Peninsula
First owner: Jerome Pratt		Current owner: Molly Levin	
Kalkaska	13	1859	Williamsburg
First owner: William Copeland		Current owner: Bonnie Krzysik	
		1859	Williamsburg
First owner: William Copeland		Current owner: Richard L. Copelan	
Lake	13	1866	Chase Twp.
First owner: Henry Gaedcke		Current owner: Mrs. John C. Gaedcke	
Leelanau	41	1855	Port Oneida
First owner: Fredrick & Margret Werner		Current owner: Charles & Catherine Miller	
Manistee	45	1847	6504 River Rd., Manistee
First owner: Samuel & Anna Potter		Current owner: Leonard L. Potter	

County	Number	Oldest farm	Location
Mason First owner: Jeremiah & Almanza Phillips	54	1852	Ludington Current owner: Alice L. Hull
Missaukee First owner: Thomas Lutke	16	1873	S. 7 Mile Rd., Marion Current owner: Harvey and Ruth Lutke
Osceola First owner: Henry Bittner	65	1862	200th Ave., Reed City Current owner: Uriah and Margaret Zimmerman
Otsego First owner: Frank Kassuba	1	1882	Kassuba Rd., Gaylord Current owner: Albert and Ann Kassuba
Wexford First owner: Andrew M. Larson First owner: ? First owner: Andrew Gentle	20	1870 1870 Clam 1870 W.	S. 31 Rd., Cadillac Current owner: Vernon D. Larson Lake Twp. Current owner: George Rock M-42, Manton Current owner: Kenneth and Janet Tidey

Michigan Historic Preservation Office

TOURISM

TOURISM SPENDING

| County | Total Tourism Spending (in millions) | | State rank |
	1997	2000	
Grand Traverse	$235	$234.00	07
Emmet	$154	$121.90	15
Charlevoix	$86	$90.10	21
Otsego	$78	$78.90	26
Roscommon	$71	$77.70	28
Antrim	$64	$67.80	31
Clare	$58	$66.30	32
Leelanau	$62	$63.70	34
Mason	$48	$62.30	35
Benzie	$71	$58.80	40
Wexford	$46	$50.10	42
Crawford	$44	$45.10	48
Lake	$39	$43.70	50
Manistee	$39	$42.10	52
Kalkaska	$25	$28.60	67
Osceola	$26	$27.70	69
Missaukee	$18	$21.80	78

Types of Tourist Spending

Michigan State University breaks down tourist spending into five categories:

Motel visits – visitors who stay overnight in hotels, motels, cabins, B&B's and related lodging

Camp – Guests who stay overnight in campgrounds, public or private.

Seasonal homes – Parties who spend overnights in seasonal homes.

Friends and relatives – Parties who spend overnights with friends or relatives.

Day trips – Visitors from outside the area (50 miles or more) who do not stay overnight.

In northern Michigan, Grand Traverse County has the highest spending from motel visitors – nearly three times the amount of 2nd-ranked Emmet County.

Mason County, with beautiful Ludington State Park, leads in the category of camper spending.

Roscommon County, with many second homes on the big lakes, has the highest spending from visitors in seasonal homes.

Traverse City residents are used to entertaining family and friends during the summer months, which helps explain the large margin it has in tourist spending from those people in the guest bedroom.

And, when it comes to tourist spending from visitors who don't spend the night, Crawford County leads the way, probably due to its convenient location on I-75, fishing trips to the Au Sable, and Hartwick Pines State Park.

County	Motel visits	Camping	Seasonal home residents	Visits with Friends and relatives	Day trips
Antrim	26.3	1.9	26.0	5.9	7.7
Benzie	25.5	2.4	16.0	4.1	10.9
Charlevoix	46.5	1.7	22.1	6.6	13.1
Clare	7.8	5.8	43.3	7.9	2.0
Crawford	11.2	5.9	20.7	3.6	45.1
Emmet	59.7	3.7	25.4	8.0	25.2
Grand Traverse	154.2	6.5	15.3	19.7	38.4
Kalkaska	2.6	1.2	19.3	4.2	1.3
Lake	1.4	3.1	35.6	2.9	0.8
Leelanau	26.2	3.8	20.7	5.4	7.6
Manistee	10.3	4.4	17.6	6.2	3.6
Mason	23.2	7.9	19.0	7.2	5.0
Missaukee	0.9	2.0	14.3	3.7	0.8
Osceola	0.4	3.5	17.0	5.9	1.0
Otsego	40.0	2.5	19.2	5.9	11.3
Roscommon	7.8	4.9	55.9	6.5	2.7
Wexford	19.3	6.4	11.1	7.7	5.6

Number of Rooms in Commercial Lodging Establishments (2000)

Grand Traverse	3,500
Emmet	2,043
Otsego	1,513
Charlevoix	997
Mason	992
Antrim	912
Roscommon	845
Manistee	703
Benzie	684
Wexford	663
Crawford	659
Leelanau	534
Clare	429
Kalkaska	136
Lake	115
Missaukee	61
Osceola	50
17-county total	**14,836**

Source: MSU Tourism Resource Cener, Tourism Profile, 2000

Historic Hotels, Inns and B&B's

Park Place – Traverse City
This downtown Traverse City landmark opened in 1873 as the Campbell House. Henry Campbell built the hotel two years after establishing the region's first stagecoach line, which served most of northern Michigan. He sold the hotel in 1879 to the Hannah, Lay & Co., which renamed it the Park Place Hotel. In 1930 a new owner, R. Floyd Clinch, added the tower, which expanded the hotel from 50 to 121 rooms. The dome, annex and pool were added in 1964 under the ownership of Eugene Power, who renamed it the Park Place Motor Inn.

In 1988, Indiana businessman Arthur Curry purchased the struggling hotel and the Perry Davis in Petoskey. He promised major renovations, but his cash flow didn't keep up with his ambition. In a bizarre turn of events, Curry was convicted of kidnapping a wealthy Bloomington, Indiana woman as a means of raising capital.

The decaying hotel, seen as a city landmark and key to a successful downtown shopping district was saved in 1989 when the Traverse City Rotary Club purchased it and invested millions in its restoration. Today it is operated by Regency Hotel Management.

Stafford's Perry Davis – Petoskey
Built in 1899 by former dentist Norman J. Perry, who gave up the profession after a patient died in his chair. The Hotel Perry was the first brick hotel in Petoskey, and the only one left standing of the twenty that were open in 1900. In 1919, Perry sold to doctors John and George Reycraft who wanted to convert it to a hospital. They were talked out of that, and

in 1926 their nephew built a four-story addition. Auto executive John R. Davis purchased the hotel in 1961 and changed the name to the Perry-Davis Hotel. Alan Gornick owned the Perry in the 1970's, and in 1988 it was sold to Arthur Curry, whose ambitious renovation plans were cut short by a bizarre kidnapping plot. (See Park Place Hotel.) Since 1989 Stafford's Hospitality has owned and operated it as Stafford's Perry Hotel.

The Doherty Hotel – Clare

Former Senator Alfred J. Doherty built this four-story hotel in 1924 anticipating the popularity of the automobile. Unlike earlier hotels built near railroad stops, the Doherty was built in the center of town. The original hotel included 60 rooms, a coffee shop, the Wedgewood Room for dining, a soda fountain, barbership, the Clare Public Library and Senator Doherty's office.

The rich history of the Doherty includes the 1938 murder of Isaiah Leebove, the chairman of the Mammoth Oil Company. He was gunned down as he dined in the grillroom by Jack Livingston, an oil promoter who lived at the Doherty. Attorney Byron Goller, who was with Leebove, survived after being shot twice by Leebove.

Now under the guidance of the 4th generation of Doherty's, the hotel has 157 guest rooms and there are plans to add a 10,000 square foot conference center.

Old Mission Inn – Traverse City

Continually operated as a hotel since it was built in 1869 as Hedden Hall. The original owner, George Hedden, ran the local post office from the inn. From 1902 to 45 it was owned by Alfred and Ella Porter, and renamed the Porter House.

Under the ownership of Norman and Doris Nevinger between 1945 and 98 indoor plumbing and electricity was installed. They also opened a restaurant to service summer residents and visitors to the beach across the street. In 1998, Angie and Bruce Jensen bought the inn and began an intensive restoration project. The inn features a 100-foot front porch overlooking the large lawn and Old Mission harbor. Among the names signed on the old guest registers: Babe Ruth!

Stafford's Bay View Inn – Petoskey

The historic inn somehow manages to stand out from the colorful, perfectly preserved Victorian homes that surround it in the Bay View

Baseball Hall of Famer, Babe Ruth once stayed at the Old Mission Inn (Author photo)

Association. Opened in 1886 as the Woodland Avenue House, it included 16 guest rooms and dining room. Within a few years it was renamed the Howard House after owner J.W. Howard, whose name remains laid in stained glass over the front entrance. By the mid 1890's he had added a shuffleboard court, porches, more dining space and a larger lobby, resulting in the new name: The New Howard Hotel.

Between 1901 and 1918 the hotel went through a series of owners until the bank foreclosed on it. Two former managers, Horace Rose and Harry F. Bart, bought the inn, changing its name to the Hotel Roselawn. They added 30 new rooms, and went bankrupt in the process. The next owner, Mr. Arthur Twarz, named it the Bay View Inn, and ran it until 1952 when he sold to Dr. Roy Heath. The Heath family operated the Bay View Inn for eight years before selling in 1961 to former desk clerk Stafford Smith. At 22, he became the youngest hotel owner in Western Michigan. Together with his wife Janice, the Stafford added central heat and private baths for every guest room. They continue as innkeepers today.

Walloon Lake Inn –
Walloon Lake
Just after the turn of the cen-

tury the Fern Cottage opened on the shore of Walloon Lake. For years guests arrived by steamboat, with a dock at waters edge. Today the Walloon Lake Inn caters to many regulars who return each year to the quaint lakeside inn recently named by *Traveler* magazine as one of its "Best Kept Secrets."

Terrace Inn (Bay View) –
Petoskey
The Terrace Inn is situated within the community of Bay View on a natural terrace overlooking Little Traverse Bay. Built in 1911, it is included with the other Bay View homes and structures as a National Historic Landmark. The Terrace Inn is the only building in Bay View that remains open during the winter months. Under the ownership of Mo and Patty Rave since 2004.

Fountain Point Resort –
Lake Leelanau
Opened as a resort in 1889 on the shore of Lake Leelanau next to a rushing spring. It started in 1860 when Anrdre de Beloit, a French fur trader, used an archaic apparatus to drill for oil. He never found the Texas Tea, but in 1867, at about 900 feet, he hit a geyser of water, hence the name Fountain Point.

In 1889, Mrs. Lydia Morrison of Cincinnati opened the Fountain Point House as a resort. She sold it in 1812 to Albert Meafoy, who upgraded and added cottages. Since 1936 the resort has been under the ownership of the Gebhardt family. The original white clapboard hotel building and cottages have been continually updated and well maintained to the point it was placed on the National Registry of Historic Places in 2003.

The Canfield House – Portage Lake
Built in 1900 as a summer home for a lumber baron, the Canfield House sits on 20 feet of Portage Lake shoreline and just steps from Lake Michigan. Completely renovated in 1998.

Wellington Inn – Traverse City
Built in 1895 by William Cary Hull, son of the owner of the Oval Wooden Dish Company, one of Travese City's largest employers at that time. The company relocated to New York in 1915, and in the 1920's the large Hull home was split into four separate living units. In the late 1990's, a Traverse City police officer was fatally shot on the home's front porch as he negotiated with a resident. The home sat empty until 1999 when Barb and Hank Rishel purchased it. Ignoring advice to tear it down rather than restore, the couple invested four years and substantial financial assets to bring it back to its original state. The Hull house has been open since 2003 as the Wellington Inn B & B.

Stonewall Inn – Frankfort
Built as the first home to show any sense of architectural design in Benzie County, the grand Victorian Italianate house was built in 1860 by the Frankfort Land Company. Owners Dave and Sandy Jackson have taken great care in restoring the home and take pride in its Civil War theme featuring many antique furnishings from the Civil War. Listed on the National Register of Historic Places in 1995.

Portage Point Inn – Onekama
Opened in 1903 as a summer resort for the Portage Point Assembly consisting of families primarily from the Chicago and Milwaukee areas. Like other northern Michigan resorts of the early 20th century it was marketed for health reasons, offering fresh air breezes from the big lake and healing mineral springs. Listed among its early clientele are writers Orson Welles and William Shirer, and rumors persist that the notorious Chicago gangster, Al

Capone, used the Portage Point Inn for R & R.

Several different owners operated the inn during the 1920's and 30's, including John Blodgett, who renamed it the Blodgett Inn. For most of the 1940's and 50's it was run by J.J. Smith, who also owned the Piney Ridge Resort on Hamlin Lake near Ludington. The Portage Point Inn changed hands several times over the next few decades until 1988 when the IRS foreclosed on it. The complex of buildings was added to the National Register of Historic Places in 1985, and today is known as the Portage Point Inn – Historic Inn & Yacht Club. Today Northwoods Development, headed by Michael and Jane DeVoe of Indianapolis, are the current owners.

Riverside Inn – Leland

In 1902 sawmill owner Jacob Schwarz built the Riverside Inn to take advantage of the growing tourist trade. By 1924 Schwarz and his wife had died, leaving the property to their daughters, who were in charge when fire destroyed the inn in 1924. Without skipping a beat the family set up innkeeping in the dancehall Schwarz had built on the banks of the Leland River. A second story was added to accommodate more guests, and the inn remained under the same management until 1957.

Since 1997 the mother-daughter team of Barb and Kate Vilter have owned and operated the Riverside, adding improvements and restorations to the five guest rooms over the Riverside Inn dining room on the Leland River.

The Inn at Watervale – Benzie County

The Inn and associated clapboard cottages with screened porches that overlook the beach are all part of the Watervale Historic District. This former sawmill town on the shore of Lower Herring Lake near Lake Michigan was established in the early 1890's. After the mill shutdown, Dr. Oscar Kraft of Chicago bought the land for a family vacation retreat, then in 1917 turned it into a resort. Today it includes an 18-room hotel and a dozen cottages. The Watervale Historic District includes 24 buildings on 225 acres on the southern edge of Lower Herring Lake.

Schoenberger House – Ludington

Another former lumber baron home, this one a 1903 neoclassical mansion. Owned by the Schoenberger family for over fifty years, the B & B features intricate woodwork, extravagant chandeliers, five fireplaces and a library. Featured in *Historic Homes of America* and *Grand Homes of the Midwest.*

Neahtawanta Inn Bed and Breakfast – Traverse City
Opened in 1906 as the Sunrise Inn on Bowers Harbor on Old Mission Peninsula. The first innkeeper was still running the operation when she died in 1970 at the age of 99. Since 1985 it's been under the ownership of Bob Russell and Sally Van Vleck. Features a 44-foot front porch, 325 feet on Bowers Harbor, and organic breakfasts.

Hanson House B & B – Grayling
The lumber baron Rasmus Hanson, who donated land for Hanson Hills Recreation Area and Camp Grayling, had this home built in 1881 for his wife, Margrethe. Its architectural highlights include: hand-painted murals from 1892, three ornately carved fireplaces, antique Roman tile, and plenty of beveled and stained glass. The home, which offers four guest rooms and a Bridal Suite, is in pristine condition. Owned and operated by Dave and Jill Wyman.

Sylvan Inn – Glen Arbor
Opened in 1885 as a hotel for lumbermen and ship workers, the Sylvan Inn retains its historic architecture, including the wraparound porch. Operated by Ralph & Rose Gladfelter.

Nationally Historic Resort – Idlewild
Located in the heart of Lake County, near Baldwin, Idlewild was founded at the start of the 20th century when developers purchased 2,700 acres around Idlewild Lake. Two businessmen from White Cloud saw a demand from upwardly mobile African-American families for vaction property since segregation prevented them from enjoying established resorts.

Original lots were marketed in Chicago, Detroit, Cleveland, and other Midwestern cities. The original $35 dollar price was a good investment as the Idlewild's popularity grew quickly. During its heyday between 1930 and the 1950's an average of 22,000 people summered at the Lake County resort.

During the 1920's Idlewild was given a major boost when W.E.B. Dubois purchased lots at Idlewild. The NAACP founder and first African-American Ph.D. graduate of Harvard, often wrote of the resort and its value to

Bathing beach at Idlewild Resort near Baldwin

the African-American society. Another prominent citizen at that time was Dr. Daniel Hale Williams, who in 1893 performed the first successful open heart surgery. He was the only African-American doctor among the 100 charter members of the American College of Surgeons. His presence at Idlewild brought credibility and investors.

Idlewild is probably best known for its entertainment. Starting the 1930's through the Civil Rights Movement of the 1960's the top entertainers in the country performed at Idlewild. Many, including several Motown greats, actually got their start at Idlewild. On any given night during the summer any one of the following were found performing or vacationing at Idlewild: Sarah Vaughan, Cab Calloway, Louis Armstrong, Della Reese, Dinah Washington, B.B. King, The Four Tops, Aretha Franklin, Sammy Davis, Bill Cosby, T-Bone Walker and Fats Waller, to name a few.

During this time several prominent African-Americans bought homes at Idlewild. Among the most popular was boxing legend Joe Louis who spent a lot of time at the resort.

By the mid sixties African-American artists were afforded the opportunity to perform at

traditional white-only resorts. Eventually all African-Americans under the Civil Rights Movement were allowed to vacation at these resorts, and Idlewild lost its allure. By the 1980's it became virtually a ghost town, riddled with poverty and drugs. Recently there has been a movement to restore and reclaim Idlewild's rich heritage. Several African-American developers have been working to restore the community. Regardless of its future, Idlewild will forever be remembered as the country's most important African-American cultural community and for giving the world some of the best entertainers it has known.

D.H. Day Estates: The Summer White House?

David Henry (D.H.) Day and a group of investors began work in 1922 on a resort overlooking Lake Michigan and Glen Lake. Day Forest Estates was to include an 18-hole golf course, polo field, tennis courts, toboggan runs and other recreational attractions. Home sites of five acres and larger were platted out, a road was built to the top of Alligator Hill, and work began on the golf course.

The resort was marketed as an exclusive playground with uncomparable views, and it was touted as a possible permanent summer home for the president of the United States. However, the Great Depression spoiled the grand plans, and the resort never materialized.

In 1950, lumberman Pierce Stocking bought the property and created a park, which included a winding road through the forest and dunes overlooking Lake Michigan. In the late 1970's the property was acquired as part of the Sleeping Bear Dunes National Lakeshore, and the 14-miles of scenic road are now known as the Pierce Stocking Scenic Drive.

Royal Frontenac Hotel– Frankfort

Built in 1900 on the shore of Lake Michigan in Frankfort by the same man who built the Grand Hotel on Mackinac Island. Like the Grand, the hotel was built by a railroad – the Ann Arbor Railroad – to bring tourists north. The three-story Frontenac had 250 rooms, wrap around porches at every level, beautiful views, fresh air, mineral springs, and plenty of recreation.

To the shock of Frankfort citizens, on January 12, 1912, the landmark hotel burned to the ground. Arson was suspected, although no cause was ever established.

A MONUMENT TO TOURISM

One of the most unusual monuments in the state is a rock pile on the 45th parallel overlooking US 31 in Antrim County. The cairn, made up of 83 rocks - one from each county - is a monument to Hugh J. Gray of Grand Rapids, regarded in some circles as the "father of tourism."

Gray worked for the Pere Marquette Railroad in Grand Rapids and Chicago until 1917, when resort operators in west Michigan asked him to promote Michigan as a tourist destination. As manager of the West Michigan Tourist and Resort Association he worked at first without pay, and eventually earned a small salary.

Under Gray the association spread promotional literature to points in Detroit, Cincinnati, Chicago, Cleveland, Ft. Wayne, Indianapolis and other metro towns of the Midwest. By the 1940's Michigan's tourism industry was bringing $400 million into the state, a credit to Gray's efforts. He also helped establish the boundary lines for the Manistee National Forest, and obtained an annual budget from the legislature to promote Michigan as a tourist destination.

The plaque on the cairn honoring Hugh J. Gray's contributions to tourism in West Michigan (Author photo)

Monument to tourism: Cairn on 45th parallel near Kewadin (Author photo)

The Cairn

Location: Cairn Highway, one-and-a-half miles north of Kewadin, east from US 31 N. *(Near the 45th parallel)* When the cairn was built this was US 31, but in 1955 a new segment of highway opened north of Elk Rapids. Cairn Highway, lined with orchards and old farms, is little traveled today.

Designer: Phillip Troeger, chief landscape architect for the State Highway Dept.
Dedication date: June 28, 1938
Height: 16 ft.
Weight: 17,000 lbs.
Base: 12 feet square

Cost: $306, paid by Antrim County. The Pennsylvania Railroad and Pere Marquette Railroad hauled stones from all over the state to Traverse City at no charge. Petoskey Cement Co. donated the cement. The flagpole was a gift from the citizens of Elk Rapids, and Traverse City Light and Power installed it at no charge.

Heaviest stone: Midland County's stone weighs over 800 pounds.

Last stone to arrive: Gladwin County's arrived eight days before the dedication.

Unusual stones: Wexford County's rock is actually a two by two foot piece of hardened rubber, symbolic of the prominent rubber industry in Cadillac.

Emmet County's stone is actually from Brunswick, Georgia. It originally lay at the foot of the tree where John Wesley preached his first sermon. The A.L. Duell family of Harbor Springs donated it to the cairn project.

Grand Traverse County's rock has a raised image of Chief Pontiac on its face. The A.W. Rickerd Monument Works of Traverse City etched the words "Grand Traverse" in an arc over Pontiac's head. The rock came from the William Love farm near Yuba.

There's a small road next to the cairn so drivers can pull off the highway. A plaque on the cairn displays and image of and dedication to Hugh J. Gray.

A crypt beneath the plaque contains newspapers and tourist literature from 1938.

TOP 5 SUMMER DRIVING DESTINATIONS

1. Mackinaw City
2. Traverse City
3. Ludington
4. Sault Ste. Marie
5. St. Ignace

AAA Michigan, Michigan Living Magazine

TOP TOURIST ATTRACTIONS IN EACH COUNTY
(event or permanent attraction)

Antrim

Harbor Days – Elk Rapids
Chain O'Lakes (Elk Rapids to Bellaire)
Shanty Creek-Schuss Mountain
White Pine Stampede
Mancelona Bass Festival
Jordan Valley Park
Grace Memorial Harbor
(220 slips)
Deadman's Hill Scenic
Overlook – Fall Colors

Deteriorating Antrim County rock in touism cairn (Author photo)

Benzie

Sleeping Bear National
Lakeshore
Pt. Betsie Lighthouse
Platte River Campgrounds
Coho Festival and fishing– Honor
Cherry Hut
Frankfort Beach
Gwen Frostic Studio
Crystal Mountain Golf
and Skiing
Michigan Legacy Art Park
Betsie Valley Trail, 23 miles on
former Ann Arbor Railroad
corridor from Elberta to
Beulah and T'ville
Canoeing Betsie and Platte
rivers

Benzie County rock in tourism cairn (Author photo)

Charlevoix

Boyne Mountain Resort
Apple Festival
Venetian Festival
Horton Bay 4th of July Parade
Fisherman's Island State Park
National Morel Mushroom
Festival – Boyne City
Lake Charleoix
Beaver Island

Charlevoix County rock in tourism cairn (Author photo)

Clare

St. Patrick's Day celebration
Wilson State Park
Fishing and Hunting

Clare County rock at top of tourism cairn (Author photo)

Crawford

Au Sable River Canoe
Marathon
Fly fishing
Snowmobiling-Frederick
Cross-Country skiing
Forbush Corners
Hartwick Pines State Park
Grayling Fish Hatchery

Crawford County rock in tourism cairn (Author photo)

Emmet

Bay Harbor
Gaslight District– Petoskey
Boyne Highlands
Nub's Nob
Wilderness State Park
Petoskey State Park
Mackinaw City
Ft. Michilmackinac
Mackinac Island ferries

Emmet County rock in tourism cairn (Author photo)

Grand Traverse

Grand Traverse Resort
National Cherry Festival
Traverse City State Park
Interlochen State Park
Interlochen Summer Arts
Festival
Tall Ships
Dennos Museum
Downtown Traverse City
Turtle Creek Casinos
Old Mission wineries
Boardman River

Grand Traverse rock with Chief Pontiac (Author photo)

Kalkaska

National Trout Festival
Fishing and hunting

Kalkaska rock at base of tourism cairn (Author photo)

Lake

Irons Flea Roast and Ox
Market
Shrine of the Pines
Blessing of the Bikes
Hunting and fishing

Lake County rock at base of tourism cairn (Author photo)

Leelanau

Sleeping Bear Dunes
Suttons Bay Jazz Festival
Leland Wine Festival
Fishtown
Homestead Resort
Leelanau State Park and G.T.
Lighthouse
Leelanau wineries
Leelanau Sands Casino

Leelanau County rock in tourism cairn (Author photo)

Manistee

Riverwalk
Manistee Huron Forest Festival
Ramsdell Theatre
Orchard Beach State Park

Fishing
City of Milwaukee Ferry

Manistee County rock in tourism cairn (Author photo)

Mason

Ludington State Park
Nordhouse Dunes
White Pine Village

Barely legible Mason County rock at base of tourism cairn (Author photo)

Missaukee

Greatest 4th in the North
(Lake City)
Lake Missaukee

Missaukee County rock in tourism cairn (Author photo)

Osceola

Pere Marquette and
White Pine trails
Dulcimer Festival *(Evart)*

*Osceola County rock in tourism cairn
(Author photo)*

Otsego

Otsego State Park
Hidden Valley Resort
Golf Trail Gaylord
Alpenfest
Otsego Lake

*Otsego County rock in tourism cairn
(Author photo)*

Roscommon

Houghton Lake
Higgins Lake State Parks
Fishing and boating
Fireman's Memorial

*Roscommon County rock in tourism
cairn (Author photo)*

Wexford

Chestnut Festival
North American Snowmobile
Festival
Mitchell State Park
Carl T. Johnson Center
Mesick Mushroom Festival
Lake Mitchell and Cadillac

*Wexford County rock in tourism cair.
(Author photo)*

NATIONAL CHERRY FESTIVAL
TRAVERSE CITY

Northern Michigan's largest festival runs for eight days every July just before harvest time. It started back on May 22, 1925 as the Blessing of the Blossoms to celebrate the fruit that gave Traverse City the title of "Cherry Capital of the World." The event included a parade and the crowning of the first Cherry Queen on a Friday. The actual blessing of the blossoms was offered up on Sunday.

The start of the 2004 Cherry Royale Parade (courtesy of National Cherry Festival)

The following year the event received national attention when it was captured on film by a newsreel service.

In 1927 the local cherry crop was damaged by a late frost, so a festival wasn't held.

1926 Blessing of the Blossoms parade on Front St. (courtesy of G.T. Pioneer & Historical Society)

In 1928 the event was moved to July, and renamed the Michigan Cherry Festival.

In 1931 the first National Cherry Festival was held and attracted a crowd of 100,000 for the Grand Parade. Seven ships from the U.S. Navy Great Lakes training fleet sailed into West Bay as part of the festival program.

Traverse City Record Eagle editor, Jay P. Smith is credited as one of the founders of the Cherry Festival, and served as its first Chairman in 1925 (courtesy of G.T. Pioneer & Historical Society)

US Navy Blue Angel over West Grand Traverse Bay 2004 (courtesy National Cherry Festival)

In 1949 the Festival Air Show featured military jets – four F-80's from Selfridge Air Base.

In 1978, the U.S. Navy Blue Angels made their first of many appearances at the National Cherry Festival. The Blue Angels Precision Flight Team appeared at the Festival in: 1988, 1992, 1994, 1996, 1998, 2000, 2002, and 2004.

The traditional military visit continues today in the form of the annual Festival Air Show, highlighted every other year by the U.S. Navy Blue Angels.

In 1935, the first aerial event took place at the National Cherry Festival – a skywriter buzzed overhead spelling out "Chevrolet" with the exhaust from his plane.

In 1936, the first festival airshow included the queen and her court arriving in seven separate planes. Military aircraft from the Selfridge Air Base put on a show later in the day.

Due to World War II the Festival was not held from 1942-47.

In 1948, the Festival Air show featured a Coast Guard float plane in a rescue demonstration on West Bay and an Army aircraft searchlight which tracked a plane flying at 20,000 feet.

In 1982, brothers John and David Williams begin a tradition that lasts 20 years – sneaking a spoof float into the Cherry Royale Parade. The first float featured the Hay Fever Queen, Anna Histemann. The queen and her court, seated on bales of hay, stopped every five minutes along the parade route to sneeze in unison. Other Williams brothers' floats over the years have included: The Weber Precision Grill Team; the Speed Queen float featuring the queen and her court seated on, or in washing machines followed by the world's longest human clothesline; the world's largest marching cow pasture; an Egyptian themed entry featuring the Queen of De-Nile, and the last entry in 2002 was entitled, "Definitely Not the Williams Brothers." The simple entry was two women dressed like Venus and Serena Williams waving to the crowd from the back of a convertible.

Annual attendance:
500,000+ over eight days

Financial impact: Pumps
$26,000,000 into local
economy each year

National Cherry Festival
spends over $1,000,000
annually with local vendors
from paper supply companies
to insurance companies to
porta-jons, etc.

Program: 150 events and
activities (85% are free)

*Cherry pit-spitting event with one
of the Cherry Festival Princes(courtesy of National Cherry Festival)*

Mission of Festival: To promote the cherry industry, promote tourism and community
involvement, and to cultivate
the business, entertainment,
and cultural interests of the
Grand Traverse region.

Operation: Minimum of
35,000 volunteer hours and
10,000 staff hours
There are nearly 1,000
Cherry Festival volunteers in
the Ambassador Program.

RECOGNITION

Annually rated in top 100
Festivals and Events in North
America by the A.B.A.

Named Michigan's Favorite
Festival by AAA Michigan
Living Magazine –

**Special guests and dignitaries:
Spencer Christian, ABC's
Good Morning America
Weatherman** – 1989, 1993
and 1998
**Phoenix Suns Dan
Majerle**–1991
U.S. Navy Blue Angels–
1988, 1992, 1994, 1996,
1998, 2000, 2002, 2004
**Former Astronaut James
Lovell** --1985
Budweiser Clydesdales –
1984, 1996
**Today Show Weatherman
Willard Scott** – 1983
**Hockey great Gordie
Howe** –1982
**U.S. Air Force
Thunderbirds** – 1978,
1990
Bob Hope – 1978
Arthur Godfrey – 1952
President Gerald R. Ford –
1975
Boxer Joe Louis – 1941

Special Kids: Only event like
it in the Midwest -- allows
mentally and physically chal-
lenged kids to take part in all
types of activities: free hot air
balloon rides, elephant rides,
and the carnival midway,
"fun and games" program.

NATIONAL CHERRY QUEENS

1935 National Cherry Queen and her Court (courtesy of G.T. Pioneery & Historical Society)

There have been 74 queens since Gertrude Brown, a Traverse City High School senior, was selected at the first Blessing of the Blossoms Festival in 1925.

Of the 74 Queens...

23 were from Traverse City
3 from Gaylord
2 queens each from: Elk Rapids, Charlevoix, Boyne City, Frankfort, Manistee, Cadillac, Reed City, Alpena, and Battle Creek

The first queen was chosen by pulling names from a hat. The following year queen candidate's photos were published in the Traverse City *Record Eagle,* and the winner was selected by popular ballot.

The only foreigner ever to wear the National Cherry Queen crown was Christine Michels of Chile in 1941. Her father was the Chilean Ambassador and good friends with Senator Arthur Vandenberg, who may have pulled some strings for his friend's daughter.

White House Visits
The 1932 Cherry Queen, 17-year-old Carolyn Hazzard of Ludington, traveled to the White House where she presented a large cherry pie to President Herbert Hoover.

In 1937, Cherry Queen Eliene Lyon of Old Mission delivered a pie to President Roosevelt at the White House.

FDR received an 80-pound pie the following year from Queen Josephine LaFranier.

In 1939, Queen Jean Halmond of Leland visited the White House dropping off a 50-pound cherry pie and enjoying a quick visit with President Roosevelt.

Courtesy of Larry Wakefield

WATER PARKS

It seems water park mania has hit northern Michigan with four parks open, and at least two others proposed. It all started in 2003 with the opening of **The Great Wolf Lodge in Traverse City.** The giant log cabin-like resort offers a 38,000 square foot indoor water park highlighted by the following:

- Eight waterslides
- Five pools
- 4-story interactive tree house water fort
- 1,000 gallon bucket that spills water from four stories above
- Two whirlpools
- An outdoor pool and spa
- 3-D theatre
- Two themed restaurants

Owned and operated by Great Wolf Resorts, Inc. the largest owner and developer of drive-to family resorts featuring indoor water parks. As of 2005 they own and operate seven indoor water park resorts.

NASDAQ: WOLF

On the web:
www.greatwolresorts.com

Avalanche Bay Indoor Water Park – Boyne Mountain
Billing itself as Michigan's largest indoor water park, Avalanche Bay opened Memorial Day 2005 with 88,000 square feet at the new Mountain Grand Lodge. Avalanche Bay offers the following in a Swiss-Austrian themed village:

- Multi-level play structure with water sprays and an 800-gallon avalanche of water that dumps on swimmers below
- The Cannonbowl sends riders round and round, faster and faster into the pool below
- Indoor surfing on the Rip Zone
- For tubers, the Boyne River flows through the entire park
- Several waterslides including water toboggans and the Super G

On the web:
www.avalanchebay.com
Owned by Boyne USA Resorts and New Frontiers Capital, LLC.

Here it comes! 1,000 gallons of water (courtesy of Great Wolf Lodge, Traverse City)

Aqua-Grand Mackinaw Inn and Water Park–Mackinac City

The only indoor water park in Mackinaw City, the Aqua-Grand is on a smaller scale than the mega water parks like the Great Wolf and Avalanche Bay. With over 5,000 square feet it offers:

- Water cannons and geysers
- Dump buckets
- Large jacuzzi
- Two indoor pools

On the web:
www.grandmackinaw.com

Thunder Falls Family Water Park–Mackinaw City

This outdoor only water park on 20 acres features the following:

- 12 waterslides
- Large wave pool with four foot waves
- A lazy river for floating
- Comfort-heated water

The Water Playground – Crystal Mountain Resort

This outdoor fun pool opened in the summer of 2004. It features lots of spraying water, water cannons, a water slide, and a multi-level play unit that includes a water dump. On over an acre it includes a 4,200 square foot pool with special features for children of all ages.

Proposed water parks:

Glacier Bay–Elmwood Township adjacent to Traverse City.
This ambitious project calls for a 200,000 square foot outdoor water park and an 80,000 square foot water park in Phase I. Later phases would include two more water parks, all as part of a $100 million dollar development that includes a hotel, several hundred condo units, golf course, riding stables, and two restaurants.

Developers: Owners of the Wilderness Resort in Wisconsin Dells, Wisconsin.

Wild Buffalo Lodge–Blair Township (south of Traverse City).
To be located just a few miles south of the Great Wolf Lodge in Traverse City. Developers plan a 61,000 square foot indoor water park to include a three-story water slide and wave pool. The proposal also calls for 170+ condo units, some of which would be rented as hotel units.

Michigan is third nationally in water park development.

MACKINAC ISLAND

One of America's favorite summer vacation spots: famous for fudge, motorless streets, the Grand Hotel, and storybook Victorian cottages. Michigan's top summer vacation destination has thrived on tourism since the 1880's when the Grand Hotel was built. Visitors can rent a bicycle, a horse-pulled carriage, or walk to the island's favorite attractions, most of which bring alive the history of Mackinac Island long before it became a destination of leisure.

Mackinac: Named by Indians

Many writers claim the name Michilimackinac comes from the Chippewa word, Mi-she-mi-ki-nock, roughly translated as "tremendous mud turtle." The common story is that the Indians believed the island looked like a large turtle rising out of the water. Native American writer and historian, Andrew J. Blackbird, considers this tale to be false.

In his *History of the Ottawa and Chippewa Indians of Michigan*, Blackbird writes of an ancient tribe of Indians who fished the waters of the Straits and lived on Mackinac Island during the warm months. The tribe was nearly annihilated by the Seneca tribe of New York. Two members of the Straits tribe managed to survive the attack by hiding in island caves. This ancient tribe was named Mi-shi-ne-macki-naw-go by modern Ottawa and Chippewa leaders, and from that comes Michilimackinac, and eventually, Mackinac.

As far as we know, the first European to encounter Mackinac Island was the French explorer, Jean Nicolet, who in 1634 paddled his canoe from the east into the Straits, possibly stopping for a breather on the island, before continuing west to discover Lake Michigan. By the mid 1600's French priests were establishing missions in the Straits and the first military fort was built.

There would be a military presence on Mackinac Island for most of the following 200 years.

Timeline of Mackinac Region

1634	Nicolet becomes first European on record to enter the Straits.
1650's	French Jesuit missionaries plant first lilacs on Mackinac Island. These are first lilacs planted on American soil.
1670	Father Claude Dablon spent the winter on Mackinac Island. He built a chapel out of bark and ministered to the Indians. (A replica of this chapel is open to visitors.)
1671	Father Jacques Marquette establishes mission at modern day St. Ignace.
1673	Father Marquette leaves the mission with explorer, Louis Joliet, to explore the Mississippi River. Marquette becomes ill on the return trip and dies at Ludington or Frankfort.
1677	Marquette buried at St. Ignace. *A statue of Father Marquette stands in Marquette Park, dedicated in 1909, just beneath Fort Mackinac.*
1679	The *Griffin*, the first commercial sailing ship on the Great Lakes, reaches the Straits.
1690	French build Fort DeBaude at St. Ignace. It is later abandoned.
1701	First fur trading post built on Mackinac Island.
1715	French build Fort Michilimackinac at present day Mackinaw City.
1761	British take over the Fort Michilimackinac following the French and Indian War.
1763	Massacre at Fort Michilimackinac. Angry

	Chippewas, led by Chief Pontiac, kill nearly all of the British soldiers at the fort. At least one survivor taken to Mackinac Island and hidden away in Skull Cave. British regain control the following year.
1781	During Revolutionary War, British move fort to a more secure location on Mackinac Island, and rename it Fort Mackinac. Island purchased from Chippewas for 5,000 pounds.
1780's	Island is becoming important link in the growing fur industry. French trappers and Indians sell their pelts to traders who ship them to Montreal, bound for Europe. The beaver, fox, and rabbit furs are coveted for hats and coats.
1783	Revolutionary War ends. British refuse to give up Fort Mackinac.
1795	British finally vacate Fort Mackinac and turn it over to Americans.
1809	John Jacob Astor opens fur trading post on Mackinac Island.
1812	War of 1812 breaks out. British troops from St. Joseph Island, armed with cannons, sneak on to Mackinac Island at night, gain high ground, and force Americans to surrender the island.
1814	American naval forces fail in attempt to take back island. 64 casualties recorded.
1815	War of 1812 ends. British hand over Fort Mackinac to Americans.
1817	John Jacob Astor builds the Stuart House, headquarters for his American Fur Company. *(Now a museum.)* Astor dominated the fur trade after buying British-owned trading posts. After the War of

Soldiers at Fort Mackinac (courtesy of Travel Michigan)

	1812 Congress limited trade with Indians to U.S.– owned companies.
1819	First steamboat on the Great Lakes, the *Walk-in-the-Water*, stops at Mackinac Island.
1822	American Fur Co. does $3,000,000 in business, its best year. As furs were depleted, the industry declined. After 1850 the economy on Mackinac Island was centered on fishing.
1829	Mission Church, first Protestant church on Mackinac Island, built.
1838	Indian Dormitory built on Mackinac Island by Federal Government.
1881	Ferry service to Mackinac Island is started by the Arnold family.
	Doud's Mercantile store opens. Today it's believed to be the oldest family-owned grocery store in Michigan.
1887	Grand Hotel built by railroad and steamship interests.
1894	Remaining troops leave Fort Mackinac.
1895	Mackinac Island become Michigan's first State Park.
1898	Motorized vehicles banned from island.
1946	"This Time for Keeps," starring Jimmy Durante and Esther Williams, is filmed at the Grand Hotel.
1957	Mackinac Bridge opens.
1980	"Somewhere in Time," starring Christopher Reeves and Jane Seymour, is filmed at the Grand Hotel.

Mackinac Island Data

Area: 3.47 square miles, about three miles wide and 2 miles north to south

Shoreline: 8 miles

Highest point: Fort Holmes is 320 feet above the Straits

Year round population: approximately 500

Owner: 1,800 of the island's 2,200 acres *(about 80%)* are part of the Mackinac Island State Park. The rest is under private ownership.

Mackinac Island State Park became our 2nd National Park in 1875. *(Yellowstone was first in 1872.)*
Mackinac became Michigan's first State Park in 1895.

Town: Harrisonville is tucked away between the airport and Grand Hotel's Jewel Golf Course. Most of the year-round residents make their home in Harrisonville.

Roads: About 144 miles of roads and trails
(61 miles within Mackinac Island State Park)

State Highway: M-185, "The Safest Highway in the Country," has never had an auto accident. The 8-mile loop around the island has no beginning and no end!

School: The Mackinac Island Public School is K-12 with fewer than 100 students enrolled. Average class size is six. A staff of six teachers handles all grades. All students must walk or ride a bike to school, except in the winter when snowmobiles and horse-drawn carriages are used.

Access: Ferry service operates between the island and St. Ignace in the U.P. and Mackinaw City in the Lower Peninsula between May and the end of October.

Great Lakes Air operates daily flights between the island and St. Ignace. Round trip fare is $36 during winter months.

After the Straits freeze over, usually in January, some residents cross over the "ice bridge" on foot or by snowmobile to St. Ignace. After island residents take down their Christmas trees they are used to mark a path across the ice.

MACKINAC ISLAND TOURISM

The big draw on Mackinac Island, besides the natural beauty of its setting in the Straits, is the lack of automobiles. Mackinac is known around the world as the island where cars are not allowed. Visitors experience today much what the first tourists did in the late 19th century: travel by horse and buggy or bicycle, beautiful Victorian cottages, and the smell of fresh lake breezes mixed with the fresh byproduct of the large horse population.

Motorized vehicles were banned from the island in 1896. Carriage operators, who had been providing transportation and tours on the island for over 25 years complained that the loud road machines spooked their horses. It was the carriage operators, led by Thomas Chambers, who convinced the village council to ban motorized transportation from the island.

Today, fourth and fifth generation members of the Chambers family run Mackinac Island Carriage Tours, Inc. It is the world's largest, oldest and continually operated horse and buggy livery.

Number of horses on the island: 600 – summer, 30 – winter

Number of carriages: approximately 100

Where they go in the winter. The horses are ferried off the island and stabled in the Upper Peninsula. Horses raised by Mackinac Island Carriage Tours are trained specifically for their work on the island.

Motor vehicles permitted on island: snowmobiles, construction equipment, and police and fire vehicles. All other motorized vehicles are by permit only, and only if the work at hand cannot be handled by horse drawn cart or wagon.

Annual visitors: 850,000 – 1,000,000 between May and October

Busiest day: 2nd Tuesday of August is historically the most crowded on the island. Saturdays tend to be the busiest overall, and Thursdays the slowest.

Number of hotels and inns: 46

Number of guest rooms: 3,000 est.

Oldest continuously operated hotel: Lake View Hotel opened in 1858

Oldest building housing a hotel: Part of the Harbour View Inn dates back to 1820, when a fur trader built it.

Hotel Iroquois has made Conde Nast Traveler Magazine's *"Gold List" on three occasions, 1997, 2000, and 2005.*

Number of bicycles available for rent on typical day: 1,325

Most popular tourist sites: Tie between Fort Mackinac, Marquette Park, Arch Rock and Grand Hotel

Fort Mackinac includes the oldest standing structures in Michigan, including the oldest. The Officers' Stone Quarters built in 1780.

The 4th of July celebration held at Fort Mackinac every year includes 38-gun salute. The 38 represents the number of states in the Union when the fort was occupied by the U.S. 23rd Regiment, 1884-1890.

Number of weddings performed on island per year: about 1,500

Oldest church: Mission Church, built in 1829, is the oldest surviving church building in Michigan, a Protestant church built by the early settlers of the island. It has been restored, and is a Michigan registered Historic site.

The Mission Church was used for Catholic services while Ste. Anne's Catholic Church was under construction.

Mackinac Island is home to Michigan's first and oldest continuously played 9-hole golf course. Designed by Alex Smith in 1898, Wawashkamo, meaning walk a crooked path, was named by the Ojibwe Chief Eagle Eye. The course is built on a battlefield from the War of 1812, and is now a National Landmark.

*Arch Rock
(courtesy Travel
Michigan)*

Awards and recognition

- One of the Top Ten Islands in the World by *Conde Naste Traveler* in 2002
- National Historic Landmark by National Trust for Historic Preservation
- Lilac Festival one of Top 100 Events by American Bus Association
- Marquette Park–One of Top 10 Lawns by Briggs and Stratton

Fudge

The term **"fudgie"** to describe a tourist in northern Michigan may have started on Mackinac Island where the chocolate treat has been marketed to visitors since the 1880's. During a typical summer, fudgies will buy over 10,000 pounds from 15 fudge stores on the island.

Murdick's Fudge proudly proclaims to be the original on Mackinac Island since 1887. Murdick's was recognized with a Centennial Business Award from the Historical Society of Michigan. Several locations on Main St., and in Mackinaw City, St. Ignace and Martha's Vineyard.

Ryba's Fudge may not be the original, but claims to be "Mackinac Island's Favorite." Ryba's has been voted #1 for three years in a row by readers of the *Detroit News*. Several locations downtown.

May's Famous Mackinac Fudge may not be the original or the favorite, but does claim to be "From the Family That Made Fudge Famous." The May family has been making fudge since 1881 in Atchison, Kansas. The Mackinac Island shop opened in 1930 and is now managed by third generation fudge makers with help from the fourth generation.

Joann's Fudge touts "authentic Mackinac Island Fudge."

Kilwin's has two stores on the island and notes the island is famous for its ban on the automobile, Indian legends, and Kilwin's Fudge!

Murray Hotel Fudge Co. makes and markets fudge in the hotel!

<u>GRAND HOTEL</u>

Known around the world for having the longest front porch, the famous veranda measures 660 feet and is visible for miles. Non-guests must pay $10 to walk the famous porch. The charge is waived after dinner, but there is a dress code, jacket and tie for men, and ladies in "their finest."

"The Grand" was built in 1886 out of Michigan white pine by railroad and shipping interests including: Michigan Central Railroad, Grand Rapids & Indiana Railroad, and the Detroit Cleveland Steamship navigation Company. The hotel opened the following year charging room rates between $3 and $5 a night. Visitors arrived by rail and steamship.

Longest front porch in the world (courtesy of The Grand Hotel)

<u>Historical Timeline</u>

1887	Opens
1895	Mark Twain stays as a guest and gives lectures
1897	West wing added
1933	William Stewart Woodfill who started work as a desk clerk, buys the hotel
1949	"This Time for Keeps," starring Jimmy Durante and Esther Williams is filmed at

	the Grand. Pool built for the movie is named Esther Williams Pool.
1979	Dan Musser II, who joined the staff in 1951, and wife Amelia purchase the hotel
1980	"Somewhere in Time" starring Christopher Reeve, Jane Seymour and Christopher Plummer is filmed at the hotel.
1989	Dan Musser III is named President of the Hotel. East Wing added Named National Historic Landmark
1998	Five new rooms, all named for first ladies, are added to West Wing: Lady Bird Johnson, Betty Ford, Rosalynn Carter, Nancy Reagan, and Barbara Bush (in addition to the Jacqueline Kennedy Suite).
2001	Millennium Wing added: 42 new guest rooms and 300 seat addition to Main Dining Room. Largest addition since original construction.

Miscellaneous Facts

Number of guest rooms: 385

Number of guests per season: 115,000

Tipping policy: No tipping. Not expected and not accepted. There is an added charge to the daily room rate.

Extras: A full breakfast and five-course dinner is included for all guests.

Attire: Evening wear—coats and ties for men and dresses or pantsuits for women—are required for dinner, and in all areas of the hotel at night.

Favorite dessert: More than 50,000 Grand Pecan Balls are served each season.

Readers of Travel & Leisure Family Magazine *voted Grand Hotel as one of the 10 kid-friendliest resorts in North America.*

Number of geraniums on the Grand's front porch: 2,000 planted in 260 planting boxes with seven tons of potting soil

Number of annuals planted on the grounds: 105,000

Number of bulbs planted: 24,000 tulips and 3,000 daffodils planted annually

Presidents who have stayed at Grand Hotel: (5) Presidents Clinton, George H. Bush, Ford, Kennedy and Truman

In 2005 the Grand Hotel held its earliest opening ever. The Millennium Wing and Masco Cottage opened on March 1st. President Dan Musser III noted two factors in the early opening: some regular guests have expressed interest in seeing the hotel and island in the off season, and changes in the temporary visa rules for foreign workers who staff the hotel each summer.

Listed in Travel and Leisure Magazine's *annual listing of the 500 greatest hotels in the world in January 2004 issue* (only Michigan hotel included).

Named Michigan's Best Hotel by Zagat Surveys.

Mackinac Island Fun

Stone Skipping and Gerplunking tournament held every 4th of July since 1964 at Windermere Beach next to the Iroquois Hotel.

Winter Stone Ice Stone Skipping Contest has been held each February since 1995

Lilac Festival celebrated in mid-June every year since 1949. The lilacs on Mackinac Island are among the country's oldest and largest. Ten-day festival includes crowning of Lilac Festival Queen, a parade, 10 K running race, and concert.

Chicago to Mackinac Island Yacht Race at 333 miles is the world's longest freshwater race and one of the most prestigious in the U.S. First race held in 1908. Held in mid-July every year.

Port Huron to Mackinac Island Yacht Race is held the weekend after the Chicago race. Hosted by the Bayview Yacht Club of Port Huron since 1924.

Somewhere in Time Weekend held mid-October each year. Brings together fans of the movie shot at the Grand Hotel starring Christopher Reeve and Jane Seymour. Both Reeve and Seymour have been guests at this event.

Fudge Festival held in late August features fudge tastings, fudge throwing, fudge & stone skipping, fudge relay races, fudge facials, best fudgie contest. The first fudge festival was held in 2004.

Starting in mid-October many of the island stores feature big sales as the high season winds down. The crowds aren't as big, and you may see some of the island horses paraded bareback down Main St. headed toward the ferry docks and their winter homes in the U.P.

REGISTERED WATERCRAFT – BY COUNTY:

October 2002 – September 2003

County	Registered watercraft
Grand Traverse	13,305
Roscommon	6,244
Leelanau	5,646
Emmet	5,533
Antrim	5,197
Charlevoix	5,070
Clare	4,618
Wexford	4,483
Mason	4,336
Benzie	4,011
Manistee	3,802
Otsego	3,174
Crawford	2,852
Osceola	2,707
Kalkaska	2,669
Lake	2,351
Missaukee	2,075

STATE PARKS

There are 18 State Parks in northwestern lower Michigan, including White Pine Trail State Park, which cuts through Wexford and Osceola counties. Most of these State Parks are situated on, or in between, beautiful lakes, and offer modern camping.

Counties without a State Park

Antrim	Benzie
Kalkaska	Lake
Missaukee	Osceola

Largest Park

Hartwick Pines is the largest State Park in northern lower Michigan. With 9,762 acres it is also the largest State Park in the entire Lower Peninsula.

Hartwick Pines includes 49 acres of old-growth pine and a 300-year old Monarch Pine.

Oldest Park

In 1875, three years after Yellowstone, Mackinac Island became our country's second National Park. Those 1,800 acres, about 80% of the island, were turned over to Michigan in 1895 to become the first State Park.

Interlochen State Park was the first to be established by the legislature. In 1917 the State, wanting to preserve pine forests which were rapidly disappearing at the hands of loggers, paid $60,000 for 200 acres originally known as Pine Park.

Newest Park

White Pine Trail State Park was dedicated in July of 1994. This unique State Park does not offer camping. It's a 92-mile long trail between Cadillac and Comstock Park near Grand Rapids. It is also the longest State Park!

Northern Michigan State Parks Ranked by Size

Park	County	Acres
Hartwick Pines State Park	Crawford	9,762
Wilderness State Park	Emmet	8,286
Ludington State Park	Mason	5,300
Fisherman's Island State Park	Charlevoix	2,678
Leelanau State Park	Leelanau	1,350
Mackinac Island State Park	Mackinac	1,800
S. Higgins Lake State Park	Roscommon	962
Young State Park	Charlevoix	563
N. Higgins Lake State Park	Roscommon	429
Mitchell State Park	Wexford	334
Petoskey State Park	Emmet	303
Orchard Beach State Park	Manistee	201
Interlochen State Park	Grand Traverse	187
White Pine Trail State Park	*	92
Otsego Lake State Park	Otsego	62
Traverse City State Park	Grand Traverse	47
Wilson State Park	Clare	36
Colonial Michilimackinac Historic State Park	Emmet	0

*Trail runs through following counties: Wexford, Osceola, Mecosta, Montcalm and Kent

Most Camp Sites

Interlochen State Park, with 428 modern campsites, has the most of any in the State Park system.

Camp Sites Ranked

Park	County	Camp sites
Interlochen State Park	Grand Traverse	428
S. Higgins Lake	Roscommon	400
Ludington State Park	Mason	344
Traverse City State Park	Grand Traverse	343
Wilderness State Park	Emmet	250
Young State Park	Charlevoix	240
Mitchell State Park	Wexford	215
N. Higgins Lake State Park	Roscommon	174
Orchard Beach State Park	Manistee	168
Petoskey State Park	Emmet	168
Wilson State Park	Clare	160
Otsego State Park	Otsego	155
Hartwick Pines State Park	Crawford	100

Rustic Camp Sites

Park	County	
Fisherman's Island State Park	Charlevoix	81
Interlochen State Park	Grand Traverse	62
Leelanau State Park	Leelanau	52

State Parks with No Camping

White Pine Trail State Park	*
Mackinac Island State Park	Mackinac
Colonial Michilimackinac Historic State Park	Emmet

Trail runs through following counties: Wexford, Osceola, Mecosta, Montcalm and Kent

State Parks in Northern Michigan

Park	County	Acres	Opened
Hartwick Pines	Crawford	9,762	1927

The Lower Peninsula's largest State Park features the Hartwick Pines Logging Museum, built in the mid 1930's by members of the Civilian Conservation Corps. Park includes 49 acres of virgin pine trees that escaped the cross saws of the late 1800's. There are numerous trails for hiking, mountain biking and cross-country skiing.

Within the park boundaries are Bright Lake, Glory Lake, and the East Branch of the Au Sable River. Fishing and hunting are permitted in season.

Year round camping is available.

Named after: Major Edward E. Hartwick. His widow inherited the land from her father, a Grayling lumberman. After her husband's death, she donated the land to the State as a memorial to her husband.

Wilderness State Park	Emmet	8,286

Features 26 miles of Lake Michigan shoreline at the tip of the Lower Peninsula. Approximately 16 miles of hiking trails, and 20 miles of cross-country skiing trails wind through a dense conifer forest and some open meadow. Habitat is home to black bear, bobcat, coyote, mink, otter, deer, beaver, ruffed grouse, duck, and other critters. Local Indian tribes claim to have observed cougar within the park, although that has not been confirmed with the DNR.

Two campgrounds with 250 developed campsites. Winter camping available.

Hunting allowed with some exceptions.

Ludington State Park   Mason   5,400

Situated between Lake Michigan and Hamlin Lake, often cited for having one of the best beaches in Michigan. Six miles of Lake Michigan shoreline, with additional beachfront on Hamlin Lake. Features include beautiful sand dunes, mature forests, some marsh and wetlands.

Modern camping sites: 398   Year round camping available.

Features a Visitors Center with exhibits on Great Lakes and State Park history.

Hunting permitted with exceptions.

Fisherman's Island State Park   Charlevoix   2,678   1973

Features a 10-acre island and five miles of undeveloped Lake Michigan shorline. Rolling dunes, some hardwoods, and three trout streams running through property. One mile-long beach with large picnic ground. 90 rustic campsites. Seven miles of trails for hiking, biking and skiing. Fishing permitted, hunting with exceptions.

Leelanau State Park   Leelanau   1,300

At the tip of the Leelanau Peninsula featuring the Grand Traverse Lighthouse, now a museum and open during the summer. Over eight miles of trails for hiking and skiing. Fifty rustic camping sites open April – December.

Mackinac Island State Park	Mackinac	1,800	1895

Michigan's first State Park makes up most of the island. Features 70 miles of roads and trails, most of which are wooded and used by hikers, bikers and horseback riders. No autos permitted on island. Historical highlights include the oldest buildings in Michigan scattered around Fort Mackinac. The highest point on the island is at Fort Holmes, and offers beautiful views of the Straits area.

Accessible by ferry or plane only.

S. Higgins Lake State Park	Roscommon	2,000+	1927

County Road 100 splits the park in half with Higgins Lake on the north and Marl Lake to the south. Nearly a mile of shoreline on Higgins Lake known for perch and lake trout fishing. Marl Lake is surrounded by 700 acres of woods. Higgins Lake campground includes 512 sites open April – December. One of the most popular State Parks in Michigan.

Young State Park	Charlevoix	560	1921

Located on Lake Charlevoix near Boyne City. Popular with sail and power boaters, fishermen and beachgoers. 240 modern campsites open May – November. Five miles of nature trails for hiking and skiing.

N. Higgins Lake State Park	Roscommon	429	1963

Established on land that was once the world's largest seedling nursery. Features 195 camping sites split between the forested west side and the grassier east side near the Ralph A. McMullan Conference Center. Over eight miles of trails for hiking, biking and skiing. Nice, sandy beach with volleyball court.

Civilian Conservation Corps Museum across the street features a replica of the barracks that housed the Corps, and a nature trail leads through the nursery area, established in 1903 as the first re-forestation project in Michigan.

| Mitchell State Park | Wexford | 334 | 1919 |

Set between Lake Cadillac and Mitchell Lake the park features an historic canal connecting the two lakes. In the winter the canal freezes first, but after the lakes freeze up, the canal becomes unfrozen. The Carl T. Johnson Hunting and Fishing Center features several exhibits on the history of hunting and fishing in Michigan. 270 modern camping sites. Sandy beach, picnic area and playground. 2.5 mile nature trail.

| Petoskey State Park | Emmet | 305 | 1969 |

One mile-long sandy beach on Little Traverse Bay known as a good spot for Petoskey stone hunting. Features include "Old Baldy" dune, accessible by trail, with great views from the top. 168 campsites.

| Orchard Beach State Park | Manistee | 201 | |

On a bluff overlooking Lake Michigan with stairs down to the beach. Very popular with fishermen, especially during salmon runs in August and September. 176 campsites.

| Interlochen State Park | Grand Traverse | 200 | 1917 |

First State Park established by legislature. Situated between Green and Duck lakes, adjacent to the Interlochen Arts Academy. 490 campsites. Interpretive display of 1890's logging life in middle of park and self-guided nature trail.

| Otsego State Park | Otsego | 62 | 1920 |

Donated to the State by a lumber company. Features a long sandy beach on Otsego Lake. 155 campsites, most are elevated with view of lake, some are closer to the beach and water. Popular for picnics, sunbathing, boating and fishing. Several buildings in the park were built by the Civilian Conservation Corps in the mid 1930's.

Traverse City State Park	Grand Traverse	45	1920

US 31 North runs between the beach on E. Grand Traverse Bay and the campgrounds amidst a hardwood forest. Beach accessible by pedestrian overpass. 342 camping sites. Paved biking and hiking trail leads to downtown Traverse City (about 3 miles).

Wilson State Park	Clare	36	1927

Located on Budd Lake. 160 camp sites, and a popular Rent-A-Teepee program in the park. Donated to the City of Harrison by Wilson Brothers Sawmill in 1901. Turned over to State in 1920, and dedicated in 1927. Good fishing, boating and swimming lake. Two buildings constructed by Civilian Conservation Corps.

Colonial Michillimackinac Historic State Park

Reconstructed 1715 French fur-trading village and military outpost, later occupied by British military, and traders. Today features re-enactments from British 1770's occupation/American Revolution era. National Historic Landmark. Accredited by American Association of Museums.

SNOWMOBILING AND TOURISM

Snowmobiling is big business in northern Michigan, and especially in the U.P. where winter-tourism spending often outpaces summer, thanks to snowmobilers.

Number of registered snowmobiles in Michigan: 390,000

Average annual tourism-related spending per snowmobiler: $5,700

Average annual spending by all snowmobilers in Michigan: $321 million

Percent of spending from out of state snowmobilers: 37%

Impact on Michigan economy: over $1 billion per year

Jobs created by snowmobiling in Michigan: 6,455

Miles of snowmobile trails in Michigan: 6,200

From a study conducted by the Michigan Department of Park, Recreation and Tourism Resources and Michigan State University.

Snowmobile Capital of Northern Michigan:
Frederic, Crawford County

Snowmobile Ownership

County	No. of snowmobile registrations (2003)	% of households w/snowmobile*
Grand Traverse	5,437	15%
Manistee	3,802	38%
Roscommon	3,512	31%
Otsego	3,356	37%
Emmet	2,951	23%
Charlevoix	2,866	27%
Wexford	2,555	21%
Antrim	2,363	25%
Clare	2,104	17%
Kalkaska	2,006	31%
Leelanau	1,705	20%
Crawford	1,643	29%
Osceola	1,625	18%
Mason	1,571	14%
Benzie	1,474	23%
Missaukee	1,351	24%
Lake	938	20%

Snowmobiling at Mackinac Lighthouse (courtesy Travel Michigan)

Snowmobile Ownership
Top Ten Counties

County	No. of snowmobiles registered
Oakland	23,686
Macomb	18,058
Wayne	16,351
Genesee	13,055
Kent	10,385
Saginaw	7,501
St. Clair	6,783
Livingston	6,529
Ottawa	6,377
Bay	5,798
Grand Traverse	5,437 (11th in state)

Skiing and Snowboarding
Tourism Impact

Amount spent in Michigan per year: $146 million

Annual skier visits (statewide): 2.2 million

Percent to northern Michigan: 45%

$63.7 million   Direct ski revenue
$41.3 million   Food, beverage, retail at ski resort
$41.4 million   Other tourism businesses

Amount spent in northern Michigan: $80.2 million (55%)

Most visitors live nearby, although overnight guests spend the most money. The breakdown on skier/snowboarder categories:

(36%) LOCAL	Live within 60 miles of ski area.
(27%) MOTEL	Stay in commercial lodging at or near the resort
(21%) VFR/SH	Stay with friends or relatives, or in a seasonal home
(15%) DAYTRIPPERS	Live more than 60 miles away, but do not stay overnight

Daily Spending by Types of Visitor:

MOTEL	$112
VFR/SH	$57
DAYTRIP	$50
LOCAL	$45

What They Spend It on:

(44%)	Lift tickets, equipment rental and lessons
(20%)	Restaurants and bars
(20%)	Groceries, gas, retail
(16%)	Lodging

Information from 2001 study by Daniel J. Stynes and Ya Yen Sun of Michigan State University's Department of Park, Recreation and Tourism Resources

DOWNHILL SKIING

Resort	County	Vertical drop	Runs	Longest	Lifts	Lift capacity (per hour)
Boyne Highlands	Emmet	545 ft.	44	5,200+ ft.	10	17,400
Boyne Mountain	Charlevoix	500 ft.	52	5,000+ ft.	13	18,600
Caberfae	Wexford	485 ft.	34	3,960	6	9,207
Shanty Creek	Antrim	450 ft.	46	5,280	11	
Nub's Nob	Emmet	427 ft.	41	4,620	8	15,000
Crystal Mt.	Benzie	375 ft.	45	2,640	7	12,400
Homestead	Leelanau	375 ft.	13	3,960	5	3,300
Hidden Valley	Otsego	350 ft.	17	2,600	7	
Hickory Hills	Gr. Traverse	240 ft.	8	1,500	5*	
Treetops Sylvan Resort	Otsego	225 ft.	19	2,200	7	6,600

Resort	County	Vertical drop	Runs	Longest	Lifts	Lift capacity (per hour)
Hanson Hills	Crawford	225 ft.	11	2,640	4	1,800
Missaukee Mt.	Missaukee	220 ft.	5	1,320	16	300
Skyline Ski Area	Crawford	210 ft.	14	1,800	6	5,400
Mt. Holiday	Gr. Traverse	200 ft.	16		7	
Petoskey Winter	Emmet	200 ft.	1	600	1*	
Mt. McSauba	Charlevoix	152 ft.	8	1,000	3*	

*rope tows only

Catching some air at Boyne Mountain (courtesy Boyne USA)

Boyne Highlands opened in 1955 as Harbor Highlands. In 1962, Everett Kircher of Boyne Mountain purchased the Harbor Springs resort and began expansion. Today it offers the largest vertical drop in northern Michigan.

Boyne Mountain (Boyne Falls) opened in 1947 after Detroit Studebaker dealer, Everett Kircher, bought the land for one dollar. He installed a double chair lift and went on to make history in the ski world by inventing snow making systems and multi-person chair lifts.

Caberfae (Cadillac) opened on January 16, 1938 as the result of a collaboration between the U.S. Forest Service, Civilian Conservation Corps, Cadillac Chamber of Commerce and local volunteers. Caberfae is a Gaelic word meaning "stag's head."

Shanty Creek (Bellaire) opened as ski and golf resort in early 1960's by Roy Deskin. In 1978 it was sold and became part of the Hilton hotel chain.

Schuss Village (Mancelona) opened in 1968 by Chicago stock-broker, Daniel Iannotti who's vision was to create a ski village with a European atmosphere. Sold to Club Resorts, Inc. in 1984.

Cedar River Village (Bellaire) opened in 1997 after private investors purchased the Shanty Creek and Schuss Mountain properties from Club Resorts, Inc.

Nub's Nob opened on New Years Day, 1959. Owners Norm and Doris Sarns enlisted friends and volunteers to carve out three runs on the tree covered hills near Harbor Springs. Nub's was sold to the Fisher family in 1977, and now has 43 slopes.

Crystal Mountain (Thompsonville) opened as Buck Hills Ski Area in December 1956. Started by businessman Ward Creech and community volunteers. In 1960, it was purchased and renamed Crystal Mountain by a group of investors headed up by Toledo businessman Ed Abbey. In 1966, it was sold to three investors headed by George Petritz – one of the original Buck Hills volunteers. Today Crystal is run by Petritz's daughter and son-in-law, Chris and Jim MacInnes.

George Petritz survived a hellish POW experience in WWII and was awarded the Navy Cross. After the war he and his wife, Althea, produced a line of frozen cherry pies that were sold nationally. In the 1950's they sold out to Pet Milk company and to this day you can find a pet-RITZ frozen pie crust at your local grocery store.

Homestead Resort (Glen Arbor) opened downhill ski area in the mid 1980's.

Hidden Valley (Gaylord) opened in 1939 as the Otsego Club, a private club formed by Donald McLouth, president of McLouth Steel Company in Detroit. Purchased in 1955 by Alan Gornick one of the "Whiz Kids" recruited in the 1950's by Henry Ford II. Gornick sold to his son, Kieth, in 1981. In the 1960's the Otsego Club's Alpine theme was adapted by the downtown district of the City of Gaylord. Open to the public on weekends until Christmas, and from March until the end of the ski season.

The Otsego Club is America's oldest private ski club with its own facility.

Hickory Hills (Traverse City) opened in 1950 on land owned by the City of Traverse City. Convenient in-town location and low city-subsidized fees has made it a popular place for families and newcomers to the sport.

Treetops Sylvan Resort Hanson Hills (Grayling) Opened in 1929 as the Grayling Winter Sports Park – the first to offer downhill skiing in Michigan. The park offered toboggan rides, and a ski jump was added in 1934. Property was willed to the State of Michigan by lumber baron Rasmus Hanson for military and/or recreational use. Known for a long time as Bear Mountain, a judge ordered it shut down in 1973 after heirs to the Hanson estate objected to some of the for-profit operations. Now under the control of the non-profit Grayling Recreational Authority.

Missaukee Mountain (Lake City) opened in 1940. Operated by a non-profit board as a low-priced community ski area.

Skyline Ski Area

Mt. Holiday (Traverse City) opened in 1951 on State land east of Traverse City. Local business leaders received permission from the State to clear out a few runs and add a tow rope. Volunteers played a big role in the founding of Mt. Holiday as they do today. The facility closed for two winters following the death of the owner. Community volunteers raised over a million dollars to buy the property and re-opened it in 2003.

Mt. McSauba (Charlevoix) The Mount McSauba Recreation Area features huge, rolling sand dunes that slope down to the Lake Michigan shoreline. This is a primitive natural area with no life-guards or other facilities. Behind the dunes is a series of well-kept trails through a beautiful canopied wooded area. Mount McSauba offers excellent family skiing and is only about a half-mile from town.

Petoskey Winter Sports Park Family park owned by the City of Petoskey.

Everett Kircher

With land in Boyne Falls purchased for one dollar, Everett

Kircher built a ski and golf empire stretching from Michigan to Florida to Utah, Montana, Washington and British Columbia. A shrewd businessman with an engineer's problem-solving skills, Kircher brought northern Michigan its first chairlift and artificial snowmaking equipment. He was also responsible for the beginning of the golf boom in northern Michigan.

The St. Louis, Missouri native moved to Detroit in 1916 when he was three months old – his father was drawn there by Henry Ford's five dollar-a-day wage. That didn't last long as the elder Kircher became a self-employed mechanic, passing along his entrepreneurial skills to Everett. After graduating high school in 1935, Kircher went to the University of Michigan, but only for a year, opting instead to run his own business. Kircher opened a business selling camping trailers, and eventually he took on a Studebaker auto dealership.

He bought his first pair of skis one year out of high school from J.L. Hudson's in downtown Detroit. Skiing was confined to vacation time out west or in New England. His love for the sport sent him looking for a mountain closer to home.

After a search of northern Michigan in 1947, Kircher and two partners prepared to make an offer on 40 acres in Boyne Falls. The owner, William Pierson – a former state legislator – told the men, "Anybody damn fool enough to want to build a ski hill, well… I'll give you the property." So Kircher made it legal by paying Pierson the sum of $1.00 for the land.

Before opening for the winter of 1947-48, Kircher purchased, for $2,000, a single chair lift from Sun Valley – the first one built in the world. He engineered it into a double lift for Boyne Mountain, then set out to create ski runs. He and his partners used only saws and dynamite to cut down hundreds of trees and remove the stumps. The first major run was named Hemlock, after a large tree that was left standing in the middle of the run. The first winter drew about 2,000 skiers and Boyne quickly became the place to ski in the Midwest.

Kircher was able to expand and improve the resort with money earned on a venture in Tennessee. After newspaper articles reported on the dou-

Everett Kircher with Boyne Mt. Lodge in background (courtesy Boyne USA)

ble chairlift in northern Michigan, a hotel owner in Gatlinburg asked if Kircher would build a chairlift for sightseers in the Smoky Mountains. Kircher agreed to build a lift on the steep mountainside, but only if he could be the owner. The deal was drawn up, and has provided a steady means of cash into the Boyne operations ever since.

To attract more interest in skiing, Kircher reasoned, you have to teach people how to ski. For that task he landed Stein Eriksen, who won three gold medals at the 1954 World Championships, and the Olympic gold medallist Othmar Schneider.

In 1953, one of Kircher's managers read about artificial snow being made at a New England resort. Using a water hose, sprinkler and air compressor, Kircher became a pioneer in snowmaking. He invented the Boyne Snowmaker and later patented the Highlands Snow Gun, which is in use at ski resorts around the world.

In 1962, Kircher purchased Harbor Highlands from a group of local shareholders. Since then it has expanded from five to 44 runs and has northern Michigan's highest vertical drop.
As the winter crowds at Boyne grew, so did the need to move them up the moun-

Former Studebaker dealer Everett Kircher (courtesy Boyne USA)

tain. Kircher responded in 1963 by installing the first triple chair lift in the world at Boyne Highlands, and in 1965 with the first four-person lift at Boyne Mountain. In 1990 he installed the Midwest's first high-speed quad lift at Boyne Highlands, and followed with the first-in-the-world six-person lift at Boyne Mountain.

Kircher took advantage of Boyne's reputation as the best ski resort in the Midwest by expanding to golf. In the mid 1950's he had the 9-hole Executive course built at Boyne Mountain. In 1967, he hired noted golf architect, Robert Trent Jones, to design the Heather course at Boyne Highlands, a move that started a golf course-building boom in northern Michigan.

The Boyne operations expanded beyond Michigan in 1976 with the purchase of Big Sky Resort in Montana. In 1986 Brighton Ski Bowl in Utah was added to Boyne USA, and in the 1990's the holdings expanded to include Boyne South in Florida, and Crystal Mountain in Washington. Boyne USA also became part owner of the Crooked Tree Golf Club, and agreed to manage the Bay Harbor Golf Club, both in Petoskey.

Kircher passed away at 85 on January 16, 2002. He was remembered by then

Michigan Governor John Engler as "a hero to American tourism." Kircher's contribution to northern Michigan tourism and to the ski and golf world is immeasurable. Today his four grown children share duties managing the Boyne USA properties around the country and in Canada.

GREAT LAKES CRUISES

A fairly new market for the northern Michigan tourism industry is the cruise ship industry. Cruise ships on the Great Lakes were a common sight in the 1930's and 40's, but disappeared by mid-century. In 1997, cruising returned to the Great Lakes, with the number of ships and passengers increasing since then.

A study conducted by the Great Lakes Cruising Coalition in 2004 shows the industry generating nearly $37 million in the U.S. and the equivalent of nearly $50 million in Canada. Those figures are based on nine ships and 82 departures from U.S. and Canadian ports in 2004. The study was designed to be unbiased and has been approved by an independent economist.

The Great Lakes cruising season runs between June and October.

Number of ports on Great Lakes and St. Lawrence Seaway prepared for cruise ships: 30-35

Northern Michigan ports: Mackinac Island, Mackinaw City, Northport, Traverse City, Ludington, Manistee

Ships offering Great Lakes cruises with stops in northern Michigan: 7

Ship	Year built	Length	Accommodations
Orion	2003	336 ft.	24 staterooms 29 suites
MV Columbus	1997	420 ft.	142 outside cabins and suites/63 inside cabins
Nantucket Clipper	1984	207 ft.	51 staterooms

Grand Caribe	1997	103 ft.	50 cabins
Grand Mariner	1998	183 ft.	50 cabins
Niagara Prince	1994	175 ft.	42 cabins
Le Levant	1998	335 ft.	45 cabins

SHIPWRECK PRESERVES

Michigan has nearly 1,900 square miles of underwater preserves protecting shipwrecks and other artifacts. The bottomlands preserves were created in 1980 through the urging of sport divers. State laws created at that time make it a felony to disturb or remove artifacts from the Great Lakes. Protecting these historic underwater scenes has led to the finest sport diving in the Midwest. Two of the nine preserves are in northern Michigan.

Manitou Passage Underwater Preserve

There are an estimated 58 wrecks scattered on the floor of Lake Michigan between the Manitou islands and the mainland shore.

The favorite dive sites include the wreck of the *Three Brothers* steam barge fifty feet off the shore of South Manitou Island. The 160-foot ship sank in 1911, but wasn't discovered until 1996 after a sandslide exposed it in shallow water. It's easily accessible for divers and snorkelers.

The *Francisco Morazan* ran aground during a snowstorm in December of 1960 at the southern tip of S. Manitou Island. This 246 foot freighter lies in 15 feet of water, much of it above the surface. Divers can explore the hull, including the engine room.

The *Walter L. Frost* is a wooden steamer that ran aground in 1905. When the *Francisco Morazan* ran aground in 1960, it landed on top of the *Frost,* breaking it up and moving it a few hundred yards to the south. Divers can explore the remains of the hull, including the boilers, machinery. and other artifacts.

The schooner *Alva Bradley* was discovered in 1990 between

North and South Manitou islands. Divers will find many small artifacts from the wreck including its cargo of steel billets and some rigging.

Straits of Mackinac Underwater Preserve

Divers have to go to greater depths to discover the many wrecks in the Straits area. The *Cedarville,* a 588-foot freighter that sank in 1965, rests in 110 feet of water. It went down on a foggy night after colliding with another ship. Divers can explore the freighter's superstructure and cabins.

The 110-foot *Sandusky,* a two-masted sailing vessel, sank in 90 feet of water during high winds in September of 1856. It sits upright, and is well preserved featuring a figurehead, anchor, pin rail, wheel and tiller.

The *C.H. Johnson* was a schooner that ran aground during a storm in 1895. It was carrying a load of sandstone blocks which can be seen at the wreck site. It rests in 10-15 feet of water and is a good adventure for divers of all skill levels.

Divers can also look for the **"Rock Maze,"** a few hundred yards east of Mackinac Island. This rock formation looks like a maze and is a popular hangout for large schools of fish.

The Straits of Mackinac Underwater Preserve Committee sponsors an annual treasure hunt on the last Sunday of August.

Scuba North's Top 10 Shipwrecks

1. *Cayuga* – Sank on May 10, 1895 in 100 feet of water between Cross Village and Beaver Island. Went down in a dense fog after collision with the *Joseph I. Hurd.* This 290 foot steel steamer sits upright. There is a sunken barge from a failed recovery operation about 40 feet from its midsection.

Divers inspect the Ebar Ward (courtesy Scuba North)

2. *Ebar Ward* – Sank in Lake Michigan due to ice damage on April 20, 1909. This 213 foot wooden steamer went down in 140 feet of water and rests upright with the bow pointing south. For experienced divers there are two decks to penetrate and two anchors at 110 feet.

3. *Minneapolis* – 226 foot wooden steamer lies in 124 feet of water about 100 yards west of the Mackinac Bridge. Sunk

Wreck of the steamer, Minneapolis *(courtesy Scuba North)*

Schooner William Young *with wheel still attached (courtesy Scuba North)*

The Congress, *one of the many ships to sink in the Manitou Passage (courtesy Scuba North)*

Diver amidst the wreck of the William H. Barnum *(courtesy Scuba North)*

on April 4, 1894, due to damage. A favorite for advanced divers, however, caution is urged as a strong current runs through the area.

4. *Cedarville* – Ten lives were lost when this 588 foot steel freighter sank on May 7, 1965, about a mile east of the Mackinac Bridge, after colliding with the *Topdalsfjord.* Divers can see the cargo of limestone spilled on the bottom of the lake, as well as conveyor arms and other machinery. The ship can be pentetrated by experienced divers, but several have died after getting trapped inside.

5. *William Young* – This 139 foot wooden schooner sank on October 5, 1891, in bad weather. It sits upright with anchors out, capstan intact, and wheel still in place in 110 feet of water one mile east of the Mackinac Bridge.

6. *Congress* – Sank in the South Manitou Harbor on October 5, 1904, after catching fire. This 265 foot wooden schooner lays upright, with hull intact. The superstructure is gone, which allows for easy viewing of its twin boilers and engine. Bottom of hull is 150 feet below the surface of Lake Michigan. Experienced divers only.

7. *Sandusky* – Sank on September 20, 1856, about six miles west of the Mackinac Bridge in 84 feet of water. 110 foot wooden sailing brig offers a lot of artifacts with a figurehead, outboard wheel and steering mechanism, masts, bowsprit and belaying pins. Very accessible dive for all recreation divers who wish to see a fairly intact vessel over 200 years old.

8. *Keuka* – Sank in August of 1932 in Lake Charlevoix a half mile from the public boat launch at the end of Stove St. This 172 foot schooner barge last served as a floating dance hall with maple decking, canopy cover with lifts and a copper still for its elaborate parties during prohibition. Cause of wreck believed to be old age and neglect. It sits upright in 45 feet of water. A favorite wreck for divers.

9. *William H. Barnum* – 218 foot wooden steamer went down in Lake Huron eight miles east of the Mackinac Bridge on April 3, 1894. When it sank, in bad weather, it was considered the fastest vessel on the Great Lakes. It sits upright, mostly intact, in 75 feet of water.

10. *Three Brothers* – Sank on September 29, 1911, in bad weather at Sandy Point on South Manitou Island, but wasn't

discovered until 1996, as it was buried in sand. This 162 foot wooden steamer it totally intact and exposed in depths of ten to forty feet of water. It became exposed after a sandslide. It can be enjoyed by divers and skin divers, as it is only fifty feet from shore.

Thanks to Jack Spencer of Scuba North.
13380 S. West Bayshore, Traverse City, MI, 49684
www.scubanorth.com

Underwater Shrine Dedicated to Divers

A one-ton marble crucifix lies at the bottom of Little Traverse Bay, a shrine for all divers, living and deceased. The Superior Marine Divers Club of Wyandotte purchased the crucifix from a man in Bad Axe who had ordered it for his son's grave, however it arrived from Italy damaged. The diver's club dropped the crucifix into 25 feet of water in Little Traverse Bay on August 12, 1962. During the submersion one of the arms broke off; reattached 35 years later. Harbor Springs diver Dennis Jessick has led viewing tours of the crucifix through the ice on the bay since 1986.

BIG STUFF

Mackinac Bridge:
Longest suspension bridge in the western hemisphere. Until 1998 it was the longest suspension bridge in the world; now the third longest in the world. *(courtesy MDOT)*

Grand Hotel Front Porch:
At 660 feet, the longest porch in the world!
(courtesy Grand Hotel)

National Trout Monument:
17-foot long trout rises 12 feet out of his pond in downtown Kalkaska, home of the National Trout Festival since 1935. Built in 1966.
(courtesy Laura Jolly)

Big Shoe in Manistee:
This shoe belonged to 8' 11" Robert Wadlow, the tallest man in the world. As a representative of International Shoes, he was the guest of Snyder's Shoe Store for the 1940 Manistee National Forest Festival. He became ill after marching in the parade and died in Manistee. His size 37-AA shoe is on display at Snyder's Shoes on River St.

Murdick's Fudge Box:
Long a visual symbol of the Grand Traverse region the big fudge box was added to Doug Murdick's Acme store, six miles east of Traverse City, in 1965. Despite the location on East Bay, at that time Acme was considered "out there," so Murdick figured the large box of fudge would get the attention of passing drivers.
(courtesy Laura Jolly)

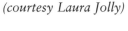

Largest Hockey Stick:
Hockey Heroes Museum, Kitchen and Bar: this 45-foot long hockey stick was constructed by Brown Lumber of Traverse City and Lonnie Smith. It stretches diagonally across the entire front dining room.

Kaleva Grasshopper:
Students in the Service Learning program from Brethren High School and Manistee Intermediate School District built this 18-foot long, 500-pound insect out of recycled metal. A monument to the Finnish St. Uhro, who ridded the farmers' fields of grasshoppers. *(Author photo)*

Big Headstone for Big Cow:
Traverse Colantha Walker was the name of the world champion cow buried on the grounds of the old Traverse City State Psychiatric Hospital. Her grave marker states: **World Champion Cow.**

Milk: 200, 114.9 pounds, **Fat:** 7,525.8 pounds... Bred, owned and developed by Traverse City Hospital." The gravestone stands near the century-old barns on the former hospital property.

Traverse City's pie tin (Author photo)

The current title of World's Largest Cherry Pie belongs to the town of Oliver in British Columbia, where a 37,740 pound pie, 20 feet in diameter, was baked in 1990.

Charlevoix's pie tin (Author photo)

Big Cherry Pies:
Within a 50-mile stretch, and within a period of nine years, two cherry pies set world records. In 1976 Charlevoix set the record with a 17,420 pound pie over 14 feet in diameter. It contained 5,850 lbs. of red tart cherries. The pan and leftover slice are hanging over the giant Medusa oven in which it was baked.

Traverse City set a new record during the National Cherry Festival in July of 1987. Weighing in at 28,330 pounds, the pie measured 17 feet in diameter. The pie tin is on display at the entrance to Sara Lee on Cass Rd. in Traverse City.

Elk Rapids Swan:
The big swan is on the lawn of the Elk Rapids Chamber of Commerce where it greets drivers on US 31 and boaters at the adjacent ramp to Elk Lake. It was designed originally to carry Miss Elk Rapids on a float in the 1966 National Cherry Royale Parade. Dr. John Tschudy and Joseph F. Yuchasz built the 15 foot high swan using scrap lumber and chicken wire. It maintained a busy parade schedule for several summer seasons before coming to its permanent spot in the early 1970's. The dent in the front side of the swan is courtesy of a local radio station DJ who backed into it.

The Chamber didn't discover who the culprit was until hearing him talk about it on the radio.

(courtesy Laura Jolly)

Cross in the Woods:
The largest crucifix in the world, the Cross in the Woods project began in 1952 with the search for a large enough tree. A 2,000 year old California Redwood from Oregon was located and brought to the Pioneer Log Cabin Co. in Roscommon in November of 1953. Eight

months later the cut tree emerged as a 55-foot high cross. It was erected on August 5, 1954. The 7-ton corpus was sculpted by Marshall Fredericks of Royal Oak, Michigan. In 1957 a plaster mold was poured in New York, and then shipped in sections to Oslo, Norway, where the bronze was poured. It arrived back in Indian River on

August 3, 1959, and took six days to attach to the cross. The cross towers 77 feet from its perch on Calgary Hill. It weighs 14 tons without the bronze statue of Christ. The corpus stands 28-feet head to toe, and 31 feet across.

MUSEUMS

Northern Michigan is dotted with small museums that preserve its rich history from the lumber boom to the early maritime industries to fishing and agriculture. There are some unusual museums that feature the likes of the largest collection of dolls dressed as nuns, or an exhibit of antique toys hanging from the ceiling, a history of Coca Cola, and a collection of furniture crafted from tree stumps, logs and roots.

Antrim

Alden Depot Par and Museum
(231) 331-4274
Alden
Old 1908 train depot houses artifacts and photos of lumber and railroad days dating back to 1849.

Bellaire Historical Museum
(231) 533-8943
Bellaire
Logging memorabilia from the region, and other artifacts documenting life in Bellaire from the 1860's through the modern era.

Elk Rapids Historical Museum
(231) 264-9333
Elk Rapids
Located inside the restored Township Hall, the museum features historical displays on the lumber and iron works industries of the late 1800's and early 1900's.

Benzie

Benzie Area Historical Museum
(231) 882-5539
Benzonia
Nice selection of books and information about the Pulitzer Prize-winning historian Bruce Catton, who grew up in Benzonia. Exhibits on the lumber era, Ann Arbor car ferries, and other local history.

Charlevoix

Beaver Island Marine Museum
(231) 448-225
Beaver Island
Housed in original 1906 building designed as a net shed. Exhibits tell the story of Beaver Island's busy turn-of-the-century commercial fishing industry.

The Protar Home
Beaver Island
Preserved to look as it did when "Doctor" Protar lived here between 1893 and 1925. Although not educated as a physician, Protar was able to heal many a sick islander, and wouldn't accept money for his services. When he died, the locals erected a tomb outside the hand-hewn cabin, and inscribed it as follows: *"To our Heaven-Sent Friend from his people of Beaver Island."*

**Old Mormon Print
Shop Museum**
Beaver Island
King Strang built the print shop in 1850 and published northern Michigan's first newspaper from this location. Today the print shop holds hundreds of historic photos, oral history tapes, diaries, genealogical records and features exhibits on the King Strang story, the island's Irish history and Native American history.

The Toy Museum and Store
(231)448-2480
Beaver Island
Over 150 antique toys on display, most hanging from the ceiling of this store that sells everything from plastic army men to old marbles.

Boyne City Historical Museum
(231) 582-2839
Boyne City
Loaded with historic photos and information on the town's rich lumbering and railroad history. Many displays of late 1800's domestic life.

**East Jordan Portside
Arts & Historical Museum**
(231) 536-7351
East Jordan
Art gallery and history museum.

Harsha House Museum
(231)547-0373
Charlevoix
Large collection of historic photos, documents, books and artifacts of the region. Housed in an 1891 Queen Anne-style house donated to the local Historical Society in 1979. Open for researchers and tours.

Crawford

**Crawford County
Historical Museum**
(989) 348-4461
Grayling
Nice exhibit on the famous bow hunter and archery entrepreneur Fred Bear. Also an old trapper's cabin, one-room schoolhouse, antique fire engines and an early railroad caboose, all displayed in a former railroad depot.

**Hartwick Pines
Logging Museum**
(989) 348-2537
Grayling
Excellent collection of exhibits bringing back to life the boom days of northern Michigan's lumber era. Exhibits include a logging camp, log buildings, and rooms depicting life in the lumber days.

**Lovells Township
Historical Museum**
Lovells
The history of fly fishing on the AuSable is captured through displays of antique reels, bamboo rods, and flies all housed in this log cabin of a museum.

Emmet

Andrew J. Blackbird Museum
(231) 526-7731
Harbor Springs
Located in the home that Blackbird bought around 1858. Blackbird, the son of an Odawa (Ottawa) chief, was educated at Eastern Michigan State University, and wrote a history of the Odawa people. From this home he also ran the local post office.

Little Traverse History Museum Center
Petoskey
Located in the old railroad depot, the museum features a permanent display of Ernest Hemingway memorabilia, including signed first edition books and other material related to his time spent as a young man in the Petoskey area. Other exhibits highlight Chief Petoskey, inventor Ephraim Shay, the sculptor Stanley Kellog, and the evolution of Petoskey from its founding through the lumber industry to the development of the tourism industry.

Grand Traverse

Dennos Museum Center
(231) 995-1055
Traverse City
Northern Michigan's premier art museum features exhibits on loan from the Detroit Institute of Arts and other top museums. The permanent exhibits include one of the largest collections of Inuit art from the Canadian Arctic. The hands-on Discovery Gallery is popular with children, and the Milliken Auditorium features year-round performing arts.

Great Lakes Children's Museum
(231)932-4526
Traverse City
Lots of hands-on exhibits including a mini Great Lakes freighter complete with weather station, a lighthouse, interactive (wet) exhibits explaining the water table and water cycle, and a schooner exhibit. Due to move into new building in 2005.

Music House Museum
(231) 938-9300
Acme
This unique museum is set in a large, sturdy old barn across from the Grand Traverse Resort and Spa. It houses a large collection of unique musical instruments; a huge Belgian dance organ, nickelodeons, music boxes and pipe organs. Also features a display of antique radios, and is the home of the Miniature City, replicating many of the downtown Traverse City buildings.

Con Foster Museum
(231) 995-0313
Traverse City

Located inside the Heritage Center in the old Carnegie Library on the Boardman River. The museum houses permanent exhibits on local Native American history and the old State Psychiatric Hospital. The museum houses an expansive historical weapons collection, as well as artifacts from the lumber days and Victorian era.

Fife Lake Historical Museum
(231) 879-4544
Fife Lake
Indian artifacts, an old schoolroom, barber shop, and country store, plus historic toys and clothing.

Hockey Heroes Museum, Kitchen & Bar
Traverse City
Formerly Gordie Howe's restaurant, it still houses an impressive collection of NHL memorabilia, including autographed photos, sticks, and uniforms, and an NHL reference library. Highlights include a display of signed sticks by the only 33 players ever to score over 500 goals in their career, the World's Largest Hockey Stick, and what may be the world's largest puck collection!

Kalkaska

Kalkaska County Historical Museum
Kalkaska
Located in the old train depot, the museum includes artifacts from the lumber days and houses one of the five remaining Elmer automobiles built by Elmer F. Johnson in Kalkaska in 1898.

Lake

Shrine of the Pines, Inc.
Baldwin
After 1910 the lumber industry was gone and left behind a lot of stumps and logs. Raymond Overholzer, without the aid of nails or fasteners of any kind, crafted over 200 furniture items out of the leftover stumps and logs. Displayed in a log cabin on the banks of the Pere Marquette River, the collection includes a table made from a 700-pound stump with detailed inlays in its surface, a rocking chair made of tree roots, and a fireplace built with 70 tons of local stone.

Leelanau

Leelanau Historical Museum
(231) 256-7475
Leland
Changing exhibits on local maritime, lumber and agriculture industries, and extensive historical archives including

Elmer Car built by Elmer Johnson of Kalkaska (courtesy G.T. Pioneer & Historical Society)

photographs, manuscripts, books on local history, local periodicals, and governmental records.

Empire Area Museum
(231) 326-5568
Empire
Displays highlight the lumber and railroad history of the region. They include: a turn-of-the-century saloon, one-room schoolhouse, and a collection of horse drawn equipment in the barn.

Manistee

Arcadia Area Historical Museum
(231) 889-4754
Arcadia
Local artifacts, furniture and history.

Babcock House
(231)723-9803
Manistee
Ornate brick Victorian home built in 1881 for lumberman Simeon Babcock includes a turret, working gas lighting, coin-operated pianos and antique phonographs.

Kaleva Bottle House Historic Museum
(231) 362-2080
Kaleva
A three-bedroom home made out of 60,000 bottles! Built in the 1940's by John Makinen, owner of the Northwestern Bottling Works, using damaged bottles.

Mansitee County Historical Museum
(231) 723-5531
Manistee
Housed in the old A.H. Lyman store, which appears exactly as it did in 1905. Includes one of the largest collections of Victorian antiques and photographs in the State.

Mansitee County Historical Museum
Manistee
The first historical museum inside the 1881 waterworks building includes displays on the lumber and maritime industries.

Kaleva Historical Museum
Kaleva
Located inside the old train depot, which was restored by local high school students. It now houses model train collections and displays from the N.W. Train Enthusiasts Club.

Mason

Historic White Pine Village
(231)843-4808
Ludington
The Village transports visitors back to life in the 1800's with its hundreds of artifacts and displays spread though 22 different buildings, including five museums.

• Abe Nelson Lumbering Museum – original arti facts from Ludington's rich

lumber history housed
in an old lumber camp
building

- Rose Hawley Museum –
furniture, clothing and
household items from
the past
- Maritime Museum – big
lighthouse lenses, uniforms,
photographs, china, and
even a propeller - and
other artifacts from the
Lake Michigan ferries
- Village Time Museum – the
"Clock Shop" houses many
antique clocks and an original Pantograph engraving
machine invented by
Andrew Halberg of the
Star Watch Case Co. which
operated in Ludington for
many years
- Museum of Music – nice
display of antique musical
instruments and the defini-
tive history of the Scottville
Clown Band

Otsego

Bottle Cap Museum
(989) 732-1931
Sparr, just east of Gaylord
Nice collection of Coca-Cola
memorabilia from the 30's,
40's and 50's. Tours include
history of the Coca-Cola
Company.

Call of the Wild
(989) 732-4336
Gaylord
Wildlife displays depicting
sixty animals in their natural
habitat, and a Wildlife Theater.

Roscommon

AuSable River Center
(989)821-5274
Roscommon
Interpretive displays on the
history of the AuSable River.
Main building constructed
in 1936 by the Civilian
Conservation Corp.

**Civilian Conservation
Corps Museum**
(989) 821-6125
Roscommon
Tells the story of the young
men who served in the
Civilian Conservation Corp
during the 1930's. Set in a
replica of the barracks where
the men lived.

Wexford

**Wexford County
Historical Museum**
(231) 389-2615
Cadillac

Mackinac Bridge Museum
Mackinaw City
Largest collection of original
artifacts from construction of
the bridge in the mid 1950's.
J.C. Stillwell, one of the iron-
workers who built the bridge
across the Straits, opened the
museum in Mama Mia's
Pizza, a restaurant he operates. Artifacts include iron
workers hardhats, large
wheels which spun the wire
inside the giant cables, tools,
workbelts and more. A video
of the construction shot by

the American Bridge Division of U.S. Steel airs on a large-screen TV, and there is an honor roll dedicated to the five men who died during construction.

**Surrey Hill Square
Carriage Museum**
(906) 847-6109
Mackinac Island
Working blacksmith shop and antique carriage museum. It's on the list of stops for island carriage tours.

Dr. Beaumont Museum
There are hands-on exhibits, artifacts and interpreters to help visitors learn about Dr. Beaumont's discoveries. In 1822 he aided a French Canadian voyageur who had been shot in the stomach. After the bullet wound healed there was still a hole in the patient's stomach. Beamont was able to conduct experiments on the digestive system, and published his groundbreaking discoveries years later.

Nun Doll Museum
(231) 238-8973
Indian River
Over 500 dolls dressed as nuns from religious orders around the world. Sally Rogalski, who started the collection, donated the dolls to the Cross-in-the-Woods in 1967. In 1988 Pope John Paul II proclaimed the Rogalski collection at the Nun Doll Museum to be the largest of its kind in the world!

MANUFACTURING

Grand Traverse Auto, first auto dealer up north, opened by Henry Ford's brother-in-law, Milton Bryant (courtesy G.T. Pioneer & Historical Society)

MANUFACTURING

Traverse City – Tops for Business

"The road to boomtown travels up through the heartland of America and arrives at a place called Traverse City, Mich." - *Site Selection Magazine,* March 2004

Traverse City has been the #1 small town in America for new and expanded businesses for two of the last three years, according to *Site Selection Magazine.* Traverse City was ranked #1 in 2002 and 2003 with a total of 79 new or expanded plants. It finished in 2nd place in 2004, and ranked 3rd in 2001. *Site Selection* writes that from 2001 to 2003 Traverse City produced more new and expanded industrial plants than any other small town in the country. The magazine cites Traverse City's work force, quality of life and pro-business climate as it competitive edge in attracting new businesses.

Newer Plants Highlighted by Site Selection

Britten Media	$2.7 million addition 45,000 sq. ft.	Custom banners for special occasions and national sporting events
Laitner Brush	$2 million new plant 40,000 sq. ft.	Brushes and brooms
Trantek	22,000 sq. ft. new plant	Automation systems
D & W Mechanical	20,000 sq. ft. new plant	Mechanical contracting
Graceland Fruit	$15 million expansion 60,000 sq. ft	Dried fruit and vegetable processing
Federal Screw Works	$37 million expansion	Bolts, nuts and screws
Tower Automotive	$30 million plant	Auto parts

- Cadillac attracted 22 new or expanded manufacturing plants between 2001-2003, making it the second highest ranked small town in Michigan.
- Michigan ranked #1 in the nation between 2000-2002 with 517 small town industrial projects.

Manufacturing Employers

County	Number of establishments/ State rank	Number of manufacturing jobs/ State rank
Gr. Traverse	233 / 18	7,299 / 22
Charlevoix	74 / 29	2,846 / 45
Wexford	67 / 44	4,884 / 28
Mason	5 / 46	2,756 / 46
Emmet	64 / 47	2,348 / 47
Antrim	61 / 49	1,829 / 53
Otsego	55 / 50	2,217 / 50
Clare	54 / 51	1,422 / 57
Osceola	52 / 53	3,946 / 33
Manistee	45 / 57	1,698 / 55
Leelanau	43 / 59	462 / 74
Missaukee	36 / 66	681 / 68
Kalkaska	33 / 68	871 / 64
Benzie	32 / 69	765 / 65
Crawford	30 / 70	643 / 70
Roscommon	30 / 71	500 / 72
Lake	11 / 81	160 / 82

Average Manufacturing Wage, by County: 2003

County	Avg. annual wage	State rank
Osceola	$48,190	18
Charlevoix	$45,502	21
Manistee	$43,522	28
Crawford	$41,353	33
Mason	$37,666	42
Grand Traverse	$35,532	46
Wexford	$36,372	47
Antrim	$36,293	49
Emmet	$35,179	53
Missaukee	$34,718	56
Otsego	$34,612	57
Clare	$34,448	59
Kalkaska	$32,582	61
Lake	$26,632	74
Benzie	$26,008	75
Leelanau	$25,536	76

AUTO MANUFACTURING

Northern Michigan never presented a serious threat to Detroit as "Automobile Capitol of the World," but it did produce three auto manufacturers in the early 20th century. Sadly there is little information and less actual evidence of their existence.

The Gaylord 30

Originally produced in Detroit, the first Gaylord automobile was driven north in 1910 to the town whose name it shared. In 1911 the Gaylord Motor Car Co. was producing two models, the DS 30 Touring Car (Gaylord 30), and the R-20 Roadster. In its first year of operation on S. Wisconsin Street 50 cars were produced, which sold for $1,000 - $1,500 each.

The Model D Runabout was added in 1913, but the plant closed down later that year due to lack of investment.

The last Gaylord 30 known to exist is on display at the Gaylord/Otsego County Chamber of Commerce. Volunteers raised $20,000 to buy it from a restorer in Washington state. The Gaylord 30 is rolled out on to the streets once a year to lead the Alpenfest parade.

The last existing Gaylord 30 on display at Gaylord/Otsego Chamber of Commerce (courtesy Gaylord/Otsego Chamber of Commerce)

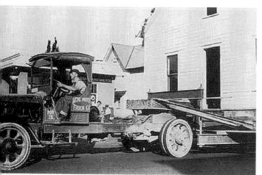

Acme Truck hauling house from ghost town of Jennings to Cadillac (courtesy of G. T. Pioneer & Historical Society)

The Acme Truck

About the time the Gaylord Motor Car Company was going out of business Walter Kysor was busy with plans to build a truck in Cadillac. The forerunner of the Cadillac Area Chamber of Commerce, the Cadillac Board of Trade, helped Walter Kysor raise the money to build an assembly plant.

The original company, the Cadillac Auto Truck Co., produced its first trucks in 1915. Later Kysor changed the name to Acme Truck Co. In the early 1920's the company built custom trailers used by its trucks to haul dozens of houses to Cadillac from the neighboring ghost town of Jennings.

The company disbanded in 1932. Kysor remained a presence in the Cadillac business community for the rest of the century.

The Napoleon

The Traverse City Chamber of Commerce, in an early instance of business recruitment, lured the company away from Napolean, Ohio by promising $74,000 and a manufacturing plant. Investors paid $10 a share and an old wood flooring plant was converted for autombile production.

The first vehicles – three passenger cars and a 3/4 ton truck – rolled off the floor in 1917. By 1919 the company produced 250 vehicles a year, but in 1920 Napoleon eliminated car production. Truck production continued for a year until a recession hit. The plant was closed for two years before finally going out of business in 1923.

The only known Napoleon still in existence is a car being restored by Dennis Kuhn of Buckley.

Ad for Acme Truck

Labor Leader Killed in Pellston Plane Crash

Organized labor lost one of its heroes in a fiery plane crash on May 9, 1970 near the Pellston Regional Airport. Walter P. Reuther served as president of the United Auto Workers union for 24 years before he was killed when a chartered Lear jet from Detroit crashed two miles short of the runway. The jet, during an instrument landing in foggy weather, went straight down and burst into flames after hitting tree tops.

The pilot and all five passengers were killed including Reuther, his wife May, her nephew, Reuther's bodyguard, and the architect of the new UAW education center at Black Lake.

Under Reuther's leadership the UAW was building a 1,000 acre family and education retreat on Black Lake in Cheboygan County. Today the Walter and May Reuther UAW Family Education Center includes camping facilities and an award winning course at the Black Lake Golf Club where UAW member receive special discounts.

Desi Arnaz and Lucille Ball honeymooned at the Maxon Lodge, which was built on the Black Lake property in 1932.

Labor leader, Walter P. Reuther, killed in Pellston plane crash

RETAIL

Retail Sales Totals and per Capita: By County

One way to track a region's economic health, according to the Northwest Michigan Council of Governments, is through retail sales. Retail sales reflect consumer confidence and indicate whether retailers are primarily servicing the local community, or serving as a regional shopping destination.

Grand Traverse County is the number one shopping destination in northern Michigan with higher per capita sales than any other county in the state. Based on per capita retail sales Wexford, Emmet and Otsego are also regional shopping destinations.

Retail Sales Totals and per Capita: By County

County	1997 total retail sales ($1,000's)	1997 retail sales per capita	State rank	2000 total retail sales
Gr. Traverse	$1,232,689	$16,916	1	$1,610,178
Otsego	$334,844	$15,382	2	$457,991
Emmet	$404,741	$14,277	3	$542,329
Wexford	$359,132	$12,330	5	$536,618
Roscommon	$266,965	$11,503		$357,185
Kalkaska	$144,296	$9,353	21	$185,026
Charlevoix	$202,772	$8,414	31	$286,495
Crawford	$115,957	$8,340		$147,257
Manistee	$189,828	$8,156	37	$293,547
Mason	$222,950	$8,027		$292,922
Missaukee	$103,144	$7,566	47	$140,772
Clare	$217,814	$7,517		$268,010
Benzie	$104,839	$7,307	56	$117,363
Antrim	$106,517	$5,079	71	$157,340
Leelanau	$91,971	$4,887	76	$131,442
Osceola	$105,457	$4,788		$162,558
Lake	$38,826	$3,626		$47,854

Sales Tax Revenue Totals and per Person: By County

Grand Traverse County ranks first statewide in the amount of sales tax paid per resident. This is due to the establishment of Traverse City as a regional shopping destination and the high number of tourists and summer residents.

County	Sales tax revenue ($1,000's)	State rank	Tax per person ($'s)	State rank
Grand Traverse	107,339	11	1,364	1
Otsego	28,348	31	1,196	2
Emmet	28,305	32	887	5
Wexford	25,834	34	839	7
Roscommon	16,597	47	641	20
Charlevoix	16,062	49	608	24
Mason	16,545	48	581	31
Kalkaska	9,693	59	557	33
Manistee	14,024	55	565	34
Crawford	6,682	64	464	47
Clare	13,839	56	437	50
Missaukee	5,673	67	386	56
Leelanau	5,631	69	262	73
Benzie	4,129	74	253	75
Osceola	5,858	66	250	76
Antrim	5,497	70	234	79
Lake	1,794	82	156	81

First Auto Dealership

Northern Michigan's first car dealer opened for business before Henry Ford invented the assembly line. In 1911, Milton Bryant, who was married to Ford's sister, opened Grand Traverse Auto on Front Street in downtown Traverse City. It remained in that location for 86 years, moving in 1997, to a brand new location just south of town.

Julius Sleder, who owned the dealership from 1964 until his death in 1999, told stories of Henry Ford sailing to Traverse City aboard his yacht to visit the business: "…he would bring his square dance band along. The dealership had three stories then, and on the third floor was a dance floor. My mom and dad would go to square dances hosted by the Ford's and the Bryant's."

Nearly 100 years after Milton Bryant began selling Model T's in Traverse City the dealership is owned by Sleder's son-in-law, Gary Moss, and still named Grand Traverse Auto.

Grand Traverse Auto, first auto dealer up north, opened by Henry Ford's brother-in-law, Milton Bryant (courtesy G.T. Pioneer & Historical Society)

TOP-SELLING VEHICLES
GRAND TRAVERSE MARKET (UNITS SOLD)

Top 10 Cars	2004	2003	
Chevy Impala	206	Saturn Ion	274
Saturn Ion	203	Chevy Impala	158
Kia Optima	150	Pontiac Grand Am	104
Honda Civic	115	Saturn L Sedan	101
Honda Accord	113	Buick LeSabre	100
Pontiac Grand Prix	104	Hyundai Electra	97
Hyundai Electra	89	Chevy Cavalier	93
Subaru Forester	87	Pontiac Grand Prix	91
Chevy Malibu	86	Subaru Legacy	89
Kia Spectra	85	Honda Civic	87

Top 10 SUV's	2004	2003	
Chevy Trailblazer	422	Chevy Trailblazer	351
GMC Envoy	276	Ford Explorer	312
Ford Explorer	252	GMC Envoy	263
Chevy Tahoe	183	Saturn Vue	199
Jeep Grand Cherokee	182	Chevy Tahoe	186
Saturn Vue	177	Jeep Grand Cherokee	163
Jeep Liberty	159	Hyundai Santa Fe	161
Hyundai Santa Fe	155	Jeep Liberty	153
Ford Escape	142	Buick Rendezvous	120
GMC Yukon	138	GMC Yukon	119

Top 10 Pick Ups	2004	2003	
Chevy C/K	616	Chevy C/K	632
Ford F Series	588	Ford F Series	484
GMC C/K Series	307	GMC C/K Series	379
Dodge Ram	223	Dodge Ram	270
Ford Ranger	108	Ford Ranger	120
Dodge Dakota	70	Chevy S 10	89
Chevy Avalanche	57	Dodge Dakota	59
Chevy S 10	56	Toyota Takoma	47
Toyota Tundra	52	Toyota Tundra	47
Nissan Titan	35	GMC Sonoma	29

Top 5 Mini Vans	2004	2003	
Chrysler Town & Country	201	Chrysler Town & Country	202
Kia Sedona	96	Dodge Caravan	131
Honda Odyssey	93	Ford Windstar	129
Dodge Caravan	79	Chevy Venture	86
Chevy Venture	53	Pontiac Montana	85

Top 5 Luxury Cars	2004	2003	
Cadillac Deville	37	Cadillac Deville	32
Lincoln Town Car	20	Lincoln Town Car	27
BMW 5 Series	17	BMW 5 Series	18
Lincoln LS	10	Lincoln LS	16
Mercedes 320 E	9	Audi A6	11

Top 5 Sport and Specialty Cars	2004	2003	
Chrysler Sebring	33	Chrysler Sebring	61
Ford Mustang	18	Hyundai Tiburon	28
Hyundai Tiburon	15	BMW 3 Series	26
BMW 3 Series	10	Ford Mustang	18
Chevy Corvette	8	Chevy Corvette	8

Top 10 vehicles overall	2004	2003	
Chevy C/K	616	Chevy C/K Series	632
Ford F Series	588	Ford F Series	484
Chevy Trailblazer	422	GMC C/K Series	379
GMC C/K Series	307	Chevy Trailblazer	351
GMC Envoy	276	Ford Explorer	312
Ford Explorer	252	Saturn Ion	274
Dodge Ram	223	Dodge Ram	270
Chevy Impala	206	GMC Envoy	263
Saturn Ion	203	Chrysler Town & Country Mini Van	202
Chrysler Town & Country Mini Van	201	Saturn Vue	19

LOTTERY SALES AND PRIZES: BY COUNTY (2004)

County	Sales of all lottery tickets ($)	Number of winners	Total prize amount ($)
Grand Traverse	8,020,328	550,198	4,137,478
Roscommon	6,080,856	425,433	7,203,780
Clare	5,357,158	395,382	2,702,947
Wexford	5,213,782	375,500	2,915,478
Otsego	3,757,674	251,879	1,918,880
Manistee	3,446,960	266,864	2,022,231
Emmet	3,242,414	227,245	1,565,536
Mason	3,086,575	225,724	1,645,667
Osceola	2,865,605	225,396	1,730,329
Charlevoix	2,676,565	184,159	1,233,726
Crawford	2,457,655	176,337	1,198,539
Antrim	2,264,527	169,435	1,109,095
Lake	2,200,360	141,290	1,126,115
Kalkaska	1,763,551	130,693	1,064,223
Leelanau	1,581,210	97,490	745,324
Benzie	1,479,159	101,492	729,366
Missaukee	1,079,070	79,812	582,265

Michigan State Lottery

LOTTERY TICKET SALES: PER CAPITA, BY COUNTY (2004)

County	Total lottery ticket sales ($)	Per person ($)
Roscommon	6,080,856	231.83
Lake	2,200,360	186.55
Clare	5,357,158	169.59
Wexford	5,213,782	166.83
Crawford	2,457,655	165.97
Otsego	3,757,674	154.84
Manistee	3,446,960	136.15
Osceola	2,865,605	121.89
Mason	3,086,575	107.60
Kalkaska	1,763,551	102.67
Charlevoix	2,676,565	100.20
Emmet	3,242,414	99.03
Grand Traverse	8,020,328	97.80
Antrim	2,264,527	93.99
Benzie	1,479,159	86.61
Leelanau	1,581,210	72.33
Missaukee	1,079,070	71.04

OIL AND GAS

Production

- Michigan ranks 17th in the country for oil production, and 11th in natural gas production.
- Average daily production of oil in Michigan: 22,677 barrels
- Average daily production of natural gas in Michigan: 790 million cubic feet
- Barrels of oil produced in Michigan since 1920: 1.34 billion
- Cubic Feet of natural gas produce in Michigan since 1920: 5.9 trillion
- Of the state's 83 counties, oil and/or natural gas are being produced in 63 of them.
- Northern Michigan counties producing gas and/or oil include:

Antrim	Manistee
Benzie	Mason
Charlevoix	Missaukee
Clare	Osceola
Crawford	Otsego
Grand Traverse	Roscommon
Kalkaska	Wexford
Lake	

Only Leelanau and Emmet counties have not had any oil or gas production.

The chemical compounds of hydrogen and carbon, which make up gas and oil, are buried thousands of feet deep into the earth. As the compounds travel up and out of the earth they become trapped by rock formations. Some of the most important gas formations in Michigan have been discovered in the north.

Antrim Shale Formation

The formation is present throughout Michigan, but has only been productive in the north, especially in Otsego, Antrim, Manistee, Montmorency, Oscoda, Alpena, and Alcona counties. Drilling began in the 1980's and doubled Michigan's annual natural gas production.

Niagaran Reef Trend

A 12-15 mile path running from Oceana County at the lakeshore northeast through Kalkaska, Otsego and Presque Isle counties. Discovered in 1968 the Niagaran Reef tripled Michigan's oil output and quintupled the state's natural gas production during the 1970's.

Glenwood and Prairie du Chein Formation

Some of the deepest wells in the state were drilled during the 1980's in this formation found in Osceola, Newaygo, Ogemaw, Bay and Arenac counties. Some of the wells were drilled over 11,000 feet deep.

Traverse, Dundee and Richfield Formations

Active in the 1930's and 40's, mainly in central and north central sections of the Lower Peninsula.

Top Oil Producing Counties (total all time production)

Hillsdale –123 million barrels

Manistee – 102 million barrels

Otsego – 100 million barrels

Top Natural Gas Producing Counties (total all time production)

Otsego – 860 billion cubic feet

Manistee – 600 billion cubic feet

Grand Traverse – 548 billion cubic feet

Kalkaska – 507 billion cubic feet

Gas and Oil Wells Drilled

Nationally, Michigan ranks 18th in number of oil wells drilled, and 8th in number of gas wells drilled.

Total oil wells currently operating in Michigan:
4,673

Total gas wells currently operating in Michigan:
6,865

Average cost to drill one well:
$162,107

Oil derrick in Manistee County (Author photo)

Number of active oil or gas wells by county

Otsego	3,415
Antrim	1,088
Manistee	462
Crawford	301
Kalkaska	226
Missaukee	167
Grand Traverse	149
Clare	123
Roscommon	81
Osceola	60
Charlevoix	58
Mason	16
Benzie	15
Wexford	11
Lake	7

Gas and Oil Employment in Michigan

Sector	No. of jobs
Oil and gas extraction	2,900
Refining	1,900
Transportation	6,800
Wholesale	5,300
Retail	27,800

In 1976, Michigan became the first State to set up a trust to buy land with revenue payments from the oil and gas industry. A percentage of oil and gas company earnings from State-leased land are made to the Michigan Natural Resources Trust Fund (MNRTF), which awards grants to help obtain important environmental and recreational land. As of January 2004, over $600 million in MNRTF grants have been awarded toward over 1,200 projects, totaling over 135,000 acres. Among them...

- 3,000 acres for the Pigeon River Country State Forest
- 14,000 acres for the State park system
- 1,000 acres for boating access sites
- 2,600 acres of water frontage for fishing access
- 37,000 acres for state wildlife areas

Petroleum Pipelines
There are no petroleum pipelines running into northern Michigan from the south. Petroleum is shipped in to marine terminals at Traverse City and Cheboygan, or trucked.

Natural Gas Pipelines
Two companies own an underground pipeline network that snakes across northern Michigan.

Great Lake Energy's line runs from the western UP to the eastern UP, and beneath the Mackinac Straits. From there it winds through Emmet, Charlevoix, Otsego, Kalkaska, Missaukee and Clare counties.

MichCon's gas lines run from Clare up through Kalkaska, Grand Traverse, Antrim, Benzie, Charlevoix and Cheboygan counties.

Gas storage fields are located in the following counties: Clare, Osceola, Lake, Missaukee, Kalkaska, Antrim and Otsego.

Michigan, with the largest underground working storage capacity of any state, is a natural gas storehouse for the Northeastern United States with 600 billion cubic feet of storage capacity.

Oil and Gas Exploration under Lake Michigan

Geologists believe there is a supply of oil and gas deep in the bedrock under Lake Michigan off the shore of Manistee and Mason counties. The extent of that supply will likely never be known as the gas and oil industry is prohibited from drilling under the lake. Although there has never been an offshore oil-rig in Lake Michigan, some companies have used directional, or "slant" drilling to reach under the lake from a point on shore.

Slant drilling operations set up a rig several hundred feet away from the shoreline, then a hole is drilled about 1,000 feet down. At that point it would be angled toward the water, where it penetrates bedrock some 5,000 feet beneath the bottom of the lake.

The practice of slant drilling under the Great Lakes started in 1972, but was permanently banned in 2002 by the State Legislature. Up to that point a total of 13 wells had been drilled under the lakes with seven of them producing oil and gas: five in Manistee County and two in Bay County. Since 1913, Canadian companies have drilled over 2,200 wells under Lake Erie.

In 1997, Governor John Engler ordered a temporary moratorium on slant drilling under the Great Lakes until a study was completed. Scientists investigated some 2,000 inland slant drilling operations, and concluded that there was little or no risk of water contamination from slant drilling under Lake Michigan. However they stated concerns about possible contamination at the well sites which led to public pressure to ban the practice.

Nordhouse Dunes
Drilling in the Nordhouse Dunes Wilderness Area has been prohibited since 1987. That ban against oil and gas drilling maintained the pristine condition of the dunes and cost State taxpayers over $100 million dollars in the process.

A year after the DNR banned drilling in the federal Wilderness Area of the dunes, a Traverse City oil company and the owners of the mineral rights under the dunes filed suit. Miller Oil had leased the mineral rights and wanted to drill in the dunes. Their argument, which eventually prevailed in court, claimed that the ban on drilling devalued their investment in the mineral rights lease. A judge ordered the State to pay Miller Oil, and the mineral rights owners, $120 million.

World's Richest Rotary Club?

In 1976 oil was discovered on property operated by Traverse City Rotary Club #754. The property is officially owned by Rotary Camps, Inc., which is operated by Rotary members. The property, over 450 acres around Spider Lake in Grand Traverse County, was purchased in 1923 for $1,100 to be used as a Boy Scout camp. To date over $40 million in oil and gas royalties has been paid to the Rotary organization.

Rotary leased the property to the local Boy Scouts for one dollar for 99 years. Rotary retained the mineral rights, and in 1975 structured the deal that paid off one year later: if oil or gas was discovered on the property, Rotary Camps would receive 25% of royalties, until all production costs were paid off, then the percentage jumped to 40% until the wells ran dry. Six wells hit oil, and the first royalty payments were made in 1977.

Rotary Club leaders set up Rotary Charities, Inc. to handle all oil and gas revenues. They didn't want the money to go directly to the Rotary Club, fearing the bonanza of cash would act as a disincentive for members regular fundraising and charitable activities. Using only the interest earned from the oil and gas fund, members of Rotary Charities hand out hundreds of thousands of dollars to local non-profit groups each year.

TRIBAL-OWNED CASINOS

Number of Slot Machines – Northern Michigan

Slot machines	Casino/town	Tribe
1,249	Little River Casino/Manistee	Little River Band of Ottawa Indians
1,192	Turtle Creek Casino/Williamsburg near Traverse City	Grand Traverse Band of Ottawa and Chippewa Indians
847	Victories Casino/Petoskey	Little Traverse Bay Band of Odawa Indians
576	Leelanau Sands Casino/Peshabestown near Suttons Bay	Grand Traverse Band of Ottawa and Chippewa Indians

Number of Slot Machines - Statewide

Slot machines	Casino/town	Tribe
4,347	Soaring Eagle/Mt. Pleasant	Saginaw Chippewa Indians
1,249	Little River Casino/Manistee	Little River Band of Ottawa Indians
1,192	Turtle Creek Casino/Williamsburg near Traverse City	Grand Traverse Band of Ottawa and Chippewa Indians
976	Chip-In's Island Casino/Harris near Escanaba	Hannahville Indian Community
903	Kewadin Shores/St. Ignace	Sault Ste. Marie Tribe of Chippewa Indians

Slot machines	Casino/town	Tribe
899	Kewadin Vegas/Sault Ste. Marie	Sault Ste. Marie Tribe of Chippewa Indians
847	Victories Casino/Petoskey	Little Traverse Bay Band of Odawa Indians
678	Lac Vieux Desert Casino/Watersmeet	Lac Vieux Desert Bands of Lake Superior Chippewa Indians
53	Bay Mills Resort Casino/Brimley	Bay Mills Indian Community
576	Leelanau Sands Casino/Peshabestown near Suttons Bay	Grand Traverse Band of Ottawa and Chippewa Indians
355	Ojibwa Casino/Baraga	Keweenaw Bay Indian Community
329	Ojibwa Casino II/Marquette	Keweenaw Bay Indian Community
275	Kings Club Casino	Bay Mills Inidan Community/Brimley
246	Kewadin/Manistique	Sault Ste. Marie Tribe of Chippewa Indians
212	Kewadin/Christmas	Sault Ste. Marie Tribe of Chippewa Indians
111	Kewadin/Hessel	Sault Ste. Marie Tribe of Chippewa Indians

Michigan Gaming Control Board

2% Payments of Slot Revenue to Local Units of Government

In 1993 seven native American tribes signed compacts with the State of Michigan requiring them to pay 2% of gross slot machine revenues to local units of government twice a year. These tribes were also required to make a semi-annual payments to the State of Michigan, but under terms of the compact that requirement was waived after casinos opened in Detroit in 1999.

Tribes signing the 1993 compact include: Grand Traverse Band of Chippewa and Ottawa Indians, Bay Mills, Sault Ste. Marie Chippewas, Saginaw Chippewas, Hannanville, Keweenaw Bay and Lac Vieux.

Grand Traverse Band of Ottawa and Chippewa Indians

2% payment to local units of government

Year	Amount ($)
1994	369,551
1995	541,252
1996	829,459
1997	1,168,406
1998	1,699,951
1999	1,830,855
2000	1,799,013
2001	1,915,279
2002	2,040,614
2003	1,882,769
Total	14,077,154

Little River Band of Odawa Indians

2% payment to local units of government

Year	Amount($)
1999	94,348 (6 months)
2000	1,189,043
2001	1,484,141
2002	1,715,218
2003	1,955,581
Total	6,438,333

Little Traverse Band of Ottawa Indians

2% payment to local units of government

Year	Amount ($)
1999	78,536 (3 months)
2000	518,783
2001	839,414
2002	978,898
2003	1,338,605
Total	3,754,237

8% of Slot Revenue Payments to Michigan Strategic Fund

Under a 1998 compact signed with the State of Michigan the following tribes agreed to make two annual payments worth 8% of their gross slot machine revenues to the State of Michigan. They also make 2% payments to a local board that dispenses the money to local units of government.

Tribes signing the 1998 compact include: Little River Band of Ottawa Indians (Manistee), Little Traverse Bay Band of Odawa Indians (Petoskey), Nottawaseppi Huron (Battle Creek), and the Polagon Band (New Buffalo).

Grand Traverse Band of Ottawa and Chippewa Indians

8% payments to State of Michigan

Year	Amount ($)
1993	423,417
1994	933,851
1995	2,439,840
1996	3,260,434
1997	4,813,873
1998	5,579,522
1999	659,036 (6 months)
Total	18,109,977

Little River Band of Ottawa Indians

8% payments to State of Michigan

Year	Amount ($)
1999	1,348,619
2000	5,133,569
2001	5,936,567
2002	6,860,872
2003	7,822,326
Total	27,101, 955

Little Traverse Bay Band of Odawa Indians

8% payments to State of Michigan

Year	Amount ($)
1999	322,549
2000	2,075,133
2001	3,357,658
2002	3,915,593
2003	5,354,420
Total	15,025,355

SHIPPING

Commercial shipping of bulk goods began in the 1600's when French voyageurs constructed large canoes to haul large quantities of fur between trading posts. The first commercial ship into Lake Michigan was the *Griffon,* LaSalle's ship that entered the Straits of Mackinac on August 27, 1679 on its way to pick up a load of furs at Green Bay. The last record of the *Griffon* was its departure from Green Bay. It was never heard from again.

Commercial shipping expanded with the opening of the Erie Canal in the 1820's and the Michigan lumber boom between 1850-1900. Ship design advanced from schooners to wood-hulled steamships to the steel-hulled propeller ships and eventually to the behemoth freighters that ply the lakes today.

Freighters on Lake Michigan are probably hauling coal, iron ore, limestone, or potash. The amount of coal shipped over Lake Michigan is a fraction of Lake Superior's volume. According to the Lake Carrier's Association, in 2003 total volume of coal shipped on Lake Michigan was 2,771,065 tons compared to 14,238,033 tons shipped on Lake Superior.

Largest freighter on Lake Michigan:
Paul R. Tregurtha at 1,013 feet, six inches

Largest freighter entering Manistee Harbor:
Courtney Burton at 690 feet.

Centennial Businesses – Over 100 Years in Business

The Island House Hotel	Mackinac Island	1852
Doud Mercantle	Mackinac Island	1854
Old Mission Inn	Traverse City	1869
Mackinac Island Carriage Tours	Mackinac Island	1869
Smeltzer Orchards	Frankfort	1872
Park Place Hotel	Traverse City	1873
Ironton Ferry	Ironton	1870's
Village Inn	Suttons Bay	1870's
Votruba's	Traverse City	1870's
Lake County Star	Baldwin	1873
Blick Dillon Insurance	Cadillac	1874
Bahle's	Suttons Bay	1876
Leelanau Enterprise	Leland	1876
Martinek's Jewelers	Traverse City	1878
Arnold Line Ferries	Mackinac Island	1878
Michigan Maple Block	Petoskey	1881
East Jordan Iron Works	East Jordan	1883
The Fly Factory	Grayling	1880's
Murray Hotel	Mackinac Island	1885
Murdick's Fudge	Mackinac Island	1887
Grand Hotel	Mackinac Island	1887
McGough's Inc.	Traverse City	1890
Carrom Games	Ludington	1890
Stafford Perry Hotel	Petoskey	1899
Riverside Inn	Leland	1902
Chippewa Hotel	Mackinac Island	1902
Hotel Iroquois	Mackinac Island	1904
Windermere Hotel	Mackinac Island	1904
Nugent Farms	Frankfort	1905

INVENTORS

Father of the Second Industrial Revolution

John T. Parsons of Traverse City is also known as the "Father of Numerical Control," a process that revolutionized manufacturing and the aerospace industry. The benefits we reap today are many; safer, faster and more affordable air travel, lower cost products from cars to clothing, and countless jobs created. In the 1940's the Parsons Corporation of Traverse City was the world's largest designer and producer of helicopter blades. Parsons was looking for a way to improve the accuracy in the manufacture of the blades, so he hired Frank Stulen from the Propeller Lab of Wright-Patterson Air Force Base. Not long after that, Parsons was asked to design a wing for a new jet bomber being designed by Lockheed.

The wing looked good on paper, but to cut out the precise curves and shapes would require hundreds of precise adjustment on the machine tools. It was 1948 when Parsons and Stulen discovered they could program a key punch computer to control the machine tools for a reliable and accurate result.

Stulen would later note, "We are today on the brink of a second Industrial Revolution. The first was the development of machines to perform mechanically what man previously did by hand. The second, now in its infancy, is the development of equipment to control these machines."

Parsons was born October 11, 1913, in Detroit. He worked in a stamping plant and did not attend college. However, he received the first honorary Doctor of Engineering awarded by the University of Michigan.

World War II patriotism (courtesy G.T. Pioneer & Historical Society)

The use of numerical data to control machines is the standard in today's manufacturing world. It has drastically cut production costs in the manufacture of everything from automobiles to clothing to computer chips.

Parsons also built the first all-composite airplane, developed technology to improve the manufacture of propellers, and produced the huge fuel line used on the Saturn booster used by NASA.

He's been hailed as a "Hero of Manufacturing" by *Fortune Magazine,* received the National Medal of Technology from President Reagan, has numerous citations from engineering and technical associations, and has been enshrined in the National Inventors Hall of Fame. Parsons Road in Traverse City is named after him, and the Northwestern Michigan College Technology Education Center (M-TEC) is named after Parsons and Stulen. Parsons resides in Traverse City.

John Parsons accepting National Medal of Technology from President Reagan (courtesy of Parsons family)

The Father of Information Theory

Were it not for Claude Shannon, you may not be surfing the net, sending e-mail, talking on your cellular phone, and listening to CD's. Shannon, a Gaylord native, was into information technology before IT was cool. His theories and discoveries in the 1940's made possible today's computer and telecommunications industry.

Shannon is considered one of the most important mathematicians of the 20th century. He was the first person to discover that information – words, pictures or sounds – could be broken down into a series of 0's and 1's and transmitted over a wire. "Nobody came close to this idea before. This was not something somebody else would have done for a very long time," said former colleague, Robert G. Gallager, a professor emeritus at the Massachusetts Institute of Technology.

Claude Shannon was born in Petoskey April 30, 1916, and raised in Gaylord. His father was a judge, and his mother was the local high school principal. Not a bad atmosphere for fostering potential genius, but the inventor's gene apparently came from Claude's grandfather, who invented the washing machine. There was another inventor in the family, a distant relative by the name of Thomas Edison. Like Edison, Shannon spent his boyhood assembling radios and playing with Morse code. During high school, he worked as a messenger for Western Union.

Shannon earned degrees in mathematics and electrical engineering from the University of Michigan. He obtained his Master's in electrical engineering, and his Ph.D. in mathematics from the Massachusetts Institute of Technology. His first job out of college, in 1941, was at AT&T Bell Laboratories, where he remained until his retirement in 1972.

In 1948 he published *A Mathematical Theory of Communication* that laid out the revolutionary idea of breaking information down into a series of binary digits, 1's and 0's, or bits to be digitally transmitted. *(Shannon was the first to use the term "bits" in his 1948 paper.)*

Shannon was a noted cryptographer, and during World War II he worked on anti-aircraft detectors that combat enemy missiles. He is credited with changing cryptography from art to science.

Claude Shannon experiments with artificially intelligent mouse

His later work explored artificial intelligence. He invented a computer that played chess, and even put up a good fight, before losing to the world champion of the day.

Colleagues at Bell Labs and MIT remember Shannon as a genius who loved to juggle while riding his unicycle down the hallway. While at Bell Labs he married Betty Moore, a numerical analyst. They had three sons and one daughter.

Shannon, a professor emeritus at MIT, received the Alfred Nobel American Institute of American Engineers Award in 1940, the National Medal of Science in 1966, the Audio Engineering Society Gold Medal in 1985, and the Kyoto Prize in 1985.

He passed away in February 2001. News of his death quickly circulated around the internet.

Ephraim Shay (7/17/1839 – 4/19/16)   Shay Locomotive
Like any great invention, the Shay locomotive solved a problem and led to higher profits for operators and lower prices for consumers. Shay's locomotive lowered the cost of harvesting trees from deep in the forest, far from the rivers needed for floating logs to the mill.

Shay operated his own mill in Cadillac. He was logging the pine forest between Cadillac and Lake City, and like other lumbermen of the 1870's, had exhausted the supply of good trees near the river. Forced to go deeper into the woods, the cost of transporting logs to the mill went up drastically. Logs couldn't be moved until there was enough snow to create narrow roads of ice. Teams of horses or oxen were used to pull sleds full of logs to the riverbanks. The logs then sat until the spring thaw when they could be floated to the nearest mill. At that time transportation of logs made up over 70% of the cost of lumber.

Shay first tried to get around this problem by building wooden tracks for a horse-dawn carriage full of logs. This increased production, and lowered Shay's cost, but took a toll on the horses that were overrun by the heavy loads on steep downhills. In 1877, he and a local machinist, William Crippen, built a locomotive to run on a two-foot wide track, which gave him more control, but the fixed wheels on the locomotive ruined his wooden track. Even with the crude new locomotive, Shay had cut his production costs by 35% and other lumbermen took note.

*Ephraim Shay
(courtesy G.T.
Pioneer &
Historical Society)*

The locomotive went into production in 1878 at the Lima Machine Works Co. in Lima, Ohio. Shay, and a machinist at Lima Machine Works improved the design of the gear-driven locomotive and in 1881 Shay was granted a patent. Lima Machine Works, built 2,770 Shay locomotives between 1880 and 1945.

Shay earned a fortune and in 1888 moved his family to Harbor Springs, where he built a six-sided house out of sheet steel called "The Hexagon." Shay built a small railroad, the Hemlock Central, used first for lumbering, and later by tourists. Using the many artesian wells around Harbor Springs, he built the town's first waterworks. In his workshop he enjoyed building sleds out of maple, which he would give to neighboring children every Christmas.

Shay's other patented inventions include several universal joints and gears used in locomotives and ships, and a fire-fighting hose cart.

Today "The Hexagon" is privately owned, and used for weekend trunk shows in the summer. It is opened for public tours during the annual Shay Days in July. Shay's waterworks is now a city-owned storage building, and there is city park named after him.

In Cadillac, Shay locomotive No. 549, built in 1898 for White & Co. of Boyne City, sits on display in a city park.

Silas C. Overpack – Big Wheels

Until the Big Wheel rolled into history, Michigan lumbermen could only move their logs out of the forest in the winter months. The only way to transport the heavy logs was on a large horse-drawn sled over an ice road. Loggers had to wait for cold temperatures and plenty of snow before such a road could be made.

Lots of lumber to haul! (courtesy G.T. Pioneer & Historical Society)

Overpack invented the Big Wheel in his Manistee carriage shop. The heavy logs were chained below the axle between the big wheels. Once the rig was rolling, it was relatively easy for the horses to pull, and allowed them to carry logs up to 100 feet long and loads equal to 2,000 board feet of lumber. The Big Wheels allowed loggers to work all year.

The wheels came in three sizes: nine, nine-and-a-half, and ten feet high. They had iron rims, and rings of iron protected the spokes. Big Wheels manufactured by Overpack were always painted red.

The wheels were a hit. At least 65 Michigan lumber companies placed orders. After Overpack exhibited his invention in 1893 at the Columbian Exposition in Chicago, orders came in from across the country and overseas. The U.S. Army used his Big Wheels in World War I.

Ray Pleva "Mr. Cherry"

It's fitting that this butcher from Cedar is known as "Mr. Cherry." After all, Ray Pleva is the guy who came up with the idea of mixing meat with cherries.

Cherry Pecan Sausage, his first concoction, debuted in 1988, and the following year earned the Best New Product award in Michigan. In 1993, he won the same award for Plevalean, his lean ground beef and cherry mixture. The awards are based on ingenuity of concept and total contribution to the State's economy.

The concept came about in 1987 when Cindy, one of Pleva's daughters, was named National Cherry Queen. She wanted to help the industry, and that was the inspiration for Ray to follow up on an idea that was born at the family dinner table: mixing lean meat with fresh cherries. Not an unusual topic considering the family's background.

Both Ray and his wife, Marge, grew up on cherry farms near Cedar. Ray learned the cherry business and started work in the family butcher shop when he was eleven. Marge was the Leelanau County Cherry Pie Baking Queen before settling down with Ray. The hardworking couple had two daughters, Cindy and Ramona, and running the butcher shop became a family affair.

Ray's talents are not limited to butchering and agriculture. He manages to find himself with the right people at the right time in the right place, resulting in millions of dollars worth of free publicity. Shortly after the debut of the Cherry Pecan Sausage ABC's Good Morning America broadcast from the National Cherry Festival. Spencer Christian, the morning weatherman, wound up eating a link of the sausage on national TV.

Soon after, Robert Vito and a camera crew from CNN were navigating their way to Pleva's Meats in Cedar. CNN wound up covering the meat and cherries story twice, while other national media from Paul Harvey to *Extra Magazine* reported on the butcher's family from small town Michigan trying to help the cherry industry by creating a new food combination.

Although it seemed odd to some, nearly all who tried the cherry sausage or cherry burgers had something nice to say. Ray knew he was on to something and contacted Michigan State University to conduct a study of his food creation.
The laboratory results: meat products, when infused with Pleva's secret cherry formula, yielded less fat, fewer calories, more fiber, were juicier and were loaded with cancer-fighting anti-oxidants! Not to mention the meat had a longer shelf life due to the cherry ingredients.

About the time these results were garnering plenty of attention from local and statewide media, a Chicago woman was in court defending a public statement she made along the lines of "I will never eat another burger." The beef industry lost its suit against Oprah Winfrey. The staff of the talk show goddess noticed an article about Pleva's healthy burgers, and that inspired a show on alternatives to the traditional burger.

Ray and his family appeared on the Oprah show in October of 1994. On the program Oprah hesitantly bit into one of Ray's freshly grilled Pleva Burgers and then looked into the camera and exclaimed, "That's good...it's delicious!"

Although a brilliant self-promoter, Pleva has always made it clear that he's pitching for all of his partners in agriculture. After his Oprah appearance, he said, "I was able to show off cherry sausage, cherry pepperoni, Canadian bacon beef, and dried cherries. Good for the beef, pork and cherry industries."

Three years later, the Plevas landed in Hollywood. They were invited by Tim Allen, the star of the hottest sitcom on television at that time. Allen had recently married a woman whose parents were in the cherry business in Leelanau County. Allen was willing to do his part to help the family and the cherry industry, so he had a small role written up for Ray, who portrayed himself before millions of viewers.

Ray and Marge Pleva with Tim Allen on the set of Home Improvement (courtesy of Pleva family)

Since the invention of Cherry Pecan Sausage in 1987, Pleva has created another 40 or so meat and cherry products. He's experimented with venison, emu, lamb and buffalo. His Plevalean burgers are served in public schools around the country, and his products are imported to Canada and Japan. His cherry and meat products have been covered in *Good Housekeeping, Cooking Light, Food & Wine, Men's Health and Fitness,* and a slew of national medical and trade journals. Even Jay Leno had a few cracks about the cherry burgers.

Pleva's mixture of meat and cherries led to the research at MSU that revealed the healthful benefits of cherries. Since then, the industry has successfully produced and promoted cherry juice and cherry tablets as health supplements that reduce and prevent joint pain.

In 2002, Pleva sold his butcher shop to a relative, but remains in Cedar and continues to promote the cherry industry the best way he knows how: by promoting Ray Pleva and Pleva Meat Products. www.plevas.com

Don Nugent – Dried Cherries

In a sense, Don Nugent made lemonade out of lemons. Actually he made dried cherries out of wasted cherries. As a cherry grower and operator of a fruit co-op in the mid 1970's, Nugent had a lot of surplus cherries, and he had to pull a lot of those off the market after a big spill in the freezer. That's where the lemonade comes in.

Nugent figured he had a lot of free cherries to experiment with. He had been considering the idea of a cherry "raisin" for a few years, and now went to work. After several years of trial and error, he wound up developing and patenting a commercial drying process. The first dried cherries hit the market in 1985.

Today Graceland Fruit is the world's largest producer of dried fruit products. The company produces dried cherries, blueberries, strawberries, peaches, cranberries, and apples. Graceland also produces dried vegetables including broccoli, carrots, celery, corn, peppers, peas and potatoes.

Since creating the dried cherry in the mid 1980's, Nugent and Graceland now buy 10% of Michigan-grown tart cherries. The company has gone from six employees to 196 year round, and an additional 150 in the summer.

Nugent was named Master Entrepreneur of the Year in 2003 by the West Michigan office of Ernst & Young. Graceland has earned the Edward R. Madigan U.S. Agricultural Export Excellence Award, the National Ag Marketer of the Year Award, Michigan Manufacturer of the Year and Michigan Exporter of the Year.

Domino Effect Started in Traverse City

The man who built an empire out of pizza crust began his working life in Traverse City. Tom Monaghan, founder of Domino's Pizza and one-time owner of the Detroit Tigers, developed his business acumen and grand tastes during his teen years in Traverse City.

His father died when Tom was four years old. His mother put him and a younger brother into an orphanage in Jackson, while she attended nursing school. She headed up north in hopes of treating her hay fever, and landed a job at Munson Medical Center. She brought her boys to live with her when Tom was in sixth grade.

In his autobiography, *Pizza Tiger,* he described a feeling of exhilaration when he got to Traverse City. "I can recall how exciting it was to be free…to be allowed to have money in my pocket, to be able to make money." After 7th grade he earned money picking cherries, selling his freshly caught fish and vegetables from his garden door-to-door, and selling the *Record Eagle* outside Milliken's Department Store.

Former Traverse City St. Francis student, Tom Monaghan

The relationship with his mother was always strained, and she eventually placed him in foster care at an Interlochen farm. Monaghan lived on several farms and enjoyed the routine and the hard work.

During early high school he grew interested in architecture and spent much time at the Traverse City Library studying Frank Lloyd Wright. At one time Monaghan owned one of the most prestigious collections of Frank Lloyd Wright furniture and homes. He had buildings at his world headquarters, and later his Ave Maria Catholic University designed in the Frank Lloyd Wright style.

Monaghan was a student at St. Francis High School and attended mass regularly. The importance of religion in his life became so great in high school that Father Passeno helped enroll him at a Grand Rapids seminary. Monaghan didn't last a year, and returned to school in Traverse City.

During 11th grade he worked at Conaway's Bowling Alley in downtown Traverse City. During that year after an argument with his mother, she had him placed in youth detention. His life changed when he was adopted by an aunt from Ann Arbor. He moved there, and after college and a stint in the U.S. Marine Corp he and his brother bought a small pizzeria. The rest is pizza history.

Pizza Tiger, *copyright 1986 by Thomas S. Monaghan with Robert Anderson, Random House, New York*

Renaissance Zones

Renaissance Zones are regions of the state set aside as virtually tax-free for any business or resident located in or moving to one of the zones. The program was designed to spark business activity in economically distressed areas of the state.

Businesses in a Renaissance Zone do not pay the following taxes:
- Single Business Tax
- 6-mil state education tax
- Local personal property tax
- Local real property taxes

Started in 1996, the Renaissance Zone program resulted in more than 6,300 new jobs and $1.7 billion in private investment in the first six years.

Renaissance Zones exist in five northern Michigan counties.

Lake County
Chase Township	24 acres
Eden Township	370 acres
Village of Baldwin	41 acres
Yates Township	21 acres

Osceola County
City of Evart	5.6 acres *(zoned residential)*
LeRoy Township	

Clare County
Freeman Township	27 acres
Grant Township	160 acres
Hamilton Township	53 acres
Village of Farwell	115 acres

Manistee County
East Lake/Filer/Manistee	376 acres
Kaleva	183 acres

Grand Traverse County
Grand Traverse Commons	20 acres

The former Traverse City State Psychiatric Hospital opened in 1885 as the Northern Michigan Asylum. The 388,000 square foot "Building 50" was designed by Detroit architect, Gordon W. Lloyd, who also designed The Whitney house in Detroit. The hospital served the mentally ill for over 100 years before it was closed by the State in 1989. Building 50 was saved from demolition by a citizens group in 2000 and is now owned by and undergoing restoration by The Minervini Group. The collection of buildings now known as The Village at Grand Traverse Commons, house a restaurant, offices, apartments, and condos (www.thevillagetc.com) (photo courtesy of John Russell)

TRANSPORTATION

TRANSPORTATION

The Mackinac Bridge

The Mighty Mac has come to symbolize the state of Michigan as much as the Great Lakes that define the State. But, the Bridge belongs solely to Michigan, and stands as one of the great achievements in the State's engineering, labor, and political history.

Looking north from the Mackinac Bridge under construction (State Archives of Michigan)

From the time it was built in 1957 until 1998 it stood as the world's longest suspension bridge. It now ranks as the longest suspension bridge in the western hemisphere, and the 3rd longest in the world, based on total suspension, or the length between anchorages.

Bridge	Total suspension	Main span (between towers)
Akashi Kaikyo Bridge, Japan	12,826 ft.	6,529 ft.
Great Belt Bridge, Halsskov-Sprogoe, Denmark	8,921 ft.	5,328 ft.
Mackinac Bridge	8,614 ft.	3,800 ft.

Largest bridges based on main span (distance between towers)

Bridge	Main span
Akashi Kaikyo Bridge, Japan	6,529
Izmit Bay, Turkey	5,472
Great Belt Bridge, Denmark	5,328
Humber, England	4,626
Jiaangyin, China	4,543
Tsing Ma, Hong Kong	4,518
Verrazzano-Narrows, New York	4,260
Golden Gate, San Francisco	4,200
Hoga Kusten, Sweden	3,969
Mackinac Bridge, Michigan	3,800

In 1999, the Michigan Section of the American Society of Civil Engineers named the Mackinac Bridge as the State's number one civil engineering achievement. The Soo Locks finished 2nd ahead of the Detroit-Windsor Tunnel. Rounding out the top 10 were: the Ambassador Bridge, Ford Motor Company Rouge complex, Detroit's Wastewater Treatment Plant, the Ludington Pumped Storage facility and the St. Clair River Railroad Tunnel.

Bridge History

The first public expression of the need for a bridge across the Straits was in 1884, when the Grand Traverse *Herald* newspaper wrote that ferry service was a failure, and that a bridge or tunnel was necessary.

That same year, a St. Ignace shop owner took out a print ad with a drawing of the just completed Brooklyn Bridge and labeled it as the "proposed bridge across the Straits of Mackinac."

In 1888, Cornelius Vanderbilt, the railroad and shipping magnate who also had a hand in founding the Grand Hotel, called for a bridge across the Straits.

The idea wasn't approached seriously until 1934 when the legislature created the Mackinac Bridge Authority to investigate the feasibility of building and financing a bridge.

Bridge Alternatives

- Former State Highway Commissioner, Horatio Earle, in 1920, suggested a floating tunnel.

- He later proposed a system of bridges, causeways and island roads that would lead from Cheboygan to Bois Blanc Island, across two island lakes, and eastward to another bridge to Round Island, to Mackinac Island, and finally over to St. Ignace.

- Charles Fowler, a civil engineer, refined the plan and submitted it as a federal public works project, but was denied.

- The State Highway Department started a ferry service for automobiles in 1923, but demand for service quickly outgrew ferry capacity.

The initial report of the Mackinac Bridge Authority found it was feasible to build a two-lane highway and one-track railroad bridge across the Straits at an estimated cost of $32,400,000. The federal government again denied funding.

Studies continued and in the late 1930's a 4,200-foot causeway was built over the water in St. Ignace. World War II brought an end to the pursuit of a bridge across the Straits, and in 1947 the legislature abolished the Bridge Authority.

Bridge promoters managed to convince lawmakers to approve a second version of the Mackinac Bridge Authority in 1950, and there next report stated the bridge could be built for $86,000,000. Several attempts to sell bonds to investors failed, but in 1953 $99,800,000 worth of bonds were purchased, and the Authority began awarding engineering and construction contracts.

Contracts

Firm	Project	Contract
David B. Steinman	Architect	$3,500,000
US Steel, American Bridge Division	Steel superstructure including towers, cables and truss spans	$43,927,806
Merritt-Chapman and Scott Corp.	Underwater and land foundations	$26,335,000
Louis Garavaglia, Centerline, MI and Johnson-Greene, Ann Arbor, MI	Paving of bridge superstructure	$2,181,093
Northern Michigan Companies		
Durocher and Van Antwerep, Cheboygan	Extension of causeway	$60,000
Erkfitz Plumbing and Heating, Rogers City	Heating and mechanical in maintenance building	$22,418
Edison Sault Electric Co.	Extension of water supply to bridge site	$19,000
Fred Hoffman, Petoskey	Tree planting and landscaping	$7,000

Construction

Start date: May 7, 1954

Finish date: November 1, 1957

Men employed at bridge site: 3,500

Men employed at quarries, shops, mills, etc: 7,500

Number of engineers: 350

Number of steel rivets: 4,851,700

Number of steel bolts: 1,016,600

Five men died while building the bridge:
Frank Pepper, September 16, 1954
James R. LeSarge, October 10, 1954
Albert Abbot, October 25, 1954
Jack C. Baker, June 6, 1956
Robert Koppen, June 6, 1956

Their names are engraved on a plaque that hangs in their honor on a bridge pillar near Colonial Michilimackinac.

Two of the men fell approximately 550 feet from a catwalk that snapped; one man fell into a caisson while welding, one fell a few feet into the water and drowned and one died in a diving accident. All but the body of one of the men who fell from the catwalk were recovered. There are no bodies buried in the concrete foundations beneath the water.

Mackinac Bridge Stats

Total length: 26,372 ft. *(5 miles)*

Width of roadway: 54 feet / 68 feet at suspended span

Length of main span *(between towers)*: 3,800 ft.

Height of main towers *(above water)*: 552 ft.

Height of roadway above water: 199 ft.

Max. depth of tower piers below water: 210 ft.

Max. depth of water at midspan: 295 ft.

Total length of wire in cables: 42,000 miles

Diameter of each wire: 0.196 inches

Number of wires in each cable: 12,580

Diameter of cables: 24 inches

Weight of cables: 11,480 tons

Total concrete in bridge: 466,300 cu. yds.

Total weight of concrete: 931,000 tons

Total weight of bridge: 1,024,500 tons

Design

The bridge is specially designed to withstand the high winds, stiff currents and moving ice in the Straits. The architect, David B. Steinman, designed the middle two lanes to be open grids instead of solid concrete, which gives the bridge added resistance to strong winds. At the center span of the bridge it is possible for it to sway as much as 35 feet in one direction under severe wind conditions.

In Lawrence Rubin's book, *Mighty Mac,* Steinman wrote: "The Mackinac Bridge represents the triumph of the new science of suspension bridge aerodynamics. It represents the achievement of a new goal of perfect aerodynamic stability, never before attained or approximated in any prior suspension bridge design."

State officials in white Oldsmobiles cross the bridge during opening ceremonies (State Archives of Michigan)

First citizen to cross the bridge
Al Carter, a Chicago jazz musician who looked for opportunities to get his name in the news by being "the first" to do something. Carter drove a 1951 station wagon across the span when it opened at 2:00 p.m., November 1st, 1957.

First snowmobile crossing
February 14, 1970. One lane of the bridge was shut down so that members of the Pathfinders snowmobile club could continue their trip from Marquette to Cadillac.

First birth on the bridge
On May 11th, 1983, Kim Shuman from the UP town of Eckerman was about to give birth to her first baby. At the time she was in a Kinross Ambulance speeding over the Mackinac Bridge towards Northern Michigan Hospital in Petoskey. Halfway across the bridge they realized there wasn't enough time to make it to Petoskey, so they turned around on the bridge and raced toward Straits Area Hospital. The baby didn't wait. The 4 lb. boy was born in the ambulance on the north end of the bridge at 5:10 p.m. The next day a banner proclaiming "It's A Boy!" hung from the bridge office.

Thanks to Karen Gould, St. Ignace News

In 1997, Yvette Johnson gave birth to her fourth child, a baby girl, halfway across the bridge as she was returning from a winning day at the Kewadin Casino in St. Ignace.

First marriage proposal
Andrew Nelson proposed to Julie Engel on the bridge in 1995. His truck stalled on the bridge, and he had to pull over even though it's illegal to stop on the bridge. State troopers pulled up as he was down on one knee popping the question.

First suicide
A Royal Oak man jumped to his death from mid-bridge on April 22, 1974.

First vehicle off the bridge
During a blizzard in September of 1989, Leslie Pluhar's 1987 Yugo went over the side rail and plunged 150 feet into the frigid Straits below. High winds contributed to the tragedy, and in 1990 State Senate recommended side rails be raised from 36 to 48 inches.

A sport utility vehicle drove off the bridge in March of 1997, but investigators believe it was a suicide.

First buggy crossing
It took an Amish family with horse and buggy one hour to cross the bridge on June 30, 1973. Bridge officials agreed to shut down one lane for the crossing.

First bridge walk
September 7, 1959. It took Governor G. Mennen Williams 65 minutes to walk from St. Ignace to Mackinaw City. An estimated 15,000 walkers joined the governor.

First plane crash
Three off-duty National Guard officers were killed on September 10, 1978, when their small plane crashed into suspension wires near the north tower during foggy conditions. The crash left an oil slick in the Straits and pieces of the plane scattered on the bridge roadway.

The man who flew under the bridge
Muskegon native, John Lappo, was a decorated Air Force Captain who made his last flight for the military over northern Michgian. He flew 28 bombing runs over North Korea, and led spy missions over the Soviet Union during the early years of the Cold War. He is best remembered, though, for a flight over northern Michigan on April 24, 1959.

Early on a Friday afternoon, while returning from a simulated bombing run and navigation mission, Lappo was flying a $3.5 million RB-47E Stratojet over northern Lake Michigan when he decided to fulfill a longtime desire: to fly a plane under a bridge. He had told friends he thought it would be the Golden Gate, but on this clear day, he saw only two cars on the bridge, and away he went. The huge bomber descended rapidly, leveled off less than two hundred feet over the water, and flew under the deck of the Mighty Mac. Mission accomplished.

RB-47E Stratojet

Lappo later told reporters that only one crew member objected to the stunt, "Of course, I had no idea at the time that he was the general's son and that he was going to go rat on me once we got back to Lockbourne."

Lappo was charged at a general court-martial in August of that year. In his defense several officers testified to his superior piloting skills, proven integrity and unquestioned courage.

Found guilty of violating an Air Force regulation that prohibited flying less than 500 feet except during take offs and landings, Lappo was ordered to pay $50 a month for six months.

Lappo and his wife moved to Alaska, where he piloted his own small plane until his death in November of 2003.

Highest wind gust recorded at Mackinac Bridge:
128 mph on May 9th, 2003

Most crossings – year:
4,936,417 in 1999

Most crossings – month:
726,400 crossings in July, 1999

Most crossings – day:
37,846 on June 29, 1996 during the Straits Area Antique Auto Show

Crossings first year:
140,518 (November and December of 1957)

Crossings first full year (1958):
1,390,390

First year with over two million crossings:
1971 with 2,090,492

First year with over three million crossings:
1987 with 3,032,547

First year with over four million crossings:
1994 with 4,333,185

50 millionth crossing:
September 25, 1984

100 millionth crossing:
June 25, 1998

Current rates

Passenger cars	$1.25 per axle
Motorcycles	$2.50
Motor homes	$2.00 per axle
All others	$3.00 per axle

Commuters can buy 24 tokens for $30.00

Bicycles, pedestrians and snowmobiles are not permitted on the bridge, but for a fee can be carried over by the Bridge Authority.

Bikes and persons	$2.00
Snowmobile and one person	$10.00

History of fares for passenger cars

1957 – 1960	$3.25
1/1/60 – 4/30/60	$3.50
5/1/60 – 12/31/68	$3.75
1/1/69 – 5/1/03	$1.50
5/1/03 – present	$2.50 (1.25 per axle)

During formal dedication ceremonies on June 25, 1958, Governor G. Mennen Williiams driver's license was expired, so he rode shotgun as his wife made the ceremonial drive over the bridge.

OTHER NOTEWORTHY BRIDGES

Mortimer E. Cooley Bridge

The high bridge on M-55 over the Pine River in Manistee County

Year built: 1934

Length: 555 feet

One of two cantilvered deck truss bridges in Michigan. In 1936 it was recognized as the most beautiful bridge in its class by the American Institute of Steel Construction.

US-31 Bridge – Manistee
Drawbridge over Manistee River near downtown Manistee

Cooley Bridge over the Pine River (courtesy of MDOT)

US 31 drawbridge from downtown Manistee (Author photo)

Year built: 1933

US 31/Island Lake Outlet Bridge – Charlevoix
Drawbridge over the Pine River Channel that connects Round Lake and Lake Charlevoix to Lake Michigan.

Year built: 1949

Replaced a swing bridge built in 1901. In an opening ceremony on July 30, 1949, the bridge was dedicated as a memorial to 22 local men who died during World War II.

The bridge opens for boating traffic every half hour, which creates congestion on Bridge Street in downtown Charlevoix during the busy summer months.

Holy Island Bridge – Charlevoix
Connects to the 11-acre Holy Island in Lake Charlevoix

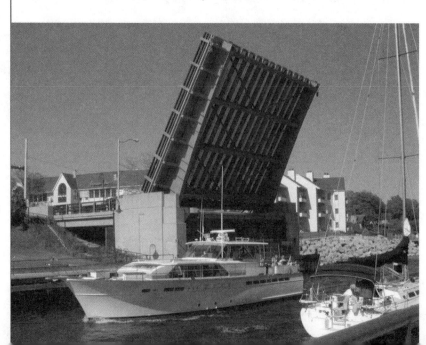

Downtown Charlevoix drawbridge opens every 30 minutes during summer (courtesy MDOT)

Year built: 1903   Installed in the 1940's

<u>Length:</u> about 50 feet

Only known surviving example of a pony truss bridge in Michigan built by the Wabash Bridge company of Wabash, Indiana.

County officials have suggested removing the bridge since it was damaged in 2003. It's capacity dropped from 14 tons to 3 tons. Water no longer runs under the bridge, as it has been filled in with sand, creating an islet out of Holy Island.

<u>Alanson Swing Bridge – Downtown Alanson</u>
Downtown Alanson over the Crooked River

Year built: 1901

May be the world's smallest swing bridge. Until the early 1960's it was opened with a hand crank. Hydraulics were installed in the mid 1960's. To open the bridge, boaters need to honk three times. Clearance is about four feet, enough for most 21' powerboats without having to open the bridge.

ROADS AND HIGHWAYS

Average Vehcile Miles Traveled – 2003	
<u>County</u>	<u>Miles traveled (thousands)</u>
Grand Traverse	765,054
Roscommon	383,828
Clare	370,729
Wexford	359,342
Osceola	339,004
Otsego	311,716
Antrim	298,429
Crawford	297,765
Emmet	290,583
Mason	268,578
Leelanau	258,648
Charlevoix	231,397
Manistee	227,400
Kalkaska	213,019
Benzie	198,732
Missaukee	136,623
Lake	122,261
Year-to-year trends in traffic	

"Little Mackinac Bridge" over the Manistee River near Reed City (Author photo)

TRAFFIC TRENDS

Cadillac

Highway/intersection	Average 1998	Daily traffic 2002	Count (ATD) 2003
M-115 at Lake Shore Blvd.	10,600	14,500	11,900
M-55/M-115 (south end of Lake Cadillac)	12,000	11,500	11,500
US-131 at Cobbs	23,200	16,700	16,500

Traverse City

Highway/intersection	Average 1998	Daily traffic 2002	Count (ATD) 2003
US-31/M-37 at S. Airport	22,800	24,300	26,600
US-31/M-37 (Division at Front)	31,400	19,800	21,700
US-31 (Grandview Pkwy) at Union	29,300	25,700	23,300
US-31 (Front St.) at Garfield	26,700	26,300	22,800
US-31 at 3-Mile (East Bay)	29,200	28,400	26,100

Petoskey

Highway/intersection	Average 1998	Daily traffic 2002	Count (ATD) 2003
US-131 at Sheridan	10,100	12,300	12,100
US-131 at US-31	16,100	19,000	18,800
US-31 at US-131	15,300	19,000	18,700
US-31/US-131 (W. Mitchell St.)	24,400	28,400	27,100
US-31 at Bay View	22,600	23,900	22,100
US-31 at M-119	28,100	30,500	27,800

2003 Average Daily Traffic Counts (ADT)

I-75	Vehicle count	Location	County
	16,100	at M-55	Roscommon
	10,600	at Crawford County line	Roscommon
	25,900	just south of Grayling	Crawford
	16,600	at Otsego County line	Crawford
	17,800	just north of Crawford County line	Otsego
	15,300	at Gaylord	Otsego
	9,100	south of Mackinac City	Emmet
	8,500	at Mackinac Bridge	Emmet

US-31			
	9,100	near Kistlers Corners	Mason
	17,900	east of Ludington (US 10/31)	Mason
	7,800	north of Custer	Mason
	8,700	south of Manistee	Manistee
	16,400	at Manistee	Manistee
	11,000	at M-22 near Onekema	Manistee
	5,400	near Bear Lake	Manistee
	3,100	at Manistee/Benzie line	Benzie
	7,600	at M-115	Benzie
	9,400	near Honor	Benzie
	15,800	Near M-137	Grand Traverse

US-31	Vehicle count	Location	County
	21,400	at Grawn	Grand Traverse
	23,800	Chum's Corner (M-31/37)	Grand Traverse
	26,600	S. Airport Rd. (M-31/37)	Grand Traverse
	26,100	at Three Mile Rd.	Grand Traverse
	21,000	at M-72 in Acme	Grand Traverse
	11,400	at Bracket Rd. in Acme	Grand Traverse
	8,400	at Antrim/Grand Traverse line	Grand Traverse
	7,700	at Elk Rapids	Antrim
	4,300	at Eastport	Antrim
	9,100	south of Charlevoix	Charlevoix
	13,700	at Charlevoix	Charlevoix
	9,300	Charlevoix/Emmet line	Charlevoix
	16,500	at US 131	Emmet
	27,800	at Petoskey	Emmet
	14,400	north of M-119	Emmet
	12,800	south of M-66	Emmet
	6,700	north of Alanson	Emmet
	4,000	near Carp Lake	Emmet

US-131

Vehicle count	Location	County
12,800	at Wexford line	Osceola
10,900	at Tustin	Osceola
12,000	at M-115 in Cadillac	Wexford
22,900	in Cadillac	Wexford
4,800	north of Manton	Wexford
4,300	near Fife Lake	Grand Traverse
5,100	north of Fife Lake	Kalkaska
11,400	just south of Kalkaska	Kalkaska
8,700	north of Kalkaska	Kalkaska
10,200	at Mancelona	Antrim
7,100	just south of Boyne Falls	Charlevoix
10,500	just south of Emmet line	Charlevoix
12,100	just south of Petoskey	Emmet

M-37

Vehicle count	Location	County
5,500	just south of Baldwin	Lake
1,800	near Luther Hwy.	Lake
2,000	at M-55	Wexford
2,700	at Mesick	Wexford
6,800	at Buckley	Wexford
6,600	at M-113	Grand Traverse
23,800	at Chums Corner (US-31)	Grand Traverse

M-37	Vehicle count	Location	County
	26,600	at S. Airport Rd.	Grand Traverse
	3,300	base of Old Mission	Grand Traverse Peninsula
	1,800	tip of Old Mission	Grand Traverse Peninsula

M-22			
	2,900	at Onekema	Manistee
	3,100	at Benzie line	Manistee
	5,600	at Elberta	Benzie
	2,500	just north of Frankfort	Benzie
	3,000	at Leelanau line	Benzie
	1,200	just south of Glen Lake	Leelanau
	4,100	at Northport	Leelanau
	2,300	at Omena	Leelanau
	6,700	at Suttons Bay	Leelanau
	8,200	at Crain Hill Rd.	Leelanau
	17,900	Elmwood Twp.	Leelanau

M-72			
	1,900	near Empire	Leelanau
	5,800	at County Rd. 651	Leelanau
	9,500	M-22, Traverse City	Leelanau
	16,700	Williamsburg	Grand Traverse

M-72	Vehicle count	Location	County
	12,500	Kalkaska	Kalkaska
	6,000	east of Kalkaska	Kalkaska
	6,800	just east of Grayling	Crawford
	8,900	just west of Grayling	Crawford
	2,300	at Oscoda line	Crawford
US-10			
	27,000	at Ludington	Mason
	17,900	at US-31	Mason
	13,700	Scottville	Mason
	5,600	Custer	Mason
	3,200	at M-37	Lake
	4,100	at Baldwin	Lake
	3,900	at Chase	Lake
	8,400	Reed City	Osceola
	7,000	Evart	Osceola
	4,200	just east of Clare line	Clare
	4,400	Lake Station	Clare
	9,200	at M-115	Clare
	9,800	M-115/US-10 north of Clare	Clare
	22,800	US-127/US-10 north of Clare	Clare

US-127	Vehicle count	Location	County
	14,600	at Clare	Clare
	22,800	US-127/US-10 north of Clare	Clare
	14,100	just south of M-61	Clare
	14,100	Harrison	Clare
	10,200	just north of Clare-Roscommon line	Roscommon
	8,200	north of M-55	Roscommon
	7,600	Higgins Lake	Roscommon
	7,300	just south of connecting point with I-75	Roscommon
M-55			
	2,800	at East Lake	Manistee
	3,100	at Wexford line	Manistee
	7,200	at N. 31 Rd.	Wexford
	12,000	at M-115	Wexford
	8,600	at Cadillac	Wexford
	5,200	at M-66	Wexford
	11,700	M-55/M-66 south of Lake City	Missaukee
	8,400	just east of Lake City	Missaukee
	5,400	Keelans Corner	Missaukee
	9,600	at Houghton Lake	Roscommon
	12,600	at Prudenville	Roscommon

M-115	Vehicle count	Location	County
	5,100	at Frankfort	Benzie
	4,600	Benzonia	Benzie
	2,900	Thompsonville	Benzie
	2,200	Copemish	Manistee
	5,600	Mesick	Wexford
	10,000	Cadillac	Wexford
	7,900	near Osceola line	Wexford
	5,500	near Gormer	Osceola
	6,200	Lake Station Road	Clare
	9,800	US-10/M-115 north of Clare	Clare

M-88			
	1,800	at Eastport	Antrim
	2,000	Central Lake	Antrim
	6,800	Bellaire	Antrim
	4,200	Mancelona	Antrim

M-66			
	13,500	Charlevoix	Charlevoix
	6,500	East Jordan	Charlevoix
	2,000	just north of Mancelona	Antrim
	10,200	M-66/US-131 at Mancelona	Antrim
	19,200	M-66/US-131 at Kalkaska	Kalkaska
	1,300	Boardman Rd.	Kalkaska

M-66	Vehicle count	Location	County
	2,300	Missaukee/Kalkaska line	Missaukee
	9,300	Lake City	Missaukee
	11,700	M-55/M-66 south of Lake City	Missaukee
	3,600	McBain	Missaukee
	2,200	Marion	Osceola
	2,200	South of US-10	Osceola

Traffic Accidents-by County (2002)

County	Number of accidents
Grand Traverse	4,029
Emmet	1,818
Mason	1,721
Clare	1,690
Wexford	1,673
Osceola	1,393
Charlevoix	1,292
Roscommon	1,221
Manistee	1,153
Antrim	1,123
Otsego	1,070
Crawford	810
Kalkaska	809
Missaukee	760
Leelanau	696
Benzie	632
Lake	594

Fatal Traffic Accidents-by County (2002)

County	Number of accidents
Antrim	4
Benzie	6
Charlevoix	2
Clare	6
Crawford	6
Emmet	4
Grand Traverse	8
Kalkaska	6
Lake	0
Leelanau	2
Manistee	5
Mason	3
Missaukee	1
Osceola	4
Otsego	4
Roscommon	4
Wexford	11

Top 10 Most Dangerous Intersections in N. Michigan (Jan. – Dec. 2003)

Accidents	Intersection	Twp./City	County
50	Garfield Rd. at S. Airport	Garfield Twp.	Grand Traverse
41	S. Airport at US-31 S.	Garfield Twp.	Grand Traverse
34	LaFranier at S. Airport	Garfield Twp.	Grand Traverse
30	US 31 N. at 3 Mile Rd.	East Bay Twp.	Grand Traverse
29	S. Airport at Cass Rd.	Garfield Twp.	Grand Traverse
23	Cedar St. at M-72	Kalkaska	Kalkaska
19	34 Road at US-131	Haring Twp.	Wexford
19	W. Main at S. Otsego	Gaylord	Otsego
18	US-131 at Bell Ave.	Haring Twp.	Wexford
18	W. Main at Dickerson	Gaylord	Otsego
18	US-10 at Brye Rd.	Amber Twp.	Mason

Most Dangerous Intersections by County (Jan. – Dec. 2003)

Antrim County

Accidents	Intersection	Twp./City
8	E. State St. at Williams	Mancelona
5	Marion Ctr. Rd. at Atwood Rd.	Banks Twp.
5	M-32 at US-131	Warner Twp.
5	Alden Hwy. at Comfort	Custer Twp.
4	US-31 at Essex Rd.	Banks Twp.

Benzie County

Accidents	Intersection	Twp./City
4	US-31 at Frankfort Hwy.	Benzonia Twp.
4	Case Rd at River St.	Benzonia Twp.
4	M-115 at Airport Rd.	Crystal Lake Twp.
3	US-31 at Benzie St.	Benzonia
3	US-31 at Marshall	Benzonia Twp.

Charlevoix County

Accidents	Intersection	Twp./City
14	Bridge St. at W. Garfield	Charlevoix
13	Park St. at Water St.	Boyne City
8	M-75 at US-131	Boyne Falls
8	Bridge St. at Clinton St.	Charlevoix
8	Bridge St. at Mason St.	Charlevoix

Clare County

Accidents	Intersection	Twp./City
10	N. McEwan at 5th St.	Clare
7	N. Clare Ave. at E. Surrey Rd.	Grant Twp.
7	Old State at Surrey	Surrey Twp.
6	McEwan Bus. 27 at 7th	Clare
6	Main St. at 1st St.	Harrison

Crawford County

Accidents	Intersection	Twp./City
8	James St. at E. M-72	Grayling
7	Peninsular at Michigan Ave.	Grayling
5	James at Michigan Ave.	Grayling

Accidents	Intersection	Twp./City
5	I-75 at N. Down River Rd.	Grayling Twp.
5	N. I-75 at 4 Mile Rd.	Grayling Twp.

Emmet

15	Spring St. at Charlevoix Ave.	Petoskey
14	US-31 at Division Rd.	Bear Creek Twp.
14	MacDonald at US-31	Petoskey
12	M-68 at US-31	Alanson
11	N. US-31 at M-119	Bear Creek Twp.

Grand Traverse

50	Garfield Rd. at S. Airport Rd.	Garfield Twp.
41	S. Airport at US-31 S.	Garfield Twp.
34	LaFranier at S. Airport Rd.	Garfield Twp.
30	US-31 N. at 3 Mile Rd.	East Bay Twp.
29	S. Airport Rd. at Cass Rd.	Garfield Twp.

Kalkaska County

23	Cedar St. at M-72	Kalkaska
6	Dresden St. at Cedar St.	Kalkaska
5	US-131 at Twin Lake Rd.	Rapid River Twp.
5	US-131 at Wood Rd.	Rapid River Twp.
4	US-131 at Boardman Rd.	Boardman Twp.

Lake County

Accidents	Intersection	Twp./City
6	W. 76th St. at S. M-37	Pleasant Plains Twp.
4	24th at M-37	Webber Twp.
3	Seventh St. at Michigan Ave.	Baldwin
3	US-10 at Jenks	Webber Twp.
3	US-10 at Nelson Rd.	Yates Twp.

Leelanau County

10	M-22 at Cherry Bend Rd.	Elmwood Twp.
5	Cty. Rd. 614 at Cty. Rd. 641	Elmwood Twp.
5	W. Bayshore Dr. at Dumas Rd.	Suttons Bay Twp.
4	S. Manitou Tr. at E. Duck Lake	Leland Twp.
3	Center Hwy. at Lakeview Dr.	Elmwood Twp.

Manistee County

16	US-31 at 1st St.	Manistee
13	US-31 at M-55	Manistee Twp.
11	US-31 at Memorial Dr.	Manistee
10	River St. at Maple St.	Manistee
8	River St. at Cypress St.	Manistee

Mason County

18	US-10 at Brye Rd.	Amber Twp.
17	US-10 at Jebavy Dr.	PereMarquette Twp.

Accidents	Intersection	Twp./City
16	US-10 at Pere Marquette Hwy.	PereMarquette Twp.
11	US-31 at US-10	Amber Twp.
10	Ludington Ave. at Nelson Rd.	PereMarquette Twp.

Missaukee County

7	M-66 at M-55	Lake City
7	Blue Rd. at S. Morey	Lake City
4	Main St. at John St.	Lake City
4	Roland St. at Euclid St.	McBain
3	Main St. at Mitchell St.	Lake City

Osceola County

7	M-115 at M-66	Middle Branch Twp.
6	US-10 Hwy. at 220th Ave.	Richmond Twp.
5	US-10 at 175th	Hersey Twp.
4	S. US-131 at 20 Mile Rd.	Burdell Twp.
4	M-115 at 20 Mile Rd.	Highland Twp.

Otsego County

19	W. Main at S. Otsego	Gaylord
18	W. Main at Dickerson	Gaylord
15	N. Center at Main	Gaylord
15	N. Wisconsin at W. Main	Gaylord
13	Meecher at W. Main	Gaylord

Roscommon County

Accidents	Intersection	Twp./City
8	Houghton Lake at Gladwin Rd.	Denton Twp.
8	W. M-55 at Reserve Rd.	Denton Twp.
6	Sullivan at M-55	Denton Twp.
5	M-76 at Steele Rd.	Gerrish Twp.
5	I-75 at M-18	Roscommon

Wexford County

19	34 Road at US-131	Haring Twp.
18	US-131 at Bell Ave.	Haring Twp.
12	N. Mitchell St. at Ayers St.	Cadillac
11	US-131 at River St.	Cadillac
10	Mitchell St. at Harris St.	Cadillac

Source: Michigan State Police Criminal Justice Information Center

Car-Deer Crashes by County

In 2003, in Michigan there were 67,760 reported car-deer crashes, with a little over 11% of them occurring on northern Michigan roads. One of the 11 fatal car-deer accidents in Michigan occurred up north, in Crawford County. Although there is the assumption that northern Michigan, with so many acres of woods, has a higher-than-average deer population, most northern counties actually rank low on the list of car-deer accidents.

About 80% of car-deer accidents take place on two-lane roads between dusk and dawn.

Vehicle-deer crashes in Michigan have increased from nearly 48,000 in 1993 to over 63,000 in 2002. In 1996, over 68,000 collisions took place between cars and vehicles, the highest number in the last 10 years.

Car-Deer Crashes

County	2002	2003	State rank (2003)
Mason	795	777	36
Clare	700	727	40
Osceola	698	777	36
Charlevoix	549	559	44
Emmet	524	548	47
Manistee	511	507	53
Grand Traverse	508	508	52
Roscommon	489	511	51
Antrim	474	449	55
Wexford	451	421	57
Missaukee	434	429	56
Crawford	388	330	65
Lake	312	226	72
Kalkaska	274	240	71
Benzie	257	283	69
Leelanau	223	275	70
Otsego	211	224	73
Total	7,798	7,791	

Michigan State Police

Northern Michigan Highways

US-31

Developed in 1920 as M-11 along the west side of Michigan, it was designated the "West Michigan Pike." When the U-S Highway system was created in 1926 it became US-31. That same year US-31 became the first highway to cross the Straits of Mackinac as it was named the official route from Mackinaw City to St. Ignace via the rail ferries. At that time US-31 continued north to US-2.

The last section of US-31 to be paved was between 1936-38 between Charlevoix and Boyne City, Charlevoix Rd.

In 1958, seven miles of new highway were opened between Elk Rapids and Kewadin. The old section, Cairn Highway, became a local road.

In 1960, new connection joined US-31 to I-75 three miles south of Mackinaw City.

In 1989-90 the freeway portion of US-31 is extended from the Mason-Oceana County line north to US-10.

In 1991 a US-31 bypass around Scottville is completed.

In 2002 plans for the US-31 Petoskey bypass are scrapped.

US-131

US-131 runs south from Petoskey about 268 miles to the State border.

In its previous life US-131 was M-13 and started at the Indiana line running through Kalamazoo, Grand Rapids, Cadillac, Kalkaska, Petoskey, and ending in Harbor Springs. When the US Highway system was created in 1926, M-13 was changed to US-131, and ran the same route, except it ended at Fife Lake in the north.

In the 1930's roads making up M-131 were linked between Fife Lake and Petoskey, and in 1938 officially became US-131 connecting to US-31 at Petoskey.

Between 1956-57 US-131 between Mancelona and Elmira, about 15 miles, is turned into a four-lane divided highway.

In 1961 the northbound lanes between Mancelona and Elmira are torn out, and the highway returns to two-lane status. (A contributor to the website, www.michiganhighways.org, claims there was too little traffic to justify the maintenance expense for a four-lane highway, and that wide open road attracted drag racers.)

M-131 between Petoskey and Harbor Springs changed to M-119 to avoid confusion with nearby US-131.

US-131 is now a four-lane freeway as far north as Manton. The four-laner was extended from LeRoy to Cadillac in 1976; from Big Rapids to LeRoy in 1986; a three-mile Cadillac bypass was competed in 2000, and the Manton segment was opened in 2003.

I-75

The first I-75 freeway signs in Michigan were put up in 1958 between Detroit and the Ohio border, and at the south end of the Mackinac Bridge running north to US-2.

With the exception of the Mackinac Bridge approach, I-75 came to northern Michigan in fragments.

- In 1960 the freeway was extended south from the Bridge to Indian River.
- In 1961 sections of new freeway were mixed with US-27 extending I-75 from Higgins Lake north to Gaylord.
- The following year 31 miles of new I-75 freeway opened up between Gaylord and Indian River.
- In 1973 a new section of M-76 opened between Roscommon and West Branch, but was changed to I-75. This completed Michigan's longest expressway, 395 miles from the Mackinac Bridge to the Ohio state line.

I-75 is the only route to cross the Straits via the Mackinac Bridge. Only two other state-designated routes have crossed the Bridge: US-27 in the late 50's when the bridge first opened, and US-31 in the 1930's via the State ferries.

M-72

Runs the width of the northern part of the mitten, 133 miles from Empire to Harrisville.

In the early 1920's it served Alcona County. In 1927, it was extended westerly to Luzerne. In 1940 it was pushed west to Grayling where it connected to M-208. At that time M-208 and M-76 near Kalkaska were re-designated as M-72. Using existing county roads M-72 was connected from Kalkaska through Traverse City to Empire.

In 1959 the last nine miles between Traverse City and Kalkaska are paved.

In 1961 M-72 is rerouted to mostly new highway construction at Barker Creek, leaving Old M-72 to local control.

In 1978 the State's only runaway truck ramp is built, at a cost of $66,000 at the bottom of a hill on M-72 west of Traverse

City. At the bottom of the hill: a shopping center, busy inter-section and West Grand Traverse Bay.

The busy Grayling to Traverse City corridor has been expand-ed to four lanes in several key areas in the past few years.

M-37

Runs 221 miles between I-94 at Kalamazoo and the tip of the Old Mission Peninsula in Traverse City.

In the early 1920's M-37 ran between Grand Rapids and Battle Creek. In 1928 it was extended north, replacing M-54, to north of Baldwin in Lake County. In 1940 M-42 north of Mesick was designated as M-37 north to the tip of the Old Mission Peninsula in Traverse City. In 1948 M-37 was con-nected between Lake and Wexford counties with a new paved segment.

M-127

Runs 214 miles from the Ohio state line to I-75 near Grayling.

Opened in 1926 as part of the new US Highway system, it was originally designed to run between Lansing and Toledo. In 1968 US-127 is extended north into Clinton County where it connects to US-27, which runs concurrently with the newer US-69 freeway. In 1999 the State Transportation Department decided to clear up any confusion by dumping the US-27 des-ignation altogether. This means US-127 is now extended from the Lansing area north to Grayling.

In 2002 all US-27 marker signs between Lansing and Grayling were changed to US-127.

M-115

Runs from downtown Clare northwesterly to meet M-22 in Frankfort, a total of 96 miles.

Opened in 1929 running between Frankfort and Benzonia, the 6.4 mile road was transferred to State control the following year and officially designated as M-115.

In 1939 two unconnected segments of M-115 is opened as "graded earth" highway between Clare and Cadillac and between Frankfort and Mesick.

In 1947 the final gravel top segment of M-115 is paved, between Benzonia and Copemish.

The diagonal M-115 is a north-south highway, however, it moves more east-west.

M-88

Runs 26 miles from US-31 in Eastport to US-131 in Mancelona.

Opened in 1921 from Mancelona to Bellaire. In 1927 it was extended 14 miles to link with US-31.

In 1929, US-31 was re-routed to M-88 between Bellaire and Eastport while 31 was being rebuilt north or Elk Rapids.

Officially named M-88 Scenic Highway.

M-119

Runs 28 miles from US-31 in Petoskey to Cross Village.

The 20-mile stretch between Harbor Springs and Cross Village is on everyone's list of favorite drives. The narrow two-lane highway snakes through "Tunnel of Trees" on the bluffs overlooking Lake Michigan.

Was identified as M-131 until 1979 when it was re-designated as M-119 to avoid confusion with nearby US-131.

There are no shoulders along the side of M-119, nor does it have a centerline.

Officially designated by the State as a Scenic Heritage Route in 2002.

Short Highways

M-212

Length: .732 miles *(shortest in Michigan)*
Opened: 1937
Runs between Aloha State Park entrance and M-33 in Cheboygan County.

Provides access from M-33 to the park and the town of Aloha.

M-168

Length: .95 miles *(3rd shortest state highway)*
Opened: 1930
Runs between M-22 in Elberta and the former Ann Arbor Railroad Ferry Docks.

The State Transportation Department created this highway to connect the rail ferry traffic to the State highway system. Similar short highways in other ports have been decommissioned by the State. M-168 is the last such car ferry feeder highway.

M-157

Length: 1.19 miles *(fourth shortest in state)*
Opened: 1931
Runs between M-55 north to M-18 near downtown Prudenville. It was built as a connector between the two highways.

M-201

Length: 1.47 miles
Opened: perhaps 1933
Runs through the town of Northport, from the M-22 on the south to the town's northern boundary.

The road has been around at least since the 1920's but did not become part of the State highway system until 1924, at which time it was not designated as M-201; it was probably a third leg of M-22. The researchers at www.michiganhighways.org believe it became M-201 in the 1930's.

M-137

Length: 2.89 miles
Opened: 1930
Runs south from US-31 in Interlochen to the entrance of
Interlochen State Park.

M-109

Length: 6.83 miles
Opened: 1928
Runs through the Sleeping Bear Dunes National Lakeshore
from M-22 in downtown Glen Arbor to M-22 a couple of
miles north of Empire.

A new State highway as of 1928 between Empire and Glen
Haven. In 1932 the road connecting Glen Haven with Glen
Arbor was added to the State highway.

From 1932 until 1997 a short connecting road from M-209
into Glen Haven was identified as M-109. At .37 miles it was
the shortest highway in the state during those years.

M-116

Length: 7 miles
Opened: 1928
Runs 7 miles between US-10 in downtown Ludington to the
Ludington State Park entrance.

Designed in 1928 to be part of US-31 between Ludington and
Manistee. However, US-31 was re-routed, so M-116 serves primarily as an entrance to the park.

M-204

Length: 7 miles
Opened: 1930
Runs 7 miles as a connector between M-22 in Suttons Bay and
M-22 in Leland.

Existing road became a State highway in 1930. Showed up on
early maps as M-304, which may have been a mistake.

M-204 is one of two east-west state highways that cut across the Leelanau Peninsula. The other is M-72.

M-185   Michigan's Safest Highway

Much of this 8.1 mile loop around Mackinac Island was built in the 19th century. It became part of the State highway system in 1930. In 1896 the City of Mackinac Island outlawed all motor vehicles, and in 1898 the Mackinac Island State Park Commission extended the ban to State park land which covers most of the island.

- M-185 is the nation's only motorless state highway.

- There has never been an automobile accident on M-185.

- In 2003, the name of M-185 through downtown was changed from Huron Street to Main Street.

AIRPORTS

Certified for carrier-use

CHERRY CAPITAL
TRAVERSE CITY, MI
ID: TVC

OTSEGO COUNTY
GAYLORD, MI
ID: GLR

PELLSTON REGIONAL AIRPORT
OF EMMET COUNTY
PELLSTON, MI
ID: PLN

AIRPORT ID'S

Airport	ID	City
Cherry Capital	TVC	Traverse City
Pellston Regional	PLN	Pellston
Otsego County	GLR	Gaylord
Charlevoix	CVX	Charlevoix
Manistee Blacker	MBL	Manistee
Wexford County	CAD	Cadillac
Antrim County	ACB	Bellaire
Boyne Mountain	BFA	Boyne Falls
Grayling AAF	GOV	Grayling
Roscommon County	HTL	Houghton Lake
Harbor Springs	MGN	Harbor Springs
Mackinac Island	MCD	Mackinac Island
Nartron Fields	RCT	Reed City
Mason County	LDM	Ludington
Fife Lake	M47	Fife Lake
Home Acres Sky Ranch	Y91	Lake City
Bunch's Half Acre	4Y9	Harrietta
Green Lake	Y88	Interlochen
Thompsonville	7Y2	Thompsonville
Lake Ann Airway Estates	4M0	Lake Ann
Frankfort Dow Memorial	3D4	Frankfort Field
Empire	3D4	Empire
Mancelona	D90	Mancelona
Torchport	59M	Eastport
Yuba International	34U	Elk Rapids
Lakes of the North	4Y4	Gaylord
Boyne City	N98	Boyne City
East Jordan	Y94	East Jordan
Roscommon Conservation	3RC	Roscommon
Houghton Lake State	5Y2	Houghton Lake Heights
St. Helen	6Y6	St. Helen
Clare	48D	Clare
Clare County	80D	Harrison
Calvin Campbell Municipal	Y65	Indian River
Pbeaaye	Y30	Topinabee
Kalkaska	Y89	Kalkaska
Baldwin Municipal	7D3	Baldwin
Evart	9C8	Evart
Sugar Loaf Resort	Y04	Cedar
Woolsey Memorial	5D5	Northport
Moorestown Airpark	6Y0	Moorestown

Woolsey Memorial Airport terminal, Northport (Author photo)

Runway Length

Airport / nearest town	Length
Pellston Regional / Pellston	6,512 paved
Cherry Capital / Traverse City	6,501 paved
Otsego County Airport / Gaylord	6,500 paved
Boyne Mountain / Boyne Falls	5,200 paved
Antrim County / Bellaire	5,000 paved
Grayling Aaf	5,000 paved
Wexford County / Cadillac	5,000 paved
Mason County / Ludington	4,998 paved
Nartron Field / Reed City	4,506 paved
Charlevoix Municipal	4,300 paved
Lakes of the North / Gaylord	4,285 paved
Harbor Springs	4,157 paved
Roscommon County / Houghton Lake	4,000 paved
Beaver Island / St. James	4,000 paved
Boyne City	3,840 paved
Home Acres Sky Ranch / Lake City	3,830 turf
Kalkaska	3,800 turf
Woolsey Memorial / Northport	3,663 turf
Roscommon Conservation	3,650 paved
Calvin Campbell / Indian River	3,600 paved
Sugar Loaf Resort / Cedar	3,519 paved
Mackinac Island	3,501 paved
Welke Airport / Beaver Island	3,500 turf
Mancelona	3,400 turf
Torchport / Eastport	3,300 turf
East Jordan	3,250 paved
Frankfort City–County	3,240 paved
Thompsonville	3,000 turf
Yuba Airport / Elk Rapids	2,975 turf
Evart	2,825 paved
Green Lake / Interlochen	2,800 turf
Clare County / Harrison	2,780 paved
Pbeaaye Airport / Topinabee	2,770 turf
Empire	2,600 paved
St. Helen	2,600 turf
Clare Municipal	2,500 paved
Bunch's Half Acre / Harrieta	2,400 turf

Cherry Capital Airport

In October of 2004, the Northwestern Regional Airport Commission opened a brand new terminal complex at Cherry Capital Airport. The 115,000 square foot terminal was built over three years at a cost of $54 million. The design was inspired by the arts and crafts style, ala Frank Lloyd Wright.

Cherry Capital Airport new terminal –2004 (courtesy of Cherry Capital Airport)

The airport features state-of-the-art security features tucked into the northern-themed décor and architecture. It was only the ninth airport in the country to install a fully integrated security system for checked baggage.

Cherry Capital Airport has the distinction of being the only airport in the country to accommodate Air Force One and Air Force Two as the first two aircraft to use the new complex. During the presidential campaign of 2004 Air Force One, with President Bush aboard, landed at the new complex in August – two months before it officially opened. Vice President Dick Cheney followed with a campaign stop in October, two weeks before the grand opening of the new terminal.

President Bush waves to the crowd as he steps from Air Force One at Cherry Capital Airport (courtesy of Cherry Capital Airport)

Air Force One shortly after landing in Traverse City 8-16-04 (courtesy of CherryCapital Airport)

Takeoffs and Landings

Year	Airlines	Military	Air Taxi	Local	Itinerant	Total
1992	11,690	9,012	5,337	60,029	45,168	131,236
1993	12,282	7,562	4,983	57,753	43,377	125,957
1994	14,024	9,041	6,579	66,587	45,936	142,167
1995	13,219	10,164	9,447	62,546	49,165	144,541
1996	12,338	12,975	8,313	64,063	43,684	141,373
1997	12,017	15,905	10,801	52,749	41,934	133,406
1998	15,668	17,788	9,111	55,478	48,548	146,593
1999	15,295	14,755	11,134	61,023	45,782	147,989
2000	15,550	12,435	12,866	56,791	44,290	141,932
2001	14,929	11,365	13,121	48,348	37,219	124,972
2002	11,931	13,435	11,478	53,151	38,738	128,733
2003	10,960	12,020	13,112	56,778	38,729	131,599

Passenger Movements

Year	Enplaning	Change	Deplaning	Change
1992	136,138		133,940	
1993	147,904	8.6%	146,095	9.1%
1994	156,980		156,670	
1995	159,684	1.7%	158,041	.9%
1996	152,811		150,411	
1997	158,469	3.7%	156,651	4.1%
1998	185,788		188,717	
1999	193,238	4.0%	191,644	1.6%
2000	201,284		196,984	
2001	190,000	-5.6%	189,103	-4.0%
2002	200,072		196,342	
2003	190,970	-4.5%	191,337	-2.5%

Enplaning – Boarding a commercial aircraft at Cherry Capital Airport

Deplaning – Getting off a commercial aircraft that has arrive at Cherry Capital Airport

Pellston Airport

In 2004, a new northern lodge-themed terminal opened at Pellston Regional Airport. The expanded terminal, complete with log exterior, three fireplaces, and cozy lodge furnishings, was built for $8.4 million.

Airport manager, Kelley Atkins, says the project started as a bathroom remodeling project, but grew into a complete expansion to meet the growing traffic.

Passenger levels

Year	Passengers
2000	64,123
2001	58,928
2002	65,261
2003	64,279

Passenger levels 1978 vs. 2000

Airport	Passenger levels		Difference	
	1978	2000	Actual	%
Manistee	5,732	1,196	(4,536)	(79.1)
Pellston	60,665	32,131	(28,534)	(47)
Traverse City	152,719	202,832	50,113	32.8

FERRIES

When we think of ferryboats today we envision high-speed ships full of smiling tourists headed to island fun spots. Four northern Michigan islands are served by full-time ferryboat operations, and shore-to-shore ferries cross Lake Michigan and Lake Charlevoix.

The first ferries were the birch bark canoes crafted by Native Americans, and the larger voyageur canoes used by French trappers and traders in the 1700's. While not commonly considered ferries, these early boats were used to ferry goods between the mainland and Mackinac Island, and later the Beaver islands. Next came the Mackinaw boats, popular with fishermen in the early 1800's. The small sailboat, usually 26 feet long, carried three sails on two masts and could easily be beached.

There are references to a regular ferry service between the Manitou islands and the mainland as early as 1860. At that time there were settlements on both islands and at Glen Arbor and Empire. The first island post office was in 1879 on South Manitou, at which time there would have to have been regular delivery service from the mainland.

In the 1870's the railroads expanded north, and at Mackinaw City reached a dead end at waters edge. The first regular ferry service at the Straits carried rail cars between Mackinaw City and St. Ignace. By the 1920's the number of automobiles on Michigan roads was increasing, as was the demand for travel across the Straits. The rail ferries obliged with limited and expensive service.

In 1876, regular ferry service across the southern arm of Lake Charlevoix began, and that same year steamboats began shuttling goods and passengers between Mackinac Island and the mainland.

In the late 1800's and early 1900's steamer ships provided regular service for vacationers and residents between the mainland and several of the islands.

In 1892 the first railroad car ferry service between northern Michigan and Wisconsin was launched from Betsie Bay in Frankfort.

The newest ferryboats include the *Emerald Isle,* launched in 1997 by the Beaver Island Boat Co., and the *Lake Express of Muskegon,* a high-speed ferry that crosses Lake Michigan in two-and-a-half hours.

Mackinac Island Ferries

All three ferry lines serve Mackinac Island from Mackinaw City in the Lower Peninsula, and St. Ignace in the U.P.

Distance to island from Mackinaw City:
a little over 6 miles

Distance to island from St. Ignace:
a little over 5 miles

Arnold Line Ferry (www.arnoldline.com)

Three catamarans, 5 traditional ferries, 3 barges, and one work boat.

Catamarans	Capacity
Straits Express	400
Mackinac Express	300
Island Express	350

Ferries	Capacity
Chippewa	600
Ottawa	600
Algomah	600
Huron	250
Straits of Mackinac II	180

Arnold Ferry catamaran approaches dock (courtesy Arnold Line Ferry)

Barges

Corsair	Carries up to two semi-trucks
Mackinac Islander	
Beaver	

History: Began in 1876 as steamer line with ports in Detroit, Chicago, Cleveland, Port Huron, Traverse City and Sault Ste. Marie. Founder George T. Arnold ran business until his death in the 1920's, when his wife took over the business. It was purchased in the 1950's by the Brown family, which continues to run it today.

Season: Regular service May through October. Serves island residents through early January, or until ice forms. Service resumes when ice is broken.

Number of trips during peak season: 50 daily round trips between two ferries

Estimated annual trips to island: 9,000+

Busiest day: 2nd Tuesday in August, 10,000 + passengers per day

Unusual cargo: Transporting the horses to and from the island at the beginning and end of each tourist season

Shepler's Ferry (www.sheplersferry.com)

Five ferries and one barge

Ferry	Capacity
Welcome (1968)	120+
Felicity (1972)	150+
Hope (1975)	150+
Wyandotte (1979)	265+
Captain Shepler (1986)	265+

The Shepler's fleet speads out in the Straits (courtesy Shepler's Ferry)

Freight

Sacre-Blue	150 gross ton, 325 persons

History: The Sheplers began service to Mackinac Island with two speed boats in 1945. They added two cruisers to the fleet in the 1950's. For a while the family's boats provided service to offshore oilrigs.

Season: May through November 1st. Frieght service is offered until the ice forms.

Number of trips during peak season: 59 round trips per day

Estimated annual trips to island: 7,200 trips

Busiest day: 4th of July and Labor Day, 3,000 passengers
a day

Shepler's also offers lighthouse cruises in Lake Michigan and
Lake Huron, and a cruise up the St. Mary's River with an
overnight stay in Sault Ste. Marie.

Unusual cargo: Clydesdale horses

Star Line Mackinac Island Ferry (www.mackinawferry.com)

Ferry	Capacity
Nicolet	150
LaSalle	150
Joliet	150
Cadillac	150
Radisson	350
Marquette II	325

History: Began service from St. Ignace in 1977. Full service
from St. Ignace and Mackinaw City started in 1978.
Following year added hydroplane hull boats built in Marquette.

Season: May through end of October

Estimated number of trips during peak season:
over 60 per day

Unusual cargo: During summer of '04 on a run from St.
Ignace the crew spotted a deer flailing in the water. As
passengers watched, the crew lassoed the deer and pulled
it aboard, where they tied its legs, and sat on it to prevent
it from running around on deck. After the scheduled stop at
the island, the crew radioed ahead to the DNR in St. Ignace,
who picked up the deer and returned him to the woods.

*Star Line Ferry
(courtesy Star
Line* Mackinac
Island *Ferry)*

Beaver Island Ferries

Beaver Island Boat Co. (www.bibco.com)

Service between Charlevoix and Beaver Island

Length of trip: 32 miles

Time: over two hours

Ferry	Capacity
Beaver Islander (1962)	200 persons 11 automobiles
Emerald Isle (1996)	298 persons 20 automobiles Can also transport buses and semi-trailers

History: Regular service between Charlevoix and Beaver Island started over 100 years ago. (See list of ferries below)

Season: 3rd week in April through last week of December

Busiest day: July 22nd

Passengers per year: 40,000

Other Beaver Island ferries as listed in "The Journal of Beaver Island History": *Volume 1, 1976 (copyright 1976, Beaver Island Historical Society)*

Emerald Isle
*Beaver Island
Ferry (courtesy
Beaver Island
Boat Co.)*

Ferry	Service date
Emerald Isle	1955
Mary Margaret	1937
North Shore	1937
Marold II	1933-1937
Ossian Bedell	1931-1933
James E. Sanford	1920-1931
Bruce	1917-1920
Irene	1917-1920
Columbia	?-1917
Beaver	1903-1915
Hackley	1899-1903
Nellie	1890-1899

Manitou Island Transit Co. (www.leelanau.com/manitou/)

Runs daily from Leland to both North and South Manitou islands between the end of June and Labor Day.

Distance to S. Manitou: 15 miles (1.5 hour trip)
Distance to N. Manitou: 11 miles (1.25 hour trip)

Ferry	Length	Capacity
Mishe-Mokwa	65'	133 passengers
Manitou Isle	52'	66 passengers

History: Service began in 1917 by Tracy Grosvenor who lived on N. Manitou. He eventually moved to the mainland and continued with mail deliver and ferry service to the two islands. His son, George Firestone Grosvenor, took over the service, and passed it on to his son, George Michael, who passed it on to his son, (George) Michael Jr. A fifth generation is in line to continue the historic ferry service to the Manitou islands.

Mishe-Mokwa *ferry. (courtesy of G.T. Pioneer & Historical Society)*

Ironton Ferry (www.charlevoixcounty.org)

One 50-foot ship designed specifically for its location at the mouth of the south arm of Lake Charlevoix.

Capacity: Four automobiles and passengers

Length of trip: 620 feet across the lake; takes about two-and-a-half minutes

*Ironton ferry
(Author photo)*

*Plaque on side
of pilot house
(Author photo)*

Season: Mid-April (depending on ice) through Thanksgiving evening Operates daily, 6:30 a.m. – 10:30 p.m.

History: Ferry service for humans and livestock began in 1876. The current ferry has been in service since 1926. The ferry saves motorists a twenty-mile trip around the south arm of Lake Charlevoix.

In 1976 the ferry was named a Michigan Historic Landmark.

Ripley's Believe It Or Not featured the Ironton ferry and Captain Sam Alexander noting that he "traveled 35,000 miles, and was never farther than 1,000 feet from his home!" A plaque of the Ripley's article is displayed on the south wall of the ferry.

<u>Lake Michigan Car Ferry Service</u> (www.ssbadger.com)

The *S.S. Badger* offers the largest cross-lake passenger-oriented service on the Great Lakes, traveling between its home port of Ludington and Manitowoc, Wisconsin.

S.S. Badger was built in 1952 by the Christy Corporation of Sturgeon Bay, Wisconsin for $5 million dollars.

Length: 410 ft, 6 inches
Width: 59 feet, 6 inches
Height: 106 feet, 9 inches
Weight: 4,244 gross tons

Two solid 4-blade cast steel propellers, 15 feet in diameter, weighing 15,400 pounds each

Average sea speed: 18 mph
Top speed: 24 mph

Capacity: 620 passengers, 180 automobiles; can carry tour buses, R.V.'s, and semi-trucks; 42 state rooms and 84 berths

Season: Mid-May through mid-October

Passengers: Over 100,000 annually

Famous passengers include: Cary Grant, Artie Shaw, The Who, Tammy Wynette and Weird Al Yankovich.

History: The *S.S. Badger* was idle for a year and a half until the summer of 1992 when the current owner. the Lake Michigan Carferry Service, Inc., purchased it.

The first ferry service was started in 1875 by the Flint and Pere Marquette Railway, when it chartered the steamer, *John Sherman,* to move grain, freight and passengers from Ludington to Sheboygan, Wisconsin.

In 1892 the Ann Arbor Railroad started the first open water railroad ferry in the world with the launching of the 260-foot *Ann Arbor I,* which traveled from Frankfort to Kewaunee, Wisconsin. The Flint and Pere Marquette Railroad followed in 1896 with the first steel-hulled rail ferry, the 350-foot *Pere Marquette.* Grand Trunk Railroad followed with its own ferries, and by 1917 the three railroads combined were operating 11 car ferries between Ludington and Wisconsin.

All three railroads added several ferries to their fleets during the 1920's. The final two ferries were added in 1952: the *S.S. Spartan* and the *S.S. Badger.*

Great Lakes car ferry service peaked in 1955 when 6,986 lake crossings were made, carrying 205,000 passengers and 204,460 freight cars.

By the early 1980's advances in railroad technology along with the high cost of fuel and labor were leading to the extinction of the railroad ferry. The C & O Railroad, which had purchased Pere Marquette Railroad, sold its last three ferries to the newly formed Michigan Wisconsin Transportation Co. The new company, struggling to survive on auto and passenger traffic alone, announced the final trip of the *S.S. Badger* would be November 16, 1990.

The end of Ludington's car ferry history was short-lived. Charles Conrad, who as a boy made dozens of cross-lake ferry trips with his father, a former Chief Engineer with Pere Marquette Railway, purchased the *Badger* and two other ships in 1991. The retired entrepreneur said he always believed the ferries would be a part of his hometown: "The ferries are a part of Ludington. They've been on the lake for the past hundred years, and I want to do whatever I can to assure they'll be running for the next hundred."

Conrad passed away in 1995. His Lake Michigan Carferry Service lives on.

Northport to Manistee

Between 1902 and 1908 carferry service existed between Northport at the tip of the Leelanau Peninsula, and Manistique in the Upper Peninsula. The Traverse City, Leelanau and Manistique railroad was built to connect to Manistique.

Mackinaw City to St. Ignace Ferries

The State Transportation Department got into the ferry business in 1923 as the number of complaints rose about the rail ferry rates and service. For the first year the State operated the 20-car capacity *Arial*. The next year, as demand increased, the State picked up two 40-car ferries, the *Sainte Ignace* and the *Mackinaw City*.

In 1928 the *Straits of Mackinac* joined the fleet. Originally it held 35 automobiles; it was later expanded to carry 90 cars and 400 passengers. The *Straits of Mackinac* operated until 1958, when ferry service ended.

The 85-car *City of Cheboygan*, a former rail ferry, was acquired in 1937, and another former rail ferry, the *City of Munising*, 105 car capacity, was added the following year.

In 1940 the *Sainte Ignace* and *Mackinaw City* were sold to the government, so a new ship was added: the 105-car *City of Petoskey*, another converted rail ferry.

In 1952 the final ship, the *Vacationland*, was added to the fleet. This brand new ferry could carry 150 cars and trucks.

By 1955, the five-ship fleet set a record by transporting 900,000 vehicles across the Straits. During 34 years of operation the ferries carried approximately 12 million vehicles and 30 million passengers across the Straits. On November 1, 1957 the State

Transportation Department ceased ferry operations for good, as the Mackinac Bridge opened, and a new era began.

Railroads Operating in Northern Michigan

CSX Transportation: A Class I railroad, CSX runs from Lake County west to Ludington and north to Manistee. It is remnant of the old Pere Marquette Railway Co.

Lake State Railway: Runs from Pinconning northwest through Roscommon County to Grayling, and north to Gaylord. Primary cargo is stone, potash and gravel.

Tuscola & Saginaw Bay: Runs from Clare to Irons to Cadillac where it maintains a rail yard. From Cadillac it runs north to Kalkaska, Manton, Boyne Falls and Petoskey. Also splits off and runs to Traverse City.

Railroad Timeline

Logging companies built the first railroads into northern Michigan. As loggers depleted the supply of trees near rivers, they advanced deeper into the woods further away from the rivers they needed to float logs to the mill.

Year	Railroad	Route
1870	Flint & Pere Marquette	From Averills in Midland County to Clare, to Newaygo County
1871	Flint & Pere Marquette	Newaygo County to Evart to Reed City
1871	Grand Rapids & Indiana	Clam Lake (Cadillac) to Fife Lake
1872	Grand Rapids & Indiana	Walton Junction to Traverse City
1873	Jackson, Lansing and Saginaw *Traverse City Railroad builds 26 miles of track.*	Otsego Lake to Gaylord
1874	Grand Rapids & Indiana	Fife Lake to Petoskey
1877	Lake George & Muskegon River	Michigan's first logging railroad runs seven miles between Clare and the Muskegon River

Great Railroad Strike of 1877

	Vanderbilt family acquires control of the Michigan Central railroad. Ephraim Shay of Cadillac invents smaller, maneuverable locomotive that could make tighter turns and move better on steep terrain in the woods.
1880	Grand Rapids & Indiana began summer-only tourist trains to resorts north of Petoskey.
	Flint & Pere Marquette Clare to Harrison
1881	Railroad car ferry service across the Straits of Mackinac is started by the Mackinac Transportation Company, a joint venture between three railroads: Grand Rapids & Indiana, Michigan Central, and Detroit, Mackinac & Marquette. First ferry was the *Algomah* which hauled cars on the barge, *Betsy*.
1882	Bay View, Little Traverse and Mackinac Railroad connect Bay View to Harbor Springs.
	The Grand Rapids & Indiana publish a tourist guide promoting hotels and resorts along its line, which it bills as "The Fishing Line." Towns highlighted include: Omena, Northport, Old Mission, Elk Rapids, Charlevoix, Bay View and Harbor Springs.
	Michigan Central opens new depots in Grayling, Topinabee and Mackinaw City.
	Flint & Pere Marquette buys two wooden steamers to rail road cargo across Lake Michigan.
1883	Chicago & West Michigan Pentwater to Baldwin
	The Northern Hay Fever Association opens a resort at Topinabee on the Michigan & Central line.
1884	Cadillac & Northeaster Cadillac to Lake Missaukee
1887	Toledo, Ann Arbor and Northern reaches Cadillac
	Chicago & West Michigan reaches Wellston
	Grand Hotel opens on Mackinac Island

By 1887 Michigan had 89 logging railroads in operation, more than any two states combined.

1888	The *St. Ignace,* a wooden car ferry, becomes first ship to carry rail cars between Mackinaw City and St. Ignace.	
	The highest railroad bridge in Michigan is built by the Chicago & West Michigan Railroad over the Manistee River between Baldwin and Kaleva (built from wood timbers and concrete).	
	Manistee & Northeastern	Manistee to Beecher near Thompsonville
1889	Toledo, Ann Arbor and Lake Michigan	Cadillac to Beecher
	Frankfort & South Eastern	Frankfort to Beecher
	Chicago & West Michigan	reaches Kaleva and Thompsonville
1890	Jennings & Northeastern	Lake City to Kalkaska
	Chicago & West Michigan	Baldwin to Traverse City
1891	Chicago & West Michigan	Traverse City to Elk Rapids
1892	Manistee & Northeastern	Interlochen to Traverse City (3rd railroad into TC)
	Ann Arbor No. 1 becomes first railroad car ferry across Lake Michigan and first railroad ferry service in the world across open water, running from Frankfort to Kewaunee, Wisconsin. Ann Arbor & Toledo Railroad start with two ferries, *Ann Arbor No. 1* and *Ann Arbor No. 2.*	
	Ann Arbor & Toledo buys Frankfort & South Eastern	
	Michigan Central	Grayling to Lewiston

1894	Ann Arbor & Toledo begin rail ferry service between Frankfort and Menominee.
1895	Ann Arbor & Toledo begin rail ferry service between Frankfort and Gladstone.
1898	Ann Arbor & Toledo buy 3rd car ferry. *The Ann Arbor No. 3* is first steel, double-hulled ferry. Operates through 1960.
1899	Chicago & West Michigan, Flint & Pere Marquette, and Detroit, Grand Rapids & Western are consolidated into one new company: The Pere Marquette Railroad.
1901	Ann Arbor & Toledo Railroad build the Royal Frontenac Hotel at Frankfort.
1910	Manistee & Northeastern Kaleva to Grayling
1918	Manistee & Northeastern goes bankrupt.

www.michiganrailroads.com

Sail and Rail, *by Lawrence & Lucille Wakefield, copyright 1980 by Lawrence M. Wakefield*

Old Railroad Nicknames

Grand Rapids & Indiana
• Fishing Line

Pere Marquette
• Stump Jumper (Grand Rapids to Traverse City)
• Brine Run (Ludington to Midland)

Detroit & Mackinac
• Turtle Route
• Huron Route
• Sugar Beet Belt Route

Humorous Nicknames

Pere Marquette
  • Poor Management

Manistee & Northeastern
  • Manistee & Nowhere Else

Cadillac & Lake City
  • Catastrophe & Lost Cause

Empire & Southeastern
  • Empire Slow & Easy
  • Empire & Something Else

Amboy, Lansing & Traverse City
  • Awfully Long & Terribly Bumpy

Detroit & Mackinac
  • Defeated & Maltreated

Named Freight Trains

Resort Special	Pere Marquette	Detroit to Bayview
Night Express	Pere Marquette	Chicago to Traverse City
The Torpedo	Ann Arbor & Toledo	Frankfort to Toledo
Northern Arrow	Pennsylvania	Cincinnati to Mackinaw City
Northland Express	Pennsylvania	Mackinaw City to Cincinnati
North Star	Pennsylvania	Mackinaw City to Chicago
Timberliner	New York Central	Detroit to Mackinaw City

GOVERNMENT/
POLITICS

POLITICS

Higher Office

Of Michigan's 47 elected governors, two were born in northern Michigan. The state's 31st governor, Fred W. Green, was born in Manistee. William G. Milliken, Michigan's 44th governor, was born, and still lives in, Traverse City.

Governor Fred Green

Fred Warren Green was elected governor in 1926 and re-elected in 1928 at a time when governors served two-year terms. Green was the third in a string of four Republicans to serve as Michigan's chief executive between 1917 and 1932.

Green was born in 1872 in Manistee. He spent his boyhood years in Cadillac and attended the University of Michigan, where he earned a law degree. After serving in Cuba during the Spanish-American War, he returned to Michigan to practice law in Ypsilanti. Green later opened a furniture store in Ionia and served twelve terms as the town's mayor.

During Green's administration in Lansing, the Conservation Department was strengthened, fish plantings were expanded, and seven State parks were added to the State's holdings.

He retired in 1931, and spent five years pursuing his favorite pastimes of hunting and fishing. He died in 1936 in Munising.

Green's mission-style home, built in 1924 in Ionia, is highlighted by a Michigan Mile Marker.

Governor William Milliken

Michigan's longest serving governor, William Grawn Milliken, took office in 1969 and remained there for 14 years. He took office in January 1969 replacing Governor George Romney, who left to head up the U.S. Housing and Urban Development Department. Milliken was elected governor the following year, and re-elected twice after that.

Milliken was born into a political family on March 26, 1922, in Traverse City. His grandfather, James W. Milliken, founded Milliken's department store in 1873, and went on to serve as a state senator. Milliken's father also served in the state senate, and as Traverse City's mayor for six years.

Milliken attended Traverse City Senior High School, where he played on the 1940 Class B State Champion basketball team, and served as governor of the senior class. At Yale, his education was interrupted by a call to service in the Army Air Force where, as a B-24 waist-gunner, he flew 50 combat missions, earning a Purple Heart on his 25th mission. After the war, Milliken married Helen Wallbank, and began business studies at the University of Michigan. Before completing his studies, Milliken got a taste of the real business world when he was summoned back to Traverse City, in the wake of his father's illness, to run the family store.

Like his father and grandfather, Milliken was elected to the state senate, where he served from 1960 to 1966, at which point he was elected lieutenant governor on the ticket with Governor George Romney.

Milliken's middle name, Grawn, is from his maternal grandfather, Charles T. Grawn, who served as superintendent of Traverse City Schools and as president of Central Michigan State Normal School, now Central Michigan University. (The oldest building on CMU's campus is Charles Grawn Hall.) The town of Grawn, near Traverse City, is named after the governor's grandfather.

Governor's Summer Residence

One of the great perks of being governor in Michigan is the summer residence on Mackinac Island. The three-story arts and crafts style cottage was built in 1902 for a Chicago family, and later owned by a Detroit family. It was sold in 1944 for $15,000 to the Mackinac Island State Parks Commission. Since then the 11 bedroom, 9-bath home has served as a summer residence for nine Michigan governors. In 1997 it was named to the National Register of Historical Places.

The governor's summer residence is open for public tours on Wednesday mornings during the summer. Boy and Girl Scouts from around the State who are members of the Mackinac Island Scout Service Camp act as guides for the tours. You can tell if the governor is in, if the Michigan flag is raised.

Senator Robert Griffin

No other northern Michigan officeholder came closer to
the White House than Robert Griffin. He served two terms as
a U.S. senator, most of that time as minority whip, his party's
second highest post in the Senate. Griffin was elected as U.S.
representative by the citizens of the Grand Traverse area five
times before his appointment to the upper chamber following
the death of Senator Patrick McNamara in 1966.

While in the House, Griffin became
good friends with fellow Michigander
Gerald Ford, and helped lead the
charge to push Ford up the leadership
ladder. Ford was House Minority Leader
in 1973, when Vice President Spiro
Agnew resigned. President Richard
Nixon appointed Ford as his Vice-
President, and Senator Griffin suddenly
had a good friend in the White House.

According to former U.S. District Judge
John Feikens, Griffin was on the short
list to be Nixon's running mate in 1968. However, Griffin
had promised to support Governor George Romney at the
Convention, and effectively took his name off the list.

*Senator Robert
Griffin with
President
Eisenhower
(courtesy of
G.T. Pioneer &
Historical Society)*

Although it was not his intention, Griffin may have indirectly
helped his friend from Michigan advance to the White House.
During the final days of the Watergate scandal, while flying
home to Traverse City, Griffin realized the facts were closing
in on President Nixon. He wrote a personal note to the president, advising him to resign in order to avoid a painful
impeachment hearing. Back in Washington on Monday, Griffin
stood before the Washington press corps, urging the president
to resign. These two actions helped nudge the president toward
his decision, three days later, to resign the presidency. By
Friday of that week Griffin had watched from the White
House as the Nixon's waved a final farewell, and his friend
from Grand Rapids was sworn in as the 38th president of the
United States.

Griffin's position in Washington and his friendship with
President Ford resulted in the first and only presidential visit
to the National Cherry Festival in 1976. The president and
first lady were the parade marshalls for the Grand Royal

Parade. Afterwards they relaxed with other friends, including
Governor Milliken, at the Griffin's home on Long Lake.

Griffin was elected to the U.S. Senate in 1966 and 1972,
before losing to Carl Levin in 1978. He returned to Michigan,
and before retiring served an eight-year term on the State
Supreme Court, from 1986 to 1994.

Born: November 6, 1923 in Detroit, MI
Graduated Fordson High School, Dearborn, MI: 1941
U.S. Army, 71st Infantry Division: 1943-46, European theater
Two Battle Stars
Central Michigan University: Bachelor of Science, 1947
Married: Marjorie Jean Anderson, 1947
University of Michigan Law School: Law degree, 1950
Law practice: Traverse City, 1950-57
U.S. House of Representatives: 1957-66
U.S. Senate: 1966-77
Michigan State Supreme Court: 1986-94

Now retired, Robert and Marjorie Griffin spend summers
at their home on Long Lake.

In the 2004 presidential election he publicly endorsed
President Bush, two weeks after his friend and fellow
Traverse City Republican Bill Milliken announced his
support for Democrat John Kerry.

Griffin's son, Rick serves on the State Appeals Court, and was
appointed in 2002 by President Bush to the Sixth Circuit U.S.
Court of Appeals. The nomination had been held up in the
Senate, and was just confirmed in June 2005.

While serving in the U.S. House, Griffin hired a young aide by
the name of Donald Rumsfeld, who went on to win his own
seat in the House, and later served in the administrations of
Presidents Ford and George H. Bush.

Senator Debbie Stabenow

In 2000, Debbie Stabenow became the first woman from
Michigan elected to the U.S. Senate. Her political career
began in 1974 with election to the Ingham County Board of
Commissioners. In 1977, at age 27, she became the youngest
person ever and the first woman to chair that body.

Stabenow grew up in Clare where her father and grand
father owned an Oldsmobile/Cadillac dealership. She was
the valedictorian of her senior class at Clare High School.
Stabenow played clarinet in high school, and took piano
and guitar lessons. She is known for her love of music, citing
among her favorites Barbra Streisand and Carol King.

While earning her Master's degree from MSU, Stabenow ran
against, and beat, the man who defeated her husband for a
seat on the Ingham County Board of Commissioners. She was
re-elected several times, and in 1978 won election to the State
House.

She later served in the State Senate before moving on to the
U.S. House and U.S. Senate, becoming only the second woman
to serve in both houses of a state legislature and U.S. Congress.

*Clare native,
Senator Debbie
Stabenow
(courtesy of
Senator
Stabenow)*

Born: April 29, 1950, Gladwin, MI
Graduated: Clare High School, Clare 1968
Michigan State University: Bachelor's Degree, 1972
Michigan State University: Master's Degree in Social
Work, 1975
Ingham County Board of Commissioners: 1974-78
State House of Representatives: 1979-90
State Senate: 1991-94
U.S. House of Representatives: 1996-2000
U.S. Senate: 2000 – present
Married: Tom Athans
Children: Todd and Michelle *(both grown)*

Presidential Elections *Winners*
1860   **1864**

Republican	Democrat	Republican	Democrat
*(Lincoln)	(Douglas)	*(Lincoln)	(McClellan)
Mason	Charlevoix	Mason	Charlevoix
Manistee	Emmet	Manistee	Emmet
Benzie		Benzie	
Leelanau		Leelanau	
Grand Traverse		Grand Traverse	
Antrim		Antrim	

1864
Republican
(Lincoln)

Otsego
Crawford
Roscommon
Missaukee
Wexford
Osceola
Lake
Clare
Kalkaska

1868		**1872**	
Republican	**Democrat**	**Republican**	**Democrat**
*(Grant)	(Seymour)	*(Grant)	(Greeley)
Same results as 1864		**All except Emmet	Emmet

1876		**1880**	
Republican	**Democrat**	**Republican**	**Democrat**
*(Hayes)	(Tilden)	*(Garfield)	(Hancock)
Same results as 1872		**All counties	0

1884		**1888**	
Republican	**Democrat**	**Republican**	**Democrat**
(Blaine)	*(Cleveland)	*(Harrison)	(Cleveland)

Mason	Manistee	Same result as 1884
Benzie	Emmet	
Leelanau		
Grand Traverse		
Antrim		
Charlevoix		
Otsego		
Crawford		
Roscommon		
Missaukee		
Wexford		
Osceola		
Lake		
Clare		
Kalkaska		

1892
Republican   **Democrat**
(Harrison)   *(Cleveland)

Republican (Harrison)	Democrat *(Cleveland)
Mason	Manistee
Benzie	Charlevoix
Leelanau	Emmet
Grand Traverse	
Antrim	
Charlevoix	
Otsego	
Crawford	
Roscommon	
Missaukee	
Wexford	
Osceola	
Lake	
Clare	
Kalkaska	

1896
Republican   **Democrat**
*(McKinley)**   **(Bryan)**

**All counties voted
  Republican

1900
Republican   **Democrat**
*(McKinley)**   **(Bryan)**

All counties in Michigan except
St. Joseph voted Republican

1904
Republican   **Democrat**
*(Roosevelt)**   **(Parker)**

All counties in Michigan
voted Republican

1908
Republican   **Democrat**
*(Taft)**   **(Bryan)**

All counties in
Michigan
voted Republican

1912
Republican   **Progressive**   **Democrat**
(Taft)   **(Roosevelt)**   *(Wilson)**

Republican (Taft)	Progressive (Roosevelt)	Democrat *(Wilson)
Charlevoix	Manistee	Mason
Otsego	Benzie	
Crawford	Leelanau	
	Gr. Traverse	
	Antrim	
	Roscommon	
	Missaukee	
	Wexford	
	Osceola	
	Lake	
	Clare	
	Kalkaska	

1916
Republican (Hughes)	Democrat *(Wilson)

**All counties except Crawford voted Republican

1920
Republican *(Harding)	Democrat (Cox)

All counties in the Lower Peninsula voted Republican

1924
Republican *(Coolidge)	Democrat (Davis)

All counties in Michigan voted Republican

1928
Republican *(Hoover)	Democrat (Smith)

All counties in Michigan voted Republican

1932
Republican (Hoover)	Democrat *(Roosevelt)
Osceola	Mason
Wexford	Manistee
Missaukee	Leelanau
Kalkaska	Grand Traverse
Benzie	Roscommon
Antrim	Lake
Charlevoix	Otsego
	Crawford
	Emmet
	Clare

1936
Republican (Landon)	Democrat *(Roosevelt)
Leelanau	Mason
Benzie	Manistee
Charlevoix	Gr. Traverse
Missaukee	Emmet
Roscommon	Osceola
	Wexford
	Kalkaska
	Antrim
	Lake
	Otsego
	Crawford
	Clare

1940
Republican (Wilkie)	Democrat *(Roosevelt)

**All counties voted Republican

1944
Republican (Dewey)	Democrat *(Roosevelt)

**All counties voted Republican

1948
Republican (Dewey)	Democrat *(Truman)

**All counties voted Republican

1952
Republican *(Eisenhower)	Democrat (Stevenson)

**All counties voted Republican

1956
Republican | Democrat
*(Eisenhower) | (Stevenson)

**All counties voted
Republican

1960
Republican | Democrat
(Nixon) | *(Kennedy)

**All counties voted
Republican

1964
Republican | Democrat
(Goldwater) | *(Johnson)

Missaukee | **All counties
except Missaukee
voted Democrat

1968
Republican | Democrat
*(Nixon) | (Humphrey)

**All counties Lake
except Lake
voted Republican

1972
Republican | Democrat
*(Nixon) | (McGovern)

**All counties Lake
except Lake
voted Republican

1976
Republican | Democrat
(Ford) | *(Carter)

**All counties voted
Republican

1980
Republican | Democrat
*(Reagan) | (Carter)

**All counties Lake
except Lake
voted Republican

1984
Republican | Democrat
*(Reagan) | (Mondale)

**All counties voted
Republican

1988
Republican | Democrat
*(Bush) | (Dukakis)

**All counties Lake
except Lake
voted Republican

1992
Republican | Democrat
(Bush) | *(Clinton)

Antrim | Benzie
Emmet | Charlevoix
Gr. Traverse | Clare
Leelanau | Crawford
Mason | Kalkaska
Missaukee | Lake
Osceola | Manistee
Otsego | Roscommon
| Wexford

1996 Republican (Dole)	Democrat *(Clinton)	2000 Republican *(Bush)	Democrat (Gore)
Antrim	Benzie	Antrim	Clare
Charlevoix	Clare	Benzie	Lake
Emmet	Crawford	Charlevoix	Manistee
Gr. Traverse	Wexford	Crawford	Roscommon
Leelanau	Kalkaska	Emmet	
Missaukee	Lake	Gr. Traverse	
Otsego	Manistee	Kalkaska	
	Mason	Leelanau	
	Osceola	Mason	
	Roscommon	Missaukee	
	Osceola	Otsego	
		Wexford	

*Denotes winner of presidential election
**All 17 counties in Northern Michigan Almanac coverage area

Source: Atlas of Michigan, Lawrence M. Sommers, Michigan State University Press, 1977

Michigan Department of State, Bureau of Elections

MILITARY

COAST GUARD

Air Station Traverse City

Commissioned: 1946 as Search and Rescue service for Great Lakes

Staff: 26 officers, 2 warrant officers, 2 Public health officers, 100 enlisted personnel

Facility: 50,000 square foot hangar, administrative offices and workshops

Aircraft: Five HH-65A "Dolphin" helicopters

Current missions: Winter and spring ice patrols, Search and Rescue, Aids to Navigation, Marine Environmental Response, and training

Notable Missions

In 1961, during gale wind conditions over four days, Coast Guard personnel in HU-19 helicopters assisted in evacuating the crew of the *Francisco Morazan,* a freighter that ran aground at S. Manitou Island.

In 1965, Coast Guard personnel rescued 25 survivors from the collision of the freighters *Cedarville* and *Topdalsfjord* in the Straits of Mackinac.

In 1979, 19 survivors of a fire aboard the Canadian freighter *Cartiercliffe Hall* were rescued by Traverse City Coast Guardsmen.

A violent wind storm in 1987 kept the Coast Guard busy with 32 search and rescue missions.

Another sudden windstorm in 1988 resulted in the rescue of two persons clinging to a capsized sailboat in Lake Michigan.

Also in 1988, Coast Guard pilots from Traverse City, flying in thick fog at night, located a downed aircraft near Marquette. All six aboard survived.

In 1986 while flying an air evacuation mission from Alpena to Traverse City, a premature baby boy was delivered aboard an HU-25A Coast Guard helicopter.

Later that year a Coast Guard helicopter was called to Florida to take part in the recovery search for the Space Shuttle *Challenger.*

The Traverse City Coast Guard Air Station has been called in to provide logistical support for floods in 1986 and 1993 and helped with an oil spill clean up in Pennsylvania.

They've also assisted the state DNR by transporting trout fingerlings to inland wilderness lakes, and assisted the National Park Service with acid rain research in Isle Royal National Park.

Station Manistee

Commissioned: 1878. Built in 1879
as U.S. Lifesaving Service.
At that time Manistee was 2nd to
Chicago as the busiest port on Lake
Michigan.

Manistee Coast Guard boat (courtesy of US
Coast Guard Manistee station)

Staff: approximately 20

Facility: 14,000 square foot complex opened in 2004

Watercraft: 47-foot Search and Rescue boat, 25 foot boat, and
21 foot inflatable

The community of Manistee saved the Coast Guard station
from being phased out of the system in 1996 by forming the
"Save Our Station" group, which successfully lobbied local
and federal officials to keep the station open.

Station Manistee is the parent command to Stations Ludington
and Frankfort.

Station Ludington

Commissioned: 1878. Built as U.S. Lifesaving Station in 1879.

Staff: approximately 9

Watercraft: 30-foot UTM boat and 21-foot rigid hull inflatable

In 2004, a decommissioned 44-foot rescue boat based at
Ludington between 1965-2000 was returned to the community. Coast Guard Motor Lifeboat 4435 had been stored in
Grand Haven after it's decommissioning. While based in
Ludington the boat was involved in many successful rescue
operations and will now become part of a community maritime
history display.

Station Frankfort

Commissioned: 1886 as U.S. Lifesaving Station

Staff: 9

Watercraft: 30 foot UTM boat

Station Charlevoix

Commissioned: 1900 as U.S. Life Saving Station. Original Life Saving Station demolished in 1965. Original Coast Guard Station was located at west end of the Pine River channel near its outlet to Lake Michigan. Moved to its current location on Round Lake in early 1960's.

Staff: 25

Facility: Offices and outbuildings on channel between Round Lake and Lake Charlevoix

Mission: Search and Rescue, Law enforcement and Homeland Security

Watercraft: 41' utility boat

Coast Guard Acacia

Staff: 50

Facility: located at city dock on Round Lake

Watercraft: The *Acacia*, a 180-foot buoy tender has made Charlevoix homeport since 1990.

Mission: Maintenance of Lake Michigan and Lake Huron buoys, lighthouses and navigational aids, search and rescue, and icebreaking.

The *Acacia* is scheduled for decommissioning in summer of 2006. Present plans do not call for a replacement ship in Charlevoix. Aids to navigation duties will be split between Coast Guard ships in Port Huron and Mackinaw City.

The *Acacia* replaced the *Mesquite,* another 180-foot buoy tender that ran aground in December of 1989 off Keweenaw Point on Lake Superior. All 53 crew members survived, but the ship was decommissioned, and sunk as a diving attraction.

Another 180-foot buoy tender, the *Sundew,* was stationed at Charlevoix from 1958-80. During its first year of operation it responded to the mayday calls of the freighter, *Carl D. Bradley,*

Buoy tender, Acacia, Charlevoix (courtesy U.S. Coast Guard, Charlevoix)

which broke in two and sank during a nasty November storm. The *Sundew* rescued the only two survivors.

The *Acacia* was named after a Coast Guard cutter that was sank by a German U-Boat during World War II.

Coast Guard buoy tenders are named after trees, shrubs and plants.

U.S. Lifesaving Service Stations

N. Manitou Island	Built in 1874
Beaver Island	Built in 1875
Charlevoix	Built in 1890
S. Manitou Island	Built in 1901
Sleeping Bear Pt	Built in 1901
Frankfort	Built in 1886
Manistee	Built in 1879
Ludington	Built in 1879

U.S. Lifesaving Station, Sleeping Bear Pt. – 1901 (courtesy Leelanau Historical Society)

Camp Grayling

Acres: 147,000 in and around Grayling in Crawford County Camp Grayling is...

- the country's largest National Guard training site
- the largest military installation east of the Mississippi River
- the largest State-owned and operated field-training site in the U.S.

Camp Grayling provides year around training for the National Guard and active and reserve units from the Army, Navy, Air Force and Marine Corps. Training exercises include: small arms, mortars, tank, heavy artillery, and multiple launch rocket system firings.

Other training: helicopter door gunnery and anti-armor gunneries, land tactics and navigation, water operations, parachute drop zones and air-to-ground munitions delivery for fixed wing aircraft

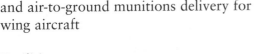

Camp Grayling from above (courtesy of Camp Grayling)

Facilities
- An Army Airfield with air traffic control tower, operations center, troop quarters, and 60 helipad tie down areas
- Housing for 6,144 enlisted personnel and 725 officers at the airfield
- Tent shelter for another 6,780 personnel
- Total housing capacity: 13,649 personnel
- 70 dining facilities to feed up to 11,900 personnel
- 527 tracked vehicles and 77 M-1 tanks
- An Ammunition Supply Point (ASP) to handle all ordinance requirements
- Bulk fuel facilities

Officer's Club at Camp Grayling (courtesy of Camp Grayling)

History: Lumberman Rasmus Hanson made his fortune from the forests around Grayling and wasn't about to turn his back on the area. In 1911, as the lumber industry was running out of trees, Hanson offered a huge tract of land to the Michigan National Guard, figuring it would be good for the local economy. Two years later the Guard accepted the land, and the first troops began training in 1914.

The original name was Camp Ferris, as the land transfer took place under the administration of Governor Woodbridge Ferris.

Cherry Capital Airport – WWII

Cherry Capital Airport in Traverse City was converted into a naval air station and testing site for aircraft drones during World War II. Navy pilots tested the TDR-1 Assault Drone, which was a forerunner to the cruise missile.

Before World War II started the War Department identified Cherry Capital Airport as having "strategic value." With that designation federal funds were approved for widening the existing runway and construction of a new one. That was in 1941, a few months before the Japanese attack on Pearl Harbor.

Within a few months of the attack commercial air service out of and into Cherry Capital was suspended, and plans were announced to expand it into a naval air station. Construction began in 1942, and hundreds of enlisted men, some with families, flooded into Traverse City. Many stayed at the Park Place Hotel until their quarters were completed.

TDR-1 drone flying over Long Lake in Grand Traverse County (courtesy of G.T. Pioneer & Historical Society)

The naval air station at Traverse City was officially commissioned in July of 1943. Among the units housed there was the Special Weapons Test and Tactical Evaluation Unit, NAS. Their work involved testing of the TDR-1 Assault Drone, an unmanned twin-engine aircraft that could be crashed into enemy targets to deliver a 2,000-pound bomb.

Pilots recall long-distance test flights over Lake Michigan using a lighthouse, probably at Waugoshance Point, for target practice. Other targets included small boats and some of the smaller islands around Beaver Island and off Waugoshance Point.

The TDR-1 program was classified, so little was known about it until many years after the end of the war. In 1990, Secretary of the Navy, H. Lawrence Garrett, noted in a letter to all members involved in the TDR-1 testing that one of the drones was successfully used against the enemy on October 27, 1944. Garrett called this "the first true guided missile," marking a new era in warfare.

Today the TDR-1 tested in Traverse City is considered the first generation of guided missiles leading up to the current cruise missile program.

Empire Air Force Base

For 33 years, starting in 1950 the U.S. Air Force had a presence in the lakeshore community of Empire. The 752nd Aircraft Control and Warning Squadron set up the Empire Air Force Station in 1950. Their mission was to monitor, with powerful radar, unidentified airborne activity moving toward U.S. borders. The radar were housed in three large domes along the Lake Michigan shore.

At its peak, in the early to mid 1950's, the base was home to 300 men. As new technology was put into use elsewhere the base population decreased gradually, until it closed in 1983. At that time the unit operating there was known as Operating Location AB, 20th Air Defense Squadron.

Evart's World War I Hero

On May 18, 1918 one day after entering the front line of battle, Joseph Guyton was cut down by German machine gun fire. The Evart native became the first American soldier killed on German soil during World War I.

Guyton was born June 10, 1889 in Evart. He attended the local school and worked in the oil industry in Ohio. He married Winona Baker of Lake City, and together they had one child, Olive Clara, in 1911.

Guyton was a member of the Red Arrows Division National Guard Unit out of Camp MacArthur at Waco, Texas. He was killed on the battlefield in Alsace (Elsass) Germany, and buried temporarily at a nearby church. When Guyton's remains were returned to the U.S., President Harding placed a wreath on his flag-draped coffin and said the following:

"In the name of the republic, I bestow this tribute on the casket of the first soldier who perished on the soil of the enemy... I chose it because I am offering the tribute to the one returned whose death on enemy soil marked the day when our civilization went face forward and the assault on our present day civilization knew it had failed. May 24, 1918, is the date on which this soldier was killed, and the name is that of Joseph W. Guyton, Company I of the 126th Infantry, a resident patriot and hero of the State of Michigan of the United States of America."

Guyton was posthumously awarded the Grand Cross of Honor by the French government. His remains were sent home to Evart where they are buried in the Forest Hill Cemetery. In Evart the local American Legion post, a park and bridge are named after Guyton, and there is an elementary school named in his honor in Detroit.

EDUCATION

School Districts

Traverse Bay Intermediate School District (TBAISD) includes sixteen public school districts, three public school academies, and fourteen private and parochial schools. The district covers Antrim, Benzie, Grand Traverse, Kalkaska and Leelanau counties.

Student enrollment runs about 26,500 in the public schools, and 2,600 in the private and parochial schools, and the district includes over 2,200 teachers.

School district	Students	Operating expenditures per student ($)	MEAP passing rate
Alba	185	8,423	48.6
Benzie Central	1,997	7,072	57.1
Buckley	460	7,171	35.4
Crawford	34	7,543	na
Elk Rapids	1,526	7,485	66.3
Forest Area	875	7,580	44.6
Frankfort	592	8,659	56.0

School district	Students	Operating expenditures per student ($)	MEAP passing rate
Glen Lake	946	6,888	66.6
Kalkaska	1,904	7,231	46.2
Kingsley	1,393	6,606	54.5
Leland	412	8,898	69.0
Mancelona	1,062	7,887	46.7
Northport	277	10,221	51.3
Suttons Bay	1,067	7,746	56.4
Traverse City	10,877	7,302	66.0

Total Students   23,607
(Public schools)

Charlevoix-Emmet Intermediate School District (Char-Em ISD) includes 11 public school districts, six private schools and three public school academies.

The district covers 1,005 square miles in Charlevoix and Emmet counties. Student enrollment runs about 11,450, and there are 800 school personnel in the district.

Crawford School is one of the last one-room schoolhouses in Michigan. The Excelsior District 1 covers two square miles and is located between Kalkaska and Grayling. Total teachers on staff: 3 Students (K-8): 34 (courtesy of Laura Jolly)

School district	Students	Operating expenditures per student ($)	MEAP passing rate
Beaver Island	92	13,378	44.2
Boyne City	1,308	7,684	54.7
Boyne Falls	326	7,300	43.8
Central Lake	511	8,032	45.4
Charlevoix	1,376	8,194	63.4
East Jordan	1,292	7,016	46.0
Ellsworth	245	8,206	58.9
Harbor Springs	1,099	7,981	66.3
Littlefield-Alanson	456	7,908	51.8
Pellston	763	7,385	48.2
Petoskey	3,029	7,226	61.7

Total students   10,497

Wexford-Missaukee Intermediate School District serves over 11,000 public and private school students in the two-county coverage area.

School district	Students	Operating expenditures per student ($)	MEAP passing rate
Cadillac	3,487	7,112	54.3
Lake City	1,317	6,970	53.6
Manton	1,013	7,394	47.1
Marion	823	7,601	40.6
McBain	1,067	6,438	56.1
Mesick	914	7,383	43.8
Pine River	1,350	7,790	55.7
Total students *(Public schools)*	**9,971**		

Manistee ISD includes approximately 4,300 students. Over four public school districts, two public academies and three private schools.

Bear Lake	357	7,652	53.9
Kaleva Norman Dixon	955	9,163	49.5
Manistee	1,730	7,659	54.8
Onekema	582	8,159	54.4
Total students *(Public schools)*	**3,624**		

Cheboygan-Otsego-Presque Isle serves 10 school districts within the counties of Cheboygan, Otsego, and Presque Isle. Districts not included in the Almanac's coverage area include: Onaway, Posen, Cheboygan and Rogers City.

Gaylord	3,362	7,261	58.3
Vanderbilt	264	7,870	35.7
Johannesburg-Lewiston	853	8,063	55.5
Mackinaw City	244	8,070	63.2
Inland Lakes	1,106	6,893	49.0
Wolverine	306	8,900	51.7

Mason - Lake ISD serves eight public school districts, one public academy and West Shore Community College. One school district not included in the Almanac's coverage area is: Pentwater.

School district	Students	Operating expenditures per student ($)	MEAP passing rate
Baldwin	738	11,021	32.8
Free Soil	192	6,494	32.7
Ludington	2,491	7,953	67.8
Mason County Central	1,645	7,556	51.3
Mason County Eastern	614	7,993	55.3

Crawford, Oscoda, Ogemaw, Roscommon (COOR ISD) covers 2,400 square miles and six public school districts. The three not included in the Almanac's coverage area are: Mio AuSable, Fairview, and West Branch-Rose City

Crawford AuSable	2,107	7,423	46.0
Houghton Lake	2,122	7,902	44.8
Gerrish-Higgins	1,889	7,295	53.1

Mecosta Osceola ISD serve five school districts and one public academy. Districts not included in the Almanac's coverage area include: Big Rapids, Chippewa Hills, and Morley Stanwood

Evart	1,306	7,083	47.8
Reed City	1,991	6,681	45.7

Clare Gladwin Regional Education Service District (RESD) serves five public school districts and three private schools. Districts not included in the Almanac's coverage area are: Beaverton Rural and Gladwin

Clare	1,546	7,269	54.3
Harrison	2,236	7,669	47.2
Farwell	1,597	7,300	43.5

Average Teacher Salaries - ranked by district

School district	2002	2001	2000	1999
Beaver Island	56,575	60,636	51,325	47,255
Mason County Central	56,200	52,670	48,005	45,689
Elk Rapids	55,625	53,982	48,421	45,846
Boyne City	55,217	54,225	51,048	49,331
Leland	55,080	51,278	48,595	48,559
Frankfort	53,653	47,966	45,224	48,596
Ludington	53,436	51,741	50,696	49,282
Gaylord	52,746	50,888	50,265	50,216
Harbor Springs	52,442	50,422	50,870	49,537
Littlefield-Alanson	52,377	48,301	46,721	46,523
Central Lake	52,085	46,118	48,051	49,201
Clare	52,042	46,877	45,218	49,810
Manistee	51,234	49,879	48,858	44,393
Petoskey	51,128	48,525	50,115	49,099
Traverse City	50,537	47,215	45,537	44,767
Mason County Eastern	50,522	46,715	44,139	45,814
Farwell	50,319	49,515	45,633	44,699
Kaleva Norman Dixon	49,241	38,122	40,245	37,541
Johannesburg-Lewiston	49,428	48,213	48,599	46,402
Glen Lake	48,824	49,872	51,638	47,224
Harrison	48,371	45,682	45,140	42,544
Mancelona	48,347	46,056	43,127	44,781
Gerrish Higgins	48,046	47,703	45,618	40,645
Cadillac	46,961	45,233	43,319	40,762
Northport	46,941	44,053	44,924	42,893
Pine River	46,262	45,060	43,642	43,008
Benzie Central	46,074	46,279	44,962	43,911
Inland Lakes	46,024	43,914	40,395	41,207
Charlevoix	46,024	45,943	45,048	46,455
Kingsley	45,605	44,376	44,973	42,119
Evart	45,531	42,157	42,521	40,185
Ellsworth	45,370	46,385	44,572	44,249
Pellston	45,244	44,495	43,897	41,694
Manton	45,176	44,054	42,733	43,249
Suttons Bay	45,160	44,920	43,412	42,337
Mackinaw City	44,904	46,294	39,975	44.145
Forest Area	44,884	44,451	41,646	40,554
Bear Lake	44,868	49,915	27,548	45,454
Crawford AuSable	44,618	44,287	44,785	38,513
Marion	44,301	42,114	42,481	40,318
Reed City	44,259	42,090	42,702	42,067

Houghton Lake	43,896	43,476	40,590	38,242
Lake City	43,766	41,910	39,109	36,449
Mesick	43,434	40,039	43,471	41,136
Baldwin	42,234	47,076	41,536	43,688
Onekema	40,989	43,931	44,943	44,763
Wolverine	40,991	40,630	38,343	38,105
Kalkaska	40,711	39,452	43,745	40,783
McBain	39,617	41,666	46,668	43,800
Boyne Falls	38,934	32,589	38,381	37,276
Buckley	38,073	37,723	40,103	38,298
Vanderbilt	37,236	39,488	33,038	37,548
Alba	33,796	34,329	29,920	36,354
Free Soil	30,596	32,094	27,845	32,739
Crawford	25,415	21,078	0	50,446

Higher Ed – Two Year Community Colleges

Northwestern Michigan College
Founded: 1951
Student enrollment (Spring 2005): 4,222
Student mean age: 26.6
Male students: 1,736
Female students: 2,486
Campus: Traverse City

North Central Michigan College
Founded: 1958
Student enrollment (Fall 2004): 2,699
Student average age: 31
Male students: 862
Female students: 1,837
Campus: Petoskey (300+ acres)

West Shore Community College
Founded: 1967
Student enrollment (Fall 2004): 1,380
Student average age: 27
Male students: 477
Female students: 903
Campus: Scottville (360 acres)

Kirtland Community College
Founded: 1966
Student enrollment (2003): 1,826
Student average age:
Male students: 719
Female students: 1,107
Campus: Roscommon (180 acres)

First College in Northern Michigan

In 1863, Reverend Charles Bailey, a Congregational minister from Ohio, organized Grand Traverse College in Benzonia, the town he founded five years earlier. The first classes met in 1867 inside a log building with thirteen students in attendance. Eventually the campus included three buildings: a boys dormitory, a girls dorm and housing for the principal, and a classroom/library building.

The college was renamed as Benzonia College and was known as the Benzonia Academy when it closed in 1918. The principal's building now houses the Benzonia Library.

Great Lakes Maritime Academy

The Great Lakes Maritime Academy (GLMA) opened in 1969 on the shore of West Grand Traverse Bay near downtown Traverse City. It is the only freshwater maritime academy in the country.

The GLMA is a division of Northwestern Michigan Community College and a partner with Ferris State University whose graduates are prepared to serve as Merchant Marine officers and business professionals aboard Great Lakes and ocean ships.

The Academy has state-of-the-art classrooms and a training ship at its facility on the Great Lakes Campus of Northwestern Michigan College.

State of Michigan *learning ship docked in Ludington (courtesy of Great Lakes Mariime Academy)*

PUBLIC LIBRARIES

Most books and serial volumes per capita

Library	No. of books	Service population	Books per capita
Beaver Island	14,636	404	36.2
Mackinac Island	10,445	469	22.3
Betsie Valley-Thompsonville	4,369	2,074	21.0
Helena Twp. (Alden)	18,476	994	18.6
Leelanau Twp (Northport)	19,000	1,694	11.2
Carp Lake Twp.	12,937	1,193	10.8
Idlewild Public Library	6,136	585	10.5
Mackinaw Area	40,281	4,081	10.0
Indian River Area	37,198	3,886	9.6
Fife Lake Library	12,756	1,344	9.5
Benzie Shores Library	19,636	2,159	9.1
Elberta Library	8,510	984	8.6
Wolverine Community	14,120	1,835	7.7
Pathfinder Community	22,000	6,595	7.7
Leland Twp. Library	32,800	4,529	7.2
Interlochen Library	23,633	3,677	6.4
Bellaire Library	29,284	3,054	6.3
Beulah Library	13,900	2,368	5.9
Topinabee Library	7,600	1,314	5.8
Peninsula Library (TC)	25,056	4,340	5.8
Falmouth Area Library	4,594	854	5.4
Glen Lake Library	4,100	2,637	5.3

Fewest books and serial volumes per capita

Library	No. of books	Service population	Books per capita
Alanson Area Library	4,320	4,252	1.0
Kalkaska Library	22,402	13,497	1.7
Traverse Area District	142,969	70,284	2.0
Harrison Comm. Library	25,828	11,918	2.5
Boyne Dist. Library	16,500	6,081	2.7
Reed City Library	22,128	7,522	2.9
Mancelona Twp. Library	13,205	4,465	3.0
McBain Community Library	15,241	5,098	3.0
Otsego County Library	56,329	17,957	3.1
Missaukee Dist. Library	33,175	7,381	3.1

Public Libraries – Most books

Library	County	No. of books
Cadillac-Wexford Community Library	Wexford	155,000
Traverse Area District Library	Grand Traverse	142,969
Baldwin Public Library	Lake	137,222
Manistee County Library	Manistee	101,908
Mason County Library	Mason	94,000
Otsego County Library	Otsego	56,329
Houghton Lake Public Library	Roscommon	47,310
Mackinaw Area Public Library	Emmet	40,281
Gerrish Higgins School Dist. Library	Roscommon	38,430
Petoskey Public Library	Emmet	37,463
Indian River Area Library	Cheboygan	37,198
Missaukee District Library	Missaukee	33,175
Leland Twp. Public Library	Leelanau	32,800
Jordan Valley District Library	Charlevoix	30,825
Evart Public Library	Osceola	28,199

ARCHITECTURE

ARCHITECTURE IN NORTHERN MICHIGAN

From the book, *Buildings of Michigan,* by Kathryn Bishop Eckert, copyright 1993, Oxford University Press.

Ms. Eckert selected architecturally important buildings from each of Michigan's 83 counties for this book she wrote while serving as State Historic Preservation Officer in the Bureau of History. She now resides in Leelanau County.

Antrim County

Henry Richardi House – One of the finest Queen Anne homes in northern Michigan has fronted many a magazine cover, and the cover of *Buildings of Michigan.* Gables, bays, overhangs, and a square corner tower with bell define the home, built for the owner of the Bellaire Wooden Ware Co. Intricate hand carved woodwork throughout, including a lion's head over the entrance. Included on National Register of Historic Places by the Department of the Interior. Built in 1895.
402 Bridge St., Bellaire.

Grand Victorian B&B, Bellaire (courtesy of Grand Victorian)

Mancelona Municipal Building – Original building, before additions, was 60 by 60 feet with barrel roof, rounded stone pillars at the front corners, and between the doors of the front façade. Built as a Fire Hall in 1933.
120 West State St., Mancelona.

Wayside Chapel – Probably the smallest chapel in northern Michigan, it was designed for travelers along US 31. Interior holds four pews. East side of US 31 .2 of a mile north of Atwood.

Wayside Chapel built in 1968 (courtesy Laura Jolly)

Wayside Chapel interior, seats four (courtesy Laura Jolly)

Elk Rapids Township Hall built in 1882-83 (courtesy Laura Jolly)

Elk Rapids Township Hall – The town's original governmental center is a long building constructed with local fired bricks. Features a mansard roof and round-arch windows. Seats 600. Built 1882-83. Corner of River and Spruce, Elk Rapids.

Hughes House – Two-and-a-half story home built as an inn to serve stagecoach travelers. Built late 1860's. 109 Elm St., corner of Elm and Traverse, Elk Rapids.

Benzie County

Gwen Frostic Studio – Pioneer Michigan artist and business woman, Gwen Frostic created her studio, print shop and business operations in a fieldstone and cedar structure. Described as "cave-like" the structure is set on the Betsie River, and wraps around a pond. Built in the 1960's. 5140 River Rd., Benzonia.

Leelanau Avenue Homes – Three large intricate homes set on a hill. At one time they overlooked Betsie Bay, but newer structures have cut off the views. Built between 1899-1903. 211, 219 and 231 Leelanau Avenue, Frankfort.

Kristin Acre House – Neo-Gothic castle-like home constructed with concrete block. Built in 1900. 503 Crystal Ave. (M-22), Frankfort.

Pt. Betsie Lighthouse – Gambrel-roofed light keeper's house attached to 100-foot high light tower at Betsie Pt. Original light built in 1858, replaced in 1880's. Home built in 1858, remodeled in 1895. Pt. Betsie Rd, Lake Township.

Charlevoix County

Earl Young – Stone Houses of Charlevoix
Earl Young never earned a degree in architecture or engineering, but he did design and oversee the building of some of the most noteworthy homes and buildings in northern Michigan. With their wavy roofs and rounded edges, the stone homes have been called everything from "Hobbit Homes" to "mushroom houses." Young, who was born in 1889 in Mancelona, moved to

Charlevoix when he was ten. He seemed always to have a fascination with rock collecting, even hiding his favorite large rocks in rivers and lakes, or buried in the ground. He did attend the University of Michigan, but didn't graduate. After college he opened an insurance agency and married Irena Harsha, his high school sweetheart.

Earl Young Stone Houses (courtesy of Laura Jolly)

He built his first stone house at 304 Park Avenue a few blocks west of US 31 in downtown Charlevoix. In 1924 he purchased 37 acres of waterfront near the Charlevoix Area Hospital, and began building. Today the neighborhood, known as Boulder Park, is dominated by Young-designed stone homes. Over a period of fifty years he designed and built 30 stone houses and commercial buildings, including the Weathervane Terrace Hotel and Weathervane Restaurant.

A favorite story about Earl Young has to do with the building of the Weathervane Restaurant. In 1928 he "found" a boulder, weighing over 9 tons that was shaped like the Lower Peninsula of Michigan. After measuring the rock, he buried it for safekeeping. During construction of the Weathervane he told the crews to leave an opening in the roof precisely large enough so the large Michigan boulder could be lowered through – Young's idea was to use it as the centerpiece of the fireplace. However, the roof opening wasn't large enough to fit the rock through, so the crews had to make a larger hole. Pressed for an explanation, Young did not question his measurements or memory; he said the boulder must have grown after all of those years underground.

Young houses can be seen in Boulder Park along the lakeshore near Charlevoix Area Hospital, and in the area bordered between Grant, Clinton and Park Streets in the same neighborhood west of US 31 a few blocks from downtown.

Earl young built only one home outside of Charlevoix and that was for a friend in Alma.

Lincoln Logs Motel – Rustic, log cabins with log furniture and fireplaces. Designed for the early automobile tourists. 820 Petoskey (US 31, one mile NE of Bridge St.), Charlevoix

On of the log cabins at Lincoln Log Cabins Motel (Author photo)

Chicago Club – The original clubhouse built by the First Congregational Church of Chicago as a summer resort included 27 rooms and large dining hall. The structure includes a two-story wrap around veranda and decorative stick construction. The hillside leading to Round Lake was billed in with large summer homes. Built in 1880. Cherry Street overlooking Round Lake. *(private association)*

Belvedere Club – Originally the Charlevoix Summer Resort Association started by Baptists from the Kalamazoo area. In the first year a bathhouse and six cottages were built on terraces overlooking Round Lake. Now a community of 86 summer homes, mostly wooden, some large with intricate woodwork, others designed as basic seasonal homes. Framed boathouses line the association shoreline on Round Lake. Original buildings date to 1876. On Lake Charlevoix and Round Lake in Charlevoix.

Loeb Summer House – Neo-Norman home designed by Arthur Heun, a student of the Prairie style. Built with native fieldstone on property overlooking Lake Charlevoix. U-shaped floor plan with 12 bedrooms upstairs. Original property covered 2,200 acres and included a farm built for and by Albert Loeb, Vice President of Sears, Roebuck and Co. at the time. Built in 1917. M-66 (east side), 3 miles SE of US 31, Eveline Township.

Greensky Hill Mission Church – Methodist-Episcopalian church built by the Chippewa minister, Peter Greensky. Built with hewn timbers with solid dovetailing at the corners. Built 1864-65. Greensky Hill Rd, off US 31, Hayes Township.

Greensky Hill Mission Church (courtesy of Laura Jolly)

Wolverine Hotel – Three-story building with wrap around porches; tile mosaic floors and custom oak woodwork in the first floor lobby. Built 1911. 300 Water St., Boyne Falls.

Boyne Mountain Lodge – Hand-hewn oak beams, local limestone, and stucco used in the A-frame lodge centered in a Bavarian-style village. Built 1950's -70's.
Boyne Mountain Road off US 131, Boyne Falls.

Crawford County

Ray's Canoe Livery – Rustic log building on the Au Sable River inspired by the design of the Logging Museum at Hartwick Pines State Park. Site once occupied by Indian Chief, Shoppenagon, one of the early river guides. Built in 1941.
James St. (Business I-75), at Au Sable River.

Ray's Canoe Livery and the Fly Factory on the Au Sable River in Grayling (Author photo)

Rialto Theater – Tan brick theater with centered entrance and marquee. Designed by R.V. Gay of St. Johns. Built – 1930. Michigan between Peninsular and Spruce, Grayling.

The Rialto (Author photo)

Wa Wa Sum – Large summer fishing camp on the Au Sable River built for J. Secour and James Brown Bell of the Champion Spark Plug Co. Six log cabins, a main lodge, dining room, caretaker's building, recreation building, river guide's cabin and boathouse and barn. Built with red pine logs, some with fieldstone foundations and chimneys. Today the compound is used by Michigan State University as a fish and wildlife research facility. Earliest structures built in late 1890's. Lodge built in 1921-22. Wa Wa Sum Drive off of Whirlpool Dr. Grayling Township.

Hartwick Memorial Building – Memorial to Edward Hartwick who was killed in World War I. His wife, Karen, donated land to the State, which became part of the Hartwick Pines State Park. This log structure was built by Civil Conservation Corps workers and includes a huge stone fireplace and porch that runs the length of the building. Built in 1934. M-93 at Hartwick Pines State Park.

Clare County

Clare Middle School – Two-story arch windows with over-hanging pent roof covered in tiles, and decorative bricks highlight the exterior. Inside there are four Gerald Mast murals depicting the academics, peaceful endeavors and the oil and gas, and agriculture industries. The Works Progress Administration sponsored the murals, painted in 1938. The murals were restored in 1988 and are valued at over $20 million. School built in 1922. Wheaton Ave. between State and Pine in Clare.

George and Martha Hitchcock House – Designed by renowned Detroit architects, Mason and Rice for timberland owner, George Hitchcock. The two-and-a-half story Queen Anne is built with Basswood, Golden Oak, Tiger-eye maple, cherry, birch, ash, and pine. Hitchcock selected much of the lumber from trees on his land. Built in 1889. 205 E. Michigan St., Farwell.

Emmet County

Little Traverse Regional Historical Society Museum – Former train depot built by Chicago and West Michigan Railroad. Built 1891-92. Pioneer Park on West Lake St., Petoskey.

Former train depot, now serving as Little Traverse Regional Historical Society Museum (Author photo)

Town and Country Log Homes – Model home built with cedar log walls that are available in hand-peeled, rough-sawn, or smooth finish. Homes are designed on computer but rustic look fits well in the deep woods. Built in the 1980's.
4772 US 131 S., Bear Creek Township.

Bay View Association – Private community originally established as a Methodist camp. It features 437 privately owned summer cottages, two hotels and 29 other structures on a hillside overlooking Little Traverse Bay. Most of the cottages are of Victorian design, built in the late 18th century. The winding streets of the original plan were modeled after Martha's Vineyard, Massachusetts. First buildings – 1876.
US 31 N., north of Petoskey.

Harbor Inn on the Bay – Large white resort hotel with red metal roof. Octagonal tower with four wings. Built in 1910.
200 Beach Rd, south of M-119.

Ephraim Shay House – Two-story octagon center section with six wings – each wing with one room. The exterior and most of the interior walls are covered in pressed metal. Built in 1892 by the inventor of the Shay locomotive.
396 E. Main St., Harbor Springs.

Holy Childhood of Jesus Church and School – Neo-Romanesque, white, wooded church with center steeple and bell tower. Three story brick school lies just northeast of the church. 150 West Main St., Harbor Springs.

Earl H. Mead House – Designer of many cottages from the early 20th century, Mead's own home sits on a steep bluff overlooking Lake Michigan. It features a steep pitched hip roof and dormers, its appearance of no particular period or style. Built in 1910. 151 East Bluff Dr., Harbor Springs.

Marina Village – Condo development on Little Traverse Bay designed by Charlevoix architect, Jack Begrow. The triangular shapes created by the shed roofs and tall chimneys leave the impression of sailboats in the harbor. Among the first condominiums built in northern Michigan. Built in 1968-71.
East Bay St. and Zoll St., Harbor Springs.

Wequetonsing – Private association formed in 1877 as the Presbyterian summer resort. Early members hailed from Allegan, Michigan and Elkhart, Indiana. Resort was built on eight acres given to the association by the City of Harbor Springs. Hotel was built in 1880 and assembly hall in 1899. Noted architect, Earl Mead, designed over 20 of the cottages in Wequetonsing. Established in 1877. On Little Traverse Bay north of Beach Dr. between First and Fifth Avenue, Harbor Springs.

Harbor Point – Described as the most exclusive of the eight summer resorts established around Harbor Springs by 1910. Organized by group of businessmen from Lansing on 52 acres of land at the tip of Harbor Point. Over 80 cottages and a casino were built by 1900. Harbor Point was a summer playground for the likes of the Wrigley's of Chicago, the Whitney's of Detroit, and the Gambles of Cincinnati. No automobiles are allowed past the entrance. Established in 1878.

Telgham and Anna Pickering Summer House – Ornate cottage designed by Earl Mead, featuring towers, dormers, covered porches, balconies, stairways and large windows. Built 1898-1902. Lot 27, Harbor Point, Harbor Springs.

Albert and Carrie Lois Stafft Goodrich Summer Cottage – Built for Albert W. Goodrich, owner of the largest steamship line on the Great Lakes at the time. Two-and-a-half story rectangular building with large verandas. Built in 1900. Lot 2, Harbor Point, Harbor Springs.

James Douglas House – International style house designed by noted architect, Richard Meier. Situated on a 45-degree bluff dropping to Lake Michigan below. From the road only the roof and entry level are visible, however, there are drops four levels down the hillside. Bright white home against backdrop of greenery is well visible from the water. Built 1971-73. 3490 Lake Shore Dr., Friendship Township.

Saint Ignatius Church – Simply designed clapboard church situated on the site of original Jesuit mission established in 1741. Built in 1889. Lower Shore Rd., Middle Village, Friendship Township.

Legs Inn – Polish immigrant Stanislaw Smolak used a recycling philosophy in building this restaurant that overlooks Lake Michigan. Constructed with local fieldstone and found objects, natural and manmade. The parapet around the roof is lined with legs from old cast iron stoves, hence the name. Interior construction and furnishings make good use of local driftwood, logs, branches, etc. Built 1921. 6425 Lake Shore Dr., Cross Village.

Redpath Memorial Presbyterian Church – Designed by Earl Mead using fieldstone and cobblestones. Features broad Gothic-pointed arch windows, flared eaves, and a cupola with bell. Built in 1921. Named after Reverend John Redpath. 6532 Lake Shore Dr., Cross Village.

Colonial Michilimackinac – Established by French Canadians as a fur trading post, and later served as a fort. In 1730's the settlement was rebuilt. Built 1715-81.
Under the Mackinac Bridge, Mackinaw City.

Mackinac Bridge – Built 1954-57. Architect-David B. Steinman.

<u>Grand Traverse County</u>

Grand Traverse County Courthouse –
Red brick and sandstone Richardsonian Romanesque with clock tower. Similar in appearance to Antrim County's Courthouse. Initial design by Rush, Bowman and Rush of Grand Rapids. Completed by Cassius M. Prall, who designed some of the buildings for the old Traverse City Sate Hospital. Built 1898-89. Corner of Boardman and Washington, Traverse City.

Grand Traverse County Courthouse is a near duplicate of Antrim County's Courthouse (Author photo)

Traverse City Opera House – Three-story red brick and sandstone structure on main retail block in downtown district. Ground floor is retail; second and third stories contain the main stage, a large open floor and the balcony. Designed by E. R. Prall who also designed some of the buildings on the Traverse City State Hospital campus. Built – 1891. 112 E. Front St., Traverse City.

Since its opening in 1891 the Traverse City Opera House has been used for plays and musicals, concerts, sporting events, town meetings, weddings and other activities, but never has an opera been performed on its stage. (Author photo)

Temple Beth El – Oldest synagogue in continuous use in Michigan. Two-story clapboard building constructed for $1,000 on land donated by lumberman, Perry Hannah. Built 1886 by J.G. Holiday. 311 S. Park St., Traverse City.

The oldest synagogue in continuous use in Michigan, located just south of the Park Place Hotel (Author photo)

Boardman Neighborhood – Some of the oldest, and most ornate homes in Traverse City lie to the east of downtown. Many of the larger homes were built in the late 19th century for executives from lumber and wood products companies.

Cary Hull Home – Exterior highlighted by large Ionic columns at the entrance. Designed in style of Academic Classicism with a hipped roof and gable dormers. Designed for the son of the Oval Wood Dish Company, the largest employer in Traverse City in the late 1800's. In the late 1990's a city police officer was shot and killed by the lone resident of the home. It sat vacant for several years, but has since been restored and now as the Wellington Inn, serves as an elegant B & B. 230 Wellington, corner of Wellington and Washington, Traverse City.

The former Cary Hull home, now the Wellington Inn B&B (Author photo)

Henry S. Hull House – Across the street from the William and Lola Hull house this ornate Queen Anne was built for the founder of the Oval Wood Dish Company at an estimated cost of $20,000. The wrap-around porch features columns in groups of three and an ornamental railing. The interior is awash in rich, ornate carved wood. Built – 1894. 229 Wellington St., Traverse City.

William Hull house across the street from Wellington Inn (Author photo)

Fine Arts Building, Northwestern Michigan College – Designed by the Architects Collaborative of Cambridge, Massachusetts. Slanted A-frame style roof with floor-to-ceiling slanted glass walls. Praised for blending with the pine and oak trees surrounding its exterior. Built – 1973.
1701 E. Front St., Traverse City.

Northwestern Michigan College Fine Arts Building (Author photo)

The Tower at Grand Traverse Resort Village (courtesy of Travel Michigan)

Grand Traverse Resort Village – A 15-story tinted glass-over steel frame tower erected in a former cherry orchard. Designed by Greyheck, Bell and Kline of Traverse City.
Tower built 1983. 6300 US 31 North, Acme.

Interlochen Center for the Arts – Well-known Michigan architect, Alden B. Dow designed several campus buildings including dormitories, Library, the Dow Science Building, C.S. Mott Language Arts Building, Kresge Auditorium and Corson Auditorium. Campus established –1928. Dow designs added in 1950's, 60's and 70's. M-137 just south of US 31, Interlochen.

Kalkaska County

Kalkaska County Historical Museum – Red brick building with hipped roof formerly served as the Grand Rapids and Indiana Railroad depot. Replace original depot destroyed by fire.
Museum is adjacent to the National Trout Festival Memorial. Built – 1920.
Cedar St., between Elm and Oak, downtown Kalkaska.

Excelsior Town Hall – Gable roof building built for $1,085. Served as high school between 1907-27. Still serves as public meeting hall. Built – 1900.
Corner of County Rd. 571 and Wagenschultz Rd., Excelsior Township.

Lake County

Shrine of the Pines – A large L-shaped log cabin with over 200 pieces of pine-carved furniture inside. Raymond Overholzer spent most of his life creating dining tables, chairs, beds, and other furniture from pine logs, tree roots and branches. Overholzer's home is now a public museum. Built in 1939.
East side of M-37, south of Baldwin.

Idlewild – One of the country's most popular African-American resorts during the mid-20th century. Over 500 buildings, mostly cottages, dotted the rolling hills around several lakes in the community. Most of the cottages were simple

bungalows, and gable-roofed cottages. The Paradise Club was built in 1923, and was the scene of many classic shows from the likes of Louis Armstrong to Bill Eckstine. Large clubhouse built on an island in Idlewild Lake was connected to mainland by a footbridge and vehicle bridge. Built 1915-1935.
South of US 10, east of Baldwin, Idlewild.

Leelanau County

Fishtown – One of the last commercial fishing villages in the state. Old wooden fish shanties line the docks along the Leland River between Lake Leelanau and Lake Michigan. The shanties now operated by merchants selling fudge, fish, T-shirts, and other gifts. Fishing village dates back to 1870's. Current shanties built between 1900-1930's. Leland River below the dam, Leland.

South Manitou Island Light –Yellow brick, two-story light keeper's house built in 1858 next to lighthouse built in 1870. Owned by the National Park Service. Southeastern part of S. Manitou Island off the shore of Leland.

Northport Indian Church – Wooden, gable-roofed mission church with open belfry and short steeple. Built by the Northport Indian Mission in 1882. M-22 northeast of Swede Rd., two miles southwest of Northport.

Grand Traverse Lighthouse – Brick, two-story home with light tower. Stone garden sculptures in the yard created by former lighthouse keepers. Built – 1858.
County Rd. 629 at Leelanau State Park, north of Northport.

Omena Presbyterian Church – New England-style white steepled church built by Presbyterian missionary, Peter Dougherty. Built – 1858.
M-22 just north of County Rd. 626, Omena.

Super Bingo Palace and Leelanau Sands Casino – Five large, wood-sided, one story, gable-roofed buildings designed so as not to interfere with the small Indian village surrounding the operation. Built in 1983-84.
M-22, four miles north of Suttons Bay, Peshawbestown.

Holy Rosary Church and School – Red brick buildings designed by Breilmaier and Sons, a prominent Milwaukee design firm. Church established in 1888. Built –1921-23. Corner of Shomberg Rd. and County Rd. 645, Isadore.

Sleeping Bear Inn – Two-story structure built on Lake Michigan shore as a hotel for steamship travelers. Built – 1857 with additions in 1890. Sleeping Bear Drive in Glen Haven.

Sleeping Bear Point Life Saving Station – Four wood-frame buildings; one housed the crew, the large double-door building housed the boats, one was a work shed, and one for storage. A signal tower also remains. Coast Guard operations from this station ceased in 1944. Built in 1901 and 1931. Sleeping Bear Dr., Glen Haven.

D.H. Day Farmstead – Queen Anne farmhouse and barns, including the 116-foot long dairy barn marked by octagonal cupolas with bell roofs. Lumberman and tourism pioneer, started a large dairy and hog operation here in the 1870's, and planted thousands of cherry trees in the early 20th century. Built in 1851 –1928. 6141 M-109, Empire.

The Homestead – The landscape architect firm of Johnson, Johnson and Roy of Ann Arbor are credited with preserving sand dunes and vegetation in carving out this slope side resort overlooking Lake Michigan and the Crystal River. They used terraces and decking to protect the dunes and create maximum views for guests. Original inn designed by Harbor Springs architect, Earl Mead as a dormitory, dining hall and class-rooms for the Leelanau School. Remodeled in the 1970's as a resort. Original inn built in 1929. M-22, two miles north of Glen Arbor.

Sleeping Bear Dunes (photo courtesy of National Park Service)

Ramsdell Theatre (Author photo)

Manistee County

Ramsdell Theatre and Hall – Described as "the finest of several opera houses built in small Michigan cities at the turn of the century." Designed by Chicago architect, Solon S. Beman. Built in 1903. 101 Maple St., Manistee.

Ramsdell Building – Richardsonian Romanesque bank and office building designed by Frederick Hollister of Saginaw. Community leader, Thomas Ramsdell, invested financed the Ramsdell Theatre, as well as this building, which was home to the Manistee County Savings Bank. Built in 1891. 399 River St., corner of River and Maple, Manistee.

River Street Commercial District – Many of the buildings are Victorian Italianate in design.

Vogue Theatre – Reinforced concrete with cement plaster face and two-tone brick veneer. Designed by Chicago theatre architects, Pereira and Pereira. Built in 1938. 385 River St., Manistee

Haley Block – This commercial block was built by sisters Ellen, Eliza, and Kate Haley, who operated a fabric store. The stores were built out of brick, replacing wood sided stores destroyed in several fires. Built in 1883. 419-423 River St., Manistee.

Vogue Theatre, Manistee (Author photo)

Buildings on Haley Block, River St., Manistee (Author photo)

The Manistee Fire Hall is the oldest fire station in continuous use in Michigan (Author photo)

Manistee Fire Hall – Richardsonian Romanesque styled building with gables and tower designed for hose drying. Originally red pressed brick exterior, now painted bright red. Built in 1888. 280 First St., Manistee.

Danish Lutheran Church – One of the oldest existing Danish Lutheran churches in the country. Highlighted by bell tower with octagonal spire and weather vane above gabled roof. One of the few buildings to survive the fire of 1871. Built in 1868-1870. 300 Walnut, Manistee.

First Congregational Church, Manistee, built 1888-92 (Author photo)

First Congregational United Church of Christ – Designed by William Le Baron Jenney, Chicago architect noted for his contribution to developing the steel-frame skyscraper. Large bell and clock tower top off the pressed red brick and limestone structure. Seating for 610. Built in 1888-92. 412 Fourth St., corner of Fourth and Oak, Manistee.

E.P. and Belle Randall Case House – Designed by William Le Baron Jenney, Chicago skyscraper architect. L-shaped wooden clapboard on limestone foundation. Picket fence design borders the peak of the front gabled dormer. Built in 1880.
467 Fourth St., Manistee.

Case House designed by Chicago sky-scraper architect, William Le Baron Jenney (courtesy of Laura Jolly)

Patrick and Susan Agnes McCurdy Noud House – Red brick Neo-Georgian house designed by Holabird and Roche, noted Chicago architects. Built for lumberman, and former mayor, Patrick Noud and family, it features superb interior wood-work. Built in 1894-95.
202 Maple St., corner of Maple and Second, Manistee.

McCurdy Noud House at Maple and Second, Manistee (courtesy of Laura Jolly)

John and Alice Swainson – George and Caroll Whitehead Vacation House – Built in the woods of Lakeland Subdivision on the shore of Lake Michigan. Irregularly shaped wood shingles, wraparound deck, inward balconies and fieldstone fireplace in this non-traditional home help it blend into nature. Winner of Michigan Society of Architects award in 1966. Built in 1965.
Professional Drive, Lakeland Subdivision, Filer Township.

Mason County

Mason County Courthouse – A Richardsonian Romanesque style public building designed by Grand Rapids architect, Sidney J. Osgood. Interior includes original plaster wainscoting, ceramic tile floors, pressed metal ceilings and wood chimney pieces. Built in 1893-94. 300 East Ludington, Ludington.

Ludington Post Office – Built during the Depression under the federal Public Works Administration. A classical building with five bays, each with round-headed windows, the middle bay acting as entrance. Built in 1932-33.
202 East Ludington St., Ludington.

Epworth Heights – Summer resort association founded by Assembly of Methodists in the 1890's. Unique cottages line the dunes leading to Lake Michigan. Hotel built in 1894. North of Ludington.

Mason County Road Commission Office and Garage – Works Administration Project designed by R.V. Gay. Built in 1940. 510 East State St., Scottville.

Osceola County

Livingston House – Intricate Queen Anne built in 1890 by carpenter and builder, Henry Marzoff. 343 W. Upton, Reed City.

John and Elizabeth Downing Wilkinson House – Queen Anne finished in knotless pine siding. The Evart Planing Mill crafted the railing and post in the central hall staircase. Built in 1884. 408 Main St., Evart.

Charles Warden Round Barn – Fewer posts are required due to the unique joint and joist system, therefore floor space is maximized. Built in 1907. 5660 M-66, mile north of US 10.

A round red barn! (courtesy Laura Jolly)

Otsego County

Hidden Valley (Otsego Ski Club) – Designed as a Swiss Alpine village for Donald McLouth, founder of McLouth Steel in Detroit. Detroit architect, Hugh T. Keyes who designed many Georgian Revival homes in Grosse Pointe designed cabins and lodges using fieldstone foundations and vertical log exteriors. McLouth is said to have been one of the promoters or carrying the Alpine theme over to the town of Gaylord, where it prevails today. Built in 1939. M-32, one mile east of Gaylord.

Roscommon County

First Congregational Church of Roscommon – Redwood exterior and interior with exposed beams. Exterior dominated by towering, slender A-frame gable. Designed by Dow-Howell-Gilmore-Associates. Built in 1961.
109 S. Main St., Roscommon.

Wexford County

Old City Hall (Author photo)

Old Cadillac City Hall and Fire Station – Rectangular structure with arched entrance, arched doors in old fire hall, and rows of arched windows on second floor. Three story building has been remodeled for commercial purposes. Built in 1900-01. 201 N. Mitchell St., corner of N. Mitchell and West Mason, Cadillac.

Michigan Dept. of Transportation Headquarters – Beaux-Arts Classical structure designed by George D. Mason of Detroit as offices for Cadillac's largest lumber company. Cobbs and Mitchell, Inc. Interior is finished in nine different woods from the Cobbs and Mitchell forests. Built in 1905-07. 100 East Chapin St., corner of E. Chapin and S. Mitchell, Cadillac.

MDOT Headquarters building (Author photo)

Frank and Maude Belcher Cobbs House – Large clapboard, gambrel-roofed home of Colonial Revival design. Home of Frank Cobbs, partner in the town's largest lumbering firm at the turn of the century. Built in 1898 by James R. Fletcher. 407 E. Chapin, Cadillac.

1898 Belcher Cobbs Home (courtesy of Laura Jolly)

Kysor Industrial Corporation World Headquarters – The Parthenon of Wexford County - a large white, symmetrical building supported by pillared columns similar to those found in ancient Greece. Built in 1981-82. 1 Madison Ave., near M-115 and US 131, Clam Lake Township.

CULTURE

Betty Beeby painting mural at Ft. Michilimackinac
Visitor's Center, 1974 (photo by Sarah Gay Dammann)

CULTURE

Interlochen Center for the Arts

Founded in 1928, by Joseph P. Maddy, as the National High School Orchestra Camp, Interlochen today is an internationally acclaimed center for the arts and arts education. The original summer music camp was set on 60 acres of lakefront property and drew 115 high school musicians. Today the year round Interlochen is spread out on over 1,200 acres and attracts hundreds of students and summer campers from every state and dozens of countries.

Interlochen includes:

- Interlochen Arts Academy, the nation's first high school dedicated to the arts, and the premier arts boarding school in the country.

- National Music Camp offering summer arts programs for 3rd –12th grade students from around the world.

- Interlochen Pathfinder School, a pre-school through 8th grade school serving the local Grand Traverse area.

- Interlochen Public Radio including two FM stations focused on classical music, and one FM station devoted to news and talk.

Early photo of the Interlochen Bowl (courtesy of Interlochen Center for the Arts)

In early 2005 Interlochen announced it was adding a film studies program to the academy and summer camp. The Aaron and Helen L. DeRoy Center for Film Studies at Interlochen was scheduled to open in a new facility in the fall of 2005.

History

By the early 1920's Joseph P. Maddy was an accomplished classical and jazz musician, with a passion for teaching. His first professional job was at 17, playing viola with the Minneapolis Symphony Orchestra. There, he was passed over for promotion because of his young age. That experience planted a notion in his head that proven talent, not age or seniority, should determine the advancement of musicians within an orchestra.

He was able to test that theory while organizing a high school orchestra in Richmond, Indiana. Although some parents and fellow educators were upset that some students were being demoted during tryouts, the system was well-received by the students who were the ones voting on their fellow students performances. Today that method of tryouts is the standard for school and professional orchestras around the world.

During his time in Richmond, Maddy met Thaddeus P. Giddings, who would encourage Maddy's educational vision of bringing music to schoolchildren and developing talented American musicians. Together the pair authored several music education manuals, including *Universal Teacher*, which became the standard for music teachers across the country.

In 1925, while teaching in Ann Arbor, Maddy was asked

National High School Orchestra (courtesy of Interlochen Center for the Arts)

to assemble a national high school orchestra to perform at the upcoming National Music Educators Conference in Detroit. At that time it was rare for high schools to have a music program, let alone a full orchestra. It was unheard of to assemble the best students from across the country in one town, rehearse, and perform any concert of note.

Maddy was able to attract over 200 talented high school musicians to Detroit, where

they stayed with local families. The respected director of the Detroit Symphony Orchestra, Ossip Gabrilowitsch, reluctantly agreed to conduct. He avoided the student musicians until the final rehearsal in which they performed Beethoven's Eroica, after which he proclaimed it "the music miracle of the century."

After the performance there were calls for the orchestra to perform in other cities, which they did, but when it came time to go home there were many tears. The students begged Maddy to bring them together so they could perform again. The search for a summer music camp began.

Within 15 months of the tearful goodbyes Maddy had opened the first National High School Orchestra Camp at Interlochen. He was contacted by Willis Pennington who operated a boys camp and girls camp along with his Hotel Pennington on Green Lake and Duck Lake, as we know them today. The men struck up a deal: Pennington gave Maddy 60 lakefront acres for his music camp in exchange for exclusive rights to board campers at his hotel, and a percentage of the early profits.

Maddy used his own money, along with loans from music publishers and instrument manufacturers, to build cabins and the Interlochen Bowl for performances. After one season, Maddy was in debt to the tune of $40,000, but was able to attract enough support for a second season, rang up more debt but was seen as an educational success.

Within four years of opening the camp Maddy's National High School Orchestra had performed before President Hoover, had played in the finest concert halls in the east, and were given a weekly program on CBS radio.

The Interlochen Movie
In 1941 Paramount released a movie about the National Music Camp, entitled "The Hard-Boiled Canary", starring Susanna Foster and Alan Jones. Foster played a New York burlesque performer brought to Interlochen by the son of the camp director. Maddy successfully lobbied to have the title changed to "There's Magic in the Music," which improved the box office and the image of Interlohcen. Maddy would not allow his campers to be extras in the film, so the Interlochen scenes were shot at Lake Arrowhead, California.

National Music Camp - Today
Today the National Music Camp attracts 2,100 students from all 50 states, the District of Columbia, Puerto Rico and more than 41 other countries. They study dance, acting, writing, visual arts, and music. Interlochen is the home of the World Youth Symphony Orchestra, which performs concerts every Sunday throughout the summer.

Interlochen Arts Academy
In 1962, Maddy opened the the country's first independent high school dedicated to the arts. The Interlochen Arts Academy attracts over 450 students a year from across the nation and around the globe. They come to study music, dance, theatre, visual arts, creative writing and college prep academics.

Over 300 staff and a distinguished faculty mix with the students on the wooded 1,200-acre campus between two lakes.

95% of IAA grads go on to universities and music conservatories. The Academy has produced 35 Presidential Scholars in the arts and academics, more than any other high school in the country.

Interlochen alumni comprise more than 10% of the members of the nation's major symphony orchestras.

Interlochen founder Joe Maddy (right) at entrance to National Music Camp (courtesy of G.T. Pioneer & Historical Society)

FAMOUS INTERLOCHEN ALUMNI

Josh Groban as student at Interlochen in 1998 (front row, far right) (courtesy of Interlochen Center for the Arts)

Christie Hefner	Chair and CEO of Playboy Enterprises, Inc.
Josh Groban	Pop and classical singer, Warner Bros. recording artist
Norah Jones	Jazz singer and pianist, Blue Note Records artist
Bruce Johnston	Member of the Beach Boys
Peter Yarrow	Member of Peter, Paul & Mary
Jewel (Kilcher)	Grammy Award-winning singer and songwriter

Returning to Interlochen in 2004 as an international singing sensation, Josh Groban performs with summer campers (courtesy of Interlochen Center for the Arts)

Jewel, 1992 graduate of Interlochen Arts Academy, returned 10 years later a as successful recording star. Before her performance she spent time with some of the summer campers. (July, 2002) While attending Interlochen, Jewel worked as a waitress in downtown Traverse City and performed at Ray's Coffee House. (courtesy of Interlochen Center for the Arts)

Jessye Norman	Soprano, youngest recipient of Kennedy Center Honors
Cathy Guisewite	Creator of the comic strip, Cathy
Doug Stanton	Author, *In Harm's Way*
Meredith Baxter	Actress, Family Ties and films
Sara Gilbert	Actress, Roseanne

	and films
Felicity Huffman	Actress, Desperate Housewives
Tom Hulce	Actor, Amadeus (nomi nated for Academy Award)
Linda Hunt	Actress, The Year of Living Dangerously (Academy Award – Best Supporting Actress)
Dermot Mulroney	Actor, My Best Friend's Wedding
Mike Wallace	Correspondent, CBS 60 Minutes
Sean Young	Actress, Ace Ventura: Pet Detective, No Way Out

1981 Interlochen grad Felicity Huffman majored in Theater Arts. She is one of the stars of the hit ABC soap, "Desperate Housewives." (courtesy of Interlochen Center for the Arts)

Interlochen alumni have excelled in the world outside of arts.

Lawrence Page is co-founder and CEO of Google, Inc., one of the most successful Internet companies in the world.

The former head coach of the Minnesota Vikings, **Jerry Burns** is an alumni grad, as is **Steve Fisher,** coach of the San Diego State University basketball team, and head coach of the 1989 National Champion Michigan Wolverines.

MOVIES AND TV

Michael Moore:
April 23, 1954

Birthplace:
Davison, MI

Connection to northern Michigan: He splits time between homes in northern Michigan and New York City, but considers home on Torch Lake as his primary residence.

Career: Moore started the alternative paper the *Flint Voice* in 1976 and published the weekly for 10 years before launching the *Michigan Voice*. During this time he observed the effects of General Motors closing up factories in Flint and decided to make a documentary film about it. In 1989 he released "Roger & Me" and the popularity of the film set Moore on the course as America's new Ralph Nader. He became the editor of *Mother Jones* and left after a short tenure to work for Ralph Nader. In 1994 he launched "TV Nation,"a series that covered news ignored by mainstream press. He filmed his debut episode at Shanty Creek Mountain in Bellaire. In 2000 he launched the hit program "Awful Truth" where he satirized big corporations and politicians. Moore has published three best selling books *Downsize This, Stupid White Men* and *Dude, Where's My Country*.

In 2002 he produced the Academy Award winner "Bowling for Columbine," shooting some of the scenes in Traverse City. Local musician Jeff Gibbs, a lifelong friend of Moore's, produced the films musical score while Traverse City photographer John Robert Williams designed the films promotional poster. In 2004 Moore released the controversial "Fahrenheit 9/11" winning best film honors at the coveted Cannes Film Festival.

Best known for: His 2003 acceptance speech at the Academy Awards. At a time when the country was divided over President Bush's Iraq policy, Moore's speech was highly critical of the president and made international headlines. It also resulted in piles of horse manure left on the driveway of his Torch Lake home.

Charlton Heston:
(John Charles Carter)
October 4, 1924

Birthplace:
Evanston, Illinois

"Moses" spent a lot of time on the water around his boyhood home in the St. Helens area. As a young boy Heston learned to hunt and fish in northern Michigan before moving to Winnetka, Illinois as a teenager.

In recalling those days during a 2000 interview with *Outdoor World* magazine, Heston said "It was the ideal boyhood. We had a community of 25 families living among the cutback timber. There was a one-room schoolhouse with 13 kids, three of whom were my cousins." In speeches Heston has reminisced of his days of hunting, running the fields with dogs, ice fishing on the big lakes, and the smell of campfires.

Heston owns a 1,200-acre spread near Roscommon that includes the 80-acre Russell Lake, named after his father. The property, which is surrounded by state land, includes a six-bedroom lodge. As of February 2005 it was for sale, listed at $1.6 million.

James Earl Jones:
January 17, 1931

Birthplace:
Arkabutla, Mississippi

Connection to northern Michigan: Moved to Dublin (near Manistee) at the age of 5 to live on his grandparents' farm. Graduated from Brethren High School in 1949. From 1953 through 1957 he acted in 28 productions at the Ramsdell Theater in Manistee under the stage name of Todd Jones and even served as the theater's stage

manager. Returns periodically to visit friends and the area.

Career: It has been said that moving from Mississippi to northern Michigan was so traumatic for Jones that he developed a stuttering problem. He overcame his stuttering to become one of Hollywood's most famous and popular actors, his voice has become legendary in commercials and as Darth Vader in the Star Wars films and Mufasa in the Lion King films.

Best known for: For those who knew the young Jones, he was a bright student (he graduated from University of Michigan) and excelled in athletics while at Brethren High. Getting his acting start in Manistee, Jones maintains a fondness for the community and the Ramsdell Theater and has lent his name and support to its preservation.

Tim Allen:
June 15, 1953

Birthplace:
Denver, Colorado

Connection to northern Michigan: Maintains a summer home near Northport.

Career: Allen moved to Bloomfield Hills at the age of 13. After high school he attended Central Michigan but transferred to Western

TODD JONES as OTHELLO

Painting of Todd (James Earl) Jones at Ramsdell Theatre in Manistee where in high school he played the role of Othello (Author photo)

Traverse City native David Wayne as the Mad Hatter on the TV show Batman.

Michigan University obtaining a communications degree. After college he worked in advertising for a small Detroit agency but left after a successful night at the Detroit Comedy Castle. Allen made an appearance at the club's amateur night and was a hit and began a stint on the comedy club circuit. After appearing in commercials and making a name in the stand up comedy world he moved to Los Angeles in 1990. Allen landed his own special on Showtime called Men are Pigs and it caught the attention of Disney's Jeffery Katzenberg, who hired Allen to develop and star in the hit series "Home Improvement." Allen also stared in the hit films "Santa Clause" and "For Richer or Poorer." He also was the voice of Buzz Lightyear in the Toy Story films.

Best known for: In 1995 Allen brought the cast and crew of Home Improvement to northern Michigan where they shot a couple of episodes on Torch Lake. He also recorded his "Toy Story II" voice over at Rich Brauer's studio in Traverse City. Allen and Brauer became friends when Brauer was commissioned by Entertainment Tonight to film a behind the scenes look of Home Improvement. Allen is often spotted eating dinner in Northport and driving around northern Michigan in his convertible Mustang.

David Wayne:
January 30, 1914 -
February 19, 1995,

Birthplace:
Traverse City, MI

Connection to northern Michigan: Born in Traverse City as Wayne McKeekan. His father was an insurance executive, his mother died when he was four. Left after high school to attend Western Michigan University. After college he worked in Cleveland where he landed his first professional acting job with a Shakespearean repertory company. During World War II he volunteered as an ambulance driver in North Africa.

Career: After World War II he landed roles on Broadway and in 1947 became the first actor ever to win a Tony Award. "Finian's Rainbow." Had roles in 27 movies starting in 1948 as Gus O'Toole in "Portrait of Jenny." His last movie role was a minor role in "The Fence" in 1994.

Best known for: His role as the Mad Hatter in the 1960's television series, Batman; Digger Barnes in the TV series, Dallas; Inspector Queen in the 1970's TV movie and series, Ellery Queen.

Lane Smith:
April 29, 1936

Birthplace:
Memphis, TN

Connection to northern Michigan: Graduated from the Leelanau School as Walter Lane Smith. Returned for Alumni Days in the late 1990's.

Career: Has appeared in over three dozen motion pictures, and dozens of television series, mini-series, and TV movies and on Broadway.

Major roles include:
The Prosecutor in "My Cousin Vinnie"; Grantland Rice in "Legend of Bagger Vance"; Perry White in the TV series Lois and Clark: The New Adventures of Superman; Coach Jack Riley in "The Mighty Ducks"; Dick Dodge in "The Distinguished Gentleman," and earned a Golden Globe nomination for his portrayal of President Richard Nixon in "The Final Days."

Recent appearances on the following television shows:
Judging Amy, The Practice, Walker; Texas Ranger, Clueless, and Murphy Brown.

He received a Drama Desk Award for his work in the Pulitzer Prize winning play "Glengary Glen Ross."

Best known for: "My Cousin Vinnie," Lois and Clark

Carter Oosterhouse:
September 16, 1976

Birthplace:
Traverse City, MI

Connection to northern Michigan: Born and raised in Traverse City, graduated in 1995 from Traverse City St. Francis High School. Attended Central Michigan University obtaining a degree in nutrition and communications.

Career: After college he moved to Los Angeles to pursue a television and film career. He landed several "behind the scenes" positions with various productions. Eventually his good looks led to modeling contracts and the role of carpenter on the popular TLC series Trading Spaces replacing Ty Pennington.

Best known for: In 2003 made People magazine's "Sexiest Man Alive" list leading to several commercial opportunities including the new leading man for the Schick Razor commercials. Locally Oosterhouse was known for his athletic prowess and was a star on the local rugby scene. As for carpenter skills, he picked those up while working summer jobs with various northern Michigan contractors.

Lane Smith, graduate of the Leelanau School

Katie Brown:
1963

Birthplace:
Petoskey, MI

Connection to northern Michigan: Born and raised in Petoskey, graduated from Petoskey High School in 1981; owns antique shop on Mackinac Island; granddaughter of the late Senator Prentiss M. Brown whose leadership in Lansing earned him the title, "Father of the Mackinac Bridge"; her brother-in-law, Daniel Musser, is president of the Grand Hotel, and her parents operate the Arnold Ferry line.

Career: Raced on the U.S. Ski Team then earned Art History degree from Cornell University in 1985. Began acting career in New York, which included a handful of national commercials. In 1990, while living in Los Angeles, a stray bullet from a drive-by shooting hit her in the knee. The resulting injuries slowed her down, but didn't prevent her from opening her own L.A. restaurant, Katie's Foods, which morphed into a boutique she called *GOAT*. Her cooking, catering and decorating caught the eye of the Hollywood elite.

In 1997, Martha Stewart was accelerating down her career path, which was taking her popular program from the Lifetime cable network to CBS. Lifetime executives turned to Mackinac Island, where they found Katie Brown at her second location of *GOAT*. She was labeled as Generation X's answer to Martha Stewart and *Next Door with Katie Brown* became the #1 show on Lifetime.

In 2000, Harper Collins published her first book, *Katie Brown Entertains*. She followed up two years later with *Katie Brown Decorates*.

Her show, *All Year Round with Katie Brown*, airs on the A&E network, and she has appeared in commercials for Kodak, Lipton, Microsoft, MasterCard, and other national brands. In 2004 she signed a four–book deal with Time Warner's Bullfinch Press, and was scheduled to begin a weekly column through the New York Time Syndicate.

Best know for: *Next Door with Katie Brown,* her first TV show made a big splash as she was touted as the "next Martha Stewart." She now has her own brand identity and large following as evidenced by her popular A&E television show, book sales, and licensing agreements.

In 2003 Katie Brown married William Corbin, an executive

with the A&E network. The couple's first child was born in July 2004, a girl named Prentice, after Katie's grandfather.

Amy Smart:
March 25, 1976

Birthplace:
Topanga Canyon

Connection to northern Michigan: She's a frequent visitor to Omena where her parents own a summer home.

Career: Amy was a relatively new arrival when she first gained notice for her supporting roles in the 1999 hit teen films "Varsity Blues" and "Outside Providence." The Los Angeles native got her start in TV-movies and made her feature debut in Stephen Kay's "The Last Time I Committed Suicide" screened at 1997's Sundance Film Festival. She was briefly seen in Paul Verhoeven's big-budget sci-fi actioner "Starship Troopers" and had an impressive turn in the vastly different, quirkily independent "How to Make the Cruelest Month." The by-the-numbers horror film "Campfire Tales" followed in 1998, along with the topically chilling but clumsily executed Internet stalker thriller "Dee Snider's StrangeLand."

Best known for: Amy donated her time to appear in a television commercial for the Leelanau Land Conservancy.

Julie Kavner:
September 7, 1951

Birthplace:
Los Angeles, CA

Connection to northern Michigan: Kavner summers on Torch Lake

Career: She gained fame for her role as Brenda Morgenstern in the popular seventies situation comedy Rhoda. In the eighties she starred in several Woody Allen films including a pivotal role in "Hannah and Her Sisters." She has several Emmy nominations including wins for her work on Rhoda and also for her most famous role as the voice of Marge Simpson on the award winning show The Simpson's. When in Michigan Kavner records her Marge Simpson voice at Rich Brauer's studio in Traverse City. From 1987 through 1990 she was a regular on the Tracey Ullman Show where she and other cast members developed the Simpson characters. In 1990 Kavner starred with Robert DeNiro and Robin Williams in the "Awakenings."

Best known for: Being Bart Simpson's mom and his aunts Patty and Selma Bouvier.

Chuck Pfarrer:
April 13, 1957

Birthplace:
Boston, Mass.

Connection to northern Michigan: Pfarrer splits his time between Florida and his Bellaire home.

Career: During the late seventies and early eighties he served as a Navy Seal. He was with the infamous anti-terrorist unit Team 6 and while with Team 4 was part of several rescue operations in Beirut. He was present during the 1983 marine barrack bombing in Beirut. After retiring from the Seals he began writing screenplays and in 1990 his first was for the film "Navy Seals" that starred Charlie Sheen. That same year his screenplay "Darkman" starring Liam Neeson hit the big screens. In 1993 he acted in the film "Hard Target" that he wrote, which starred Jean Claude Van Damme. Pfarrer's biggest hit came with "The Jackal"; released in 1997 it starred Bruce Willis, Richard Gere and Sidney Poitier. His 2000 screenplay "Red Planet," starring Val Kilmer, Terrance Stamp, Benjamin Bratt and Tom Sizemore was also a major hit. In 2004 he

published his biography *Warrior Soul*.

Best known for: Pfarrer's film "The Jackal" was filmed partly during the Chicago to Mackinac sailboat race.

Jim Cash:
January 1, 1940–2000

Birthplace:
Boyne City, MI

Connection to northern Michigan: Born in Boyne City.

Career: Cash earned his English degree at MSU in the early 1970's and in 1974 began as a writing instructor. He went on to teach film and screenwriting, and teamed up with former student, Jack Epps to write screenplays. Their first big hit was 1986's "Top Gun" starring Tom Cruise. The pair also collaborated on "Legal Eagles," "Turner and Hooch," "Sister Act" and "Dick Tracy." The successful writing team rarely saw one another, as Epps preferred Hollywood, and Cash remained in East Lansing where he continued to teach through 1991. Cash also owned the Silver Screen Café in Lansing for a short time. He was quoted in a 1985 *State News* article after "Legal Eagles," starring Robert Redford and Deborah Winger, was released: "I want to live a normal life. I have a beautiful wife, four terrific kids and a wonderful house in a great place to live. That's what I want more than anything. I need my family, my teaching, my values."

Cash passed away on March 24, 2000 at the age of 60.

Best known for: "Top Gun," one of the highest-grossing films of the 1980's.

James Gartner:
September, 24, 1950

Birthplace:
Detroit, MI

Connection to northern Michigan: Lives in Traverse City. Has used northern Michigan settings in several of the national commercials filmed by Gartner, his company with offices in New York and Los Angeles. Gartner was chosen to sit on the Motion Picture Arts advisor Board for the new Motion Picture Arts program at the Interlochen Arts Academy.

Career: Studied advertising at Ferris State University before starting a career in radio broadcasting. Was a rock jock at WLAV in Grand Rapids, WQXI-Atlanta, and a Los Angeles radio station. Tired of the radio scene, Gartner landed a copywriting/art director position at Bonneville Communications

in Salt Lake City, Utah, where he worked on television commercials. Demonstrating a talent for telling a story in the medium of film, he worked his way up to become one of the most respected and successful directors of television commercials in the world. His commercials for companies like VISA, AT&T, IBM, FedEx, Apple, and other major corporations have starred the likes of Tony Bennett, Tiger Woods, and Garth Brooks—whose scenes for a Dr. Pepper commercial were filmed at the Old Mission General Store.

Gartner chooses to work near his home in Traverse City whenever possible: he shot an AT&T commercial at a home on Sixth St. in Traverse City; made it snow in the summer for a Blockbuster spot filmed in Old Town Traverse City, and used downtown Manistee for a parade scene in a Texaco commercial. Gartner's wife, Lauri, is a Traverse City native, and the couple has raised three children there.

In 2004 he accepted an offer from Jerry Bruckheimer and Disney to direct "Glory Road," based on the true story of the 1966 NCAA basketball championship. Texas Western College coach, Don Haskins, recruited mostly black ballplayers, and in the NCAA finals started an all black team against the all white team from Kentucky. Gartner referred to the event as a "kind of Jackie Robinson story of basketball." The game is credited with opening more university doors and opportunity to blacks in the racially charged 1960's. As of February 2005, the film was in post-production and scheduled for release later that year.

Rich Brauer:
September 15, 1954

Birthplace:
Ann Arbor, MI

Connection to northern Michigan: Brauer summered on Crystal Lake as a kid and attended Northwestern Michigan College where he met his wife Marty. After graduating from the Brooks Institute of Photography in California he went back to Ann Arbor to start his film production company but in 1977 after just one year in Ann Arbor he moved his company and family to Traverse City where he has lived since.

Career: Produced several commercials for local businesses and international corporations. Produced and filmed full-length motion pictures "Sleeping Bear," "The Lost Treasure Sawtooth," and "Barn Red" in northern Michigan. The latter of the two starred Ernest Borgnine. Brauer's studio in Traverse City has been used by Tim Allen to do voice-overs for "Toy Story" and Julie Kavner uses the studio for her Marge Simpson voice-over. Brauer befriended Michigan native Jeff Daniels and served as director of photography on Daniels films "Escanaba in Da Moonlight" and "Super Sucker."

Best known for: His commitment to make and produce films in northern Michigan that promote the northern Michigan lifestyle and preservation of the land.

FOX NEWS – TRAVERSE CITY CONNECTION

Two of the Fox News correspondents – Molly Henneberg and Bill McCuddy – can share memories of Traverse City.

Bill McCuddy is the network's entertainment correspondent. McCuddy lived for a short time in Traverse City and attended Traverse City Senior High. His big break came in the 1995 when he won a national contest sponsored by the now defunct America's Talking cable TV network.

The prize: His own talk show. He's been with Fox News since 1996.

Molly Henneberg handled reporting and anchoring duties for TV 7 & 4, and won 1999 Michigan Association of Broadcasters Award for Best Series Reporting. She parlayed an overnight news-writing job at Fox into an on-camera position that has taken her to Iraq on several occasions. She's also covered the 2004 presidential campaigns and election, and reports frequently from the White House. She maintains many friendships in Traverse City, and has been a guest speaker at Bay Pointe Community Church.

ROCK AND ROLL

<u>Kenny Olson:</u>
November 12, 1967

Birthplace:
Royal Oak, MI

Connection to northern Michigan: Moved to Traverse City in 1981 and attended Traverse City High School. His rock guitar prowess turned heads at Union Street Station Open mic nights from the mid-Eighties to the early-nineties.

Career: In 1995 he met up with Kid Rock and currently heads up Rock's band Twisted Brown Trucker. Olson's lead-guitar work appears on albums that have sold over 20 million copies collectively including the

Devil Without a Cause that has sold 12 million units and remains the single best selling album of all time from any Michigan artist. He has performed on all the major late night TV shows and traveled with several celebrities to perform for the troops in the Middle East.

In late 2004, Olson formed Pack of Wolves with vocalist, Chris Van Dahl, Howlin Diablos drummer Shannon Boone and Legs Diamond bassist Adam Kurry. Their first public performance was in March of 2005 at Sreeter's in Traverse City.

Best known for: His guitar playing caught the attention of Al Hendrix, father of guitar legend Jimi Hendrix. The senior Hendrix said of Olson, "he is the only one out there who has truly captured my son's spirit." The Hendrix family asked Olson to play on the Jimi Hendrix tribute CD *Power of Soul* that feature's guitar legends Eric Clapton and Carlos Santana and singers Sting and Prince.

In the summer of 2002 Olson married in Traverse City on the beach of his parents East Bay home. His guest list featured a who's who of Detroit rock royalty. Several rockers including Kid Rock, Uncle Kracker, members of Bob Seger's band all came to Union Street Station for a

Traverse City native, Kenny Olson (photo by Don Rutt)

post-wedding reception jam. As for returning to northern Michigan, Olson hopes to return someday when the ride is all over. "This where my heart is, I always tell everyone I am from Traverse City, the people are real up there. I get home as often as possible."

The Nuge!
(photo by Eric Amundson)

Ted Nugent:
December 13, 1948

Birthplace:
Detroit, MI

Connection to northern Michigan: Nugent sightings throughout northern Michigan are quite common, and local folklore has him owning a hunting cabin in just about every community. Actually Nugent owns a large hunting preserve outside of Baldwin where he visits often when not touring. He celebrates Michigan's firearm deer opener there each November. His sister lives near Irons.

In 2002 Nugent released his cookbook *Kill It & Grill It* at Borders in Traverse City and over 5,000 waited in line to meet the rocker.

Career: The Motor City Madman ruled the concert scene in the 1970's with hits like "Catch Scratch Fever," and "Wango Tango." He performed at the Traverse City Fairgrounds (now the Civic Center) in 1970 and was detained by local police for possessing a large hunting knife. The incident didn't diminish Nugent's love for the area where he has reached legendary status with hunters. Nugent befriended famed hunter and Grayling resident Fred Bear (passed away in 1988) and celebrated their friendship by writing and recording in 1992 what has become the hunters anthem "Fred Bear."

When he started his career he said he was going to rock and roll until his "balls fell off" and then he was going to "buy the U.P." To date neither has happened though the outspoken Nugent is now considering a run for governor of Michigan. A more likely office to be obtained will be that of president of the National Rifle Association.

Nugent has recorded over 25 albums and has sold nearly 40 million copies worldwide. He got his start in 1967 with the Amboy Dukes as part of the emerging Detroit rock scene. After enjoying regional success he became a solo artist in the early seventies. From 1977 through 1979 he was the top grossing tour act on the rock music circuit. In 1989 he formed the super group Damn Yankees with Jack Blades of Night Ranger and Tommy Shaw of Styx. The group released two albums selling more than 5 million copies. Nugent returned to his solo career in the mid nineties.

Best known for: Coming out on stage on the back of his pet buffalo "Chief" while wearing a loincloth. Nugent has enjoyed a duel career as one of the godfathers of the heavy metal guitar and now the chief spokesperson for hunting rights. His PBS show Spirit of the Wild has raised over 3 million dollars for station affiliates nationwide.

Bob Seger:
May 6, 1945

Birthplace:
Dearborn, MI

Connection to northern Michigan: Owns a home on Lake Michigan near Harbor Springs. Spotted often in Traverse City playing golf at the Grand Traverse Resort and downtown visiting good friend and former road manger, Mike Parshall, who owned the now closed New Moon Records.

Career: He became the voice of the Detroit rock and roll scene in the seventies and eighties. While Detroit life served as a foundation for his songs so did northern Michigan where Seger performed several times in the early 1960's at the Tanz Haus outside of Traverse City.

Married with young children Seger has all but retired from his music career. While rumors always swirl about a new album or tour, he seems content on fatherhood, perfecting his golf game and his passion for sailing. In 2001 and 2002 he won the Port Huron to Mackinac race with his 53' sailboat *Lightning*. During the height of his music career Seger performed at Castle Farms outside of Charlevoix in the summers of 1979 and 1980.

Several of Seger's former band mates have resided in northern Michigan over the years. Keyboardist Robyn Robbins lived on Lake Huron in Cheboygan during the 1980's where he built a studio and formed a band with former members of the Baby's and the Doobie Brothers. Lead guitarist Drew Abbott moved into a home on 8th Street in Traverse City and played around Traverse City in the Blue Highway Band. Drummer Charlie Martin also resided in Traverse City.

Best known for: The song "Old Time Rock and Roll" in which Hollywood hunk Tom Cruise danced in "briefs" while lip-syncing the song in the movie "Risky Business." Seger is also credited with helping slumping auto sales by lending his song "Like a Rock" to Chevrolet for the company's truck commercials. The success of his commercial opened the doors for other rockers of his generation like Led Zeppelin and the Who to musically endorse Detroit based automakers. In 2004 Seger joined the Rock and Roll Hall of Fame.

Mark Farner:
September 29, 1948

Birthplace:
Flint, MI

Connection to northern Michigan: Moved to Onaway during the 1970's and currently lives outside of Petoskey.

Career: In 1969 he founded Grand Funk Railroad, rock music's first power trio with Flint friends Mel Schacher and Don Brewer. His vocals and lead guitar work on such songs as "We're an American Band," "Closer to Home/I'm Your Captain," and Some Kind of Wonderful," led to 12 platinum albums for the band.

Burned out, the group broke up in 1977 with Farner seeking solitude in Onaway. Eventually Farner would begin a solo career and move to Petoskey where he resides today. From 1983 to 1994 he would record four Christian albums and would climb to number two on the Contemporary Christian charts with "Isn't It Amazing." In 1996 he joined Ringo Starr's All Starr Band and performed at the Grand Traverse Resort.

He reunited with the original members of Grand Funk in 1997 and they toured together for three years. In 2000 Farner returned to solo career and currently tours with his band Nr'g" performing classics from his Grand Funk days along with a mix of originals.

Best known for: In 1971 Grand Funk sold out Shea Stadium in New York faster than any band including the Beatles.

Mel Schacher:
April 8, 1951

Birthplace:
Owosso, MI

Connection to northern Michigan: Schacher lives near Traverse City.

Career: Along with Mark Farner and Don Brewer he founded Grand Funk Railroad in 1968. Prior to Grand Funk, Schacher at the age of 16 became a member of Question Mark and the Mysterians when the bands original bass player was drafted for service in Vietnam. The group had a number one hit "96 Tears." His "lead-bass" style helped to create the signature power sound that Grand Funk became known for. He moved to Traverse City in the 1980's where he built a home studio for fellow musicians and friends. He and Don Brewer continue to tour as Grand Funk Railroad.

Best known for: Credited with popularizing the heavy bass sound that inspired several heavy metal bands.

Chris Van Dahl:
October 22, 1966

Birthplace:
Detroit, MI

Connection to northern Michigan: Family and friends attracted Van Dahl to northern Michigan from Los Angeles. He moved to Traverse City in 2002 and spends his nights in his home recording studio.

Career: Rock vocalist Chris Van Dahl flirted with various bands during the dying Detroit music scene of the 1980's. He ventured west and formed the popular Los Angeles-based metal band Cherry Street. Van Dahl replaced Axl Rose as lead singer for LA Guns, which sold over 6 million albums worldwide during the 1990's.

Looking to get away from the destructive LA music scene, Van Dahl took a hiatus from the music business. In late 2004 he formed a new band Pack of Wolves with Kid Rock Guitarist Kenny Olson, Howlin Diablos drummer Shannon Boone and Legs Diamond bassist Adam Kurry. The foursome has been work-

ing with legendary sound engineer Kenneth "Pooch" Van Druten of Motley Crue, KISS and Kid Rock fame. They performed publicly for the first time in March of 2005 at Streeter's in Traverse City.

Pack of Wolves lead vocalist, Chris Van Dahl (photo by Don Rutt)

Best known for: His first northern Michigan performance at Streeters in 2004 where he joined band members of the Rolling Stones, the Faces, Bob Seger and the MC5 for a tribute to rock and roll photographer Tom Wright.

Brian Schram:
September? 1980

Birthplace:
Mancelona, MI

Connection to northern Michigan: While Schram currently resides in the Detroit area, he returns to northern Michigan often to perform with his Brian Schram Band.

Career: Schram caught the attention of area rock music enthusiasts while in the Amanda Waggener Band performing at clubs throughout northern Michigan. Kid Rock and Uncle Kracker spotted his "flashy" high-powered guitar attack at guitarist Kenny

Brian Schram photographed by legendary rock and roll photographer Tom Wright

Olson's wedding in Traverse City, and Schram was immediately offered a contract to join Uncle Kracker's band. He toured with Uncle Kracker performing at major concert venues and on the Tonight Show. Schram's guitar wizardry also attracted the attention of Mario Ciccone (Madonna's brother) who became Schram's manager. In 2003 Schram left Kracker and under Ciccone's direction formed his own band. By late 2004 Schram and his band were entertaining offers from various labels for a major record deal.

Best known for: He finished in the top 10 at the national guitar championships, with nearly 10,000 contestants.

Brian Schram photographed by legendary rock and roll photographer, Tom Wright (photo by Tom Wright)

ROCK AND ROLL PHOTOGRAPHER

Tom Wright:
March 17, 1944

Birthplace:
Birmingham, Alabama

Connection to northern Michigan: He moved to the Torch Lake area in 1999 to organize his collection of more than 200,000 photographs of rock stars Pete Townshend, Joe Walsh, the Rolling Stones, Rod Stewart, Bob Seger, Ted Nugent and numerous others. In 2004 the International Debut of Wright's collection of rock and roll photographs appeared at the Dennos Museum Center in Traverse City and attracted rock stars and media from around the world.

Career: In 1961 Wright attended the famed Ealing Art School in London where he befriended Pete Townshend. The two became fast friends and when Townshend formed the Who, he called on Wright to be the band's road manager and official photographer.

During the 1960's Wright toured with the Who, Rod Stewart and the Faces, Joe Walsh and the James Gang and numerous other bands, capturing them with his Nikon.

He also recorded 2,000 hours of conversations between the

legends backstage, in hotel rooms and on the tour buses. During the late 1960's Wright managed the legendary Grande Ballroom in Detroit during the clubs heyday that included bands such as Led Zeppelin, Pink Floyd, the Who and the MC5 performing on a regular basis.

Wright's photos have appeared on numerous album covers, in various magazines and several books. A Wright original is a prized possession and many hang in homes of the world's elite rock stars. In the 1990's Wright donated his collection to the Center for American History at the University of Texas. He is currently cataloguing his collection to be completed by 2007. He is writing his memoir, which is scheduled for release in 2006.

Best known for: His collection of albums of blues, jazz and R&B legends was renowned in music circles in London in 1961. He put several singles on the jukebox at the coffee shop across the street from the college. It would become a favorite hangout for future stars Paul McCartney, Mick Jagger, Keith Richards and Pete Townshend all who were said to have been inspired by the collection.

JAZZ

<u>Bob James:</u>
December 25, 1939

Birthplace:
Marshall, Missouri

Connection to northern Michigan: Along with his wife Judy, the James' have resided near Traverse City full time since 2000, and have been part-time residents since the mid-eighties when their daughter Hillary began attending the Interlochen Arts Academy. James has given benefit concerts and allowed his artwork to be auctioned to raise funds for the restoration of the Traverse City Opera House.

Career: After graduating from U of M he formed a jazz trio, which won just about every category at a jazz competition at the University of Notre Dame in 1962. Legendary producer Quincy Jones was in the audience, and eventually hired James to play on several albums. As a result, he became a top session musician and performed and recorded with the likes of Sarah Vaughan, Grover Washington Jr., Paul Simon, Aretha Franklin, and Neil Diamond.

In the 1970's his solo career as a jazz artist and composer took off. He composed and performed the award-winning theme song for the hit TV show "Taxi." In 1990 he formed the jazz super group Fourplay featuring Lee Ritenour, Harvey Mason and Nathan East (Ritenour was later replaced by Larry Carlton). The group has had several number one albums on the Billboard Jazz Charts. James maintains a successful solo career touring and recording with his Bob James Trio.

He has reached mythical proportions in the hip-hop and rap communities. His compositions from the 1970's and 1980's are among the most sampled in the rapindustry. "Bob James is from the world above the radar and he is definitely in the top five most important musical influences for those who pioneered rap and hip-hop," said rapper Jay-Z. "Shit, Bob James is the man and those of us from the streets know that. There ain't a hip-hop kid around who don't know Bob James."

Best known for: Composing and performing the theme song to the 1980's hit sitcom, "Taxi."

<u>Jeff Haas:</u>
May 9, 1949

Birthplace: Detroit, MI

Connection to northern Michigan: Well known for his work as a jazz pianist and promoter of jazz shows in northern Michigan.

Career: Son of the late Karl Haas who hosted "Adventures in Good Music," that aired on several NPR stations around the country. Jeff Haas is credited with bringing jazz to the forefront of the northern Michigan music scene in the 1980's. He spent his early teen years studying piano, theory and composition at the famed Hochschule fur Musik in Berlin and moved to Traverse City in 1972, taking a position as a social worker. Jeff's music came to the attention of legendary jazz pianist Dave Brubeck who said, "In combining these great musical traditions, [Haas] has created a soulful music that transcends ethnic barriers. I congratulate him and his colleagues for their fine playing." In 1998, Jeff received a commission to write an original jazz suite commemorating the sesquicentennial celebration of metro Detroit's Jewish community. The critically acclaimed composition, "The Bridge Lives," portrays a significant and timely social message about building bridges between cultures, generations and identities.

Best known for: Creating a northern Michigan jazz scene in the 1980's and starting the

"Jazz at the Museum," concert series at the Dennos Museum. He has produced over 350 jazz concerts and festivals in the Traverse area and also created the Northern Michigan Jazz Society to promote local jazz musicians.

Harry Goldson:
February 27, 1929

Birthplace:
Chicago, IL

Connection to northern Michigan: Harry Goldson and his wife Piper moved to Suttons Bay in 1990.

Career: Goldson grew up in the same neighborhood as Benny Goodman and attended the famed Austin High School that produced several jazz greats including Goodman and Jimmy McPartland. He began his musical career as a teenager primarily playing clarinet with some of Chicago's early jazz legends. His reputation as one of the country's top reedmen led to touring opportunities with such jazz greats as Bill Russo, Claude Thornhill and Chuck Foster. A call to serve his country led a brief stint in the army. After returning home from the Korean War, Goldson put his clarinet in the closet and pursued a very successful banking career. He retired to Suttons Bay in 1990, and at the encouragement of his wife began playing again. He has recorded 8 CDs since resuming his career and his quartet remains in high demand and even performed at the Academy Awards pre-party performance in 1999.

Best known for: What was suppose to be just a few gigs for fun in the early nineties has led to a second career for Goldson. The popularity of his quartet has helped to reintroduce the big band jazz sound in northern Michigan. He performs annually each July at the Suttons Bay Jazz Festival, a festival started by he and his wife that has attracted such legendary jazz masters as Ramsey Lewis and Marian McPartland.

Madonna:
August 16, 1958

Birthplace:
Bay City, MI

Connection to northern Michigan: Madonna's father Silvio "Tony" Ciccone owns Ciccone Vineyards and Winery near Suttons Bay. Despite rumors Madonna has no financial interest in the winery but visits often.

Career: Madonna got her start at the University of Michigan dance program, but left before graduating. She moved to New York to study dance and performed with various rock bands at night.

In 1983 the world was introduced to Madonna the "Pop Diva" and with over 2 billion dollars in worldwide album revenues in 20 years, she has become the reigning queen of the pop music industry. She has tried her hand in acting with her most notable role as the lead in the musical film "Evita." She has expanded her career to include author and published the controversial book *Sex* in 1990. Now she has become a children's author and has published five books including her 2003 debut *The English Roses*.

Sightings of the pop goddess in northern Michigan are seldom as she maintains homes in London, LA and Miami. Contrary to popular myth the superstar doesn't own property at Bay Harbor or elsewhere in northern Michigan. When not touring she occasionally seeks solitude in Sutton's Bay with her husband and filmmaker Guy Ritchie and children Lourdes and Rocco. Her favorite things to do when visiting the area includes biking and running the hilly roads of the Leelanau Peninsula and Pilate's Yoga at a local Traverse City studio. She also dines regularly with friend the author/filmmaker Michael Moore who lives on Torch Lake. She has been spotted shopping for produce at Hansen's in Sutton's Bay and at the Candle Factory in Traverse City.

Best known for: Madonna's stage shows are considered to be among the best ever in the history of pop music. The superstar made the headlines for her trend setting clothes and her men. She was married to Sean Penn and dated Vanilla Ice, Dennis Rodman, and was rumored to have dated Warren Beatty.

Edgar Struble:
September 11, 1951

Birthplace: Monroe, MI

Connection to northern Michigan: Struble grew up in the Ludington/Scottville area and maintains a summer residence there.

Career: Struble attended Michigan State University pursuing a degree in music education. In 1976 while playing piano at a Nashville hotel, country superstar Kenny Rogers discovered him. Rogers invited Struble to join his band and from 1976 through 1991 he served as Rogers musical director, composer, band conductor, instrumentalist and backing vocalist. Kenny Rogers said of Struble "I've never had to worry about the quality of my music with him." In 1991

Struble left Rogers to be at home with his young family. He began serving as musical director for several TV music specials for Rogers and other country stars. In 1996 he became music director of the Nashville Network's flagship program "Prime Time Country." He moved to Los Angeles in 1999 and began work producing musical scores for Dick Clark and television programs on the History Channel, TLC and A&E in addition to writing theme music for made for television movies on Fox.

Best known for: Struble returns to northern Michigan each summer where he maintains a home on Lake Michigan in Ludington and performs a series of summer concerts at area venues. Every other December he performs a holiday concert at the Lakeshore Community College in Scottville.

Chuck Jacobs:

Birthplace:
Bellaire, MI

Connection to northern Michigan: He grew up on 10th Street in Traverse City. Still maintains a family getaway on Torch Lake near Bellaire.

Career: Since 1977 he has been the bass player with country music superstar Kenny Rogers. He has traveled the world with Rogers and his bass guitar work has appeared on numerous platinum and award winning albums. In addition to Rogers, he has performed or recorded with Dolly Parton, Faith Hill, Garth Brooks and several other country legends. As a child he played in the family jazz band and recently reunited with his brothers Dan and Rod along with Kenny Rogers' lead guitarist Randy Dorman to form the Jacobs Brothers. His book *The Bottom Line,* is one of the all time best selling instruction books on how to play the bass.

When not touring or recording he serves as president of Simplicity Records specializing in easy listening music. If all that is not enough, his Jacobs Web Design company produces the websites for Ringo Starr and Hall of Fame Quarterback Phil Simms. He returns home each summer for a jazz jam with his brothers and members of Kenny Rogers' and Bob Seger's bands, to raise money for music scholarships in his mother's name at the Interlochen Center for the Arts.

Best known for: While not a household name, Jacobs is best known in music circles for his proficient bass playing in several genres.

Tobin Sprout:
April 28, 1955

Birthplace:
Dayton, OH

Connection to northern Michigan: Moved to Leland in 1997 after leaving the band Guided by Voices.

Career: Tobin Sprout helped to launch the American indie-rock scene in the1990's with his band Guided by Voices. The Dayton based lo-fi rockers were founded in 1983 but after touring with the band for 14 years, Sprout decided to call it quits and moved to Leland to raise his young children and pursue his other passion as a painter. He opened The Petrified Fish Gallery in Leland but has since closed the in-town gallery and plans to open a gallery above his garage in the near future. He has released a couple of albums Lost Planets and Phantom Voices in 2003 and Live at the Horseshoe Tavern in 2004 and has begun touring as a solo performer. In 2004 he rejoined his former band mates for what was the Guided by Voices final concerts.

Best known for: Bringing a melodic sound to Guided by Voices.

Mark Staycer:
January 16, 1955

Birthplace:
Mt. Clemmons, MI

Connection to northern Michigan: Moved to Traverse City in 1986 and was a popular afternoon drive DJ on the country station WTCM.

Career: A Beatles fan and in particular of Lennon, Staycer's impersonations of the Beatle become a staple of his radio show while on WTCM. Resembling Lennon, he launched a career as a Lennon impersonator in 2002, testing out his show locally. In a period of time he has risen to one of the top Lennon impersonators in the world. In 2004 he performed at the International Beatles Week in Liverpool where 300,000 fans gathered. Staycer's performance captured the "imagination" of the crowd with several hundred mobbing him after his show and chasing him down the streets of

Mark Staycer, best known for resemblance to John Lennon

Liverpool. Staycer was driven to the airport with a coat over his head. He was invited to return in 2005 as one of the events headlining acts.

Best known for: His dead on resemblance to John Lennon, combined with musical abilities keeps him in demand around the States and in Europe.

Song of the Lakes:
Summer of 1983

Birthplace:
Benzie County, MI

Connection to northern Michigan: Their music is considered to be the heart and soul of the northern Michigan lifestyle.

Career: As local favorites they have become the areas ambassadors to life on the Great Lakes. The Benzie County quartet formed in 1983 with a Maritime/Nordic/Celtic sound. They are perennial winners of "Best Folk Artist" in the *Northern Express* and they have expanded their fan base to as far away as Switzerland where they have become a favorite at the legendary Montreux Jazz Festival. In 2004 the group released their 5th album "Poets Say," and continue their popular Michigan Cultural Tour at northern Michigan State Parks.

Best known for: Playing St. Patrick's Day at Dill's and the Park Place and performing during the summer months on the tall ships *Malabar* and *Manitou* on West Grand Traverse Bay. Their song "Benzie Rover," continues to be the anthem for rural residents of the area.

Claudia Schmidt:
June 5, 1953

Birthplace:
Highland Park, MI

Connection to northern Michigan: Lived on Beaver Island for several years where she owned the Old Rectory Pub. Currently lives in Traverse City.

Career: Her 30-year performance and recording career has taken her around the States and Europe filling 4,000 seat auditoriums and performing at some of the most prestigious folk festivals in the world. She was also a regular on Garrison Keillor's popular radio program "A Prairie Home Companion." She has recently branched out into the jazz and spoken word genres and may be found performing often in the area including Poppycock's in Traverse City.

Best known for: Her appearances on "A Prairie Home Companion," gave Schmidt a national audience in folk music circles. She describes herself as a "creative noise-maker," and prefers not to be classified by typical industry titles as she explores jazz, classical and blues styles as well.

A NIGHT AT THE OPERA

Jayne Sleder:

Birthplace:
Traverse City, MI

Connection to northern Michigan: Grew up the daughter of former mayor, owner of Grand Traverse Auto and community leader, Julius Sleder. Maintains a home in Traverse City, and an apartment in New York City. Helps run the family auto dealership with her husband and gives voice lessons.

Career: Her musical training began at an early age when she was taught the "Michigan State Fight Song," by her father. She furthered her vocal skills while attending Michigan State University and eventually obtained her doctorate degree at the Cincinnati's College-Conservatory of Music. Trained under the famed Italian baritone Tito Gobbi, Sleder lived and worked the famous opera stages of Europe. She sung with the legendary Pavarotti during a recital. She remains in high demand and the mezzo-soprano star splits her time between her Manhattan apartment and Traverse City home. Her decision to live part time in Traverse City after living in some of the worlds most romantic places, "there is no place like home and at the end of the day, no place as beautiful as here."

Nicole Philobsian:

Birthplace:

Connection to northern Michigan: Voice instructor at the famed Interlochen Center for the Arts. Among her students: 1992 graduate, Jewel Kilcher.

Career: A voice instructor with the world-renowned Interlochen Arts Academy, she has carved out a vocal career at the world's finest opera houses. Her work in New York City led the *New York Times* to write, "Philibosian is a find, blessed with a beautiful full lyric soprano, good looks and sex appeal."

A graduate of the Eastman School of Music, with study at Juilliard Opera Center, the Colorado native first came to national prominence when she won the International Khachaturian Competition, and the Joy of Singing Award. The latter led to her New York recital debut in Lincoln Center's Alice Tully Hall. Her operatic repertoire is widely varied, including such roles as: Rusalka, Pamina, Donna Anna, the Countess and Fiordiligi; Mimi, Liu, Antonia, Rosalinda, Juliette, the title roles of La Calisto, Madama Butterfly, Suor Angelica, and Aida; Salome, the Marschallin in Der Rosenkavalier, and most recently, Renata in Prokofiev's Fiery Angel, which she learned on short notice for the San Francisco Opera.

Her debut at the New York City Opera was as the Countess in *Le Nozze di Figaro* as it was for Hawaii Opera Theatre, and she has sung Pamina, Juliette, Rusalka and Musetta for Seattle Opera. Her European debut was as Musetta at l'Opera de Nice, France, and she sang her first performances in the title role of Richard Strauss' Salome in concert with the Bournemouth Symphony Orchestra in England led by Andrew Litton. Miss Philibosian and Maestro Litton repeated the final scene from Salome the following season with the Dallas Symphony Orchestra on a program that also included 'Isolde's Liebestod.' She has sung Liu in Seoul, Korea.

Heartbreak Hotel

The King called him Sir. Long-time Prudenville resident, Thomas Durden, wrote "Heartbreak Hotel," Elvis Presley's first #1 record and million seller.

Durden, who passed away in 1999, moved to the Houghton Lake area about three years after penning the song with a schoolteacher friend in Florida. The inspiration for the song came from a suicide. Durden remembered reading about a man who took his own life, and when found was clutching a note that read, I walk a lonely street."

At the time Durden was playing in a country band in Florida. Later in his career he played with Johnny Cash and Tex Ritter. He never played with the King, but received Christmas cards from him and met him once – Elvis addressed him as "sir."

In the early 80's Durden wrote the song Come to "Tip-Up Town," with sales proceeds benefiting the local high school band.

WRITERS

Hemingway as a boy fishing at Horton Creek, near Horton's Bay, Charlevoix County (courtesy of John F. Kennedy Library)

Windemere, the Hemingway family cottage on Walloon Lake (courtesy of John F. Kennedy Library)

Ernest Hemingway in Northern Michigan

Like Key West and Cuba, Paris and Spain, northern Michigan is Hemingway country. The most celebrated American author of the 20th century developed his passion for hunting and fishing during summers spent at the family cottage on Walloon Lake. As a teen, Hemingway discovered romance during summers up north, and when the time came for marriage, he chose Horton Bay as his wedding site. Although none of Hemingway's published works were written in northern Michigan, his experiences there were the basis for some of his finest early work.

Hemingway was born in Oak Park, Illinois on July 21, 1899, one year after his family first vacationed on Walloon Lake. They stayed at the Echo Beach Hotel and liked it enough to buy an acre of lakefront property for $200. Dr. Clarence Hemingway had a cottage built the following year naming it Windemere after a lake in England.

Ernie's first visit to Walloon Lake came a few weeks before his first birthday. He returned every summer for the next 18 years. He fished Horton Bay and Horton Creek, boated on Walloon Lake, camped and hunted in the woods, and roamed the North Country on foot and rail looking for adventure. His family bought a 40-acre farm across the lake from the cottage, which they named Longfield, and grew vegetables and fruit trees.

In her memoir, Hemingway's younger sister, Madelaine, "Sunny," writes, "Together, we really made what we thought was a 'fist full of money' peddling the extra fresh vegetables that grew on our farm across the lake from the cottage. We used our launch, the *Carol*, to take the vegetables around and had regular customers that had good enough docks for landing our launch. People looked forward to our now-and-then trips. We sold beets, carrots, lettuce, and even ice to very special people…When Ernest became famous, some people boasted that he had been their "iceman.""

In becoming a professional writer, Hemingway relied on his true-life experiences to generate plot ideas, settings and characters. Much of his early fiction is set in and around Petoskey, Walloon Lake and Horton Bay, and he used himself as the model for the Nick Adams character. In his first published book, *Three Stories and Ten Poems* (1923), Horton Bay is the setting in the story "Up in Michigan," which Hemingway wrote in Paris. Following is a timeline of events in Hemingway's life as it relates to northern Michigan.

1899:
Born at Oak Park, Illinois

Parents:
Dr. Clarence and Grace Hemingway

1900:
First trip to Walloon Lake. Returned every summer through 1918.

1917:
Passed on college to work at Kansas City *Star* newspaper.

1918:
Volunteered as American Red Cross ambulance driver in Italy during World War I. In April he came to northern Michigan for a final fishing trip before heading overseas.

1919:
Following war injury, Hemingway returned to Walloon Lake to spend the summer with parents. He had leg injuries after getting hit by mortar and machine gun fire.

Remained up north in the fall, living at Dilworth's in Horton Bay, and later moved to Potter's Rooming House on State Street in Petoskey. During this winter Hemingway worked on his writing and spent many hours at the Petoskey Library.

1920:
Moved to Toronto for a reporting job with the Toronto *Star Weekly*.

Spent summer with family at Walloon Lake, then moved to Chicago where he met Hadley Richardson.

Returned to Horton Bay where he married Hadley Richardson on September 18, 1921. The couple honeymooned at Windemere then returned to Chicago where they lived for a short time before moving to Toronto, and then Paris.

1923:
First book published, *Three Stories and Ten Poems*, includes "Up in Michigan," set in Horton Bay.

Hemingways at Windemere (from top: Ernest's mother, Grace, Ernest, and sisters Marce, Sunny, Ursula and Carol (courtesy of John F. Kennedy Library)

The house on State St. in Petoskey where Hemingway stayed after returning from World War I (courtesy of Laura Jolly)

Charlevoix restaurant: "Hemingway never ate here." Truth in advertising? (Author photo)

Old Petoskey Library which Hemingway frequented in the winter of 1919-20 (courtesy of Laura Jolly)

1924:
First Nick Adams story published. *Indian Camp* was included in the first edition of *in our time*, published in Paris. (*In Our Time* was later published in the States with upper case letters in the title.)

1925:
Hemingway completes his first novel, *Torrents of Spring* in ten days. The book parodied the writing style of Sherwood Anderson, who at one time acted as a mentor to Hemingway. Hemingway and Anderson shared the same publisher, but Hemingway wanted out of his contract so he could sign with Scribners, so his first novel parodied the firm's top writer.

Torrents of Spring

Hemingway's first published novel was a parody of Sherwood Anderson's *"Dark Laughter."* Part One is entitled, "Red and Black Laughter," and the very first sentence mentions the pump factory in Petoskey, probably referring to the old Blackmer Rotary Pump Factory. Later in the first paragraph, reference is made to the G.R. & I. railroad station, which is where the Hemingways arrived by train from Harbor Springs each summer. The station now serves as the Little Traverse Historical Museum and houses Hemingway artifacts.

Ten Northern Michigan References in *"Torrents of Spring"*:

1. In the second paragraph of the first chapter we discover the character Scripp's O'Neil has two wives; "One lived in Mancelona and the other lived in Petoskey."

2. Chapter two starts off with Scripp's staring into the windows of Mancelona High School.

3. In chapter three, one of Scripp's wives leaves him, so he leaves Mancelona. "What had a town like that to give him?" He's walking up the "Boyne Falls grade" of the G.R. & I. railroad tracks hoping to hop a train to Petoskey.

4. Scripp's arrives at the train station in Petoskey where he notices a pile of deer on the station platform "shipped down by hunters from the Upper Peninsula of Michigan." Scripp's addresses a telegrapher behind a window in the station. Today a mannequin sits behind the same window, now an exhibit in the Little Traverse History Museum.

5. Petoskey's "Main Street" is described in chapter six as "a handsome, broad street, lined on either side by brick and pressed-stone buildings.

6. Scripp's scores a job in the

pump factory working with Yogi Johnson. When asked by Scripp's if he was in the war, Yogi replies, "Yes. I was the first man to go from Cadillac."

7. Scripp's Petoskey wife, the waitress Diana, is competing for his attention with a younger, well-read waitress. Diana is described at the end of chapter nine, as "walking through the frozen streets of the silent Northern town to the Public Library," to read the *Literary Digest* "Book Review."

8. Yogi is walking home from the pump factory in chapter eleven, thinking about the librarian at the Petoskey Public Library as he "walked on up the hill and turned to the left onto the Charlevoix road. He passed the last houses of the outskirts of Petoskey and came out onto the open country road. On his right was a field that stretched to Little Traverse Bay....Across the bay the pine hills behind Harbor Springs. Beyond, where you could not see it, Cross Village, where the Indians lived. Even further beyond, the Straits of Mackinac with St. Ignace...."

9. Chapter twelve Yogi meets up with two Indians on the outskirts of town. "Through the night down the frozen road the three walked into Petoskey...they came down

the hill past the feed store, crossed the bridge over the Bear River...and climbed the hill that led past Dr. Rumsey's house and the Home Tea-Room up to the pool room."

10. Hemingway ends chapter twelve with a "P.S. – From the Author to the Reader." His remarks are rather sarcastic as he points out the story is not autobiographical. "Please, reader, just get that idea out of your head. We have lived in Petoskey, Mich., it is true, and we lived it then. But they are other people, not the author. The author only comes into the story in these little notes. It is true that before starting this story we spend twelve years studying the various Indian dialects of the North, and there is still preserved in the museum at Cross Village our translation of the New Testament into Ojibway...."

Hemingway reportedly returned to the Petoskey area in the 1950's. Author Constance Cappel Montgomery, in her book, *Hemingway in Michigan*, writes about an old friend who had dinner with Hemingway, and asked if he'd ever come back to live in northern Michigan. Hemingway's reply: "No. It's too civilized now."

The family cottage, Windemere, was designated a

National Historic Landmark in 1968. Ernie Mainland, Hemingway's nephew, who still lives in the area, owns and maintains the cottage. After restoring the original outhouse, he hung a sign on it reading, "Ernest Hemingway Sat Here."

For further reading on Ernest Hemingway in Michigan

Hemingway in Michigan, by Constance Cappel Montgomery, copyright 1966 by Fleet Publishing Corporation, New York

Along with Youth: The Hemingway Early Years, by Peter Griffin, copyright 1985 by Oxford University Press

Ernie: Hemingway's Sister "Sunny" Remembers, copyright 1975 by Madelaine Hemingway Miller, Crown Publishers, Inc., New York

Hemingway: Up in Michigan Perspectives, edited by Frederic J. Svoboda and Joseph J. Waldmeir, copyright 1995 by Michigan State University Press

A good source for Hemingway history and books is through John Hartwell at the Red Fox Inn, next door to the Horton Bay General Store.

"The best sky was in Italy and Spain and Northern Michigan in the fall..."

–from Green Hills of Africa, and painted on a wall at the Red Fox Inn, Horton Bay.

Jim Harrison:
December 11, 1937

Birthplace: Grayling, MI

Connection to northern Michigan: While born in Grayling, Harrison grew up in Reed City before attending Michigan State University. After graduating, Harrison returned to northern Michigan and lived for several years on a 160-acre farm on the Leelanau Peninsula. He now divides his time between Arizona and Montana and returns to northern Michigan often to visit friends.

Career: Harrison is known worldwide for his writing, a career that has spanned 40 years with success in fiction, non-fiction, poetry, and screenwriting. His works have appeared in several mainstream publications including regularly in *Sports Illustrated* and *Esquire* and on occasion in *Rolling Stone* and *The New Yorker*. His non-fiction works on outdoor/hunting life and food and wine gained him fame in those circles. Growing up and living in northern Michigan served as inspiration for many of his writings. His 1979 book of novellas, *Legends of the Fall,* led to two motion pictures: the 1990 film "Revenge" starring Kevin Costner and Anthony Quinn and "Legends of the Fall" that starred Brad Pitt, Anthony Hopkins and Aidan Quinn and grossed over 160 million dollars worldwide. Actor Jack Nicholson befriended Harrison and bought early screenplay rights to Harrison's works during the early 1970's, keeping the burgeoning author financially afloat. His books have been translated in 22 languages, preserving his international literary legacy.

Other films based on Harrison works:
"Wolf" (1994) starring Jack Nicholson and Michelle Pfieffer based on the novella of the same title; "Carried Away" (1996) starring Dennis Hopper and Amy Irving based on the book *Farmer*; and "Dalva" (1996) starring Farrah Fawcett based on the book of the same title. Harrison teamed with Thomas McGuane in 1989 for the comedy "Cold Feet," starring Kieth Carraidne, Sally Kirkland and Tom Waits.

Best Known For: Some of his most popular novels and novellas include: *Wolf* (1971), *A Good Day to Die* (1973), *Farmer* (1976), *Legends of the Fall* (1979), *Warlock* (1981), *Sundog* (1984), *Dalva* (1988), *The Woman Lit by Fireflies* (1990), *Julip* (1994), *The Road Home* (1999) and *True North* (2004).

James B. Hendryx:
(1880 – 1963)

Birth place:
Sauk Centre, Minnesota

Connection to northern Michigan: Lived on 300-acre waterfront estate on Lee Point near Suttons Bay with his wife, two daughters and a son. Wrote many of his popular adventure books for boys from a cabin on the property. His one surviving daughter, Hermione (Mittie), still lives on the property. In nearby Bingham Township there is a Hendryx Park on land donated by his wife.

Career: Hendryx wrote over 70 novels, most set in the rugged Northwest – Montana, Alaska, and Canada. His adventuresome tales of justice triumphing in the great unsettled wilderness made him a favorite author of boys growing up between the 1920's and 60's. Many a young boys bookshelf would include Hendryx books next to *Call of the Wild* or *White Fang* by Jack London. Hendryx grew up the son of a newspaper publisher in central Minnesota, where he enjoyed hunting, fishing, and playing poker with boyhood pals, including Sinclair Lewis. Hendryx abandoned college to pursue adventure out west. He worked as a cowpuncher, woodchopper and panned for gold in Alaska, before returning east to work for his father at a Cincinnati newspaper. His first fiction was published during his newspaper years, after which Hendryx said he "stopped punching the time clock forever."

His first book, *The Promise,* was published in 1915. He followed up with four more books before 1920, and around that time established a friendship with Harold Titus, an adventure writer from Traverse City. Titus invited Hendryx to join him on a fishing trip on Grand Traverse Bay, and Hendryx liked the area so much he bought 300 acres on West Bay. There he built a home and writing cabin where he produced dozens of books starring the heroes Corporal Downey of the Northwest Mounted Police and Black John, who always beat the bad guys in the name of justice.

In later years he created the character of Connie Morgan an average American boy who gains knowledge and values from living outdoors and reading his Boy Scout manual. The only two Hendryx books set in northern Michigan are from the Connie Morgan series: *Connie Morgan in the Lumber Camps* (1919) and *Connie Morgan and the Forest Rangers* (1925). Five of Hendryx' books were made into movies: "The Promisev" "The Mints of Hell", "Prarie Tales," "Snowdrift" and "The Texan," which starred Tom Mix.

Best known for: *The Black John Smith of Halfaday Creek* series set during the Yukon Gold Rush, that Hendryx experienced first hand. In 1956 he appeared on the television show, "This Is Your Life." When the host Ralph Edwards asked Hendryx the difference between his writing and Sinclair Lewis', Hendryx replied, "Sinclair gets a buck a word, and I get a penny a word."

For more information on James B. Hendryx, visit **www.halfadaycreek.com.**

The Leelanau Historical Society in Leland houses the James B. Hendryx Collection, which includes books, letters, magazines, original manuscripts and other materials related to Hendryx.

Harold Titus:
(1888-1967)

Birthplace:
Traverse City, MI

Connection to northern Michigan: Nationally known outdoors and conservation writer who worked from his home in Traverse City. Books set in northern Michigan include *Timber, Smoke Chaser, Black Feather,* and *The Beloved Pawn,* which is loosely based on King Strang of Beaver Island.

Credited with being a co-founder of the National Cherry Festival with newspaper editor and Chamber of Commerce President, Jay P. Smith.

Career: His first writing job was for the *Detroit News,* covering campus events and sports while he attended the University of Michigan. Later he became a full time crime reporter for the *News.*

Titus returned to Traverse City where he married Beth Benedict, and started cherry farming. He continued to write, submitting articles to national magazines such as *Ladies Home Journal, Red Book* and *Colliers.* After serving in the Army during World War I, Titus returned home and wrote his first novel, *I Conquered,* about a young man's adventures in the Wild West. He followed that with another western, *Bruce of Circle A,* and then *The Last Straw,* which was made into a movie.

Although Titus had become a national success by the age of 24, he was bothered by what he saw around his hometown. The same woods where he learned to hunt, fish and camp as a boy were disappearing. It was 1922, and the logging industry left nothing in its wake except stumps and a damaged Boardman River.

Titus' response was an early call for conservation. After witnessing the destruction of the wildlife habitat by an unregulated logging industry, he became one of the pioneers in the movement to manage our natural resources.

The setting for his book *Timber* is the woods of northern Michigan around the fictitious town of Blueberry. As loggers ravage the woods around her, a young woman is developing a small forest of pine on land inherited from her father. This was unheard of at the time, as was the outcome of the book, which had the conservationists winning out over the logging companies.

The book was influential in bringing about management and restoration of Michigan's forests. Titus helped develop the Forest Service, and in 1927, was appointed by Governor Fred Green to the Conservation Commission.

Titus wrote ten books, hundreds of magazine articles and was Conservation Editor for *Field and Stream* magazine. In the 1920's four of his stories were produced as motion pictures, and in 1941 Eddie Albert starred in "The Great Mr. Nobody," based on Titus' *The Stuff of Heroes*.

Best known for: *Timber,* his 1922 plea for restoration and management of Michigan's forests and wildlife habitats. The book was made into a movie, "Hearts Aflame," produced by Louis B. Mayer. Outdoor writer, Ben East, said of the book, *Timber*; "That book probably did more than any other single factor between 1920 and 1925 to give impetus to the conservation movement."

Marlene Dietrich and John Wayne in 1942 version of "The Spoilers" released on DVD in 2004 (Universal Studios)

Rex Beach:
(September 1, 1877 – December 7, 1949)

Birthplace:
Between Atwood and Norwood, MI

Connection to northern Michigan: Born in Charlevoix County where he spent his first nine years before the family moved to Florida.

Rex Beach Road, that runs west from US 31, leads past the old family farm down to Rex Beach on the shore of Lake Michigan.

Career: Beach attended Rollins College in Florida, and the Chicago College of Law with an eye toward becoming an attorney. He excelled in writing and sports during college. In 1889 he dropped his studies after learning of the Gold Rush in Alaska. He joined the thousands seeking their fortunes in the great Northwest, however, after five years he had nothing to show for his troubles.

He returned to Chicago where he learned that a fellow goldrusher was earning money by selling stories about his experiences. Beach said that after hearing this he immediately sat down at an empty desk and began to write. He sold his first story to *Redbook* magazine in 1903, and within three years he was a famous best-selling author.

His ability to tell a good story caught the attention of Hollywood where Beach struck it rich. A total of 27 Rex Beach stories and books were turned into motion pictures. "The Spoilers" captured the excitement of the Yukon gold Rush, and was first filmed in 1914 starring the most popular actors of the day. It was remade three times, including the 1942 version that starred John Wayne and Marlene Dietrich. Beach was one of the first writers to work well with the Hollywood elite. He not only sold his stories, but also acted in some and produced a few films.

Beach married his one great love, Greta Crater, but the couple had no children.

Besides a road and beach named after him in Charlevoix County, Rex Beach Hall was dedicated in his honor at Rollins College in Winter Park, Florida.

Best known for: *The Spoilers* – his bestselling book that was filmed as a motion picture four times.

Eleanor Blake (Atkinson): 1899 -

Birthplace:
Hinsdale, Illinois

Connection to northern Michigan: In her late 20's she moved to Omena where she wrote a novel, *Seedtime and Harvest,* and raised her son, Wally Cox, who went on to be a famous actor.

Career: After graduating from high school in Chicago, Blake took a reporting job with the Chicago News Bureau. During the 1920's she worked for trade papers, wrote freelance articles, did publicity work, ghost wrote a book for a Chicago judge and wrote three mystery novels of her own.

Blake was born Eleanor Atkinson, sharing the name with her mother, a successful author of *Greyfriars Bobby,* and other books. To avoid confusion, she changed her name to Eleanor Blake. She is also known as Eleanor Blake Pratt, as her second marriage was to Benson K. Pratt in New York City.

Two of her novels are set in northern Michigan. *Seedtime and Harvest* (1935) follows three generations of the Martisons, a Norwegian family that settles near Traverse City because of its similarities to their homeland. Blake follows up with *Wherever I Choose,* written in 1938 in New York, about a third generation Martison girl who moves to Chicago.

While living in Omena, Blake rented a home for $18.00 a month, raised her own vegetables and two children from her first marriage.

Best known for: Mystery novels such as *Death Down East* and the previously mentioned novels set in northern Michigan.

In his book, *My Life as a Small Boy,* Wally Cox writes: "I come from many places, but the only place I like to think of myself as coming from is a northerly part of Michigan, itself a northerly state, where snow that fell in the middle of winter fell upon snow that was already there, so that the depth of it merely varied and never ended until spring showed up." He reminisces about digging snow caves, his dislike of snowballs, and inability to build a sturdy snowman.

Karl Detzer:
(September 4, 1891 – 1986)

Birthplace:
Fort Wayne, Indiana

Connection to northern Michigan: Lived on Lake Leelanau where he began his writing career after serving in World War I; Publisher of the weekly *Leelanau Enterprise-Tribune* from 1947-51; served as Leland Fire Chief; two of his books, *Pirate of the Pine Lands* and *The Marked Man* were set in northern Michigan.

Career: Worked as newspaper reporter in Ft. Wayne after high school, then entered the military. Served as captain in U.S. Army Division of Criminal Investigation, Paris Bureau, during WWI. After the war Detzer worked in Chicago as an advertising writer. He wrote screenplays in Hollywood during the mid 1930's. He wrote an article for the *Saturday Evening Post* about the Detroit Police Department's use of radio communications - a new development in the 1930's - that was the inspiration for the 1935 movie, "Car 99," starring Fred MacMurray. Detzer wrote the screenplay for "Car 99" and for the movie, "Crash Donovan," which came out the following year.

He became an Editor with *Reader's Digest* in the late 1930's, and later moved to Leland where he built on Lake Leelanau, an exact replica of the home he lived in while serving in Paris. Detzer had a keen interest in police and fire work that developed in his cub reporter days out of high school. He was a welcome and frequent guest at local fire and police departments, and eventually served as the Leland Fire Chief.

Detzer's wife Clarice was also a writer who helped him with his many projects. Clarice Detzer authored *The Island Mail* (1926) about the adventures of two girls sailing with a mail delivery in northern Lake Michigan.

Best known for: His many police and firefighter articles in national magazines; his book, *Carl Sandburg: A Study in Personality and Background* (1941), and his memoir, *Myself When Young* (1968).

William Ratigan:
November 7, 1910

Birthplace:
Detroit (Corktown), MI

Connection to northern Michigan: Lived in Charlevoix with his wife, Eleanor, and daughters, Patsy and Anne. The Ratigan's operated the *Dockside Press* and both William and Eleanor authored books. Ratigan's articles and books capture key moments and important periods of northern Michigan history from 19th century Great Lakes captains to the Mackinac Bridge to tragic shipwrecks on Lake Michigan. Ratigan also served on the faculty of Charlevoix High School.

Career: Ratigan earned his B.A. from the University of Chattanooga, where he captained the football team, before returning to Michigan to further his education at Albion College, CMU and MSU. Ratigan worked in the offices of NBC radio before WWII, then became a radio reporter during the war, and eventually was named managing news editor of NBC's western division.

Ratigan's fiction for young people includes *Young Mr. Big* and *The Adventures of Captain McCargo* about the exploits of 19th century sailors on the Great Lakes.

His book *Soo Canal,* published on the centennial of the opening of the canal, is a romantic historical novel that also highlights the building of and importance of the great Soo Canal.

Ratigan covers the story of the Mackinac Bridge in three titles: *Straits of Mackinac* (1957); *The Long Crossing* (1959), and *Highways Over Broad Waters* (1959).

Best known for: The Great Lakes maritime history classic, *Great Lakes Shipwrecks and Survivals* (1960). He followed with updated versions to include the *Edmund Fitzgerald* and *Morrell* shipwrecks. Following his coverage of the wreck of the *Carl D. Bradley* off the shore of Charlevoix in 1958, Ratigan was given artifacts from the great freighter that include a broken lifeboat oar, tiller and wooden bailing scoop.

Jerry Linenger:
January 16, 1955

Birthplace:
Eastpointe, MI

Connection to northern Michigan: Linenger lives with his wife and four children in Suttons Bay.
Career: Linenger is known for his work as an astronaut, but his credentials are endless. His official identification

with NASA reads: Jerry M. Linenger, M.D., M.S.S.M., M.P.H., Ph.D. Captain, Medical Corps, USN, Ret., NASA Astronaut. To accomplish his long list of credentials Linenger received a Bachelor of Science degree in bio-science from the U.S. Naval Academy in 1977; a doctor-ate in medicine from Wayne State University in 1981; a Master of Science degree in systems management from University of Southern California in 1988; a Master of Public Health degree in health policy from the University of North Carolina in 1989; a Doctor of Philosophy degree in epidemi-ology from the University of North Carolina in 1989.

In 1992 he joined NASA and began training for his first flight aboard the Space Shuttle *Discovery* in 1994. After the mission he became the first American astronaut to train with Russians at the Cosmonaut Training Center in Star City, Russia, that led to a four-month stay on the Russian Space Station Mir.

Linenger and his two Russian crewmembers faced numer-ous difficulties including the most severe fire ever aboard an orbiting spacecraft, fail-ures of onboard systems including the oxygen genera-tor, a near collision with a re-supply cargo ship during a manual docking system test, loss of station electrical power, and loss of attitude control resulting in a slow, uncontrolled "tumble" through space. Despite these challenges he was able to conduct all of his missions and experiments in space.

In 1998 he retired and has since written two books; *Off the Planet: Living Aboard the Russian Space Station Mir for Five Months,* and *Letters from Mir: An Astronauts Letters to His Son.* Linenger also has become a popular speaker on the motivational circuit.

Best known for: His time on the Mir Space Station and the several near fatal glitches.

Historical moment: First ever 5-hour space walk between the onetime cold war adver-saries.

Bruce Catton:
(1899 – 1978)

Birthplace:
Petoskey, MI

Connection to northern Michigan: Raised in Benzonia where his father was princi-pal at the Benzonia Academy. Family lived in Boyne City during Catton's teen years. He retired to Frankfort, where he wrote *Waiting for the Morning Train,* his memoir of growing up in northern Michigan.

Career: One of the most respected Civil War historians of our time never graduated from college. While attending Oberlin College, Catton didn't even take a history class. And this was the son of a teacher and principal. His interest in the Civil War started in Benzonia, where as a boy, he would listen to the stories of the town's Civil War veterans.

After serving in the Navy, Catton started in journalism, writing for the *Cleveland Plain Dealer* and later for the syndicated wire services out of Washington D.C. His first book, *The War Lords of Washington,* came after he served on the War Production Board during WWII.

He didn't write his first two Civil War books, *Mr. Lincoln's Army* and *Glory Road,* until after his 50th birthday. Of those first two books the *Chicago Tribune* wrote, "military history at its best." Catton completed his trilogy with *A Stillness at Appomattox,* which was awarded a Pulitzer Prize in 1954.

Among his other Civil War books are, *This Hallowed Ground, Grant Moves South,* and *Grant Takes Command.* The 1982 television mini-series, "The Blue and the Gray," which starred Gregory Peck and Lloyd Bridges, was based on Catton's Civil War histories.

In 1954, Catton became the first editor of *American Heritage Magazine,* a position he held until his death in 1978. He also wrote *Michigan: A Bicentennial History.*

Best known for: His Civil War trilogies and his memoir of northern Michigan, *Waiting for the Morning Train.*

Catton retired to Frankfort, where the street he lived on, Glory Road, was named after one of his books.

Petoskey native, Bruce Catton

Doug Stanton:
September 24, 1961

Birthplace:
Reed City, MI

Connection to northern Michigan: Attended Interlochen Arts Academy graduating in 1979. Came back to Interlochen in 1990 as the writer in residence and has lived in Traverse City since.

Career: Stanton received his writing degrees from the famed Hampshire College and Writers' Workshop, University of Iowa. A full time writer for such publica-

Traverse City author Doug Stanton

tions as *Esquire, Men's Journal* and *Sports Afield,* he has traveled extensively around the world as a literary journalist and essayist writing national stories about culture, travel, sport, and the outdoors. In 2001 he published the international best seller *In Harms Way,* which depicted the Navy's worst disaster at sea. The book remained on the *New York Times* best seller list for 9 months and took many top book honors. Stanton's next book, *The Horse Soldiers* (September 2006), gave him unprecedented access to U.S. military in this dramatic account of 12 secret U.S. soldiers who entered Afghanistan immediately following 9/11, and, riding to war on horses, defeated the Taliban.

Best known for: *In Harm's Way: The Sinking of the* USS Indianapolis

Stanton drew some of his literary inspiration while being the caretaker of Robert Frost's house in Vermont.

Kevin Dockery:
October 12, 1954

Birthplace:
Highland Park, MI

Connection to northern Michigan: Spent most boyhood summers and lived for a time in the family cottage on

Lake Skegemog. Dockery Road in nearby Williamsburg is named for his family.

Home Team: *The Undeclared War* (Harper Collins), written by Dockery and Dennis Chalker, is partially set in Leland and the Fox islands.

Career: Before becoming a full time writer Dockery served in the military. He enlisted in the U.S. Army in 1972, serving in the President's Guard of the 3rd Infantry Regiment in Washington DC. He served as a platoon sargent in the Michigan National Guard in the early 1980's while earning his communications degree from Oakland University.

In 1988 he accepted an offer to write a book about the Navy SEALS – *SEALS in Action* – that was the beginning of a strong relationship between Dockery and Navy SEALS, past and present. He has written two dozen non-fiction books, most about Navy SEALS history and operations. He has collaborated with former Command Master Chief and founding member of SEAL Team Six, Dennis Chalker, for several books, fiction and non-fiction.

Dockery was the lead historian and writer of *The Complete History of the Navy SEALS,* a two-hour documentary produced in 1999 for the History Channel. That led to a book version published in three editions.

Dockery has worked as a technical adviser for the movies "The Rock," "Eraser" and "ConAir." Dockery continues to write from his home in northern Ohio, and frequently visits family in the Traverse City area.

Best known for: *The Complete History of the Navy SEALS* – the television and book versions.

Bob Pisor:
December 7, 1939

Birthplace:
Bellefontaine, OH
Connection to northern Michigan: Pisor and his wife Ellen live in Leland and own Stonehouse Bread, a bakery/café, where they produce several varieties using only three ingredients: organic flour, well water, and sea salt. As a child his family camped on the Leelanau Peninsula, which continually beckoned to Pisor. He honeymooned on S. Manitou Island, bought a farm in Leland, while working as a television reporter in Detroit, and finally made the move there permanently in 1991.

Career: Received his Masters of Journalism from Columbia University, and embarked on a reporting career which included two years in Vietnam as a correspondent for the *Detroit News*. His writing and reporting led to numerous prestigious awards and employment with WNBC-TV and WNDT-TV in New York City. In the mid 1970's, he worked the other side of the podium as press pecretary to Detroit Mayor Coleman Young. Pisor has served as political columnist for the *Detroit News* and written many stories that have appeared in the *Washington Post,* major wire services and *Detroit Free Press*. In 1982 he authored *The End of the Line: The Seige of Khe Sanh,* the story of 6,000-trapped Marines that would become the turning point in the US involvement in Vietnam. He also worked in various capacities at WDIV TV in Detroit, ranging from news anchor to political analyst. In 1991 he left WDIV and moved to Leland to indulge his passion for pure, honest, fresh bread by launching Stonehouse Bread Company, which opened in 1995.

Best known for: Making a great loaf of bread, and all of the above.

Jerry Dennis:
October 12, 1954

Birthplace:
Flint, MI
Connection to northern Michigan: Moved to Traverse City at the age of 5, and with the exception of attending college at Northern Michigan University and the University of Louisville, has lived in the area ever since. Currently resides in a 130-year-old farmhouse on the Old Mission Peninsula with his wife Gail. His book *A Place on the Water* is a memoir of growing up in Traverse City.

Career: Jerry Dennis has been a professional full-time writer since 1986. He has authored 10 books, most notably his book *The Living Great Lakes* (St. Martin's Press, 2003) that won the Best Book of 2003 by the Outdoor Writers Association of America. In 1999 the Michigan Library Association presented him with the Michigan Author of the Year Award. His writings about nature and the environment have appeared in such publications as *the New York Times, Smithsonian, Audubon, Field and Stream,* and *National Geographic Traveler.* His essays and articles have won numerous awards and have been frequently anthologized in *The Best American Nature Essays* and elsewhere. Additional books by Dennis include *Canoeing Michigan Rivers, It's Raining Frogs and Fishes, A Place on the Water, The Bird in the Waterfall, The River Home,* and *From a Wooden Canoe.*

Best known for: Jerry Dennis is considered to be one of the top outdoor and environmental writers of his generation. His book *It's Raining Frogs and Fishes* was a national best seller.

George Weeks:
August 1, 1932

Birthplace:
Traverse City, MI

Connection to northern Michigan: Weeks was born and raised in Traverse City, the son of a former Traverse City *Record Eagle* editor. Served in the administration of former Governor William Milliken of Traverse City. Weeks, who resides with his wife near Glen Arbor, has written several books about the region including: *Sleeping Bear: Yesterday and Today* (1990, 2005), *Sleeping Bear: Its Lore, Legends and First People* (1988), and *Mem Ka Weh: The Dawning of the Grand Traverse Band of Ottawa and Chippewa Indians* (1992). He also teamed with Joyce Braithwaite to produce *The Milliken Years: A Pictorial History* (1988).
Career: Started journalism career as editor of *The Black*

& Gold student paper at Traverse City Senior High. After graduation from the Journalism School at Michigan State University, Weeks was a reporter for the UPI wire service in Lansing, and later became the foreign editor for the Washington Bureau during the Kennedy and Johnson administrations. In 1969, William Milliken, whose family maintained a long-standing friendship with the Weeks family, became governor. Weeks accepted an offer to become press secretary, and eventually served as Milliken's chief of staff. In 1980 he was awarded a fellowship at the John F. Kennedy School of Government at Harvard University, where he studied and wrote about America's outstanding governors. After Milliken left office in 1982, Weeks was offered his current position as political columnist for the *Detroit News*. In 1987 he wrote the book *Stewards of the State: The Governors of Michigan.*

Best known for: His weekly syndicated column on state and local politics that appears in several newspapers around the state including the *Detroit News* and *Traverse City Record Eagle.*

Larry Wakefield:
1914

Birthplace:
Grand Rapids, MI

Connection to northern Michigan: Has lived in Traverse City since 1941, and since 1977 has written 17 books, most of which deal with Grand Traverse area history.

Career: Born in Grand Rapids, raised in Evanston, Illinois, and off to Oberlin College where he majored in English Lit. Wakefield spent many years in the mink farming business with his father, and in 1941 moved to Traverse City to carry on the business. He left the mink business and began to write articles which appeared in national magazines such as *Esquire*. Since 1977's *All Our Yesterday's: A Narrative History of Traverse City and the Region,* he has turned out a steady stream of books, article and columns on local history.

He eschews computers, opting to write all of his material on a 1938 manual Royal Standard typewriter.

Best known for: *Queen City of the North: An Illustrated History of Traverse City From Its Beginnings to 1980's* (1988).

Ben Hamper:
September 14, 1955

Birthplace:
Flint, MI

Connection to northern Michigan: After vacationing in the Suttons Bay area, Hamper left his career in the factory and moved to Suttons Bay in 1995, where he continues to live.

Career: Growing up in Flint, Hamper did what his father, grandfather and great grandfather did before him: upon graduating from high school he went to work on the General Motors assembly line. In 1980 he stumbled across fellow Flint native Michael Moore, who was publishing the alternative paper the *Flint Voice*. Fascinated with Hamper's reflections and observations of assembly line life, Moore asked him to write a weekly column about "life on the line." The column would set the stage for Hamper's 1992 best selling book *Rivethead: Tales from the Assembly Line*. The book remains popular and in 2005 over 200 universities around the world continue to use it as a textbook in labor relations classes. Hamper took on several freelance projects during the 1990's and worked with his buddy Michael Moore on the successful television shows "Awful Truth "and "TV Nation."

Best known for: His book *Rivethead* became the mouthpiece of the stressful and, at times, destructive lifestyle of the American assembly line.

Stephanie Mills:

Connection to northern Michigan: Resident of Maple City area since late 1980's.

Career: Mills has been involved in the ecology movement since earning a Bachelor of Arts from Mills College (no relation) in California in 1969. She won the *Mademoiselle Magazine* Award that same year and was named Editor-in-Chief of *EarthTimes* magazine in San Francisco. She was a leader in the San Francisco-based group, *Friends of the Earth* through much of the 1970's. She continued to write and lecture on issues of women's rights, population control, and ecology. During the 1980's she was Editor-in-Chief of *CoEvolution Quarterly* and *California Tomorrow,* both San Francisco-based magazines. In 1996 the *Utne Reader* included Mills as one of its visionaries.

Books authored by Mills include: *Whatever Happened to Ecology* (1989), *In Service* to the Wild: Restoring and Reinhabiting Damaged Land (1995), *Turning Away from Technology* (1997), and *Epicurean Simplicity* (2002).

Best known for: Her Mills College commencement speech in 1969, in which she vowed never to have children because of overpopulation and environmental ills. The speech was given prominent coverage by news media, including a spread in *Life* magazine.

Jack Driscoll:
March 7, 1946

Birthplace:
Holyoke, MA

Connection northern Michigan: Driscoll moved to Interlochen, Michigan in 1975 to develop the creative writing program at the Interlochen Arts Academy, where he remains today as the permanent writer in residence.

Career: In addition to his work at Interlochen, Driscoll is a sought after instructor at several top writing workshops. He is also an accomplished author, winning the Pushcart's Editors Book Award in 1998 for his novel *Lucky Man, Lucky Women.* He followed in 2000 with another successful novel titled *Stardog,* that starts out with a school bus driver abandon-

ing his bus, and the young children in it, on a cold Benzie County highway! He has four books of poetry published, and in May of 2005 the University of Michigan Press published his most recent novel *How Like An Angel,* which is set in a rustic northern Michigan cabin.

Best known for: While Driscoll has won numerous awards and honors for his writing, it has been his work with young writers at Interlochen and at various workshops that he is most proud of. Over 50 of his former students have had major publishing success including Doug Stanton (see entry), Marya Hornbacher who at the age of 22 sold over a million copies of her memoir *Wasted: A Memoir of Anorexia and Bulimia* and in February 2005 published her first novel *The Center of Winter* for Harper Collins. Most recently he worked with Christopher Paolini (who at the age of 17 was labeled the next Tolkien) who published the popular fantasy thriller *Eragon.* Now 19 and on the verge of publishing the second in his series (Eldest), Paolini credits Driscoll for shaping the young writer's style.

Jack Driscoll: Lucky Guy (courtesy of Jack Driscoll)

CHILDREN'S AUTHORS

Gloria Whelan:
1923

Birthplace:
Detroit, MI

Connection to northern Michigan: Whelan lives with her husband on Oxbow Lake near Mancelona. Many of her children's books are set in northern Michigan or set against northern Michigan history.

Career: After graduating from the University of Michigan, Whelan worked in the social services field, and taught American literature at Spring Arbor College. She wrote poetry and adult fiction before moving to northern Michigan. She has written over two dozen children's books, including a series of three set on Mackinac Island before Michigan's statehood. *Pathless Woods* is a fictitious look at Ernest Hemingway's 16th summer in northern Michigan. Many of her stories take place in northern Michigan at various points in history. She also has set her stories in Russia, Vietnam, China, India, the Wild West, and Alaska.

Best known for: *Homeless Bird.* In 2000 Whelan was the winner of one of the most important author awards in the world, the National Book Award. In *Homeless Bird* she writes of a 13-year old girl in India forced by her family to get married because she was an extra mouth to feed. Shortly after marriage, the teen's husband becomes ill and dies. After that, young Coly lives the life of a slave in her husband's family, but discovers reading, and finds hope. Whelan's awards for children's literature are numerous; Michigan Author of the Year (1998), American Library Association – Best Books for Young Adults, Great Lakes Booksellers Award, honors from the Midland Society of Authors, and the National Book Award in 2000 for *Homeless Bird.*

Quote: "Many of my books take place in the summer; that's because I do a lot of my writing during northern Michigan blizzards… I tell children that one of the perks of being an author is that all the while you are writing your book, you can be anyone and anyplace you wish. Would you like to live in the days of the pioneers? Race sled dogs in Alaska? Sail across the China Sea? Live on Mackinac Island in 1812? You can. Just write a book about it. That's what I did."

Betty Beeby:
1923

Birthplace:
Detroit, MI

Residence:
Eastport, Antrim County

Beeby's name appears on dozens of books as illustrator, as she is, above all, an artist. Her children's books include *"Just Josie,"* based on her daughter, and *"Great Granny's Sturdy, Steady Picnic Tables."* Her interest in local history led her to publish two books of letters and historical records from local pioneer women: *Grace Hooper's Pioneer Notes,* and *Breath Escaping Envelopes.*

Since 1974, Beeby has lived in Eastport on the same property where her father was born. She grew up in Detroit, attending Cass Tech High School. After graduating from the Pratt Institute of Brooklyn, she went to work as a staff artist for *Time-Life,* and from there became a film artist for CBS television where she created art for the set of Captain Kangaroo.

Her most public work of art, a 50-foot mural of the Mackinac Bridge, has been covered up for years. She was commissioned to design and paint the mural in 1974 for the Visitors Center at Fort Michilimackinac. But in the 1980's it was concealed behind the newly built gift shop. In May 2005 the shop was moved and the mural is now the visible highlight of the center.

Beeby is a familiar face in local circles, and has dedicated proceeds from many of her books and paintings to local historical groups and student art scholarships.

Betty Beeby painting mural at Ft. Michilimackinac Visitor's Center, 1974 (photo by Sarah Gay Dammann)

Kathy-jo Wargin

Birthplace:
Minnesota

Connection to northern Michigan: Lives with husband and son in Petoskey. Many of her best-selling books are based in northern Michigan.

Career: Before moving to northern Michigan from Minnesota, Kathy-jo teamed up with her photographer husband, Ed Wargin, on *Scenic Driving Michigan,* which maps out the best drives for enjoying the beauty of Michigan. The couple also teamed up on *Michigan: Spirit of the Land a Photographic Tour of the State,* and *The Great Lakes Cottage Book.*

Her love of history and local folklore resulted in 1998's

Legend of the Sleeping Bear, a beautiful re-telling of the Indian legend with gripping illustrations from Gijsbert van Frankenhuyzen. The pair teamed up again for; *Legend of Mackinac Island, Legend of the Loon, Legend of Leelanau, Legend of the Lady's Slipper, Legend of the Petoskey Stone,* and *Edmund Fitzgerald.* Combined, the books have sold hundreds of thousands of copies, and continue to top best-seller lists around Michigan.
Other books by Kathy-jo Wargin include *The Michigan Counting Book,* and the *Michigan Reader for Boys and Girls.*

Best known for: The Legend books, especially the first, *The Legend of the Sleeping Bear.*

<u>Johnathan Rand:</u>
November 24, 1964

Birthplace:
Pontiac, MI

Connection to northern Michigan: Lives in Topinabee. Grew up in Grayling, and lived for a short time in Houghton Lake. During late 1980's and early 90's he was heard as Christopher Knight on WCCW-Traverse City, WKHQ-Charlevoix, and WGFM Cheboygan. Won several creative awards for his commercial writing and pro-

duction. Now a prolific children's author with several books set in northern Michigan including: *Mackinaw City Mummy's, Gargoyles of Gaylord, Poltergiests of Petoskey, Terror Stalks Traverse City* and *Mayhem on Mackinac Island.*

Career: First book, *St. Helena,* was released only as an audio book. The tale of a haunted northern Michigan lighthouse set the tone for Knight's writing career. His ten-book series, *Michigan Chillers,* has made him a favorite among young readers across the State. He's spoken at hundreds of schools, and the success of the series has led to *American Chillers,* scary tales from each state. So far he's written 14 with a goal of one book for each state. Rand, who likes to read children's books and adult fiction, lists the following among his favorite books: *My Side of the Mountain'* by Jean Craighead George, *James and the Giant Peach* by Roald Dahl and *Where the Wild Things Are* by Maurice Sendak.

Best known for:
Michigan Chillers. Thousand and thousands of Michigan school children have read all ten in this series, and anxiously await the next new title.

Johnathan Rand (photo courtesy of Johnathan Rand)

Timothy R. Smith:
1945

Birthplace:
Santa Rosa, CA

Connection to northern Michigan: An avid fisherman, Smith moved with his wife and three children to Traverse City in the 1970's. He founded the Stained Glass Cabinet Company in 1978, and began writing his children's books in 1995.

Career: Graduated with a degree in microbiology from Michigan State University in 1968. Hit the road as a pharmaceutical salesman before getting the itch to own his own business. Opened the Stained Glass Company in Traverse City, eventually selling it to his employees so he could focus on writing a children's book. After several rejections from major publishers, he invested his own funds to produce *Buck Wilder's Small Fry Fishing Guide* in 1995. Smith made a connection with Michigan astronaut, Jerry Linenger, who took the book into space with him.

Smith was instrumental in forming a partnership with the Michigan Department of Natural Resources to create a natural history program for 4th grade students. Characters from his books, including "Buck Wilder" and his "family of animal friends" were used from 1999 to 2003 in the curriculum.

Smith has given elementary school presentations to over 375,000 Michigan children. He focuses on character building in these presentations: believing that a person should "always work hard, not be afraid to make mistakes, and to try new things." This message guided him as he began writing his books after turning 50 years old!

Best known for: Creating and writing the Buck Wilder book series: *Buck Wilder's Small Fry Fishing Guide; Buck Wilder's Small Twig Hiking and Camping Guide;* and *Buck Wilder's Little Skipper Boating Guide.* To date, the books have sold over 250,000 copies.

Anne Margaret Lewis:
November 8, 1963

Birthplace:
Detroit, MI

Connection to northern Michigan: Her Mackinac Island Press is based in downtown Traverse City. Three of her books were inspired by northern Michigan: *Hidden Cherries* was named the Official Children's Book of the National Cherry Festival in 2004, *Tears of the Mother Bear* is based on the Legend of the Sleeping Bear, and *Lighthouse Fireflies* features Point Betsie Lighthouse.

Career: Liberal Arts degree from the University of Michigan. Learned the publishing business at Sleeping Bear Press in Chelsea, before moving north to write and become a publisher. Formed Petoskey Publishing, which partners with the University of Michigan Press to produce high quality and popular regional titles. Started Mackinac Island Press (MIP) to publish children's titles. Besides the three books she has authored, MIP has published *The Day the Great Lakes Drained Away* by Charles Barker, and *The Fairy Painting* by Stacey DuFord. More titles planned for 2005, including *Hidden Pumpkins* with Traverse City illustrator Jim DeWildt.

Best known for: *Hidden Cherries*

Laura Bannon:
(1894 – 1963)

Birthplace:
Acme, Grand Traverse County, MI

Millions of school children growing up in the 1940's, 50's and 60's read Bannon's colorfully illustrated books. She believed in having first hand knowledge of her sub-jects. The settings for her books were inspired by her numerous travels including extended stays in Japan, Iceland, South America, Mexico, and a year on a houseboat in California.

Bannon was from a family of eight children. She graduated Traverse City High School, the Grand Traverse County Normal School and Western Michigan College. She studied art and taught at the Art Institute of Chicago.

Bannon never married. She led a busy life traveling, and wrote over 20 children's books between 1939 and 1963. She also illustrated five books for other authors.

Only two books are set in northern Michigan. "*Who Walks the Attic*" is set atop Bunker Hill in her hometown of Acme. "*Billy the Bear*" is set in the eastern U.P. town of Cedarville.

Quote: "My greatest single help in writing and illustrating books for children is the circumstance of having come from a large family. All eight of us lived out the noisy ups and downs of childhood on a hill overlooking Grand Traverse Bay, Michigan. I baby-sat my way through Traverse City High School, tutored my way through two years at Western Michigan State College, and did odd–

very odd–jobs to earn my way through four years of training at the School of the Art Institute of Chicago. I painted on velvet, beaded lampshades, turned out designs for Christmas cards. When the rent came due, did drawings of a sinus operation, and once I repainted a man's false ear to match his suntan."

Clara Dillingham Pierson:
(around 1870 –1954)

Birthplace:
Coldwater, MI
Connection to northern Michigan: Well-known figure in Omena, where she summered in a home built in 1898, following the success of her first book.

Career: Before writing, Pierson was head of the teaching department at Alma College, and taught kindergarten in Chicago. She learned to love the outdoors as a child, and that inspired her to write. Several articles turned away by magazine editors were the basis for her first book in 1898, *Among the Forest People*. In that and the follow up books, *Among the Farm Yard People*, *Among the Meadow People*, and *Among the Night People*, Pierson entertained young readers by giving voice to the critters in her beloved outdoors.

Best known for: Her Three Little Millers series of books. Pierson adapted stories from her summers at Omena into a popular series of books for boys and girls. The fictitious Miller family, like the Piersons, spent summers at a cottage called Pencroft. In the book, Omena is changed to Trelago Point, and the Millers have two sons and a daughter, whereas the Piersons had two sons. Friends say Pierson always wanted a daughter, so she created one in her writing.

The first installment, *Three Little Millers*, was published in 1905; it was followed by *The Millers at Pencroft*, *The Millers and their Playmates*, and *The Millers and their New Home*. There are several local references throughout the books, such as taking the steamer *Columbia* from Traverse City to Trelago Point, a two hour and twenty minute ride.

Pierson died in 1954. Her sons sold Pencroft, which is still standing and known by its new owners as Green Gables.

From Omena: A Place in Time, Amanda J. Holmes, copyright 2003, *The Omena Historical Society*.

Elizabeth Howard (Mizner): 1907

Birthplace:
Detroit, MI

Connection to northern Michigan: Howard spent summers at her family's cottage on West Bay in Traverse City, and moved there permanently late in life. Many of her historical stories for young girls are set in northern Michigan.

Career: Earned a Master's Degree in history from University of Michigan and taught at a girl's school in Georgia before starting her writing career. She has said the Great Lakes played a prominent role in her life and writing. She spent time on excursion steamers in Detroit, and for a few years her family lived in a Chicago apartment overlooking Lake Michigan.

Her first book, *Sabina,* published in 1941, was about a young girl in Detroit at the time of the Mexican War. Other books include *Summer Under Sail,* which is about a young girl sailing the Great Lakes with her grandfather; *North Winds Blow Free,* which looks at slavery from the point-of-view of a northern Michigan family whose farm is on the trail of slaves escaping from the South; *A Girl of the North Country* and *Wilderness Venture,* both of which relate stories of young girls and their families in the early days of northern Michigan.

Best known for: *North Wind Blows Free.* Millions of young girls read about the Underground Railroad in this book that examines the depth of young Elspeth McLaren's compassion.

Sara Gwendolen *"Gwen"* Frostic: (1906 – 2001)

Birthplace:
Croswell, MI

Connection to northern Michigan: Founded Presscraft Papers, an 18-press print shop in Benzonia, Michigan. The shop also functions as a gallery/showroom for Gwen's linoleum-block prints and books.

Education: Frostic studied art education from 1924 to 1926 at Michigan State Normal College (now Eastern Michigan University) in Ypsilanti, Michigan, which earned her a teaching certificate. After transferring to Western State Normal College (now Western Michigan University) in 1926, she dropped out in 1927 without acquiring a degree.

Best known for: Frostic wrote, illustrated, printed and published 20 books (and contributed to four others). Her linoleum-block prints, which were inspired by her love of nature, made her a millionaire in the mid-1960's when Frostic was herself over 60 years old. And while her art and prose are what made her notable, she is also remembered, as a businesswoman of strong will, which drove her entrepreneurial spirit. Born with a high fever that resulted in some physical handicaps (possibly polio, but there was never an official diagnosis), Frostic never limited herself; she attended college, worked at the Willow Run bomber plant during World War II (which is where she was introduced to linoleum) and started Presscraft Papers in the Frostic basement in Wyandotte, Michigan. In 1950, Frostic and her father, Fred, a retired school superintentent, bought property near Frankfort, Michigan. Fred built a cottage, and Gwen quickly fell in love with the tranquil surroundings. After her father's death in 1954, Gwen closed her Wyandotte shop and moved north.

In 1978, Governor William Milliken named May 23 as Gwen Frostic Day in Michigan. In 1986, Frostic was inducted to the Michigan Woman's Hall of Fame in Lansing.

Anne Marie Oomen:

Oomen is chair of the Creative Writing Division at the Interlochen Academy of Arts, and an instructor of playwriting. She grew up on a farm in Oceana County and shares her memories in *Pulling Down the Barn*, which was named a Michigan Notable Book in 2004. Oomen is the founder of the regional literary magazine, *The Dunes Review*, and edited *Looking Over My Shoulder: Reflections on the Twentieth Century*, an anthology of writing by older adults. In 2005, her play *Wives of an American King*, depicting the King Strang years on Beaver Island, premiered in Traverse City. Her plays have been produced in Chicago, St. Louis, and Iowa City.

POETS

Terry Wooten:

Founder of the Stone Circle north of Elk Rapids where storytelling and poetry are shared over a giant bonfire on weekend nights during the summer. Wooten is one of the few, if not the only, writers in Michigan who earns a full time living solely through the writing and reading of poetry. He has a dozen books of poetry published, two CDs, and has been a guest speaker and performer at hundreds of schools around Michigan. In 2004, Wooten wrote *Lifelines: A World War II Story of Survival and Love,* a collection of poems based on his conversations with Jack and Leda Miller of Elk Rapids. Jack served in World War II and survived the Bataan Death March, as Leda waited for him back home. Wooten and Elk Rapids High School teacher, Lin Opgenorth, turned the poems into a play that served as a unique learning tool for the students who personally met with Jack and Leda before portraying the couple on stage.

Wooten was born and raised in northern Michigan and says he was inspired to follow his love of poetry and build the Stone Circle by his mentor, Max Ellison.

Max Ellison:

During the 1960's and 70's Ellison spoke to school students around Michigan, sharing his books and poetry. Born in Bellaire in 1914, Ellison attended Bellaire schools, before serving in World War II, where he earned a Purple Heart and two Oak Clusters in the Philippine campaign. He married and raised five children before becoming divorced. Later in life he let his hair down, choosing to live in a small former schoolhouse on Frog Hollow Road. Ellison attracted a strong following to his humble home when he began nightly bonfires where he would recite poetry.

Ellison's books include, *The Underbark* (1969), *The Happenstance* (1972), *Double Take* (1973), *The Blue Bird* (1977) *and Poems by Max Ellison* (1977).

Michael Delp:

Born in Greenville, Michigan in 1948. Delp is an instructor of creative writing at the Interlochen Arts Academy and has won numerous writing awards including the PEN Syndicated Fiction Award. Delp is the editor of *Contemporary Michigan Poetry: The Third Coast.* His books include: *Over the Graves of Horses* (1988), a collection of poems; *Under the Influence of Water* (1992), a collection of essays, poems and short stories; *The Coast of Nowhere: A Meditation on Rivers, Lakes and Streams* (1997), and *The Last Good Water* (2003) prose and poetry.

Notable Books:

The Library of Michigan chooses 20 books each year for its Michigan Notable

Books list. Each book is about or set in Michigan or on the Great Lakes, or written by a native or resident of Michigan.

Northern Michigan has been well represented by subject and author. Below is a list of previous years Notable Books pertinent to northern Michigan.

2005 Michigan Notable Books:

Eight Steamboats: Sailing through the Sixties, by Patrick Livingston. Wayne State University Press. Author's memoir of crewing aboard Great Lakes vessels during the 1960's.

The Indians of Hungry Hollow by Bill Dunlop and Marcia Fountain-Blacklidge. University of Michigan Press. This memoir recounts Dunlop's experiences as an Ottawa youth growing up in a Native American community in Petoskey.

On the Brink: The Great Lakes in the 21st Century by Dave Dempsey. Michigan State University Press. Environmental history of the Great Lakes including environmental threats and public policy.

Pulling Down the Barn: Memories of a Rural Childhood by Anne-Marie Oomen. Wayne State University Press. Author memoir of growing up on a farm in rural Oceana County.

The Tarnished Eye: A Novel of Suspense by Judith Guest. Scribner. Fiction base on 1960's unsolved murder in Emmet County. Book is set in fictional town of Blessed (Cross Village).

True North: A Novel by Jim Harrison. Grove Press. Set in Michigan's Upper Peninsula, this poignant novel details David Burkett's struggles with his father and his family's legacy of timberland destruction in the Upper Peninsula.

2004 Michigan Notable Books:

The Edmund Fitzgerald: The Song of the Bell, by Kathy-jo Wargin. Illustrated by Gijsbert van Frankenhuyzen. Sleeping Bear Press. Emmet County children's author, Kathi-jo Wargin tells the story of the famous 1975 Great Lakes maritime disaster and the recent recovery of the ship's bell.

The Forests of Michigan, by Donald I. Dickmann and Larry A. Leefers. University of Michigan Press. Complete with full color photographs and maps, this book details the natural history of forests in Michigan from the time of the receding glaciers, through the lumbering era, to the 20th century renewal and future prospects.

The Living Great Lakes: Searching for the Heart of the Inland Seas, by Jerry Dennis. Thomas Dunne Books. The Traverse City author explores the region's natural history, shares personal anecdotes, and experiences the adventure and true wonder of the Great Lakes as a crewmember aboard a large schooner.

Shipwrecks of Lake Michigan, by Benjamin J. Shelak. Trails Books. Lake Michigan maritime disasters, dating back to 1800.

Voelker's Pond: A Robert Traver Legacy, by Ed Wargin and James McCullough. Huron River Press. Wargin, of Emmet County provides rare photographic glimpse into Voelker's Upper Peninsula fishing retreat.

2003 Read Michigan Selections

Black Eden: The Idlewild Community, by Lewis Walker and Benjamin C. Wilson. Michigan State University Press. Incorporating oral interviews and photographs, the authors study the African-American resort community in Lake County.

Lake Michigan Passenger Steamers, by George W. Hilton. Stanford University Press. Examines the development, rise and decline of the passenger steamer industry on Lake Michigan and contains detailed corporate histories of the ten major operators.

Off to the Side: A Memoir, by Jim Harrison. Atlantic Monthly Press. One of Michigan's most acclaimed authors writes candidly and poignantly about his rugged Michigan childhood in northern Michigan, coming-of-age, literary influences, personal struggles and his passion for hunting and trout fishing.

Vintage Views of Leelanau County, by M. Christine Byron and Thomas R. Wilson. Huron River Press. Using vintage postcards and photographs the authors capture a slice of Leelanau County's history.

The Wanigan: A Life on the River, by Gloria Whelan. Illustrated by Emily Martindale. Alfred A. Knopf. National Book Award Winner, Gloria Whelan of Mancelona, tells the tale of a 19th century family working in the northern Michigan timber industry.

Windjammers: Songs of the Great Lakes Sailors, by Ivan H. Walton with Joe Grimm. Wayne State University Press. Music, lyrics and brief histories of dozens of chanteys and songs on sailing, lumbering and lake disasters.

2002 Read
Michigan Selections

Angels in the Architecture: A Photographic Elegy to an American Asylum, by Heidi Johnson. Wayne State University Press. A photographic history of the Northern Michigan Asylum located in Traverse City, supported by recollections of former patients and staff members.

Historic Cottages of Mackinac Island, by Susan Stites and Lea Ann Sterling. Photography by Lanny Sterling and Lea Ann Sterling. Arbutus Press. A pictorial look at seventy-three cottages, including the Governor's Residence, that were constructed on Mackinac Island between 1870 and 1910.

Idlewild: The Black Eden of Michigan, by Ronald J. Stephens. Images of America (series). Arcadia Publishing. This photographic compilation explores the history of the African-American resort community in Lake County, Michigan.

In Harm's Way: The Sinking of the USS Indianapolis and the Extraordinary Story of Its Survivors, by Doug Stanton. Henry Holt. Soon after delivering parts of the atomic bomb to be used on Hiroshima, the *USS Indianapolis* was sunk by the Japanese. The survivors, including Michigan resident Dr. Lewis Haynes, drifted aimlessly in the Pacific Ocean for five days, fighting off shark attacks and hypothermia, before being rescued by the U.S. Navy. (Traverse City author)

Ruin and Recovery: Michigan's Rise as a Conservation Leader, by Dave Dempsey. University of Michigan Press. An environmental history of Michigan, focusing on two public conservation efforts: the first developed in response to the excesses of the lumber industry, and the second grew from the push to clean the state's air and water in the 1960s and 1970s.

2001 Read
Michigan Selections

A Place Called Home: Michigan's Mill Creek Story, by Janie Lynn Panagopoulos, illustrated by Gijsbert van Frankenhuyzen. Sleeping Bear Press and the Mackinac Island State Park Commission. Life in the Straits area during revolutionary days. Illustrated for young readers.

Canoeing Michigan Rivers: A Comprehensive Guide to 45 Rivers, Jerry Dennis and Craig Date. Friede Publications. Traverse City author Jerry Dennis co-authors this revised edition of the authoritative guide to canoeing 1,500 miles of rivers in Michigan.

Leelanau: A Portrait of Place in Photography & Text, photos by Ken Scott, text by Jerry Dennis. Petunia Press. The author notes that Leelanau County "remains quiet and rural and slow to change, and thus increasingly important to our collective well being."

Off the Planet: Surviving Five Perilous Months Aboard the Space Station Mir, by Jerry M. Linenger. McGraw-Hill. The author, now living in Leelanau County, is among four U.S., astronauts raised in Michigan (another four attended the University of Michigan.). He offers a colorful view of the state from space.

Views of Mackinac Island, by Thomas Kachadurian. Sleeping Bear Press. Outstanding photos and text highlight the well known and little known beauty spots of the island.

Women and the Lakes: Untold Great Lakes Maritime Tales, by Frederick Stonehouse. Avery Color Studios. Zeroes in on contributions of women to Great Lakes maritime history.

BROADCASTING

Northern Michigan's First Radio Station:

A Petoskey High School teacher is credited with putting northern Michigan's first station on the air. In 1923, just three years after the first radio stations in the country signed on, Frank Jacobs was encouraged by the Petoskey Board of Education to apply for a federal radio license. Jacobs was using a ham radio to teach students the science of the medium. In January of 1924 Petoskey High School was awarded a federal license to broadcast at ten watts as station, WBBP. (Wonderful Bay, Beautiful Petoskey)

The stations' first broadcast was a live performance by Cole's Merry Midnight Serenaders from the High School auditorium. The station caused a stir in the community, enough so that $1,000 in donations was raised to cover the cost of raising power from 10 to 100 watts. WBBP broadcast live performances by local singers, musicians, and provided live broadcasts of church services, debates, service club meetings and even a few Petoskey High School basketball games. WBBP set up the "Canary Studio" in the lobby of the Perry Hotel, featuring live Sunday morning broadcasts of classical performances with live canaries in the background.

As the popularity of radio grew, so did the number of stations around the country, and with more stations on the dial, there was more interference. In May of 1928 the Federal Radio Commission announced it was canceling the licenses of 160 stations around the country, including WBBP, Petoskey. The town would be without its own radio station until 1947 when Les Biederman built WMBN.

Thanks to George Bednarik at www.michimedia.net and *Petoskey Evening News*

Northern Michigan's Broadcast Pioneer

While working as an engineer in the late 1930's at WTEL Radio in Philadelphia, Les Biederman studied a radio map of the United States. He was looking for a city in need of a radio station. With a little homework he developed a plan to build five radio stations in northern Michigan, starting in Traverse City.

By September of 1940 Biederman had rounded up a few investors to help fund construction of northern Michigan's first commercial radio station. Total cost was $12,000, which included electronics, tower, legal fees, and miscellaneous expenses. Biederman and his partner, Bill Kiker, used their engineering skills to build the station from the ground up, which kept expenses low.

WTCM AM 1370 went on the air for the first time on January 8, 1941. Until then the only radio available in northern Michigan were weak signals from Chicago, Detroit and Milwaukee. Eventually WTCM switched from AM 1370 to AM 580. Biederman went on to build four other stations: WATT-Cadillac in 1945, WMBN-Petoskey in 1947, WATC-Gaylord in 1950, and WATZ-Alpena in 1954. He called his group of five stations the Paul Bunyan Network.

In 1954, Biederman expanded his network by getting into television. He built WPBN (Paul Bunyan Network), Channel 7 on a hilltop overlooking West Bay. Today the station continues to operate from that location. He later expanded the reach of his station by building WTOM (Top of Michigan), Channel 4, in Cheboygan.

Biederman also built northern Michigan's first cable television system. In 1966, he won franchise rights to build a 12-channel system in the Traverse City region.

Biederman's vision and ability to get things done went beyond broadcasting. He is credited as being one of the founders of Northwestern Michigan College and the Great Lakes Maritime Academy in Traverse City, and a driving force behind that town's hospital expansion and its symphony.

In order to increase broadcast power of WTCM in Traverse City in the early 1980's, federal laws dictated that Biederman sell his stations in Petoskey, Gaylord and Cadillac. The Telecommunications Act of 1996 changed the ownership rules, which allowed the company to expand. Under the guidance of Biederman's son, Ross, Midwestern Broadcasting grew from two AM and two FM stations into the number one radio group in the north consisting of six FM stations, and three AM stations.

From Happy Days: An Autobiography, copyright 1982 by Lester Biederman, edited by Nancy Niblack Baxter, Pioneer Study Center, Traverse City, Mich.

WTCM's Merlin Dumbrille ready to play a stack of hot wax in the 1970's (courtesy of Merlin Dumbrille)

First Radio Station Licenses:

WBBP Petoskey	AM 1250 1924	
WKBZ Ludington	AM 1500 1928	
WTCM Traverse City	AM 1400 1940	
WATT Cadillac	AM 1240 1946	
WKLA Ludington	AM 1450 1946	
WMBN Petoskey	AM 1340 1947	
WATC Gaylord	AM 900 1950	
WMTE Manistee	AM 1340 1951	

Broadcast Veterans

Merlin Dumbrille:
WTCM, Traverse City
If he doesn't already hold it, Dumbrille is working on the record for most consecutive

years at the same radio station. The Traverse City native started at his hometown station in 1951, and has been a fixture ever since. Dumbrille has been the host of the station's agriculture program, Farm and Orchard Time, since 1963.
The former Cherry Festival Prince got the radio bug as an eight year old watching the

WTCM radio tower go up in 1940. As a boy he was known for hanging around the station, and after meeting the owner was told that there would be a job waiting for him when he grew up. Dumbrille, at age 17, returned to take up the offer, and has been at the station ever since.

From 1963 to 1974 he pulled double duty, working at the radio station, and doing weather forecasts for TV 7 & 4.

Dave Fortin:
WPBN/WTOM TV 7 & 4, Traverse City

Dave Fortin is among the few, and may be the only television reporter to work for the same station for over 40 years. The Muskegon native started with WPBN TV 7&4 in 1963, after flirting with an acting career in New York. Fortin has outlived several different owners, and survived many house cleanings of the station's news staff. In summing up his approach to

the job he said, "When there was something that needed to be done, I always stepped forward, not backward."

During the early years of his career, Fortin was in the studio as a weatherman, but eventually made his mark as a reporter. He's interviewed visiting celebrities from Bob Hope to Johnny Cash, and covered disasters, politics, business, environmental and human-interest stories. In 1986 the U.S. Small Business Administration honored him for his "Upside" series, which profiled small industrial businesses in the region. He's also won awards for his reporting from the Michigan Farm Bureau and Northern Michigan Environmental Action Council.

Each Christmas Eve since the mid 80's the station's late newscast ends with "Santa Watch:" a Fortin creation featuring a sometime elaborate story ending with a radar sighting of reindeer and sleigh in flight over northern Michigan.

Bernie Schroeder:
WMTE, Manistee

WMTE's Bernie Schroeder started at the station in 1959, one year out of college, and

When they said film at eleven, they meant film .Aboard a Great Lakes freighter on the Detroit River (courtesy of Dave Fortin)

An exclusive interview with the man in black at the Traverse City Holiday Inn (courtesy ofDave Fortin)

Hmmmm... interesting sponsor. "May is National Tavern Month" TV 7&4's Dave Fortin (courtesy of Dave Fortin)

has been there ever since. The MSU grad became news director in 1965, and now wears two hats: morning host on AM 1340 WMTE and station news director.

On December 18, 1999 – his 40th anniversary at the station – Manistee declared it "Bernie Schroeder Day." In 2004 he was nominated for the Michigan Broadcasting Hall of Fame.

EARLY TV STATIONS

WWTV/WWTU TV 9 & 10
Cadillac/Sault Ste. Marie

Owner:
Heritage Broadcasting Co.

Founded by:
Spartan Corporation of Jackson, MI.

First broadcast:
WWTV, Channel 13 in Cadillac went on the air January 1, 1954. After fire destroyed the facilty in 1961, the station went on the air as Channel 9 on May 15, 1962. WWUP, Channel 10 in Sault Ste. Marie, signed on June 15, 1962.
Network affiliate:
CBS

Notes:
Much of the development of WWTV and WWUP came during the Fetzer years. Broadcast entrepreneur and former owner of the Detroit Tigers, John Fetzer owned the stations from 1958 to 79.

The WWTV tower is situated on Briar Hill in Harrietta, the highest point in the Lower Peninsula. The base of the 1,290 foot high broadcast tower is at 1,704 feet above sea level, making it one of the tallest structures in the Great Lakes region.

The WWUP tower near Sault Ste. Marie is 1,126 feet tall and stands at 1,881 feet above sea level.

Weekend anchor John McGowan has been with the station since 1972 when he started as a production assistant. His first broadcast was as sports director in 1977.

WPBN/WTOM TV 7 & 4
Traverse City/Cheboygan

Owner:
Raycom Media, Montgomery, AL

Founded by:
Les Biederman and William Kiker (Midwestern Broadcasting)
First broadcast:
WPBN, Channel 7, went on the air September 13, 1954. In the early days the station broadcast only three hours a day.

To expand the coverage area the owners built WTOM
Channel 4, Cheboygan, which went on the air May 16, 1959.

Network Affiliate:
NBC, since day one.

Famous faces of the past:
TV 7 & 4 maintained the tradition of developing local
entertainment programming and characters through the
1980's. Don Melvoin was probably the most famous person
in northern Michigan for the latter half of the 20th century.

He started at WPBN in the 1950's as Deputy Don, host of a
children's show. His career took him to Grand Rapid where
he was known as Fireman Freddie, and then it was off to
Hollywood where he picked up bit parts on shows like
"Marcus Welby M.D.," "Bonanza," and "Night Gallery."
In the 1980's he returned to TV 7 & 4 where he recreated
Deputy Don, hosted a scary movie show as Count Zappula,
and hosted his own talk show.

Melvoin's last appearance on TV 7 & 4 was during a
Halloween special in October of 1998. He died in 2002.

Veterans:
Dave Walker has been at the news anchor desk since 1983.
Dave Fortin has been a field reporter since 1964.

Television Call Letters:

WPBN   Paul Bunyan Network

WTOM   Top of Michigan

Radio: FM

Frequency	Call letters City of license	Format	What call letters stand for
88.1	WBLW, Gaylord	Religious	We Broadcast Living Words
88.5	WDQU, Mackinaw City	Contemporary Christian	The Dove
88.7	WIAA, Interlochen	Public	Interlochen Arts Academy
89.3	WTLI, Boyne City	Contemporary Christian	SMILE
89.9	WLJN, Traverse City	Christian	We're Lifting Jesus' Name
90.7	WNMC, Traverse City	College	Northwestern Michigan College
91.9	WOLW, Cadillac	Christian	
91.3	WJOG, Petoskey	Contemporary Christian	
91.5	WICA, Traverse City	Talk	Interlochen Center for the Arts
92.1	WOUF, Beulah	Country	
92.1	WVXH, Harrison	Variety	
92.9	WJZQ, Cadillac	Smooth Jazz	
93.5	WBCM, Boyne City	Country	Boyne City, Michigan
93.7	WKAD, Harrietta	Oldies	KAD=Cadillac
94.3	WFCX, Leland	Contemporary	The Fox
94.5	WLJZ, Mackinaw City	Modern Rock	The Zone
94.9	WKZC, Scottville	Country	Z 95
95.5	WJZJ, Glen Arbor	Modern Rock	The Zone
96.3	WLXT, Petoskey	Lite Contemporary	Lite 96
96.7	WLXV, Cadillac	Contemporary	
97.3	WDEE, Reed City	Oldies	
97.5	WKLT, Kalkaska	Rock	
97.7	WVXM, Manistee	Variety	

98.1	WGFN, Glen Arbor	Classic Rock	
98.5	WUPS, Houghton Lake	Contemporary the Hits (UPS_	We Deliver
98.9	WKLZ, Petoskey	Rock	
99.3	WBNZ, Frankfort	Contemporary	Benzie
100.1	WCUZ, Bear Lake	Contemporary	
100.3	WGRY, Grayling	Country	Grayling
100.7	WKVK, Honor	Contemporary	
100.9	WICV, East Jordan	Public	
101.1	WQON, Roscommon	Contemporary	
101.5	WMTE, Manistee	Oldies	Manistee
101.9	WLDR, Traverse City	Country	*Long Distance Radio
103.5	WTCM, Traverse City	Country	Traverse City, Michigan
103.9	WCMW, Harbor Springs	Public	
104.3	WRDS, Roscommon	Info-Religious	
104.9	WAIR, Lake City	Contemporary Christian	
105.1	WGFM, Cheboygan	Classic Rock	
105.9	WKHQ, Charlevoix	Contemporary	
106.7	WKPK, Gaylord	Contemporary	
107.1	WCKC, Cadillac	Classic Rock	
107.5	WCCW, Traverse City	Oldies	*Cherry Capital of the World
107.9	WCZW, Charlevoix	Oldies	

Radio: AM

Frequency	Call letters City of license	Format	What call letters stand for
580	WTCM, Traverse City	News-Talk	Traverse City, Michigan
750	WWKK, Petoskey	News-Talk	
1110	WJML, Petoskey	News-Talk	
1210	WLDR, Traverse City	Classic Country	*Long Distance Radio
1230	WGRY, Grayling	Standards	Grayling
1240	WATT, Cadillac		News-Talk
1270	WMKT, Charlevoix	News-Talk	*Market Radio (was a business format)
1310	WCCW, Traverse City	Sports-Talk	*Cherry Capital of the World
1340	WMTE, Manistee	News-Talk	Manistee

1370	WLJW, Cadillac		Religious
1400	WLJN, Traverse City	Religious	We're Lifting Jesus' Name
1450	WKLA, Ludington	News-Talk	
1500	WDEE, Reed City	News-Talk	

Michigan Talk Radio Network

Based in Charlevoix with studios overlooking Round Lake, the network was launched in January 2001 by former Detroit disc Jockey Dave Scott. The network broadcasts Michigan-themed talk shows via satellite to several small stations around the State.

Fibber McGee and Molly

One of the most popular radio programs of the 1940's and 50's, Fibber McGee and Molly, was created by Don Quinn, who grew up in Charlevoix. Quinn was also head writer for the show between 1935 and 1951. The program ran on NBC radio until 1959.

The setting was in the Midwestern home of the McGee family where friends and neighbors dropped in and out to discuss the events of the day. Fibber and Molly were played by Jim and Marian Jordan from Peoria, Illinois. In 1931, they met Quinn, then an unemployed cartoonist, and hired him to be their writer. Shortly there after he came up with the idea for Fibber McGee and Molly.

Leelanau Sports Broadcaster

Back in the 1930's Harry Heilman was the voice of the Detroit Tigers, but it wasn't unusual to hear some play-by-play from Raymond Schaub of Leelanau County. Schaub was the radio engineer for the Detroit Tiger games and sat alongside Heilman. When nature called, Heilman turned the microphone over to Schaub.

Raymond and his brother Alvin helped their father run the local Bell Telephone operation by setting poles and stringing wire. The boys earned radio licenses and started the first wireless radio station in northern Michigan by 1924. They weren't allowed to run entertainment, and could only receive limited signals.

Alvin became a radio operator aboard ships and traveled the world.

Raymond went into radio and television. He was the engineer for famous radio programs such as "The Lone Ranger" and "The Green Hornet," and helped the Detroit Tigers and Detroit Lions set up a statewide radio and television network.

SPORTS AND RECREATION

Hockeytown North

For Detroit Red Wing fans the season starts in September in Traverse City. Since 1997* the team has held training camp at Center Ice Arena, attracting thousands of fans over the four-day camp. Wing's fans were still on a high from the teams Stanley Cup victory when it was announced they were headed north. Tickets for all games and practices sold out immediately, with many fans camping in the ticket line overnight. Watching the players prepare for another run at the Cup was one thing, but many fans enjoyed running into their favorite Wing's after practice at local nightspots.

The team travels together by bus from Detroit to Traverse City, which management and players say is a good bonding experience to start the season. They also like the warm reception from fans that fill the house just to watch a morning workout and practice, and the pampering from a large platoon of volunteers.

The person most responsible for attracting the Wings to Traverse City is Pete Correia, a leader in a non-profit group that owns and operates Center Ice Arena and the Howe Arena, also located in

Traverse City.

Correia who played hockey at MSU and continues to play in a local adult league, says he was driven as a fan to bring the Wings to Traverse City. The idea came in the early 90's after meeting Newell Brown, the coach of the Wing's Adirondack team.

Correia planted a bug in Brown's ear, and continued to contact the Wings management through two administrations. In 1994 Bryan Murray, the Wing's GM and coach at the time, agreed to bring the team north for a mini-camp before the playoffs started, however he cancelled at the last minute.

The letters continued and Correia even sent promotional videos of the Traverse City area to the Wings organization until May of 1997 when Ken Holland called. The team's new GM said he was on his way up north to play some golf and talk it over. Correia guaranteed Holland that bringing the team to Traverse City for training camp would be a positive experience, and the new GM took a chance.

Correia, with his and Traverse City's reputation on the line, took no chances. He rounded up 600 volunteers,

Fans welcome the Wings to Traverse City, Hockeytown North (courtesy of I.C.E.)

Nick Lidstrom makes their day (courtesy of I.C.E.)

Red Wing Brendan Shanahan entertains (courtesy of I.C.E.)

Shanny and Drapes taking a break (courtesy of I.C.E.)

Training camp manager, Pete Correia with assistant coach Barry Smith and head coach, Dave Lewis, 2003 (courtesy I.C.E.)

Captain Steve Yzerman and teammate Brendan Shanahan ready for practice at Center Ice (courtesy of I.C.E.) far right

many who took a week off work. They did everything from making sure the players had clean uniforms every day to driving them between the hotel and arena. They handled security and visiting media.

Volunteers worked the concession stands, and behind the scenes, and were rewarded with what has become an annual tradition: having their photo taken on ice with the

team on the last day of camp. The community benefits as many hotel rooms are filled up by players, team officials, visiting media and out of town fans. During their stay, team members sign dozens of sweaters, sticks, pucks and posters that are used throughout the year as fundraising items by local non-profit groups. Proceeds for ticket sale and concessions benefit the non-profit group that owns and runs the arena.

In 1998 Traverse City hosted the first NHL Prospects Camp the week before the Wing's arrival. Eight NHL teams sent their top prospects for the tournament that was heavily

Darren McCarty signing an autograph (courtesy of I.C.E.)

attended by the league's top scouts. The prospect tournament has also become a September tradition at Center Ice Arena. Some of the players to emerge from those games include: Jiri Fischer, Henrik Zetterberg and Pavel Datsuk of the Red Wings, and Danny Heatley and Ilya Kovalchuk of the Atlanta Thrashers.

*Except 2004 when the season was cancelled when owners and players failed to negotiate a new contract.

Dan Majerle "Thunder Dan"

Born:
September 9, 1965
Traverse City, MI

Position:
Guard

Height:
6' 6"

Weight: 215

When the Phoenix Suns announced Dan Majerle as their first-round draft pick in 1988 some fans in the audience responded by booing. Dan who? It didn't take long for fans to learn how to pronounce his name (Marley), and they surely won't forget him. Known for his trademark hustle on the court and gentlemanly off court demeanor, "Thunder Dan" quickly became one of the most popular athletes in Phoenix.

His basketball career started at Traverse City High School where he led the team to winning seasons and a quarterfinal appearance in the Class A finals during his senior year. In the 1982-83 season he scored 926 points, third highest in Michigan high school basketball history. He moved on to Central Michigan University where he was a three-time Mid-American Conference player.

He was named to the U.S. Olympic basketball team in 1988 where he gained attention for his hustle and three-point shooting ability. The U.S. took home Bronze that year. In 1994, Majerle was a member of Dream Team 2 that won the World Championship.

Career highlights and stats:

Seasons:
14 (1988 – 2002)

Games:
955

Minutes:
30,209

Points:
10,925 (ranked 199th all time)

Points per game average:
11.4

Three pointers made:
1,360

Attempted:
3,798

• Ranked 19th all time for three pointers made in a season: 1999-2000

• Set NBA record for 192 three-pointers made in a season. 1993-94 (record stood for one year)

• Holds record for three-pointers made in a playoff

series with 17 during the 1992-93 Finals against Chicago.

- Three-time NBA All Star

- Played himself in 1995 film, "Forget Paris," starring Billy Crystal

- Played for the Suns from 1988-95. Was traded to Cleveland in 1995, where he spent one season. Traded to Miami where he played for five seasons before returning to Phoenix in 2001.

- Retired in 2002.

- Opened Majerle's Sports Grill in 1992. Located in oldest building in Phoenix.

Today:

Member of the Phoenix Suns broadcast team, providing color commentary during televised games. Continues to operate Majerle's Sports Grill.

Ludington's French Open Winners

French Open doubles champions, Luke and Murphy Jensen, hail from northern Michigan. In 1993, just six months into their pro careers, the brothers stunned the tennis world by winning the French Open doubles crown. Some writers referred to the colorful siblings as "the Beavis and Butthead of Tennis." The boy's rock star personas attracted an international following that continues to this day.

"Dual Hand Luke," the older of the two was born in Grayling, and Murphy was born in Ludington. They grew up playing tennis in East Grand Rapids, and both attended University of Southern California. Both brothers, now based in Atlanta, are dedicated to promoting the sport of tennis and invest a lot of time working with youth groups.

Luke Jensen broadcasts on ESPN and network television during tennis events, and has written for *USA Today*. The brothers also are in demand on the dinner-speaking circuit.

HIGH SCHOOL RECORDS

High School Football – State Champions

Year	School	Score	Opponent	Class
1978	Traverse City	20-14	N. Farmington	A
1985	Traverse City	29-3	Troy	A
1988	Traverse City	24-14	Det. Catholic Central	A
1990	Marion	33-7	Waterford Our Lady of the Lakes	DD
1990	Frankfort	33-6	Lawrence	D
1991	Frankfort	21-7	Portland St. Patrick	D
1992	TC St. Francis	28-21 (OT)	Harper Woods Bishop Gallagher	C
1994	Glen Lake	20-10	Waterford Our Lady of the Lakes	DD
1999	TC St. Francis	23-6	Gobles	Div. 7
2003	TC St. Francis	28-14	Hudson	Div. 7

Coaching victories – career

234   Larry Sellers, Traverse City St. Francis (1973-2000 and 2002)

16th best career record in state

State record is 332 victories over 43 years by Al Fracassa of Birmingham Brother Rice

Most all-time victories - team

550   Traverse City Central (1896-2004) (550-284-50), (fourth highest in State)

Touchdowns scored in a quarter

*5   Marcus Ewing, Johannesburg-Lewiston vs. Bellaire (1st Qtr.) (9/17/99) (tied for State record)

Most extra points in a game

11   Matt Collins, Gaylord St. Mary 77, Manistee Catholic Central 6
                  (9/3/99) (Modern day record. State record of 24 was set in 1912.)

Most extra points in a season

*72   Matt Collins, Gaylord St. Mary (72 of 87) (1999)

Most extra points – career

*164   Matt Collins, Gaylord St. Mary (164 of 200) (1997-00)

Most rushing yards - game

*529   Dwain Koscielniak, Gaylord St. Mary (35 carries) (1990)

Most touchdown passes – game

*7   Craig Ream, Indian River Inland Lakes vs. East Jordan (10/12/73)
                  (tied with two others)

Longest punt return-yards

96   Kevin Tarras, Traverse City Central vs. Cadillac (10/1/99)
                  (tied for 2nd statewide)

Most interceptions - season

*18   Trent Mulder, McBain (14 games) (2001)

Most interceptions – career

*26   Kyle Klein, Frankfort (1990-92)

*State record

High School Boy's Basketball State Champions

Year	School	Score	Opponent	Class
1926	Michigamme	27-15	Alpena St. Bernard	D
1927	Reed City	18-5	Shelby	C
1929	Harbor Springs	25-20 (OT)	Flint St. Michael	C
1940	Traverse City	26-23	Detroit St. Theresa	B
1942	Leland	18-13	Whitehall	D
1946	Manton	34-33	Saginaw SS Peter & Paul	C
1959	Maple City Glen Lake	66-54	Baldwin	D
1977	Maple City Glen Lake	70-68	Detroit East Catholic	D
1980	Reed City	71-58	Grand Rapids S. Christian	C
1987	McBain NMC	56-46	Gaylord St. Mary	D
1988	Northport	80-78	Beal City	D
2002	McBain	57-48	Kalamazoo Christian	C

Northern Michigan individual records

Most points in a game: 84 (3rd highest in State)	Anton Phillips, 2/27/89 for Glen Arbor against Freesoil
Most points-season: 926 (3rd highest in State)	Dan Majerle, 1982/83 for Traverse City
Most points-career: 2,449 (5th highest in State)	Matt Stuck, 1989-92, for Manton
Most three-point field goals: 97 (3rd highest in State)	Nate Meyers, 1996-97 for Benzie Central

Most free throws made-game: 23 (tied for 2nd in State)	Ken Fitzek, 2/11/83 for Gaylord St. Mary (Former TV 7 & 4 Weatherman, Terry Camp with 25 for Ubly in 1980 holds first place)
Most free throws made-season: 194 (3rd highest in State)	Adam Kerfoot, 2002-03 for Gaylord St. Mary
Rebounds-season: 392 (2nd highest in State)	Matt Stuck, 1989-90 for Manton
Rebounds-career: 1,287 (2nd highest in State)	Matt Stuck, 1988-92 for Manton

Team records

Most victories-season: 28 (#1 in State)	Leland, 1941-42 and Reed City, 1979-80
Most points-game: 171	Glen Arbor vs. Freesoil (171-94) 2/17/89

SOCCER CHAMPIONSHIPS – BOYS

Year	School	Opponent	Class
1986	Northport	Grosse Pt. Woods University Liggett	D
1995	Petoskey	Macomb Lutheran North	B
1997	Elk Rapids	Riverview Gabriel Richard	Div. 4
1998	Elk Rapids	Muskegon W. Michigan Christian	Div. 4
2001	Ludington	Parchment	Div. 3

BOYS SKI CHAMPIONSHIPS

Year	School	Runner-up	Class
1975	Traverse City	Houghton	Open
1976	Traverse City	Okemos	Open

1978	Cadillac	Petoskey	Open
1979	Traverse City	Kingsford	Open
1980	Cadillac	Okemos	Open
1982	Petoskey	Cadillac	Open
1983	Traverse City	Petoskey	Open
1984	Petoskey	Traverse City	Open
1985	Traverse City	Petoskey	Open
1986	Traverse City	Kingsford	Open
1987	Petoskey	Traverse City	Open
1988	Traverse City	Birmingham Brother Rice	Open
1989	Traverse City	Petoskey	Open
1990	Traverse City	Petoskey	Open
1991	Traverse City	Petoskey	Open
1992	Traverse City	Glen Arbor - The Leelanau School	Open
1993	Traverse City	Marquette	Open
1994	Traverse City	Harbor Springs	Open
1995	Traverse City	Harbor Springs	Open
1996	Harbor Springs	Iron Mountain	B-C-D
1998	Petoskey	E. Grand Rapids	B-C-D
1998	Traverse City Central	Marquette	A
1999	Traverse City Central	Marquette	A
2000	Petoskey	Maple City/ Glen Lake	B-C-D
2001	Petoskey	Charlevoix	B-C-D
2002	Petoskey	Charlevoix	B-C-D
2003	Harbor Springs	TC St. Francis	B-C-D
2004	Maple City/ Glen Lake	Harbor Springs	B-C-D
2004	Petoskey	Marquette	A
2005	Petoskey	Marquette	A
2005	Harbor Springs	Maple City/ Glen Lake	B-C-D

BOYS GOLF CHAMPIONSHIPS

Year	School	Opponent	Class
1953	Petoskey St. Francis	Comstock Park	C-D
1975	Manistee Catholic Central	Mt. Pleasant Sacred Heart	D
1996	Traverse City	Grand Blanc	A
1999	Traverse City Christian	North Muskegon	Div. 4

2000	Suttons Bay	Ann Arbor Greenhills	Div. 4
2001	Suttons Bay	Ann Arbor Greenhills	Div. 4
2004	TC. St. Francis	Suttons Bay	Div. 4

GIRLS BASKETBALL CHAMPIONSHIPS

Year	School	Score	Opponent	Class
1976	Lake City	58-48	Perkins	D
1978	Maple City Glen Lake	52-32	Portland St. Pat.	D
1980	Leland	65-36	Ashley	D
1981	Leland	50-33	Ann Arbor Gabriel Richard	D
1982	Leland	54-41	Portland St. Pat	D
1982	Manistee	40-29	Fenton	B
1984	McBain	48-43	Ottawa Lake Whiteford	D

Most points - season

| *846 | Stephanie Hass, Harbor Springs Harbor Light Christian (22 games/38.5 points per game) (2001) |
| 812 | Julie Polakowski, Leland (28/29.0) (1981) (tied for 2nd in the state) |

Most points - career

| *2,732 | Stephanie Hass, Harbor Springs Harbor Light Christian (87/31.4 points per game) (1998-01) |
| | Her 31.4 per game average over 87 games (1998-01) is now tops among career per-game scoring averages |

Rebounds – season

| *417 | Liz Shimek, Maple City Glen Lake (1999) |
| *417 | Liz Shimek, Maple City Glen Lake (2000) |

Rebounds – career

*1,533	Liz Shimek, Maple City Glen Lake (1998-01)

Blocked shots – game

*22	Mandy Czapek, Grayling vs. Roscommon (8/27/03)

Three point field goals attempted –season

*684	Manistee (190 made) (1994)

Three point field goals made – season

*190	Manistee (190 of 684) (1994)

Most career victories – coach

443	Rick Guild, Johannesburg-Lewiston (1975-00, 443-137) (11th highest in State)

GIRLS VOLLEYBALL CHAMPIONSHIPS

Year	School	Opponent	Score	Class
2002	Leland	Battle Creek St. Philip	15-6, 6-15, 15-12	D

Prior to 2000 there were separate titles for the Upper and Lower Peninsulas.

Lower Peninsula champions

Year	School	Opponent	Score	Class
1978	Leland	Ann Arbor Greenhills	15-11,15-8	D
1980	Leland	North Adams	15-4, 15-13	D

Kills – season

934	Kristie Price, Reed City (1999-00) (2nd highest in State)

Kills – career

2,253	Kristie Price, Reed City (1997-00) (2nd highest in State)

Blocks – season

245	Kristie Price, Reed City (1998-99) (2nd highest in State)

GIRLS SKIING CHAMPIONSHIPS

Year	School	Runner-Up	Class
1975	Traverse City	Cadillac	Open
1976	Traverse City	Cadillac	Open
1977	Cadillac	Houghton	Open
1978	Cadillac	Iron Mountain	Open
1979	Iron Mountain	Marquette	Open
1980	Petoskey	Cadillac	Open
1981	Petoskey	Traverse City	Open
1982	Petoskey	Cadillac	Open
1983	Cadillac	Traverse City	Open
1984	Petoskey	Cadillac	Open
1985	Traverse City	Cadillac	Open
1986	Traverse City	Cadillac	Open
1987	Harbor Springs	Traverse City	Open
1988	Harbor Springs	Charlevoix	Open
1989	Traverse City	Cadillac	Open
1990	Cadillac	Traverse City	Open
1991	Petoskey	Harbor Springs	Open
1992	Petoskey	Traverse City	Open
1993	Petoskey	Traverse City	Open
1994	Petoskey	Traverse City	Open
1995	Traverse City Central	Petoskey	Open
1996	Traverse City	Cadillac	A
1996	Petoskey	Maple City Glen Lake	B-C-D
1997	Traverse City	Marquette	A
1997	Petoskey	Maple City Glen Lake	B-C-D
1998	Traverse City Central	Marquette	A
1998	Maple City Glen Lake	Ironwood	B-C-D
1999	Maple City Glen Lake	Manistee	B-C-D
2000	Harbor Springs	Petoskey	B-C-D
2001	Harbor Springs	Houghton	B-C-D
2002	Harbor Springs	Houghton	B-C-D
2003	Harbor Springs	BH Cranbrood Kingswood	B-C-D
2005	Traverse City Central	Marquette	A
2005	Traverse City St. Francis	Houghton	B-C-D

Slalom – Two-time MHSAA Champions
Libby Kutcipal, Petoskey (1992 & 1994)
Mackenzie Bickel, Traverse City Central; Traverse City West (1998 & 2000)
(and two others)

Giant Slalom – Two time MHSAA Champions
Anna Estelle, Gaylord (1991-92) (and one other)

GOLF

Walter Hagen

Professional golf pioneer: 1892 – 1969. Hagen won 2 U.S. Opens, 4 British Opens, 5 PGA Championships and was a 6-time captain of the U.S. Ryder Cup team.

Connection to northern Michigan: Retired to 20-acre estate on Long Lake near Traverse City in 1954.

"Sir Walter" was a giant figure in professional golf: The first American to earn a full time living playing the game, and the first professional athlete to earn one million dollars. His taste for fine clothes, outgoing manner, and raw talent gained him admittance to the country club set. Before Hagen, golfers were barred from the clubhouse.

In Traverse City he was a familiar site at Lil Bo's Bar and the Park Place Lounge where he would sit for hours drinking and playing cards. A retired State trooper recalls a late night when he was asked to pick up a special package at the Park Place. The package was Walter Hagen in need of a ride home.

Walter Hagen tees off

That trooper remembers Hagen enjoyed driving golf balls from his backyard into Long Lake. One early morning the trooper pointed out to "The Haig" that he was driving with a putter. Hagen realized indeed he was driving with a putter, and tossed it to the trooper saying, "This has won a lot of tournaments for me, why don't you keep it." The putter, now worth thousands of dollars, hangs over the mantel of a friend of the trooper who received it in a trade.

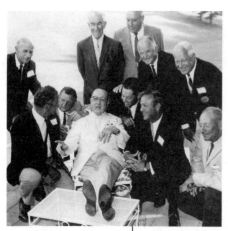

Walter Hagen at the Traverse City Country Club

Hagen was honored at a testimonial dinner in 1967 at the Traverse City Golf and Country Club. Among the professional golfers there to praise Hagen was Arnold Palmer, who said one of his biggest thrills came after winning the British Open at Troon with a course record: " Walter Hagen phoned to congratulate me from Traverse City. I didn't even know The Haig knew I was alive until then."

Today, memories of Hagen's contributions to the game of golf and and his retirement years in Traverse City are kept alive with an annual tournament at Elmbrook Golf Course. "The Haig," in which all golfers dress in period clothing and use hickory clubs, is a fundraiser for the Grand Traverse Heritage Center.

Tom Watson

Winner of 5 British Opens, 2 Masters and a U.S. Open. 4-time Ryder Cup member and captain of the 1993 team. 6-time PGA Player of the Year. Now playing on the Senior Tour.

Connection to northern Michigan: Spent boyhood summers playing at the Belvedere Golf Club in Charlevoix and Walloon Lake Country Club.

Watson started playing golf at an early age, not long after his first summer at the family cottage on Walloon Lake when he was five years old. When he was 14 he beat his father in the Walloon Lake Club championship.

In a 1999 interview with Jack Berry for *Michigan Golfer Magazine* Watson remembered his summers up north: "I love that country. It has a wonderful feel and the old Hemingway influence. Charlevoix with the petunias lining the streets. It's such a pleasant place to be. It makes you feel wonderful. Eating Shrimp at the Argonne, eating planked whitefish at Juilleret's, the Damsite Inn for fried chicken. And fudge in Charlevoix and Petoskey."

The last time Watson played Belvedere was in 2004 when he played with his father. At the 157-yard 14th he witnessed a hole-in-one by 16-year old Scott Kury of Portage. Kury said it was "the thrill of my life" when Watson asked to have his picture taken with him.

Rick Smith

Golf instructor to Phil Mickelson and other PGA stars, award-winning golf course designer, television host.

Connection to northern Michigan: Part owner and managing partner of Treetops Resort in Gaylord, which includes a Rick Smith Golf Academy. Designed the Signature, Treetops, and Tradition courses at Treetops and Arcadia Bluffs in Manistee County.

Governor John Engler named Rick Smith, Michigan's "Golf Ambassador."

Smith has been recognized for his ability to teach golfers at every level. Two-time U.S. Open Champion Lee Janzen says, "Rick is the best teacher in the world. I wouldn't see anyone else. He has a remarkable ability to adapt to each of his students." Other pro's who have called on Smith for help include: Phil Mickelson, Greg Norman, Rocco Mediate, Jack Nicklaus and Vijay Singh. He's been ranked as one of the top five golf instructors in the world by *Golf Digest* in 2000 thru 2003.

Smith is responsible for attracting and hosting the annual Par-3 Shootout at the Threetops course in Gaylord. The event attracts some of the biggest names in golf and is televised on ESPN. Smith hosted the Golf Channel reality show, "The BIG Break," which was shot at Treetops Resort in Gaylord. He's been the host of the Rick Smith Signature series seen on ESPN, Fox Sports Net and TSN (Canada). He's also been a commentator for NBC and ESPN, and hosted "Inside the PGA Tour".

He has written for several golf magazines and in 1998 authored *How to Find Your Perfect Golf Swing* (Broadway Books), considered one of the top instruction books in the industry.

Tom Doak

One of the leading golf course architects in the world.

Connection to northern Michigan: His company, Renaissance Golf Design, Inc., and the first course he designed, High Pointe Golf Club, are in Traverse City.

Doak considers High Pointe, which he designed when he was 26, his "home office." It's been named one of the Top Ten courses built in the U.S. between 1989 and 1999 by *Links Magazine*.

Doak has had a reputation for being candid since his entry into the world of professional golf design. His unconstrained criticism of some courses designed by respected architects in, *"The Confidential Guide to Golf Courses"* (Sleeping Bear Press), caused some controversy when it was published in 1996.

He's been called a radical and a traditionalist. He subscribes to the minimalist philosophy of design, in which the bulldozer is a last resort. He lists as heroes Alister MacKenzie (Augusta National, Crystal Downs), and Pete Dye, whom he credits as a mentor.

Doak started playing golf at 14 near his home in Connecticut. He played some of the countries finest courses by the time he was 15, then chose to study landscape architecture at Cornell. During college he caddied at St. Andrews and studied the great golf courses of the British Isles.

Four of Doak's 18 designs are ranked in the Top 100, including Pacific Dunes Golf Club at Bandon, Oregon, named the second best course in the country built since 1960 by *Golf Week* magazine.

As of early 2005 Doak has just finished designing courses in New Zealand and Australia, and has six courses under construction, including Sebonack Golf Club in Southampton, New York, in which he is paired up with Jack Nicklaus.

Sebonack is located between two of the best courses in the country, Shinnecock Hills and the National Golf Links of America.

Mike DeVries

Golf course architect.

Northern Michigan connection: DeVries Designs, Inc. is based in Traverse City, and his most noted design to date, the Kingsley Club, lies just a few miles to the south.

Devries was an apprentice of Tom Doak and an on-site design co-coordinator with Tom Fazio before striking out on his own. He earned a Masters in landscape architecture from the University of Michigan in 1994.

Devries was exposed to good design from the start. At age 8 he began following his grandfather around the Alister MacKenzie's Crystal Downs in Frankfort. As a teen he worked in Crystal Downs pro shop and on the grounds crew where he developed his passion for design and the work of Dr. Alister MacKenzie.

His designs, all in Michigan, include, Pilgrim's Run Golf Club in Pierson (Fourth "Best New Affordable" golf course in America, 1999, *Golf Digest*), Diamond Springs in

Hamilton, the critically acclaimed Greywalls at the Marquette Golf Club, and the Kingsley Club in Kingsley which is ranked 22nd on *Golfweek* magazine's list of America's Best Modern Golf Courses (post 1960).

As of early 2005 DeVries is designing Crosswinds, a links-style course near Muskegon, and the Mines in Grand Rapids. He has also been chosen to restore the Meadow Club – Alister MacKenzie's first course in North America – in Fairfax, California. He is also working on restoration and improvements at St. Charles in Winnipeg, Manitoba and Walnut Hills in East Lansing.

EARLY GOLF

The first golf course in northern Michigan was probably the now defunct Roaring Brook Course in Harbor Springs, which saw its first action as early as 1894. Two years later Harbor Point and Wequetonsing Golf Club (private) opened, also in Harbor Springs. Both remain open today.

The oldest nine-hole course is Wawashkamo Golf Club (semi-private), which opened in 1898 on Mackinac Island.

Chronology of Existing Northern Michigan Golf Courses

1896	Harbor Point	Harbor Springs
	Wequetonsing Golf Club	Harbor Springs
	Charlevoix Country Club	Charelvoix
1898	Wawashkamo Golf Club	Mackinac Island
1901	Grand Hotel Golf Course	Mackinac Island
	Manistee Golf and Country Club	Manistee
1910	Cadillac Country Club	Cadillac
1915	Traverse City Golf & Country Club	Traverse City
	Petoskey Bay View Country Club	Petoskey
1918	Leland Country Club	Leland
1922	Cheboygan Golf & Country Club	Cheboygan
1923	Elk Rapids Golf Club	Elk Rapids
	Grayling Country Club	Grayling
	Ye Nyne Old Holes	East Jordan
1924	Ye Olde Country Club	Roscommon

Chronology of Existing Northern Michigan Golf Courses

1926	Elk Rapids Golf Course	Elk Rapids
1927	Bel-Aire Golf Club	Bellaire
	Belvedere Golf Club	Charlevoix
	Crystal Downs Country Club (original front 9)	Frankfort
	Frankfort Golf Course	Frankfort
1929	Crystal Downs Country Club (new front)	
1933	Crystal Downs Country Club (back 9)	Frankfort
1934	Sunnybrook Golf Course	Houghton Lake
1949	Gaylord Country Club	Gaylord
1951	Garland	Lewiston
	Spruce Course – McGuire's	Cadillac
1957	Hidden Valley Classic	Gaylord
1959	Beaver Island Golf Club	Beaver Island
	Norway – McGuire's	Cadillac
1962	Burning Oak Golf Club	Roscommon
1964	Marquette Trails Country Club	Baldwin
	Wilderness Golf Club	Carp Lake
1965	Interlochen Golf Club	Interlochen
	Shanty Creek Golf Club	Bellaire
1966	Reed City Golf Club	Reed City
	Sugar Loaf Resort	Cedar
	White Deer Country Club	Prudenville
1967	Devils Knob Golf Club	Harrison
1968	Heather – Boyne Highlands	Harbor Springs
1969	Missaukee Golf Club	Lake City
1970	Alpine – Boyne Mountain	Boyne Falls
	Crystal Lake Golf Club	Beulah
	Wilderness Valley	Gaylord
1971	Antrim Dells Golf Club	Ellsworth
	Lakes of the North	Mancelona

Chronology of Existing Northern Michigan Golf Courses

1972	Alpine – Boyne Mountain	Boyne Falls
	Birch Point Golf Club	St. Helen
	Creek and Meadows	Thompsonville
	Crystal Mt.	
1974	Birchwood Farms Golf & Country Club	Harbor Springs
1975	Moor – Boyne Highlands	Harbor Springs
1978	Sugar Springs	Baldwin
1979	Spruce Run – Grand Traverse Resort	Traverse City
1980	Cedar Hills Golf Club	Traverse City
1982	Mitchell Creek Golf Club	Traverse City
	Tamaracks Golf Club	Harrison
1983	Dunes Golf Club	Empire
1984	The Bear – Grand Traverse Resort	Traverse City
	Monument – Boyne Mountain	Boyne Falls
1986	A-Ga-Ming	Kewadin
	Legend – Shanty Creek	Bellaire
1987	Swampfire – Garland	Lewiston
	Treetops	Gaylord
1988	Otsego Club	Gaylord
1989	Briar Downs	Mesick
	Donald Ross Memorial – Boyne	Harbor Springs
	High Pointe Golf Club	Williamsburg
1990	Fox Run Country Club	Grayling
	Matheson Greens Golf Club	Northport
	Monarch – Garland	Lewiston
	Reflections – Garland	Lewiston
1991	Boyne Highlands	Harbor Springs
	Dunmaglas Golf Club	Charlevoix

Chronology of Existing Northern Michigan Golf Courses

	Little Traverse Bay Golf Club	Harbor Springs
	Veronica Valley	Lake Leelanau
1992	Black Forest	Gaylord
	Chestnut Hills Golf Club	Bear Lake
	Crooked Tree	Petoskey
	Creek Course – Crystal Mountain	Thompsonville
	Eagle Glen	Farwell
	Fox Run	Grayling
	Firefly Golf Links (2nd nine)	Clare
	Little Traverse Bay	Petoskey
	Marsh Ridge Golf Course	Gaylord
	Natural	Gaylord
	Pinecroft	Benzonia
1993	Centennial Farm Golf Club	Bellaire
	Charlevoix Country Club	Charlevoix
	Chestnut Hills	Frankfort
	Grandview	Kalkaska
	Mistwood	Lake Ann
1994	Black Bear Golf Club	Vanderbilt
	Chestnut Valley Golf Club	Harbor Springs
	Manistee National	Manistee
	Quest	Houghton Lake
	Rose	Cadillac
	Snow Snake	Harrison
1995	Bay Meadows	Traverse City
	Briar Downs	Mesick
	Arthur Hills Course – Boyne	Harbor Springs
	Caberfae Peaks Course	Cadillac
	Fountains – Garland	Lewiston
1996	Bay Harbor Golf Club	Petoskey
	Ridge Course – Crystal Mountain	Thompsonville
	Hidden River Golf and Casting	Brutus
1997	Emerald Vale	Manton
	Heathlands	Onekema
	Mackinaw Club	Mackinaw City
1998	The Crown	Traverse City
	King's Challenge	Cedar

Chronology of Existing Northern Michigan Golf Courses

	Timber Wolf Golf Club	Kalkaska
	Treetops Tradition	Gaylord
1999	Leelanau Club	Suttons Bay
2000	Black Lake Golf Club	Onaway
	Cutters Ridge	Manistee

Source: www.michigangolfer.com, Art McCafferty

Golf Courses by County

Antrim County

Course	Town	Yards
A-Ga-Ming	Kewadin	6,693
Antrim Dells	Ellsworth	6,606
Bellaire Golf Club	Bellaire	6,012
Elk Rapids Golf Course	Elk Rapids	6,086
Deer Run (Lakes ofthe North)	Mancelona	6,986
Schuss Mountain Golf Club	Bellaire	6,922
Cedar River Golf Club	Bellaire	6,989
Summit Golf Club	Bellaire	6,559
The Legend	Bellaire	6,764
Windmill Farm	Mancelona	995 (9-hole)
The Chief	Bellaire	6,101
Hawk's Eye Golf Club	Bellaire	7,011
The Farm Golf Club	Bellaire	3,049 (9-hole)

Benzie County

Champion Hill	Honor	6,887
Crystal Downs	Frankfort	6,518
Crystal Lake Golf Club	Beulah	6,400
Betsie Valley (Crystal Mt.)	Thompsonville	6,357
Mountain Ridge (Crystal Mt.)	Thompsonville	7,007
Frankfort Golf Course	Frankfort	2,446 (9-hole)
Mistwood Golf Course	Lake Ann	6,695
Pinecroft Golf Plantation	Benzonia	6,447

Charlevoix County

Beaver Island Golf Course	Beaver Island	3,260 (9-hole)
Belvedere Golf Club	Charlevoix	6,715
Alpine (Boyne Mt.)	Boyne Falls	7,045
The Monument (Boyne Mt.)	Boyne Falls	7,086
Charlevoix Country Club	Charlevoix	6,600
City of Charlevoix Golf Course	Charlevoix	3,001 (9-hole)
Dunmaglas Golf Course	Charlevoix	6,897
Scotland's Yard Golf	Walloon Lake	2,555 (9-hole)
Springbrook Golf Course	Walloon Lake	6,250
Ye Nyne Olde Holles Golf Club	East Jordan	2,970 (9-hole)
Mallard Golf Club	East Jordan	5,966

Clare County

Snow Snake Ski and Golf	Harrison	6,134
Devil's Knob Golf Course	Harrison	2,995 (9-hole)
Eagle Glen	Farwell	6,602
Tamaracks Golf Course	Harrison	5,760
Firefly Golf Links	Clare	5,929

Crawford County

Fox Run Country Club	Grayling	6,293
Forest Dunes	Grayling	NA
Hawk Ridge	Grayling	NA
Grayling Country Club	Grayling	5,726

Emmet County

The Links (Bay Harbor)	Petoskey	3,432
The Quarry (Bay Harbor)	Petoskey	3,348
The Preserve (Bay Harbor)	Petoskey	3,378
Birchwood Farms	Harbor Springs	
The Heather (Boyne Highlands)	Harbor Springs	6,890
The Hills (Boyne Highlands)	Harbor Springs	7,312
Donald Ross Memorial (Boyne Highlands)	Harbor Springs	6,814
The Moor (Boyne Highlands)	Harbor Springs	7,179
Walloon Lake Country Club	Petoskey	6,484
Chestnut Valley Golf Club	Harbor Springs	6,800
Crooked Tree Golf Club	Petoskey	6,584
Harbor Point Golf Course	Harbor Springs	6,003
Hidden River Golf & Casting Club	Brutus	7,101
Little Traverse Bay Golf Club	Harbor Springs	6,895

Petoskey Bay View Country Club	Petoskey	6,249
The Mackinaw Club	Mackinaw City	6,807
The Narrows (Maple Ridge)	Brutus	6,004
The Executive (Maple Ridge)	Brutus	3,100 (9-hole)
Wequetonsing Golf Club	Harbor Springs	6,150
Wilderness Golf Course	Carp Lake	2,760 (9-hole)

Grand Traverse County

Bay Meadows Golf Course	Traverse City	2,099 (9-hole)
Cedar Hills Golf Course (CLOSED 2005)	Traverse City	2,981
Traverse City Golf & Country Club	Traverse City	6,330
The Crown Golf Club	Traverse City	6,723
Elmbrook Golf Course	Traverse City	6,131
Spruce Run (G.T. Resort)	Acme	6,700
The Bear (G.T. Resort)	Acme	7,065
The Wolverine (G.T. Resort)	Acme	7,065
High Pointe Golf Club	Acme	6,890
Interlochen Golf Course	Interlochen	6,445
Mitchell Creek Golf Course (CLOSED 2005)	Traverse City	3,253 (9-hole)
Kingsley Club	Kingsley	6,911
Lochenheath Golf Club	Williamsburg	7,000

Kalkaska County

Grandview Golf Course	Kalkaska	6,628
Timber Wolf Golf Club	Kalkaska	6,451
Twin Birch Golf Course	Kalkaska	6,133

Lake County

Marquette Trails Country Club	Baldwin	5,847
Redfoot Hills Golf Course	Luther	1,700 (9-hole)

Leelanau County

Dunes Golf Club	Empire	5,730
King's Challenge Golf Club	Cedar	6,593
Leelanau Club at Bahle Farms	Suttons Bay	6,770
Leland Country Club	Leland	5,867
Northport Point	Northport	N/A (9-hole)
Sleeping Bear Golf Club	Leland	6,813
Veronica Valley (Closed 2005)	Lake Leelanau	3,203 (9-hole)

Manistee County

Arcadia Bluffs Golf Club	Arcadia	7,300
Bear Lake County Highlands	Bear Lake	6,492
Chestnut Hills Golf Course	Bear Lake	3,500 (9-hole)
Cutter's Ridge (Manistee Nat'l)	Manistee	6,707
Canthooke (Manistee Nat'l)	Manistee	6,619
Fawn Crest Golf Course	Wellston	2,100 (9-hole)
Fox Hills Golf Course	Manistee	2,340 (9-hole)
Heathlands of Onekema	Onekema	6,569
Manistee Golf and Country Club	Manistee	6,031

Mason County

Epworth Heights Golf Course	Ludington	1,967 (9-hole)

Lakeside Links Golf Course (Play combination of any two 9-hole courses)

Lakeside Links - East Course	Ludington	2,884 (9-hole)
Lakeside Links - South Course	Ludington	3,556 (9-hole)
Lakeside Links – West Course	Ludington	2,882 (9-hole)
Hemlock Golf Club	Ludington	4,800
Lincoln Hills Golf Club	Ludington	6,168

Missaukee County

Missaukee Golf Course	Lake City	5,756

Osceola County

Tustin Trails Golf Club	Tustin	5,624
Spring Valley Golf Course	Hersey	6,439
Birch Valley Golf Course	Sears	2,405 (9-hole)
The Rose Golf Club	Leroy	5,854

Otsego County

Gaylord Country Club	Gaylord	6,452
Black Bear Golf Club	Vanderbilt	6,504
Green Trees Golf	Gaylord	3,043 (9-hole)
Black Forest (Wilderness Valley)	Gaylord	7,044
Wilderness Valley Course	Gaylord	6,495
Marsh Ridge Golf Club	Gaylord	6,141
Michaywe Lake Course	Gaylord	6,310
Michaywe Pines Course	Gaylord	6,835
Otsego Club - The Loon	Gaylord	6,701
Otsego Club-The Classic	Gaylord	6,348

Otsego Club-The Tribute	Gaylord	7,347
Beaver Creek-The Natural	Gaylord	6,355
Treetops-Tradition	Gaylord	6,467
Treetops-Masterpiece	Gaylord	7,060
Treetops-Premier	Gaylord	6,832
Treetops-Signature	Gaylord	6,653
Treetops-Threetops	Gaylord	1,400 (9-hole)
Elk Ridge	Atlanta	7,072
Black Lake Golf Club	Onaway	7,046
Little Course-Black Lake	Onaway	773 (9-hole beginner)
Garland-Fountains Course	Lewiston	6,800
Garland-Swampfire Course	Lewiston	6,854
Garland-Monarch Course	Lewsiton	7,188
Garland-Reflections Course	Lewiston	6,407
Indian River Golf Club	Cheboygan	6,692

Roscommon County

Birch Point Golf Club	St. Helen	3,201 (9-hole)
Pine View Highlands	Houghton Lake	6,100
White Deer County Club	Prudenville	6,322
Burning Oak Country Club	Higgins Lake	6,229
The Quest at Houghton Lake	Houghton Lake	6,802
Ye Olde Country Club	Roscommon	3,003 (9-hole)
Forest Dunes	Roscommon	7,104

Wexford County

Briar at Mesick	Mesick	5,817
Bunker Hill Golf Course	Cadillac	4,592 (9-hole)
Caberfae Peaks Course	Cadillac	6,682
Cadillac Country Club	Cadillac	6,017
El Dorado	Cadillac	6,836
Emerald Vale Golf Club	Manton	6,785
Lakewood on the Green	Cadillac	2,975 (9-hole)
McGuire's Resort-The Spruce	Cadillac	6,439
McGuire's Resort-The Norway	Cadillac	2,792 (9-hole)
Wedgewood Club	Cadillac	6,047

18 hole golf courses (17 county area) 113   9 hole golf courses (17 county area) 30

GOLF EVENTS

Par 3 Shootout at Threetops

Every June since 1999 four of the top golfers in the world take a break from the PGA Tour to play a relaxed, good-natured round on what some have called the best Par 3 course in the world. The Par 3 Shootout at Rick Smith's Threetops course in Gaylord may be a relaxed affair, but the stakes are high. A hole-in-one is worth a million dollars, and each hole is worth up to $30 thousand.

Each hole is worth $20 thousand plus a $10 thousand bonus for closest to the hole. To claim the money a player has to validate by winning or tying the next hole. If there isn't a winner, the money carries over to the next hole. Since 1999 only Lee Trevino has won the million dollar hole-in-one bonus by acing the 138-yard 7th hole in 2001.

The event draws a large, appreciative gallery, and a nation-wide television audience, as it is tape delayed and broadcast at night on ESPN.

Par 3 Shootout Fields

1999	2000	2001
Lee Janzen	**Ray Floyd**	**Lee Trevino**
Jack Nichols	Hale Irwin	Paul Azinger
Phil Mickelson	Lee Janzen	Phil Mickelson
Ray Floyd	Phil Mckelson	Ray Floyd

2002	2003	2004
Fred Couples	**Fuzzy Zoeller**	**Fred Couples**
Phil Mickelson	Phil Mickelson	Phil Mickelson
Lee Trevino	Lee Trevino	Lee Trevino
Arnold Palmer	Fred Couples	Fuzzy Zoeller

USA Today *included Threetops with Pebble Beach, Pinehurst, Sawgrass and Kiawah Island in its list of Ten Great Places for Dad to Golf His Day Away (Father's Day).*

LONGEST NON-STOP CANOE RACE IN NORTH AMERICA

The Weyherhaeuser AuSable River Canoe Marathon is billed as North America's Richest Canoe Race, or as it is hyped: $50,000 purse, 50,000 fans and over 50,000 paddle strokes! The race begins in Grayling on a Saturday evening during the AuSable River Festival and ends 120 miles later at the AuSable River Days Festival in Mio.

The tradition dates back to 1947 when a group of Mio residents came up with the idea to promote their town and beloved river. The first winners were Allen Carr and Delbert Case of Grayling with a time of 21:03:00. Since then, the winning times have improved but little else has changed.

Two person teams sprint 250 yards through downtown Grayling with canoes hoisted on their shoulders until they reach the river. From there the furious pace begins, 60-70 paddle strokes a minute around rocks and under branches. Much of the race takes place in the dark including six challenging portages. Support teams and fans follow the race by driving along M-72 from bridge to bridge, and updates are broadcast on local radio throughout the night.

First place finishers claim the top prize of $5,000. The record time of 13:58:08 was set in 1994 by the Canadian team of Serge Corbin and Solomon Carriere.

Most Victories – Team:

8	Serge Corbin (Quebec) and Jeff Kolka (Grayling) 1996-2003
5	Serge Corbin (Quebec) and Brett Stockton (Grayling) 1990-1994
4	Butch Stockton (Higgins Lake) and Brett Stockton (Grayling) 1982-83, 1985-86
3	Ralph Sawyer (Oscoda) and Stan Hall (Oscoda) 1967-68
3	Don Felderhauser (Grayling) and Bernie Fowler (Grayling) 1953-55

| 3 | Jay Stephan (Grayling) and Ted Engle (Gaylord) 1950-52 |

Most Victories – Individual:

17	Serge Corbin (Quebec)
9	Brett Stockton (Grayling)
9	Ralph Sawyer (Oscoda)
8	Jeff Kolka (Grayling)
5	Butch Stockton (Higgins Lake)
4	John Baker (Grayling)
4	Jerry Kellogg (Twin Lakes)
4	Irvin "Buzz" Peterson (Minnesota)

HUNTING

Deer Hunters in Northern Michigan – by County

| County | (2002) | (2001) |
	Registered deer hunters	
Manistee	15,831	14,610
Wexford	15,146	15,146
Missaukee	12,394	13,806
Kalkaska	7,529	8,520
Antrim	8,969	8,338
Gr. Traverse	7,529	8,520
Benzie	6,125	6,672
Charlevoix	6,010	5,910
Emmet	5,056	5,952
Leelanau	4,183	3,878
Beaver Island	680	828
Manitou Islands	26	50
Fox Islands	26	31

Restricted number of licenses available. Distributed by random drawing.

Island Deer Hunting
Special deer hunts are held on North Manitou and South Fox islands.

North Manitou

Special permit deer hunts have been held since 1985. Deer, four male and five female, were introduced on the island in 1926. By 1981 there were an estimated 2,000 deer on the island. The vegetation began to disappear and starvation was a factor which led to the special deer hunts.

Archery	October 1-14
Muzzleloading	October 15-20
Firearm	October 21-November 7

Permits awarded by lottery

South Fox

| Archery | October 1-28 |
| Firearm | October 29-
November 26 |

Deer Harvested 2003 – by County

	2003	2002	2001
Mason	8,459		
Osceola	8,106		
Missaukee	6,647	6,027	5,934
Roscommon	6,628		
Clare	6,001		
Manistee	5,606	8,258	6,979
Lake	5,482		
Wexford	5,182	6,751	5,137
Crawford	4,523		
Leelanau	4,379	1,443	1,328
Antrim	3,289	3,300	3,986
Emmet	3,042	2,457	2,880
Otsego	2,457		
Charlevoix	2,455	2,716	2,872
Grand Traverse	1,734	1,784	2,911
Kalkaska	1,686	2,607	3,567
Benzie	1,606	1,233	2,324
Beaver Island		474	520
Manitou Islands		0	0
Fox Islands		52	25

Michigan DNR

HISTORY OF DEER HUNTING IN NORTHERN MICHIGAN

The deer population of Michigan was confined mostly to the southern part of the State until sometime around the 1870's. By then farms had replaced much of the ground cover in the south and there was no limit on the number of deer farmers could shoot. At that same time the dense forests of northern Michigan were being thinned by loggers, which produced more openings and new vegetation for the deer to feed on.

Hunters in the north took advantage of the growing deer population and newly arrived railroad. They supplied venison for the eastern states, but without regulation, their supply of deer was disappearing. Concerned hunters formed the Michigan Sportsmen's Club in 1875, and by 1880 had pieced together enough evidence to estimate that 70,000 deer were being killed annually. In Roscommon the amount of venison meat shipped over rail was placed at 250,000 pounds.

In 1881 the state reacted by making it illegal to possess a deer unless it was for personal consumption. The only other hunting law on the books prohibited the killing of deer during certain months. Neither law was taken seriously in the wild north. In one example from Harrison, a local jury, despite solid circumstantial evidence, found two men charged with illegally killing a deer in June of 1881 not guilty.

After that the Michigan Sportsmen's Association appointed Cyrus Higby to help organize sportsmen's clubs in northern Michigan to help enforce hunting laws, and in 1887 the State created the Office of State Game Warden. By 1895, concerns about the falling deer population led to the first established deer-hunting season with limits on the number that could be harvested.

In 1913, the first State Game Preserve was established when Grayling lumberman Rasmus Hansen donated 40,000 acres to the State of Michigan. The first game raised included German deer and wild turkeys.

In 1914, with concerns of a declining deer population, hunters were limited to taking only antlered deer. The population rebounded. By 1937, the State's first deer biologist, Ilo Bartlett, estimated the herd size at 1.125 million deer, with 2/3rds of them in the northern Lower Peninsula. The population grew to 1.5 million by the late 1940's, which led to the issuance of antlerless permits.

In the 1980's the population peaked at 2 million deer. Farmers complained of crop damage, and over 40,000 car deer accidents were recorded on Michigan roads and highways. Since then the DNR has been working to thin the deer population to 1.3 million statewide.

Hunter's Heritage: A History of Hunting in Michigan, by, Eugene T. Petersen, copyright 1979 by Michigan United Conservation Clubs, Lansing, MI

Fred Bear

An international figure in the world of bowhunting, Fred Bear enjoyed a long association with the town of Grayling. Bear owned an archery company there with hundreds of employees, and his museum drew thousands of visitors.

Fred Bear was born on March 5, 1902 in Waynesboro, Pennsylvania. He moved to Detroit where he worked for the Packard Motor Company and took classes at the Detroit Technology Institute. In the late 1920's he got hooked on archery after viewing the film by the pioneer bow hunter Art Young.

A few years later Bear started Bear Products Company, a silk-screen printing shop that produced advertising literature for auto companies.

During the late 30's Bear and a woodworker named Nels Grumley began making their own archery equipment. After a few years together Bear sold the printing business to Grumley and focused on archery. By 1937 he received the first of several patents, and to this day many of his designs and materials are used in the making of bows.

Fred Bear (State Archives of Michigan)

Bear wrote books about bow hunting adventures and technique; he produced movies about the sport, wrote magazine articles, and was interviewed on national television shows – all to promote bow hunting. During a bow hunting expedition to Africa he brought along the popular radio personality, Arthur Godfrey. Bear took a bull elephant during the hunt, which Godfrey recounted to his national radio audience. That exposure, along with a profile in *Life* magazine, brought Bear national fame, and led to booming sales of his archery products. In 1947 he moved operations from Detroit to Grayling where the company became a major employer.

For many years Grayling was not only home to Fred Bear,

and Bear Archery, but to the Fred Bear Museum which housed his huge collection of archery artifacts and mounts of animals – moose, caribou, a lion and even an elephant – he had taken during his hunting adventures. In 1968 he sold his company, but remained as president for several years. Following a labor dispute in 1978 the company moved to Gainseville, Florida where it continues to operate as Bear Archery. The Fred Bear Museum also moved to Gainseville.

The Grayling Historical Museum maintains a large exhibit on Fred Bear, and the town named a local street Fred Bear Drive. Fred Bear lives on in the heart of many an outdoorsman, including Motor City rock and roller Ted Nugent, who wrote a song in memory of Bear:

The Spirit of the Woods is
like an old good friend.
Makes me feel warm and
good in-side.
I knew his name and it was
good to see him again.
Cause in the wind he's still
a-live.

Oh Fred Bear
Walk with me down the trails
again.
Take me back, back where
I be-long.
Fred Bear
I'm glad to have you at my
side my friend
and I'll join you in the big
hunt before too long
before too long.

Fred Bear (State Archives of Michigan)

World Record Whitetail Deer?

Traverse City hunter Mitch Rompola may have taken a world record whitetail with his bow and arrow in November of 1998. However he's not making that claim.

Rompola says he shot the deer on November 13, 1998 after observing it for three years in the southern part of Grand Traverse County. Controversy erupted shortly after a photo of Rompola and the deer rack appeared in newspapers and on the Internet. Some hunters claimed the rack was a fake, based on the deer's droopy ears in the photo. Rompola refused to have the buck verified by internationally respected Boone & Crockett, or Michigan Commemorative Bucks, and wouldn't talk to the press. His initial claims were that the buck weighed 263 pounds dressed, with an estimated field weight of 300 pounds.

Rompola claims three officials with Commemorative Bucks of Michigan scored the deer. The three men, all from northwestern lower Michigan, scored the deer at 216 5/8, three inches bigger than the stated world record from 1963 by Milo Hanson in Saskatchewan.

The last word on this story: The holder of the official record for largest whitetail is Milo Hanson, who in 1993, took a 213 5/8 buck near his home in Saskatchewan. The record earned Hanson some good money from endorsements and personal appearances, but that started to dry up after the Rompola story in 1998. Hanson threatened legal action against Rompola, and as a compromise the Traverse City hunter signed a document agreeing not to claim he shot the world record deer.

Elk Hunting

Biologists estimate there are 800-900 elk in the northern Michigan herd in the Pigeon River Country State Forest. The elk native to Michigan were killed off by 1875, but in 1918 seven new elk were released near Wolverine. By the early 1960's the herd had grown to an estimated 1,500, and a limited hunt was held in 1964 and 1965.

Due to poaching, and reduced quality of habitat, the herd size shrunk to about 200 by 1975. In the 1970's the DNR focused on improving the habitat and cracking down on poaching, which led to an elk population of about 850 by the year 1984.

Starting in 1984 the DNR has held a limited elk hunt for one week each December, and in some years additional hunts have been held in the fall. Hunting is limited to portions of the following counties:

Otsego, Montmorency, Cheboygan, Charlevoix, Emmet, Alpena, Antrim, Oscoda, and Presque Isle.

Number of licenses issued depends on the size of the elk herd.

Year	Hunt dates	Applications	Licenses
1984	12/11-16	45,908	50
1985	12/10-15	52,658	120
1986	12/9-14	36,348	95
1987	12/9-13	38,546	130
1988	10/25-30	38,416*	90
1988	12/6-13	40,166	145
1989	10/17-22	35,687	80
1989	12/5-12	42,310	110
1990	10/16-23	25,274	90
1990	12/11-16	32,392	140
1991	12/10-17	38,432	155
1992	9/9-15, 9/17-24	37,208	100
1992	12/8-15	49,805	170
1993	9/8-12, 9/15-20 and 9/23-29	25,128	165
1993	12/7-14	41,420	195
1994	9/7-11, 9/14-19	23,297	130
1994	12/6-13	39,094	200
1995	9/12-17, 9/19-24	23,150	165
1995	12/12-19	37,194	165
1996	9/7-13, 9/17-24	28,540	220
1996	12/9-16	42,367	200
1997	9/13-21, 12/9-16	34,801	355
1998	9/12-20, 12/8-14	39,104	360
1999	9/18-26, 12/7-12	39,725	189
2000	9/16-20, 9/26-31, 12/5-12, 1/20-26	48,652	410
2001	8/25-29, 9/19-23, 12/4-11	46,933	256
2002	12/10-17	37,464	150
2003	12/9-16	38,778	100
2004	12/7-14	40,500	124

*Selection of October 1988 hunters made from unsuccessful 1987 applicants.

Michigan DNR

Number of Hunting Licenses Purchased in Michigan – by Game

Game	2000	2001 Number of licenses	2002
Deer	810,864	800,872	788,180
Small game	354,858	347,314	327,279
*Spring turkey	84,355	95,595	98,286
*Fall turkey	25,507	19,348	21,952
Waterfowl	66,110	65,961	64,582
Fur harvester	17,346	18,871	19,386
*Bear	7,900	8,262	9,107
*Elk	365	247	142

Hunting licenses - 2004
Michigan ranks 5th in the country, behind Colorado, Pennsylvania, Wisconsin and Texas in number of hunting licenses sold.

Paid license holders: 863,946

Total licenses, tags, permits and stamps sold: 2,266,331

Revenue: $27,557,693

89% of hunters in Michigan are deer hunters.

Fishing licenses – 2004
Michigan ranks 6th in the country, behind California, Texas, Wisconsin, Minnesota and Florida, in fishing licenses sold.

Paid license holders: 1,317,605

Total licenses, tags, permits and stamps sold: 1,317,605

Revenue: $22,318,881

U.S. Fish and Wildlife Service National Hunting License Report.

Steve Smith

This Traverse City resident is an author, publisher, avid hunter, biologist, and one of the founders of Woodcock Limited. Smith has founded ten outdoor magazines including: *Pointing Dog Journal, Retriever Journal, Just Labs,* and *The Traveling Wingshooter,* all published in Traverse City.

His 1988 book *Woodcock Shooting* is a staple among like-minded hunters and fans of the sport. He's written 19 other books, and is frequently seen on the *Outdoor Life* Network's (OLN) series, *"A Dog's Life."*

Smith helped launch Woodcock Limited due to his concern over the decline in woodcock numbers and woodcock habitat. (www.woodcocklimited.org)

FISHING

State fishing records that occured in northern Michigan

Fish	Weight/length (lbs)/(inches)	Lake/County	Year
Brown bullhead	3.06/18"	Lake Cadillac/Wexford	1984
Brown Trout	34.62/40.5"	Lake Michigan/Manistee	2000
Channel catfish	40/41.5"	Houghton Lake/Roscommon	1964
Coho Salmon	30.56/40"	Platte River/Benzie	1976
Gizzard shad	3.25/19.5"	Manistee River/Manistee	1989
Hybrid Sunfish	1.44/11.25"	Arbutus Lake/Gr. Traverse	1988
Lake Herring	5.4/25"	East Bay/Gr. Traverse	1992
Lake Sturgeon	193/87"	Mullett Lake/Cheboygan	1974
Muskellunge	48"	Lake Skegemog/Kalkaska	1985
Pumpkinseed	1/10"	Thayer Lake/Antrim	1990
Smelts (family)	11.5"	Lake Michigan/Emmet	1992

Largest fish caught by lake

Lake	County	Fish	Weight (lbs)	Length (inches)	Date
Elk	Antrim	Salmon	29	42	10/10/99
Torch	Antrim	Muskellunge	40	56	5/20/01
Crystal	Benzie	Lake Trout	23.5	39.5	8/06/94
Charlevoix	Charlevoix	Chin. Salmon	36.5	43	10/04/99
Budd	Clare	Muskellunge	NA	46.75	9/29/02
Margrethe	Crawford	Muskellunge	35.31	49	2/04/00
Carp (Paradise)	Emmet	N. Pike	NA	44	6/13/98
Long	Gr. Traverse	Muskellunge	48	53	4/28/01
Duck	Gr. Traverse	N. Pike	20.25	42.25	1/29/95
Green	Gr. Traverse	Lake Trout	19.12	35.25	8/23/97
Leelanau	Leelanau	Rainbow Trout	18.63	NA	6/29/97
Glen	Leelanau	Lake Trout	20.75	36	7/27/01
Portage	Manistee	Ch. Catfish	21.47	33	7/16/03
Hamlin	Mason	Ch. Catfish	21.06	28	7/09/97
Missaukee	Missaukee	N. Pike	19.67	40	2/13/94
Otsego	Otsego	Tiger Musky	25.5	48	8/13/01
Houghton	Roscommon	Carp	39.44	39.5	6/19/04
Higgins	Roscommon	Lake Trout	35.19	46	4/15/98
Mitchell	Wexford	Bowfin	9.75	31	7/13/05
Cadillac	Wexford	N. Pike	24.50	46	2/11/98

*State record

Trout Unlimited

One of the largest and most influential sportsmen's organizations in the world, Trout Unlimited, was founded on the banks of the Au Sable River near Grayling. In July of 1959, 16 sport fishermen came together at "The Barbless Hook," George Griffith's lodge on the banks of the Au Sable. There they formed a group dedicated to promoting healthier rivers to produce a better quality trout than what was being planted by the state. Their stated principle was "take care of the fish, then the fishing will take care of itself."

After achieving some policy victories with the DNR in Lansing, other Trout Unlimited chapters formed in Illinois, Wisconsin, New York and Pennsylvania.

Today there are 500 chapters across the United States, with 125,000 volunteers.

The organization's mission is to conserve protect and restore North America's trout and salmon fisheries and their watersheds. Trout Unlimited maintains a national head-quarters in Washington D.C.

George Griffith

Griffith was an Ohio native who discovered his beloved Au Sable River while making sales calls in the 1920's. He moved to the Grayling area in his 30's and established his home, The Barbless Hook, on the north bank of the Mainstream about a half-mile above the Wakely Bridge. His inspiration to form Trout Unlimited came from his friend, George Mason, who owned a large tract of land on the river, and was active in Ducks Unlimited.

Griffith's legacy lives on not only through Trout Unlimited, but also through the George Griffith Foundation, which he established to support research on rivers and trout conservation, and Griffith's Gnat, one of the most popu-

lar flies used by fishermen around the world.

Griffith donated his Au Sable River home and property to the Michigan chapter of Trout Unlimited. Today on a granite rock on the river bank outside that home is a plaque marking the birth-place of Trout Unlimited.

Many of Griffith's rare books on fly fishing are housed in the Devereaux Memorial Library in Grayling as part of the George Griffith and Marion Wright Collection. Wright was a past President of the Mason chapter of Trout Unlimited and served on the Board of the Griffith Foundation.

Adams fly

Since 1922 the Adams fly has been a favorite of fly fish-ermen around the world. It was a success upon first test by its namesake, Charlie Adams, in the town of Mayfield, about ten miles south of Traverse City. Although named after Adams, the fly was created by his friend and fishing partner, Leonard Halladay.

Halladay owned and operated the Halladay House hotel in Mayfield where he would lead fishing excursions to the nearby Boardman River. Halladay and Adams used to fish a nearby millpond, but one night Adams grew frustrated, and asked his fishing buddy to tie up a new fly. The new fly was an immediate success, and it didn't take long for orders to come in from other fly fishermen. Since he already named another of his creations the Halladay fly, he decided to name the new one after his friend.

Orders started to roll in from around the country, so Halladay started a mail order business, while he continued to fish, and run the Halladay House.

Today the Adams fly is still in wide use, and the millpond where it first flew is now a public park in honor of Leonard Halladay and the Adams fly.

Bob Summers

Known and respected by fly fishermen around the world for his high quality bamboo fly rods. Summers, who lives on the Boardman River south of Traverse City, started making fly rods in his teens while working after school in Paul Young's shop in the Detroit area. Young's wife took over the shop after his death in 1960, and eventually moved the operation up north to Traverse City. Summers ventured out on his own to began crafting fly rods entirely from hand.

Today a fly rod from the R.W. Summers Co. commands $1,200 - $2,000, and customers wait up to two years for the privilege of buying one. It takes about 50 hours to craft on rod, and Summer turns out about 50 rods per year.

Each year Summers donates one rod to be auctioned off during a fundraiser for the Boardman River Project, a volunteer group that fights erosion on the river banks. Drawing the winner's name is always a highlight, as tickets have are purchased by avid fly fishermen from as far away as Australia and Japan.

On the web:
www.rwsummer.com

Historic Trout

The first known planting of a Brown Trout in the U.S. took place on April 11, 1884 in the Pere Marquette River in Lake County. The 4,900 tiny brookies came from Germany – the eggs were shipped to a fish hatchery in New York. From there they landed at a federal fish hatchery in Northville, and were taken to Lake County for the historic planting. The Michigan Marker sign stands at the release site on the Pere Marquette.

Fish Hatcheries

Jordan River National Fish Hatchery:

The only national fish hatchery in northern Michigan works to restock Lakes Michigan and Huron with Lake Trout. Each winter millions of trout eggs from hatcheries in Wyoming, Minnesota and the U.P. are delivered to the Jordan River Hatchery where they are incubated, hatched, marked for identification, and then by April released into the lakes. Between 1997 and 2004 the hatchery has stocked over 22 million lake trout into the two Great Lakes.

The Jordan River Hatchery was opened in 1963 on 116 acres near Elmira in the Jordan River Valley. The Department of Interior's Fish and Wildlife Service operate it on an annual budget of $995,000. Besides the hatchery the staff are responsible for *M/V Togue,* a former shrimp trawler, retrofitted for stocking lake trout. The *M/V Togue* is scheduled to be replaced in 2006 by the brand new $6.5 million *M/V Spencer F. Baird.*

The Jordan River National Fish Hatchery attracts over 14,000 visitors annually.

Lake Trout planted in Lake Michigan and Huron by Jordan Fish Hatchery

Year	# Stocked
1997	3,327,000
1998	3,581,500
1999	3,280,000
2000	3,369,700
2001	3,416,700
2002	2,898,334
2003	3,073,751
2004	3,072,917

State of Michigan Fish Hatcheries

Six State hatcheries produce up to 750,000 pounds of fish per year, which equates roughly to: 13 million trout and salmon, and 30 million walleye, muskies and sturgeon. The raising and stocking of fish in Michigan waters provides about 40% of the fish for the recreational fishing industry.

State fish hatchery locations
Marquette
Thompson (Manistique)
Wolf Creek (Mattawan)
Harrietta
Oden
Platte River

Northern Michigan State Hatcheries

Harrietta State Fish Hatchery

Location:
6801 West 30 Road, Harrietta, Wexford County
Located on 160 acres backing up to the Manistee
National Forest

Opened: 1901 – States oldest operating fish hatchery

Overview: A major facility for rearing rainbow and brown
trout, mostly for inland waters. Remodeled in 1979 and
switched from using local springs and surface water to well
water. Features an interpretive area with outdoor trails and
information on the Big Manistee watershed.

Fish Plantings from Harrieta State Fish Hatchery, 2000 – 2001

Species	Strain	Number
Brown Trout	Seeforellen	378,835
Brown Trout	Wild Rose	270,632
Brown Trout	Bilchrist Creek	94,940
Rainbow Trout	Eagle Lake	322,646
Rainbow Trout	Shasta	123,770
Total stocked: Michigan Waters		1,506,954

Oden State Fish Hatchery

Location:
8258 South Ayr Road, Alanson, Emmet County

Opened: Original Oden Fish Hatchery opened in 1921 and
operated through 2002, when a new $11 million complex,
about a quarter of a mile away, was completed built. The
old hatchery building was remodeled and re-opened as the
Michigan Fisheries Visitor Center. The Center includes a
replica rail car once used to transport fish, now serving as an
interpretation center.

Overview: Described by the DNR as one of the most
advanced fish culture facilities of its kind. The Oden hatchery
is the key broodstock station for lake and rainbow trout that
are stocked in the Great Lakes and inland waters. The brood-

stock are large captive fish that produce eggs and sperm, which are taken in late fall and early winter, for fish production. For information on hatchery tours: 231-347-4689

The Visitor Center is open Memorial Day – Labor Day: 231-348-0998

Fish Plantings from Oden State Fish Hatchery, 2000-2001

Species	Strain	Number
Brown Trout	Gilchrist Creek	87,850
Brown Trout	Seeforellen	187,002
Brown Trout	Wild Rose	239,087
Rainbow Trout	Eagle Lake	358,347
Total stocked in Michigan waters		91,019,595

Platte River State Fish Hatchery

Location:
15210 US 31 Highway, Beulah, MI 49617

Opened:
1928 as Platte River Rearing Station. Reared trout from the Harrietta Fish Hatchery until they could be planted in lakes.

Rebuilt:
1968-72 to be the major salmon hatchery in Michigan because of its location on the Platte River. Spawning salmon from Lake Michigan swim up the river, right to the hatchery.

Overview:
In the 1960's the DNR planted Coho salmon in some Michigan rivers to combat an infestation of alewives. The Coho population thrived on the little invaders from the Atlantic resulting in swarms of fishermen, from all over the Midwest, converging on Lake Michigan near the mouth of the Platte River. (When a storm swept down on the crowded lake on a September day in 1967, seven fishermen drowned.)

The Platte River Hatchery is the main egg-taking station for coho in the Upper Great Lakes, and raises coho and Chinook salmon for the Platte River and Great Lakes. The facility has been undergoing a major renovation since 2003.

Fish Plantings from Platte River State Fish Hatchery, 2000-2001

Species	Strain	Number
Coho Salmon	Michigan and Hinchenbrooke	1,849,316
Chinook	Michigan	4,106,063
Walleye	Muskegon River	5,500,000
Total stocked in Michigan waters:		11,092,542

State salmon egg take stations:

Medusa Creek (Charlevoix)
Boardman River (Traverse City)
Platte River (Honor)
Little Manistee River (two stations)
Swan River (Rogers City)

Manistee Fish Weir:
During March and April each year the weir is put up on the Little Manistee to capture steelhead for their eggs, used as broodstock at state fish hatcheries. In the fall the weir is put back up to harvest all returning salmon for their eggs. Steelhead and brown trout are counted, and passed upstream.

The Little Manistee weir is the only steelhead egg-take facility in the state of Michigan, producing the Michigan winter-run strain of steelhead.

Little Manistee Weir Salmon Harvest and Trout Passed

	Chinook	Coho	Steelhead	Brown Trout
Spring 2002			6,290	
Fall 2002	19,385	538	120	38
Spring 2003			3,209	
Fall 2003	14,419	616	1,404	43
Spring 2004			2,571	
Fall 2004	15,618	1,102	1,079	60
Average	19,684	18,416	2,362	82

Records since 1968

Chinook	39,359 (1983)	
Coho	108,400 (1970)	
Steelhead	7,622 (fall-1971)	10,480 (spring-1977)
Brown Trout	238 (1975)	

For more information on Michigan fish hatcheries and fishing related information, visit: www.michigan.gov/dnr

Grayling Fish Hatchery

Opened:
In 1914 Grayling lumber baron Rasmus Hanson founded the hatchery in an effort to restore the Grayling fish, which ironically was brought to extinction by the lumber industry. The Graylings spawning beds were filled with sand after the trees were chopped down and riverbank vegetation burned and cleared away so the logs could be floated down the river. The loss of shade from the tree cover warmed the temperature of the stream and hurt the food supply for the Grayling.

In 1916 Hanson and friends formed the Grayling Fish Hatchery Club recognizing that in order for the trout population to survive and flourish, there would have to be some help from the outside. Members of the club included Detroit auto magnates, Henry and Edsel Ford, and Charles Nash. Ponds were constructed and a hatching and rearing program begun. They failed to save the Grayling, but were successful in planting brook and brown trout in the AuSable.

Hanson sold the Hatchery for $10,000.00 to the State of Michigan in 1926, which operated it through 1964 before shutting it down. During nearly fifty years of operation the Grayling Fish Hatchery Club raised and released 50 million brook, brown and rainbow trout into nearby rivers and streams.

In 1979 a local group began lobbying the State to re-open the hatchery. Four years later the Grayling Recreation Authority and County of Crawford opened the hatchery, which has drawn 35-40,000 visitors each year between Memorial Day and Labor Day.

There are 11 ponds, with fish ranging in size form fingerlings to full size. Visitors are encouraged to buy fish food, which helps finance the operation, to feed the fish.

The hatchery has been under restoration since the volunteer Grayling Fish Hatchery Restoration Steering Committee was formed in 1999. They're raising money and working to restore the 1940 hatchery building to house educational and historic exhibits. They've created a natural trout stream in place of the old concrete raceways, and added landscaping and a children's fishing pond, among other improvements.

For more information on the Grayling Fish Hatchery restoration, visit: **www.graylingfishhatchery.com/**

SAILING

Chicago to Mackinac Island Race:

The 333-mile race from Monroe Harbor in Chicago to the Round Island Lighthouse near Mackinac Island is the longest, and oldest freshwater race in the world.

Pied Piper *in 2004 Chicago to Mackinac Island race (courtesy of Torresen Marine, www.chicago-mackinac.com)*

Started in 1898 by a few yacht club members who sailed north to the island each summer, the first race drew only five entries. The event will mark its 100th race in 2008, even though it was founded in 1898. The race skipped a few years in the beginning, and during World War I.

Sponsor: Chicago Yacht Club

Entry: By invitation only

Fastest time (any class):
18:50:15 by *Stars and Stripe*s, captained by Steve Fossett in 1998

Fastest time (monohull):
23:30:23 by Roy Disney (nephew of Walt Disney) and *Pyewacket* in 2002

Fastest time (singlehaded):
One day, 17:53:50, by Dave Rearick and *Geronimo* in 1997
The race finished at Harbor Springs twice, therefore is not included as an official Chicago to Mackinac Island Race.

Man overboard

Experienced sailors keep a close watch on the sky over Lake Michigan where fierce, life-threatening storms, can appear with little warning. Such was the case in July 2002 when a squall carrying 50-70 knot winds ripped the sails off the 44-foot triple hulled *Caliente*.

Two crewmembers, Tim Doran and Mark Muehler, stayed afloat with one working PFD between them, as the capsized craft drifted away. As night fell, the four crewmembers clinging to the hull of the boat fired a flare and radioed "mayday."

The 730-foot freighter *Algomarine* was passing through the Straits of Mackinac and had to turn around after hearing the mayday message, but due to shallow water couldn't approach the two drifting sailors.

The 55-foot *Kokomo* left the racecourse for the direction of the flare. Once in the vicinity, they followed a spotlight from the freighter, which led them to Doran and Muehler, weak and exhausted from fighting to stay afloat. The *Kokomo* was able to pull them aboard before rescuing the rest of the *Caliente* crew. Despite the crowd aboard the *Caliente,* it was able to jump back in the race, crossing the finish line after midnight. The crew of the *Caliente* was accorded a 64-minute credit for its rescue efforts, rendering it the first place finisher for its division.

The following sailors aboard the *Caliente* were awarded the Arthur B Hanson Rescue Medal from U.S. Sailing, and were officially recognized by the U.S. Coast Guard: Dr. Wesson Schulz, Dr. Rob Lovell, Dr. Kerry Kaysserian, Greg Beck, Myles Cornwell, Tom Cowell, Eugene Miller, Dan Lisuk, Mike Fisher, Erik Nelson, Ken Stepnitz, Adam Veltman, and Chuck Wyres.

The following year the Weather Channel produced a segment about the storm and the rescue on its Storm Stories program.

Port Huron to Mackinac Island Race

The first race was held in 1925 with 14 boats entered. The 56-foot *Suez* I, owned by Howard Grant was first to reach the island with a time of 88 hours and 41 minutes.

The original course ran 235 miles up the Lake Huron shoreline. In 1935 the course was lengthened, as crews had to sail around Cove Island in northern Lake Huron. That idea was scrapped the next year due to dangerous fog. Since 1972 there have two courses: the 298 mile course around Cove Island and the 235 Shore Line course.

Sponsor: Bayview Yacht Club

Fastest time Shore Line Course (overall):
25:47:19 by Wendell Anderson and the 71-foot *Escapade* in 1950.

Fastest time Cove Island Course (overall):
26:41:01 recorded in 1993 by *Windquest,* owned by Richard DeVos (co-founder of Amway), and captained by his son, Doug DeVos.

<u>**Famous Port Huron to Mac racers:**</u>

Bob Seger (*Lightning*) – rock and roller
Ted Turner (*Tenacious*) – America's Cup winner and cable television pioneer
Candice Miller – U.S. Congresswoman and former Michigan Secretary of State
Gordon Lightfoot (*Golden Goose*) – singer-songwriter (Wreck of the *Edmund Fitzgerald*)

<u>**Society of Mackinac Island Billy Goats**</u>

Any sailor who has raced in at least 25 Port Huron to Mac races is included in the society. Their names are on a plaque in the Bayview Yacht Club bar. Congresswoman Candace Miller became the fifth woman (Nanny Goat) enshrined in the Society.

In 1971, aboard the *Sayonara,* Miller was part of the first ever all-female crew to finish the race.

<u>**The Pickle Boat:**</u>

The last boat to cross the finish line is known as the "pickle boat." In England the last place finisher is called the "fisher," because they stopped to fish for herring, which they pickled, and presumably caused them to finish last.

Ted Turner

The cable television pioneer knows a thing or two about sailing, after all in 1978 aboard his yacht, *Courageous*, he won the America's Cup.

He was a prominent America's Cup competitor in 1970 when he entered the Chicago to Mackinac Island Race. Before the race Turner referred to Lake Michigan as a "mill pond."

After the race, after the 60 knot winds knocked out over half of the 167 starters, after more than a dozen masts were snapped in two, after Turner failed to conquer the "millpond," he retracted his remarks about lake racing.

After his America's Cup victory in 1978, he pursued another trophy; this time it was the Port Huron to Mackinac Island race. Turner fell behind and lost out to the 32-foot *Hot Flash*, and hasn't entered a Great Lakes race since.

From 1925 to 1939 both races were held on the same weekend. In 1939 they agreed to hold them on consecutive weekends.

GLIDING AND SOARING

The Frankfort-Elberta area has been a gliding capital since the 1920's when the Detroit Glider Council discovered the beauti-ful dunes that crawl 400 feet up from the lake surface. The height and the powerful updrafts attracted national gliding events in the late 1930's and at that time, Stan Corcoran built the Frankfort Sailplane Manufacturing Co. By the time World War II began Corcoran relocated the plant to Joliet, Illinois where he was awarded the first ever Army contract for a glider. After the war Corcoran donated one of his training gliders to Lewis University where it was restored by students and donated to the Smithsonian.

Today the Northwest Soaring Club of Frankfort offers public glider rides on most weekend during war weather. The gliders are towed by a motorized plane to an altitude of 3,000-5,000 feet before they disconnect. For the next 20-30 minutes the glider drifts, quietly and lazily, back to earth. Cost for a flight runs $100-140. The club also offers lessons.

Hang and Paragliding

The popularity of hang gliding over the bluffs near Frankfort is steadily yielding to the more convenient paragliding. It may take up to three days of lessons before one can take a solo hang glide off the sandy cliffs, whereas paragliding requires less than a day of training before the first flight. Hang gliding requires heavier equip-

Paragliding over the dunes (courtesy of T.C. Hang Gliders)

ment, which is a factor considering the long walk from parking lot to bluff's edge.

Training starts on a pilot-owned site about 75 feet above the lake surface. Pilots also fly from three sites within the Sleeping Bear Dunes National Lakeshore, some nearly 400 feet high. For more information check, www.serioussports.com and go to the Air Sports link.

In 1992 the Smithsonian Institution named Frankfort one of its nine National Landmarks of Soaring.

Bayshore Marathon

Started in 1983 the Bayshore is a qualifying event for the Boston Marathon. The race, held in late May, limits participation to the first 1,500 runners. The course is flat and scenic as much of it is along East Grand Traverse Bay. A bonus prize of $1,000 is paid to the first place male who finishes under 2:30 and first place female under 2:55.

Course record:

Male:
2:17:40 by Jeff Sharp in the first Bayshore Marathon, 1983

Female:
2:48:41 by Wanda Cousineau in 1992

Fun stuff:

Stone Skipping on Mac Island

The competition starts at 10 am on the Sunday of 4th of July Weekend on Windermere Beach at Iroquois Hotel. The Pros stones skip over the water 20-plus times before disappearing. John Kolar holds the record of 24 plus infinity skips in 1977. The counting stopped when his stone disappeared into the fog. Winners take home bragging rights and a years supply of fudge.

Fish Toss at Beaver Island:

St. Patrick's Day is special on "America's Emerald Isle," where many residents have deep Irish roots. After a long winter of isolation St. Patrick's Day is the perfect excuse to ...well, throw trout down the street. Somewhere before the annual tug-of-war and obstacle race the crowds gather to watch their neighbors see who can throw a 16 or 17 pound frozen trout the farthest.

Bowling on Main Street - Harbor Springs

Somebody once said that spring break in Harbor Springs was so quiet you bowl down Main Street. So, they did and it continues as an annual tradition on April Fools Day.

Operation petunia

Since 1982 the Thursday before Memorial Day means one thing in Charlevoix the Beautiful: **time to plant the petunias!** Volunteers by the hundreds turn out to plant colorful petunias along the curb –both sides- the length of US 31 through Charlevoix. The tradition was the brainstorm of Dale Boss and his wife Marilyn. The first year nearly 500 volunteers planted the petunias. Today it seems everyone in town shows up with a trowel to help plant the 1,000 flats. When it's all done, they hold a community picnic at East Park overlooking Round Lake.

Morel Mushroom hunting

In northern Michigan May means Morels! The mysterious yet delectable fungus sprouts in late spring, usually after warm weather and a good night of rain. It is not unusual to see vehicles parked along the wooded stretches of roads and highways, their drivers and passengers deep in the woods hunting the elusive morel.

Experienced morel hunters have several favorite locations, none of which they'll share with you. They may bring family members along, but only after blindfolding them, so as not to give away

The start of the Iceman Race

the location. The morel season is short, and they are scarce. Restaurants pay between $15-$25 per pound depending on supply.

Morel mushroom festivals are held in Boyne City, Mesick and Lewiston. Winners in the Largest Morel contests are usually in the 8 –10 inch range.

First time morel mushroom hunters should go with an experience hunter to a avoid frustration and poisoning! There are numerous guides and internet sites available describing and showing the difference between edible morel mushrooms, and similar poisonous shrooms.

Iceman race

In 1990 a handful of mountain bike racers registered for something called the Iceman Cometh Challenge, a 27-mile point-to-point race between Kalkaska and Traverse City. The course winds in and out of the woods along the hilly M-72 corridor. Oh, and its held the first Saturday in November which mean the weather can be windy and wild, the course can be snowy and frozen, or it can be dry, hot and sandy. The idea did take off, and now registration has to be limited to the first 2,000 racers, and is usually six months before the race.

Shoe tree

On US 131 north of Kalkaska on the west side of the road, stands a tree known as, the Shoe Tree. Why? Because there are dozens of shoes hanging from its branches. Nobody seems to know when it started, or why. The first sighting came sometime in early 2001.

Bridge walks

Not content to let Mackinaw City and St. Ignace own the spotlight on Labor Day, other towns have jumped into the act. Bridge Walks are now held in Horton Bay, in Glen Arbor over the Narrows, and over the Leland River.

Petoskey stone hunting

Northern Michigan never seems to run out of Petoskey stones. Locals and tourists delight in walking the beaches of Lake Michigan, and a few inland lakes, looking for the corral fossil. If you can't find one on the beach, there are plenty of polished Petoskey stones available in area gift shops. Craftspeople create everything from Petoskey stone doorknobs to key chains shaped like the State of Michigan. Check out *The Complete Guide to Petoskey Stones* (University of Michigan Press) by Bruce Mueller and William H. Wilde for good tips on the best places to find Petoskey stones.

Stone Circle

Since 1983 poets and story tellers have gathered at Terry Wooten's Stone Circle north of Kewadin. Wooten, a professional poet, says he was inspired by Bellaire poet Max Ellison who used to entertain by reciting poems by the light of a big bonfire outside his home in Frog Holler near Shanty Creek. Wooten used a John Deere orchard tractor to form the circle with 88 boulders, 88 being the symbol for infinity in Pythagorean math, and Wooten's number on his high school football jersey.

The Stone Circle draws 1,000-2,000 people per summer. Crowds number up to 200 on the busiest nights, and can dwindle to a few dozen on other nights. A unique northern Michigan experience.

Horton Bay 4th of July Parade

The wackiest parade in the North! Each year the town's residents (population 20 or so) team together to build floats to fit a specially selected theme. In 2004, election year, the theme was Political Parties, which drew intricately crafted floats with names like the Cocktail Party. The tiny town plays host to 10,000-15,000 people who line the "streets of the financial district" of downtown Horton Bay. Politicians and commercial floats are banned and parade entrants are encouraged to perform in front of the judges pavilion on the porch of the Horton Bay General Store. Great family event and unforgettable 4th of July parade.